C PRIMER PLUS

by

Mitchell Waite, Stephen Prata
and Donald Martin

Howard W. Sams & Co., Inc.

4300 West 62nd Street, Indianapolis, Indiana 46268

FIRST EDITION
THIRD PRINTING—1985

International Standard Book Number: 0-672-22090-3
Library of Congress Catalog Card Number: 84-50060

Edited by *Patricia Perry*
Illustrated by *David Cripe*

Printed in the United States of America.

PREFACE

C is a simple, elegant programming language that is the choice of a rapidly increasing number of programmers. This book (*C Primer Plus,* if you missed the cover or title page) is a friendly, easy-to-use guide to learning and using C.

The *Primer* in the book title indicates that our first goal is to guide you through the basics of C. Experience is the great teacher in programming, and you will find many examples to use, study, and play with. We've tried to use figures whenever we think they help clarify a point. The main features of C are summarized and highlighted with a blue background to make them easy to find. There are questions (and answers) to let you check your progress. We don't assume any great past computer language experience on your part, but we do make an occasional comparison with other languages to aid those readers who know them.

The *Plus* in the title represents several extras. One, already mentioned, is a question and answer section at the end of each chapter. A second plus is that we go a bit beyond the boundaries of a simple primer and discuss some of the more advanced topics, such as using structures, casts, file operations, and, in the appendix, C's handling of bits, and some of the extensions to C. A third plus is that the book covers both the UNIX and the microcomputer environment for C. For example, we discuss redirection of input and output in both environments, and we illustrate the use of ports for the 8086/8088 microprocessor. The cartoons provide another plus, a rather pleasant one.

We've tried to make this introduction to C instructive, clear, and helpful. To get the greatest benefit from this book, you should take as active a role as possible. Don't just read the examples. Enter them into your system and try them out. C is a very portable language, but perhaps you may find differences between how a program works on your system and how it works on ours. Experiment—change part of a program to see what effect that has. Modify a program to do something slightly different. Ignore our occasional warnings and see what happens. Try the questions and the exercises. The more you do yourself, the better you will learn.

We wish you good fortune in learning C. We've tried to make this book meet your needs, and we hope it helps you reach your goals.

MITCHELL WAITE
STEPHEN PRATA
DONALD MARTIN

With love to Vicky and Bill, my parents—S.P.

CONTENTS

ACKNOWLEDGMENTS

We thank Robert Lafore of the Waite Group for his editorial advice and Bob Petersen for his technical assistance. We thank Lifeboat Associates (Joshua Allen and Todd Katz in particular) for providing and supporting the Lattice C Compiler. We also thank c-systems, The Software Toolworks, Telecon Systems, and Supersoft for providing us information about their C compilers.

TRADEMARK NOTICES

1

GETTING READY

In this chapter you will find

- Whence C?
- Why C?
- Whither C?
- Using C
    - Use an Editor To Prepare Your Program
    - Source Files and Executable Files
    - Compiling C on a UNIX System
    - Compiling C on an IBM PC (Microsoft/Lattice C)
    - Another Compilation Strategy
- Some Conventions
- Advice

1. GETTING READY

CONCEPTS

C history
C virtues
Compiled languages
Running a C program

Welcome to the world of C. In this chapter we help prepare you for learning that powerful and increasingly popular language. Just what do you need to get ready? First, you need an interest in C, and most likely you already have that. But to help you along, we will outline quickly some of the more alluring aspects of C. Secondly, you need a guide to the C language. This book will serve you there. Next, you need access to a computing system with a C compiler. That you will have to arrange yourself. Finally, you will need to learn how to run a C program on your system, and we will offer you some advice about that at the end of this chapter.

WHENCE C?

Dennis Ritchie of Bell Labs created C in 1972 as he and Ken Thompson worked on designing the UNIX operating system. C didn't spring full-grown from Ritchie's forehead. It came from Thompson's B language, which came from . . . but that's another story. The important point for us is that C was created as a tool for working programmers. Thus its chief goal is to be a *useful* language.

Most languages, we suppose, aim to be useful, but often they have other concerns. One of the main goals for Pascal, for instance, is to provide a sound basis for teaching programming principles. BASIC was developed to resemble English so that it could be easily learned by students unfamiliar with computers. These, too, are important goals, but they are not always compatible with pragmatic, workaday usefulness. C's background as programming tool, on the other hand, supports its role as a programmer-friendly language.

WHY C?

C is rapidly becoming one of the most important and popular programming languages. Its use is growing because people try it and like it. As you learn C, you, too, will recognize its many virtues. Let's mention a few of them now.

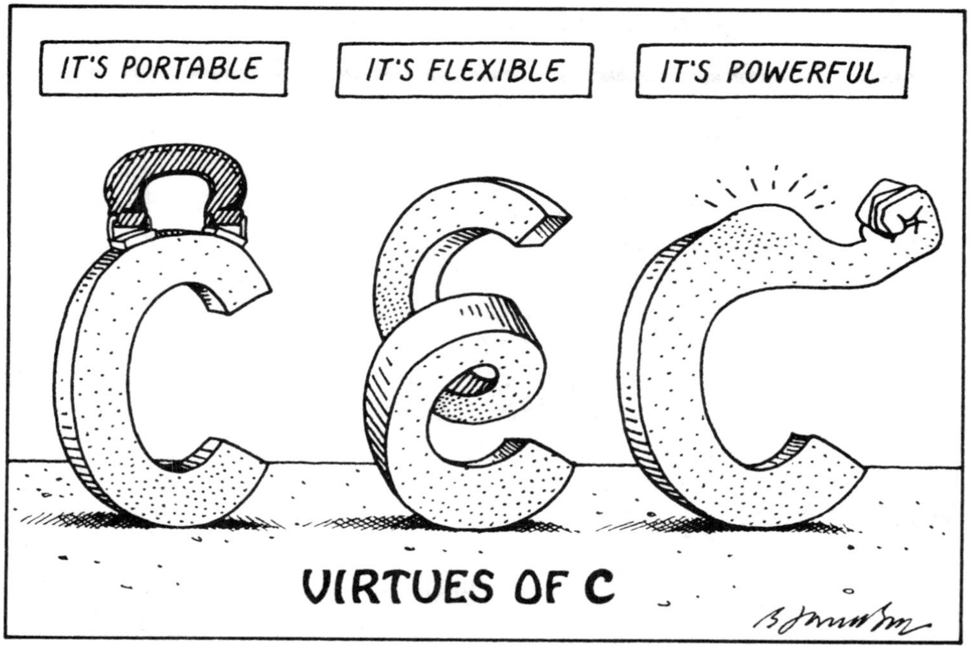

C is a modern language which incorporates the control features that computer science theory and practice find desirable. The design of C makes it natural for users to use top-down planning, structured programming, and modular design. The result is a more reliable, understandable program.

C is an efficient language. Its design takes advantage of the abilities of current computers. C programs tend to be compact and to run quickly.

C is a portable language. This means that C programs written on one system can be run with little or no modification on other systems. If modifications are necessary, often they can be made just by changing a few entries in a "header" file which can accompany the main program. Of course, most languages are meant to be portable, but anyone who has converted an IBM PC BASIC program to Apple BASIC (and they are close cousins) or tried to run an IBM mainframe FORTRAN program on a UNIX system will know that there can be many troublesome details. C is a leader in portability. C compilers are available for about 40 systems, running from 8-bit microprocessors to the world's current computer speed champ, the Cray 1.

C is powerful and flexible (two favorite words in computer literature). For example, most of the powerful, flexible (see!) UNIX operating system is written in C. This includes compilers and interpreters for other languages, such as FORTRAN, APL, Pascal, LISP, Logo, and BASIC. So when you use FORTRAN on a UNIX machine, ultimately a C program does the work of producing the final executable program. C programs have been used for solving physics and engineering problems and even for animating sequences in movies such as *The Return of the Jedi.*

C exhibits some of the fine control usually associated with assembly language. If you choose, you can fine tune your programs for maximum efficiency.

C is friendly. It is sufficiently structured to encourage good programming habits, but it doesn't bind you in a straitjacket of restrictions.

There are more virtues, and, undoubtedly, a few faults. Rather than delve further into the matter, let's ask one more question.

WHITHER C?

C already is a dominant language in the minicomputer world of UNIX systems. Now it is spreading to personal computers. Many software houses are turning to C as the preferred language for producing their products: word processing programs, spreadsheets, compilers, and the like. These companies know that C produces compact, efficient programs. More importantly, they know these programs will be easy to modify and easy to adapt to new models of computers.

Another force helping spread C to the personal computer environment is the desire of UNIX C users who want to take their C programs home. Several C compilers are available now to let them do just that.

What's good for the companies and the C veterans is good for other users, too. More and more computer users are turning to C to secure its

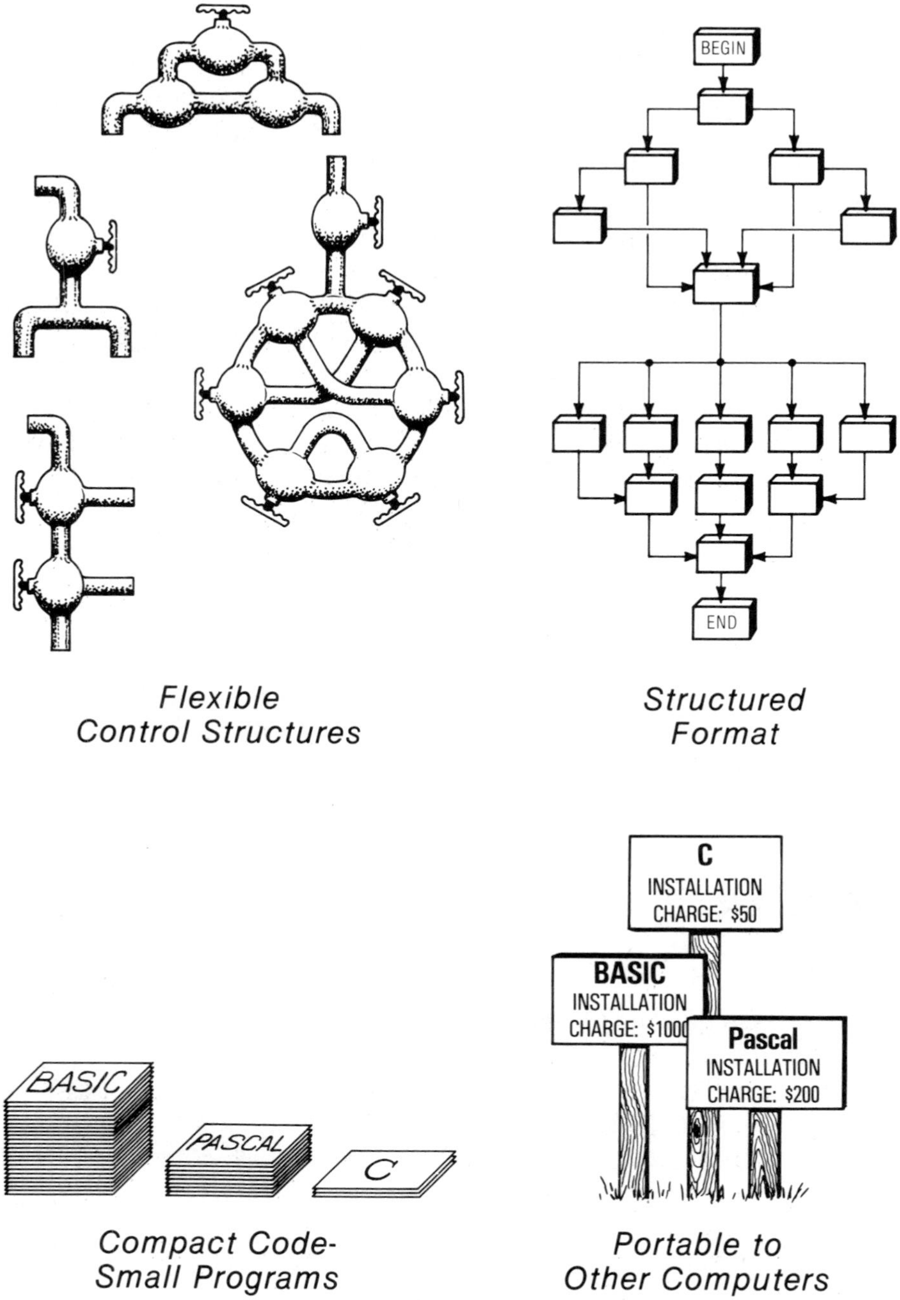

Figure 1.1
Virtues of C

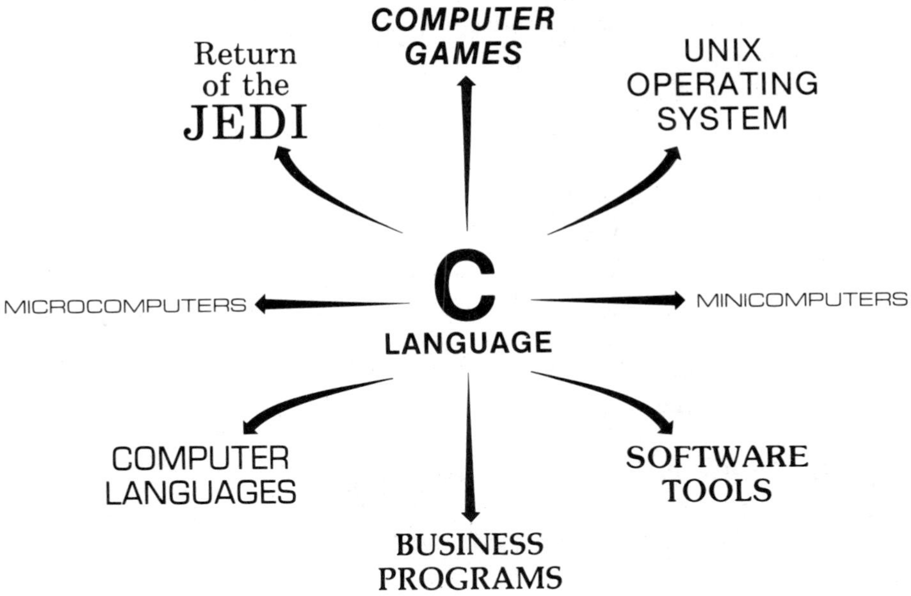

Figure 1.2
Where C is used

advantages for themselves. You don't have to be a computer professional to use C.

In short, C is destined to be one of the most important languages of the 1980s and 1990s. It is used on minicomputers and on personal computers. It is used by software companies, by computer science students, and by enthusiasts of all sorts. And if you want a job writing software, one of the first questions you should be able to answer "yes" to is "Oh say can you C?"

USING C

C is a "compiled" language. If that fails to ring a bell (or succeeds in ringing an alarm bell), don't worry, because we will tell you what that means as we describe the steps in producing a C program.

If you are accustomed to using a compiled language, such as Pascal or FORTRAN, you will be familiar with the basic steps in putting a C program together. But if your background is in an "interpreted" language, such as BASIC or Logo, or if you have no background at all, you may find the process a little strange at first. Fortunately, we are here to guide you through the process, and you'll see that it is actually pretty straightforward and sensible.

First, to give you an overview of the process, here is a simplified outline of what you do to go from writing a program to running it:

1. Use an "editor" to write your program in C.
2. Submit your program to your friendly compiler. It will check your program for errors and let you know if it finds any. If not, the compiler undertakes the task of translating your program to your computer's internal language, and it places this translation into a new file.
3. You can then cause your program to run by typing the name of this new file.

On some systems, the second step may be subdivided into two or three substeps, but the idea is the same.

Let's take a longer look at each step now.

Use an Editor To Prepare Your Program

Unlike BASIC, C does not have its own editor. Instead, you use one of the general purpose editors available for your system. On a UNIX system, that might be **ed, ex, edit, emacs,** or **vi.** On a personal system, it might be **ed, edlin,** Wordstar, Volkswriter, or any other of a vast number of editors. With some editors you need to specify a particular option. On Wordstar, for example, you would use the **N,** or nondocument, option.

Your two main responsibilities here are typing the program correctly and choosing a name for the file that will store the program. The rules for a name are simple: it must be a legal name for your system, and the name should end with **.c.** Here are two such names.

```
sort.c
add.c
```

Choose the first part of the name to remind you of what the program does. The second part **(.c)** identifies the file as a C program. In the wonderful world of computers, the part of a name following a period is called an "extension." Extensions are used to inform you and the computer about the nature of a file.

Here is an example. Using an editor we prepared the following program and stored it in a file called **inform.c.**

```
#include <stdio.h>
main()
{
 printf("A .c is used to end a C program file name.\n");
}
```

The text we just typed is known as "source code," and it is kept in a "source file." The important point here is that our source file is the beginning of a process, not the end.

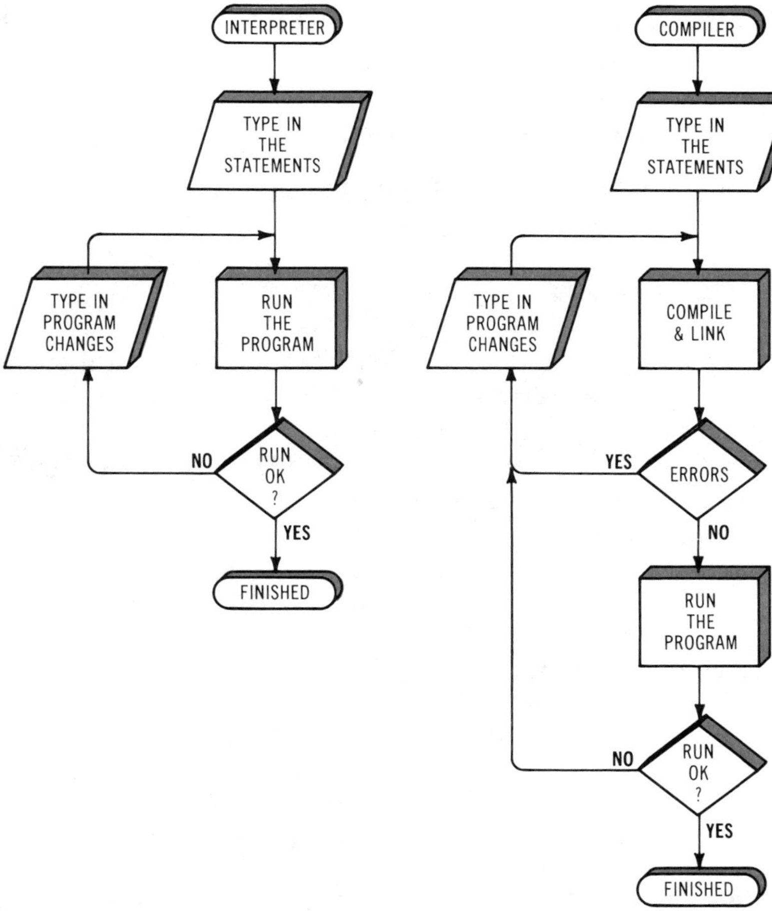

Figure 1.3
Interpreter versus compiler

Source Files and Executable Files

Our program, although undeniably brilliant, is still gibberish to a computer. A computer doesn't understand things like **#include** or **printf.** It understands "machine code," things like 10010101 and 01101001. If we want the computer's cooperation, we must translate *our* code (source code) to *its* code (machine code). The result of our efforts will be an "executable file," which is a file filled with all the machine code the computer needs to get the job done.

If that sounds tedious, don't worry. We have managed to shift the burden of this translation to the machine itself! Clever programs called "compilers" do the brunt of the work. The details of the process depend on the particular system. We will outline a few approaches now.

Compiling C on a UNIX System

The UNIX C compiler is called **cc.** All we need to do to compile our program is to type

```
cc inform.c
```

After a few seconds, the UNIX prompt will return, telling us the deed is done. (We may get warnings and error messages if we fail to write the program properly, but let's assume we do everything right.) If we use **ls** to list our files, we find that there is a new file called **a.out.** This is the executable file containing the translation (or "compilation") of our program. To run it, we just type

```
a.out
```

and our wisdom pours forth:

```
A .c is used to end a C program file name.
```

The **cc** program combines several steps into one. This becomes more obvious when we examine the same process on a personal computer.

Compiling a C Program on an IBM PC (Microsoft/Lattice C)

The exact steps here depend on the operating system and on the compiler. The particular example we give here is the Microsoft C Compiler running

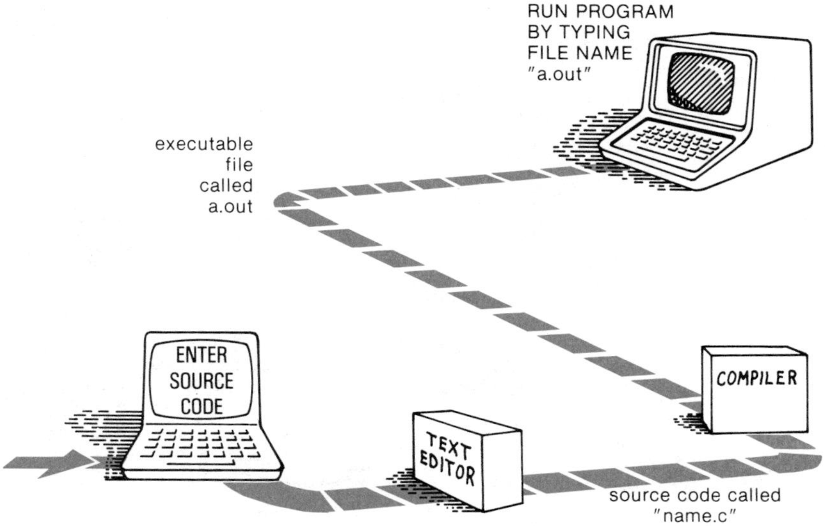

Figure 1.4
Preparing a C program using UNIX

under PC DOS 1.1. Again we start with a file called **inform.c.** Our first command is

```
lc1 inform
```

(The compiler interprets **inform** as **inform.c**). If all goes well, this produces an intermediate file called **inform.q.** Then we type

```
lc2 inform
```

and this produces a file called **inform.obj.** This contains the "object code" (machine language code) for our code. (See below for some explanation.) Then we type

```
link <disk>:cs+<disk>:filename,<disk>:filename,,lcms+lcs
```

and this leads to a file called **inform.exe**. (Specifications may change depending on the configuration of your pc. Check your Lattice C documentation if the above does not work on your system.) This is the goal, the executable file. If we type

```
inform.exe
```

or, for short,

```
inform
```

the program runs.

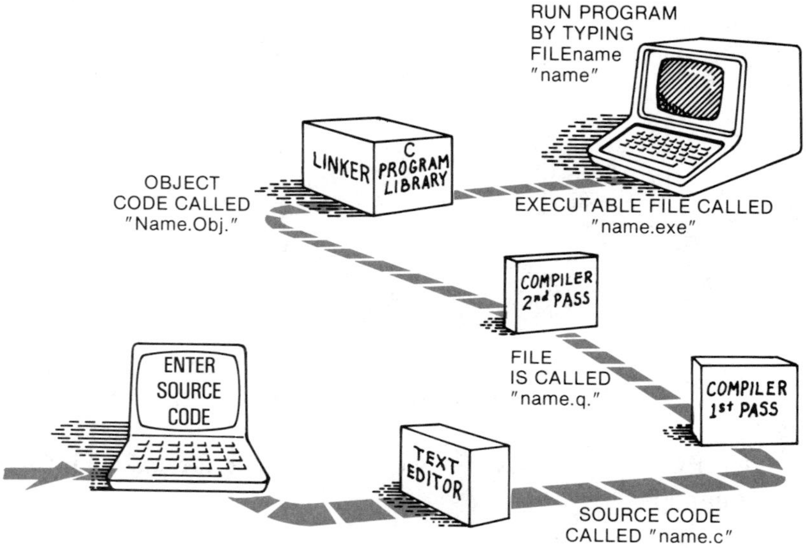

Figure 1.5
Preparing a C program in Microsoft/Lattice C

You don't really have to know what is going on to use this procedure, but here's a rundown if you are interested.

What's new here? For one thing, the file **inform.obj** is new. Since it is in machine code, why aren't we finished here? The answer is that the complete program includes parts that we didn't write. For example, we used the command **printf,** which is a program stored in the C library. A complete program needs to use some standard routines stored elsewhere. This is where the second new item, the **link** command, comes in.

Link is part of the IBM DOS operating system. It links our object code file (**inform.obj**) with a file of some standard items (**c.obj**) and searches a library we specify (**link** asks for that info while it is running), in this case, **lc.lib.** It then combines all the elements together into the final program.

The UNIX **cc** program goes through a similar sequence of steps; it just hides the fact from us, erasing the object file when it is done. (But if we ask nicely, it will give us the object file under the name **inform.o**).

Another Strategy

Several personal computer C compilers take a different route. The method we just discussed produces an object code file (extension **.obj**) and uses the system linker to produce an executable file (extension **.exe**). The alternate method is to produce an "assembly code" file (extension **.asm**) and then use the system "assembler" to produce an executable file.

Oh my! Yet another code! Assembler code is very closely related to machine code. Indeed, it is just a mnemonic representation. For example, JMP may represent 11101001, which is part of machine code telling the computer to jump to a different location. (If you visualize a computer headed towards a lake, be aware we are speaking of different *memory* locations.) Humans find assembler code much easier to remember than pure machine code, and the assembler program takes care of making the translation.

But Why?

Those of you used to BASIC may wonder about going through these steps to run a program. It may seem time consuming. It may even *be* time consuming. But once a program is compiled, it will run *much* faster than a standard BASIC program. You trade some inconvenience in getting a program running for a much swifter final product.

SOME CONVENTIONS

We are almost ready to begin now. We just need to mention some conventions we will use.

Type Face

For text representing programs, computer input and output, and the names of files, programs, and variables, we will use a type font that resembles what you might get on a screen or printed output. We already have used it a few times; in case it slipped by you, the font looks like this:

```
printf("Howdy!\n");
```

Color

We will use a pleasant blue to represent interchanges between the computer and the user. Also, to make our summaries easy to find, we will give them a blue background.

Input and Output Devices

There are many ways for you and a computer to communicate with each other. We will assume that you type in commands using a keyboard and that you read the response on a screen.

Keys

Usually you send a line of instructions onward by hitting a key that is labeled variously as "enter," "c/r," or "return," perhaps capitalized. We will refer to this key as the [enter] key. We use the brackets so that you know you type a single key and not spell the word out.

We also will refer to control characters such as [control-d]. This notation means to hit the [d] key while the key labeled "control" is depressed.

Our System

Some aspects of C, such as the amount of space used to store a number, depend on the system. When we give examples and refer to "our system," we speak of an IBM PC running under DOS 1.1 and using a Lattice C compiler.

We also occasionally refer to running programs on a UNIX system. The one we use is Berkeley's BSD 4.1 version of UNIX running on a VAX 11/750 computer.

ADVICE

You learn programming through doing, not just reading. We have included many examples. You should try running at least some of them on your system to get a better idea of how they work. Try making modifications to see what happens. Try working through the questions and exercises at the ends of the chapters. Be an active, experimenting learner, and you will learn C more quickly and more deeply.

Okay, you are ready and we are ready, so let's turn to Chapter 2.

2

INTRODUCING C

In this chapter you will find

- A Simple Sample of C
- The Explanation
    - Pass 1: Quick Synopsis
    - Pass 2: Details
- The Structure of a Simple Program
- Tips on Making Your Programs Readable
- Taking Another Step
- And While We're at It . . .
- What You Should Have Learned
- Questions and Answers
- Exercises

2. INTRODUCING C

CONCEPTS

Structure of a simple program
Declaring variables
Using comments
Readable programs

OPERATORS

=

What does a C program look like? Perhaps you have seen a sample in Chapter 1 or elsewhere and found it peculiar-looking, sprinkled with symbols like { and ***ptr++**. As you read through this book, you will find that the appearance of these and of other characteristic C symbols grows less strange, more familiar, perhaps even welcome! In this chapter we will begin by presenting a rather simple example program and explaining what it does. At the same time we will highlight some of the basic features of C. If you desire more detailed elaborations of these features, don't worry. They will come in the following chapters.

A SIMPLE SAMPLE OF C

Let's take a look at a simple C program. We have to admit that the example is pretty useless, but it will point out some of the basic features of a program in C. We will give a line-by-line explanation, but before you read that, take a look at the program and see if you can tell what it will do.

```
#include <stdio.h>
main() /*a simple program */
```

```
{
 int num;

 num = 1;
 printf("I am a simple ");
 printf("computer.\n");
 printf("My favorite number is %d because it is first.\n",num);
}
```

If you think this program will print some things on the screen, you are right! But exactly what will be printed may not be clear, so let's run the program and see what comes out.

The first step is to use your editor to create a file containing these innocent lines. You will have to give the file a name; if you are too excited to make one up, use **main.c** for a file name. Now compile the program. (Here we wait patiently while you consult the manual for your particular compiler.) Now run the program. If all went well, the output should look like this:

```
I am a simple computer.
My favorite number is 1 because it is first.
```

All in all, this result is not too surprising. But what happened to the **\n's** and the **%d** in the program? And some of the lines in the program do look a bit strange. It must be time for an explanation.

THE EXPLANATION

We'll take two passes through the program. The first pass will highlight the meaning of each line, and the second pass will explore some of the implications and details.

Pass 1: Quick Synopsis

`#include <stdio.h>`—including another file

This line tells the computer to include information found in the file **stdio.h**.

`main()`—a function name

C programs consist of one or more "functions," which are the basic

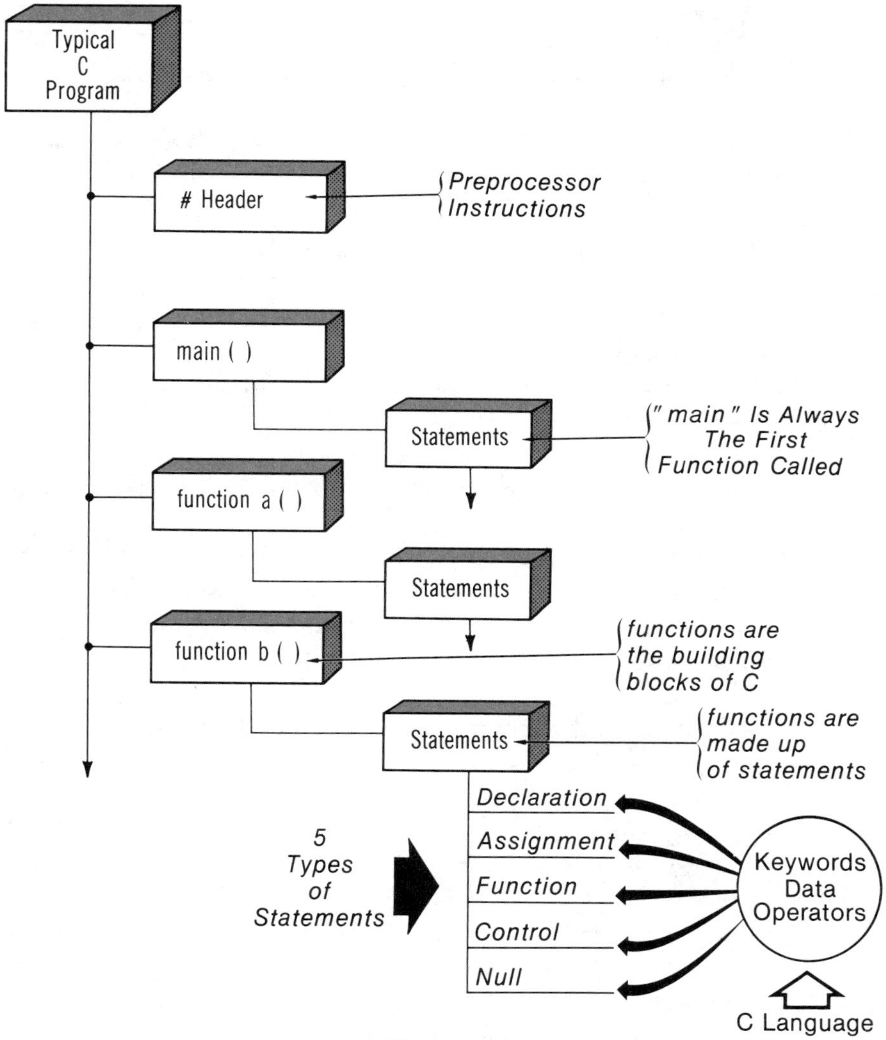

Figure 2.1
Anatomy of a C program

modules of a C program. This program consists of one function called **main.** The parentheses identify **main( )** as a function name.

`/* a simple program */`—a comment

You can use the symbols /* and */ to enclose comments. Comments are remarks to help clarify a program. They are intended for the reader and are ignored by the computer.

`{`—beginning the body of the function

This opening brace marks the start of the statements that make up the function. The function definition is ended with a closing brace, }.

`int num;`—a declaration statement

This statement announces that we will be using a variable called **num** and that **num** will be an **int**eger type.

`num = 1;`—an assignment statement

This statement assigns the value 1 to **num.**

`printf("I am a simple ");`—a print statement

This prints the phrase within the quotes:

```
I am a simple
```

`printf("computer.\n");`—another print statement

This tacks on

```
computer.
```

to the end of the last phrase printed. The **\n** is code telling the computer to start a new line.

```
printf("My favorite number is %d because it is first.\n", num);
```

This line prints the value of **num** (which is 1) embedded in the phrase in quotes. The **%d** instructs the computer where and in what form to print **num's** value.

`}`—the end

As promised, the program ends with a closing brace.

Now let's take a closer look.

Pass 2: Details

```
#include <stdio.h>:
```

The **stdio.h** file is supplied as part of the C compiler package, and it contains information about input and output (communications between the program and your terminal, for example). The name stands for **standard input/output header.** (C people call a collection of information that goes at the top of a file a "header.")

Sometimes you need this line, sometimes you don't. We can't give you a hard rule, for the answer depends on the program and on the system. On our system we don't need this line for *this* program, but you may need it for your system. In any case, including the line won't hurt. From now on, we will show this line only when it is needed for our system.

Perhaps you are wondering why something as basic as input and output information isn't included automatically. One answer is that not all programs use this I/O (Input/Output) package, and part of the C philosophy is not to carry along unnecessary weight. Incidentally, this line is not even a C language statement! The # symbol identifies it as a line to be handled by the C "preprocessor." As you might guess from the name, the preprocessor handles some tasks before the compiler takes over. We will come across more examples of preprocessor instructions later.

`main( ):`

True, **main's** a rather plain name, but it is the only choice we have. A C program always begins execution with the function called **main( ).** We are free to choose names for other functions we may use, but there must be a **main( )** to start things off. What about the parentheses? They identify **main( )** as being a function. We will learn more about functions later. For now, we will just repeat that functions are the basic modules of a C program.

The parentheses, in general, enclose information being passed along to the function. For our simple example, nothing is passed along, so the parentheses remain empty. Don't leave them out, but don't worry about them yet.

The file *containing* the program, incidentally, can have any name we want to give it, as long as it satisfies the system's conventions and ends in **.c.** For example, we could use **mighty.c** or **silly.c** rather than **main.c** as names for a file containing this program.

`/* a simple program */ :`

You should use comments to make it easier for someone (including yourself) to understand your program. One nice feature of C comments is that they can be placed on the same line as the material they explain. A longer comment can be placed on its own line or even spread over more than one line. Everything between the opening /* and the closing */ is ignored by the compiler, which is just as well, since it wouldn't understand such un-C language, anyway.

`{` and `}`:

Braces mark the beginning and the end of the body of a function. Only braces { } work for this purpose, not parentheses ( ) and not brackets **[ ].**

Braces also can be used to gather together statements inside a program into a unit or "block." If you are familiar with Pascal or Algol, you will recognize the braces as being similar to **begin** and **end** in those languages.

```
int num;:
```

The "declaration statement" is one of the most important features of C. As we said earlier, this particular example declares two things. First, somewhere in the function, we will be using a "variable" having the name "**num.**" Secondly, the **int** announces that **num** is an "integer," that is, a whole number. The semicolon at the end of the line identifies the line as a C "statement" or instruction. The semicolon is *part of the statement,* not just a separator between statements as it is in Pascal.

The word **int** is a C "keyword" identifying one of the basic C data types. Keywords are the words used to express a language, and you can find a list of C keywords in the appendix.

In C *all* variables must be declared. This means you have to provide lists of all the variables you use in a program, and that you have to show what "type" each variable is. Declaring variables generally is considered a Good Thing.

At this point, you may have three questions. First, what choices do you have in selecting a name? Second, what are data types? Third, why do you have to declare variables at all? We've prepared two boxes to answer the first and third questions.

We'll deal with the second question in Chapter 3, but here is a short summary. C deals with several kinds (or "types") of data: integers, characters, and "floating point," for example. Declaring a variable to be an integer or a character type makes it possible for the computer to store, fetch, and interpret the data properly.

NAME CHOICE

We suggest that you use meaningful names for variables. You can use up to eight characters for a name. (Actually, you can use more, but C will ignore the ones after the first eight. Thus **shakespeare** and **shakespencil** would be considered to be the same name since they have the same first eight characters.) The characters at your disposal are the lower-case letters, the upper-case letters, the digits, and the underscore _, which is counted as a letter. The first character must be a letter.

Valid Names	Invalid Names
`wiggly`	`$Z^**`
`cat1`	`1cat`
`Hot_Tub`	`Hot-Tub`
`_kcaB`	`don't`

Library routines often use names beginning with the underscore symbol. The assumption is that users are unlikely to choose names beginning with this symbol; thus there is little chance of a user accidentally using one of these names to mean something else. Resist the temptation to begin names with an underscore symbol, and you will avoid risking a clash with the library.

FOUR GOOD REASONS TO DECLARE VARIABLES

1. The gathering together in one place of the variables makes it easier for a reader to grasp what the program is about. This is particularly true if you give your variable meaningful names (such as **taxrate** instead of **r**) and if you use the comment facility to explain what the variables represent. Documenting a program in this manner is one of the primary methods of good programming.
2. Thinking about what to put into the variable declaration section encourages you to do some planning before plunging into writing a program. What information will the program need to get started? What exactly do I want the program to produce as output?
3. Declaring variables helps prevent one of programming's more subtle and hard-to-find bugs, that of the misspelled variable name. For example, suppose that in some language that shall remain nameless, you made the statement

   ```
   ANS = 19.7*BOZ0 - 2.0
   ```

   and that later in the program you mistyped

   ```
   BOZO = 32.4
   ```

   thus unwittingly replacing the numeral 0 with the letter O. The program would create a new variable called **BOZO** and use whatever value it had (perhaps zero, perhaps garbage). **ANS** would be given the wrong value, and you could have a heck of a time trying to find out why. This can't happen in C (unless you were silly enough to declare two such similar variable names) because the compiler will complain when the undeclared **BOZO** shows up.

4. Your C program will not work if you don't declare your variables. If the other reasons discussed here fail to move you, you should give this one serious thought.

```
num = 1;:
```

The "assignment statement" is one of the most basic operations. This particular example means "give the variable **num** the value of 1." The fourth line allotted computer space for the variable **num,** and this line gives it its value. We could assign **num** a different value later on if we wished; that's why we call **num** a variable. Note that the statement is completed with a semicolon.

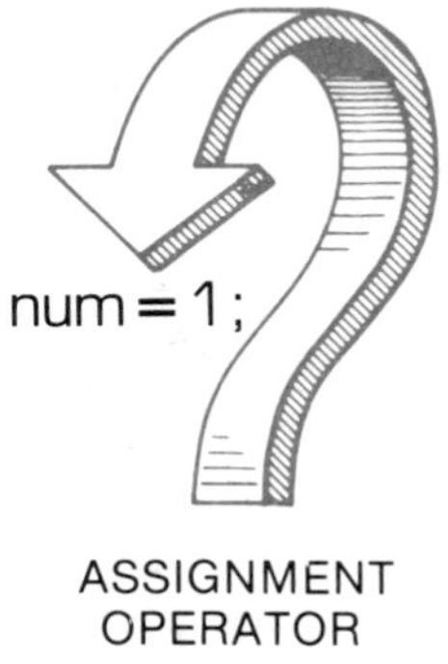

Figure 2.2
The assignment statement is one of the most basic operations

```
printf("I am a simple ");
printf("computer.\n");
printf("My favorite number is %d because it is first.\n",num);
```

These lines all use a standard C function called **printf( );** the parentheses tell us that we are, indeed, dealing with a function. The stuff enclosed in the parentheses is information passed from our function **(main( ))** to the **printf( )** function. Such information is called the "argument" of a function, and in the first case the argument is "I am a simple ". And what does the function **printf( )** do with this argument? Obviously, it looks at whatever lies between the double quotation marks and prints that on the terminal's screen.

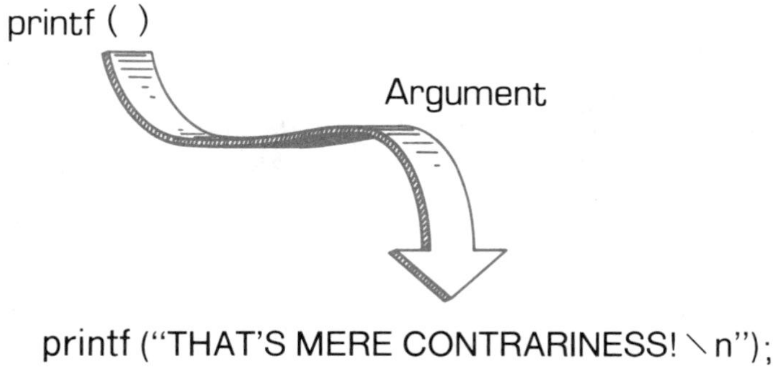

Figure 2.3
printf( ) with an argument

This line provides an example of how we "call" or "invoke" a function in C. We need only type the name of the function and include the desired argument(s) in the parentheses. When your program reaches this line, control is turned over to the named function (**printf( )** in this case). When the function is finished with whatever it does, control is transferred back to the original (the "calling") program.

But what about this next line? It has the characters **\n** included in the quotes, and they didn't get printed! What's going on? The **\n** actually is the instruction to start a new line. The **\n** combination represents a single character called the "newline" character. Its meaning is "start a new line at the far left margin." In other words, this character performs the same function as the [enter]-key of a typical keyboard. "But," you say, "**\n** looks like two characters, not one." Well, they are two characters, but they represent a single character for which there is no single-key representation. Why not just use the [enter]-key? Because that would be interpreted as an immediate command to your editor, not as an instruction to be stored away. In other words, when you hit the [enter]-key, the editor quits the current line on which you are working and starts a new one, leaving your last line unfinished.

The newline character is an example of what is called an "escape sequence." An escape sequence is used to represent difficult- or impossible-to-type characters. Other examples are **\t** for tab and **\b** for backspace. In each case the escape sequence begins with the backslash character, **\.** We'll return to this subject in Chapter 3.

Well, that explains why our three print statements produced only two lines; the first print instruction didn't have a newline character in it.

The final line brings up another oddity: what happened to the **%d** when the line was printed? The output for this line, recall, was:

```
My favorite number is 1 because it is first.
```

Aha! The digit **1** was substituted for the symbol group **%d** when the line was printed, and **1** was the value of the variable **num.** Apparently the **%d** is a kind of placeholder to show where the value of **num** is to be printed. This line is similar to the BASIC statement:

```
PRINT "My favorite number is "; num; " because it is first."
```

The C version does a little more than this, actually. The % alerts the program that a variable is to be printed at that location, and the **d** tells it to print the variable as a **digit.** The **printf( )** function allows several choices for the format of printed variables. Indeed, the **f** in **printf( )** is there to remind us that this is a formatted print statement.

THE STRUCTURE OF A SIMPLE PROGRAM

Now that you've seen a specific example, you are ready for a few general rules about C programs. A program consists of a collection of one or more functions, one of which must be called **main( ).** The description of a function consists of a header and a body. The header contains any preprocessor statements, such as **#include,** and the function name. You can recognize a function name by the parentheses, which may be empty. The body is enclosed by braces { } and consists of a series of statements, each terminated by a semicolon. Our example had a declaration statement, announcing the name and type of variable we were using. Then it had an assignment statement that gave the variable a value. Finally, there were three print statements; each consisted of calling the **printf( )** function.

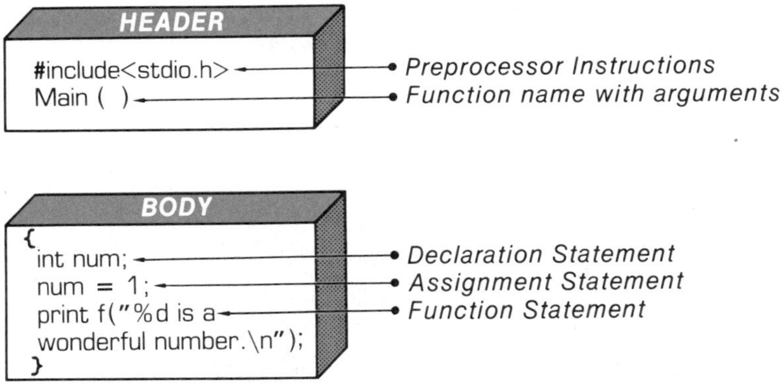

Figure 2.4
A function has a header and a body

TIPS ON MAKING YOUR PROGRAMS READABLE

Making your programs readable is good programming practice. It makes it much easier to understand the program, and that makes it easier to correct or modify the program, if necessary. The act of making a program readable also helps clarify your own concept of what the program does. We will try to point out useful techniques as we go along.

We've already mentioned two points: choose meaningful variable names and use comments. Note that these two techniques complement each other. If you give a variable the name **width,** you don't need a comment saying that this variable represents a width.

Another technique is to use blank lines to separate one conceptual section of a function from another. For example, in our simple program, we had a blank line separating the declaration section from the action section (assigning and printing). The blank line is not required by C, but it is part of the C tradition to use it as we did.

A fourth technique we followed was to use one line per statement. Again, this is a convention not required by C. C has a "free form format." You can place several statements on one line, or spread one statement over several. The following is legitimate code:

```
main() { int four; four
=
4
;
printf(
              "%d\n",
four); }
```

The semicolons tell the compiler where one statement ends and the next begins, but the logic of a program is much clearer if you follow the conventions we used in our example. Of course, there wasn't much logic to follow in our example, but it's best to develop good habits at the beginning.

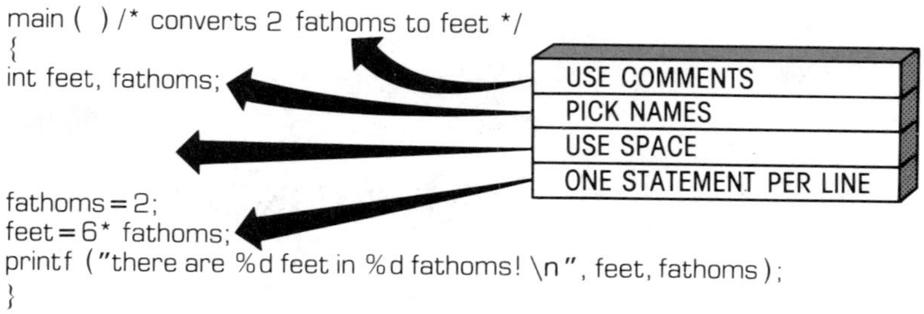

Figure 2.5
Making your program readable

TAKING ANOTHER STEP

Our first example program was pretty easy, and our next example won't be much harder. Here it is:

```
main() /* Converts 2 fathoms to feet */
{
int feet, fathoms;

fathoms = 2;
feet = 6 * fathoms;
printf("There are %d feet in %d fathoms!\n", feet, fathoms);
}
```

What's new? First, we have declared two variables instead of just one. All that was necessary was to separate the two variables (**feet** and **fathoms**) by a comma in the declaration statement.

Second, we have made a calculation. We harnessed the tremendous computational power of our system to multiply 2 by 6. In C, as in many languages, the * is the symbol for multiplication. Thus the statement:

```
feet = 6 * fathoms;
```

means "look up the value of the variable **fathoms,** multiply it by 6, and assign the result of this calculation to the variable **feet.**" (Judging from this paraphrase, plain English is not as clear as plain C; that's one reason we have developed computer languages.)

Finally, we make fancier use of **printf( ).** If you run the example, the output should look like this:

```
There are 12 feet in 2 fathoms!
```

This time we have made *two* substitutions. The first **%d** in the quotes was replaced by the value of the first variable (**feet**) in the list following the quoted segment, and the second **%d** was replaced by the value of the second variable (**fathoms**) in the list. Note how the list of variables to be printed comes at the tail end of the statement.

This program is a bit limited in scope, but it could form the nucleus of a program to convert fathoms to feet. All we need is some way to assign **feet** other values; we will learn to do that later.

AND WHILE WE'RE AT IT . . .

Here is one more example. So far our programs have used the standard **printf( )** function. Here we show how to include and use a function of your own devising.

```
main()
{
   printf("I will summon the butler function.\n");
   butler();
   printf("Yes. Bring me some tea and floppy disks.\n");
}
butler()
{
    printf("You rang, sir?\n");
}
```

The output looks like this:

```
I will summon the butler function.
You rang, sir?
Yes. Bring me some tea and floppy disks.
```

The function **butler( )** is defined in the same manner as **main( ),** with the body enclosed in braces. The function is called simply by giving its name, including parentheses. We won't return to this important topic until Chapter 9, but we wanted you to see how easy it is to include your own functions.

WHAT YOU SHOULD HAVE LEARNED

Here's a summary of some hard (but not cruel) facts we hope you have picked up. We've included short examples as room permits.

What to call the file containing your program: **eye.c** or **black.c** or **infan.c,** etc.

What name to use for a one-function program: **main( )**

The structure of a simple program: header, body, braces, statements

How to declare an integer variable: **int varname;**

How to assign a value to a variable: **varname = 1024;**

How to print a phrase: **printf("Wanna buy a duck?");**

How to print the value of a variable: **printf("%d",varname);**
The newline character: **\n**
How to include comments in a program: /* **cash flow analysis** */

QUESTIONS AND ANSWERS

Here are a few questions to help you check and extend your understanding of the material in this chapter.

Questions

1. Ichabod Bodie Marfoote has prepared the following program and brought it to you for approval. Please help him out.

```
include studio.h
main{} /* this program prints the number of weeks in a year /*
(
int s

s := 56;
print(There are s weeks in a year.);
```

2. What would each of the following examples cause to be printed, assuming they were part of a complete program?
   a. `printf("Baa Baa Black Sheep.");`
      `printf("Have you any wool?\n");`
   b. `printf("Begone!\nO creature of lard!");`
   c. `printf("What?\nNo/nBonzo?\n");`
   d. `int num;`

      ```
      num = 2;
      printf("%d + %d = %d", num, num, num + num);
      ```

Answers

1. line 1: begin the line with a #; spell the file stdio.h; place the file name in angle brackets.
   line 2: use ( ), not { }; end comment with */, not /*
   line 3: use {, not (
   line 4: complete the statement with a semicolon
   line 5: Mr. IBM got this one (the blank line) right!
   line 6: Use = and not := for assignment. (Apparently Mr. IBM knows a little Pascal.)
   52, not 56, weeks per year

line 7: should be **printf("There are %d weeks in a year.\n",s);**
line 8: there isn't one, but there should be, and it should consist of the closing brace, }.

2. a. **Baa Baa Black Sheep.Have you any wool?**
   (Note that there is no space after the period. We could have had a space by using " **Have** instead of "**Have.**)
   b. **Begone!**
   O creature of lard!
   (Note that the cursor is left at the end of the second line.)
   c. **What?**
   No/nBonzo?
   (Note that the slash (/) does not have the same effect as the backslash (\).)
   d. **2 + 2 = 4**
   (Note how each **%d** is replaced by the corresponding variable value from the list. Note, too, that + means addition, and that calculation can be done inside a **printf( )** statement.)

EXERCISES

Reading about C isn't enough. You should try writing a simple program or two yourself and see if it all goes as smoothly as it looks in this chapter. Here are a few suggestions, but you can use your own ideas if you prefer. (We'll never know.)

1. Write a program to print your name.
2. Write a program to print your name and address, using three or more lines.
3. Write a program that converts your age in years to days. At this point, don't worry about fractional years and leap years.

3

DATA, C, AND YOU

In this chapter you will find

- Data: Variables and Constants
- Data: Data Types
    - The Integer
    - The Floating-Point Number
- C Data Types
    - Types *int, short,* and *long*
    - Declaring Integer Types
    - Integer Constants
    - Initializing Integer Variables
    - Usage
    - Type *unsigned*
    - Type *char*
    - Declaring Character Variables
    - Character Constants
    - A Program
    - Types *float* and *double*
    - Declaring Floating-Point Variables
    - Floating-Point Constants
    - Other Types
    - Type Sizes
- Using Data Types
- What You Should Have Learned
- Questions and Answers

3. DATA, C, AND YOU

CONCEPTS

Interactive programs
Basic data types
Variables and constants
Declaring different types
Words, bytes, and bits

KEYWORDS

int, short, long, unsigned, char float, double

OPERATORS

`sizeof`

Programs work with data. We feed numbers, letters, and words to the computer, and we expect it to do something with these data. In these next two chapters we will concentrate on data concepts and properties. Following that, we will pounce on some data and see what we can do. But since it is not much fun just talking about data, we will do a little data manipulation in this chapter, too.

Our main topic in this chapter will be the two great families of data types: integer and floating point. C offers several varieties of these types. We will learn what the types are, how to declare them, how to use them, and when to use them. Also, we will discuss the differences between constants and variables.

Once again it's time to look at a sample program. Also, once again, you'll find some unfamiliar wrinkles that we'll iron out for you in the main body of the chapter. The general intent should be clear, so try compiling and running this program. To save time, you can omit typing the comments. (For reference, we've included a program name as a comment. We will continue this practice with future programs.)

```
/* goldenyou */
/* a program to find the value of your weight in gold */
main()
{
  float weight, value; /* 2 floating-point variables */
  char beep;           /* a character variable */

  beep = '\007';       /* assigning a special character to beep */
  printf("Are you worth your weight in gold?\n");
  printf("Please enter your weight in pounds, and we'll see.\n");
  scanf("%f", &weight);      /* getting input from the user */
  value = 400.0*weight*14.5833;
          /* assumes gold is $400 per ounce */
          /* 14.5833 converts pounds to ounces troy */
  printf("%cYour weight in gold is worth $%2.2f%c.\n",
    beep,value,beep);
  printf("You are easily worth that! If gold prices drop, ");
  printf("eat more\nto maintain your value.\n");
}
```

When you type in this program, you may wish to change the **400.00** to the current price of gold. We suggest, however, that you don't fiddle with the **14.5833**, which represents the number of ounces in a pound. (That's ounces troy, used for precious metals, and pounds avoirdupois, used for people, precious and otherwise.) Note that "entering" your weight means to type in your weight and then to hit the "enter" or "return" key. (Don't just stand on the keyboard.) Hitting this key informs the computer that you have finished typing your response. When we ran the program, the results looked like this:

```
Are you worth your weight in gold?
Please enter your weight in pounds, and we'll see.
175
Your weight in gold is worth $1020831.00.
You are easily worth that! If gold prices drop, eat more
to maintain your value.
```

The program also has a nonvisual aspect. You'll have to run the program yourself to find out what that is for sure, but the name of one of the variables should provide an unsubtle clue.

What's new in this program?

1. You probably noticed that we used two new kinds of variable declaration. Before, we used only an integer variable, but now we've added a floating-point variable and a character variable so that we can handle a wider variety of data.
2. We've included some new ways of writing constants. We now have numbers with decimal points, and we have a rather peculiar-looking notation to represent the character named **beep.**
3. To print out these new kinds of variables, we have used the **%f** and the **%c** codes of **printf( )** to handle floating-point and character variables, respectively. We used modifiers to the **%f** code to fine tune the appearance of the output.
4. Perhaps the most outstanding new feature is that this program is "interactive." The computer asks you for information, and then uses the number you type in. An interactive program is more interesting to use than the noninteractive types we used earlier. More importantly, the interactive approach lets us make more flexible programs. For instance, our example program can be used for any reasonable weight, not just for 175 pounds. We don't have to rewrite the program every time we want to try it on a new person. The **scanf( )** and **printf( )** functions make this possible. The **scanf( )** function reads data from the keyboard and delivers that data to the program. In Chapter 2 we saw that **printf( )** reads data from a program and delivers that data to your screen. Together, these two functions let you establish a two-way communication with your computer, and that makes using a computer much more fun.

This chapter will deal with the first two points, variables and constants of various data types. We will cover the last two points in the following chapter, but we will continue to make use of **scanf( )** and **printf( )** in this chapter.

DATA: VARIABLES AND CONSTANTS

A computer, under the guidance of a program, can do many things. It can add numbers, sort names, command the obedience of a speaker or video screen, calculate cometary orbits, prepare a mailing list, draw stick figures, draw conclusions, or do whatever else your imagination can create. To do these tasks, the program needs to work with "data," the numbers and characters that bear the information you use. Some data are preset before a program is used and keep their values unchanged. These are "constants." Other data may change or be assigned values as the program runs; these are "variables." (We've already used the term in the last chapter, but now you are formally introduced.) In our sample program, **weight** is a variable; and **14.5833** is a constant. What about the **400.0?** True, the price of gold isn't a constant in real life, but our program treats it as a constant.

The difference between a variable and a constant is pretty obvious: a variable can have its value assigned or changed while the program is running, and a constant can't. This difference makes the variables a little tougher and more time-consuming for a computer to handle, but it can do the job.

DATA: DATA TYPES

Beyond the distinction between variable and constant is the distinction between different "types" of data. Some data are numbers. Some are letters, or, more generally, characters. The computer needs a way to identify and to use these different kinds. C does this by recognizing several fundamental "data types." If a datum is a constant, the compiler usually can tell what type it is just by the way it looks. A variable, however, needs to have its type announced in a declaration statement. We'll fill you in on the details as we move along. First, though, let's look at the fundamental types recognized by standard C. C uses 7 keywords to set up the types. Here are those keywords.

```
int
long
short
unsigned

char

float
double
```

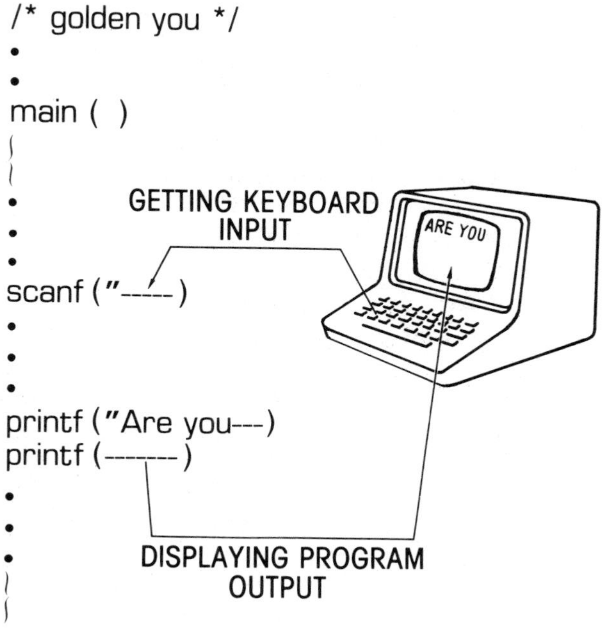

Figure 3.1
***scanf( )* and *printf( )* at work**

The first four keywords are used to represent integers, that is, whole numbers with no decimals. They can be used alone or in certain combinations, such as **unsigned short.** The next keyword, **char,** is for letters of the alphabet and for other characters, such as #, $, %, and &. The final two keywords are used to represent numbers with decimal points. The types created with these keywords can be divided into two families on the basis of how they are stored in the computer. The first five keywords create "integer" types, while the last two create "floating-point" types.

Integer types? Floating-point types? If you find these terms disturbingly unfamiliar, be assured that we are about to give you a brief rundown of their meanings. If you are unfamiliar with "bits," "bytes," and "words," you may wish to read the next box first. Do you *have* to learn all the details? Not really, not any more than you have to learn the principles of internal combustion engines to drive a car. But knowing a little about what goes on inside a computer or engine can help out occasionally. It also can help to make you a fascinating conversationalist.

BITS, BYTES, AND WORDS

The terms "bit," "byte," and "word" can be used to describe units of computer data or to describe units of computer memory. We'll concentrate on the second usage here.

The smallest unit of memory is called a bit. It can hold one of two values: 0 or 1. (Or we can say the bit is set to 'off' or 'on'; this is another way of saying the same thing.) You can't store much information in one bit, but a computer has hordes of them. The bit is the basic building block of computer memory.

The byte is a more useful unit of memory. For most machines a byte is 8 bits. Since each bit can be set to either 0 or 1, there are 256 (that's 2 times itself 8 times) possible bit patterns of 0s and 1s that can fit in a byte. These patterns can be used, for example, to represent the integers from 0 to 255 or to represent a set of characters. Representation can be accomplished using "binary code," which uses (conveniently enough) just 0s and 1s to represent numbers. We've included a discussion of binary code in the appendix; please feel free to read it.

A word is the natural unit of memory for a given computer design. For "8-bit" microcomputers, such as the Sinclairs or the original Apples, a word is just one byte. Many newer systems, such as the IBM PC and the Apple Lisa, are "16-bit" machines. This means they have a word size of 16 bits, which is 2 bytes. Larger computers may have 32-bit words, 64-bit words, or even larger. Naturally, the larger a word is, the more information it can store. Computers usually can string two or more words together to store larger items, but this process does slow the computer down.

We will assume a word size of 16 bits for our examples, unless we tell you otherwise.

For a human, the difference between an integer and a floating-point number is reflected in the way they can be written. For a computer, the difference is reflected in the way they are stored. Let's look at each of the two classes in turn.

The Integer

An integer is a whole number. It never has a fractional part, and in C it never is written with a decimal point. Examples are 2, −23, and 2456. Numbers like 3.14 and 2/3 are not integers. Integers are stored pretty straightforwardly as binary numbers. The integer 7, for example, is written

111 in binary. Thus, to store this number in a one-byte word, just set the first 5 bits to 0 and the last 3 bits to 1. See Fig. 3.2.

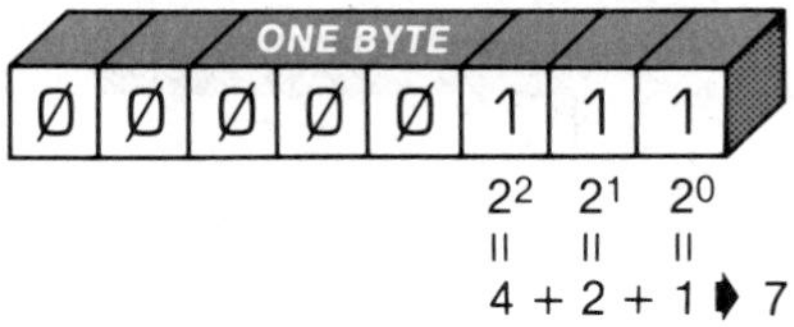

Figure 3.2
Storing the integer 7 using a binary code.

The Floating-Point Number

Floating-point numbers more or less correspond to what mathematicians call "real numbers." They include the numbers between the integers. Here are some floating-point numbers: 2.75, 3.16E7, 7.00, and 2e-8. Obviously, there is more than one way to write a floating-point number. We will discuss the "E"-notation more fully later. In brief, the notation "3.16E7" means to multiply 3.16 by 10 to the 7th power, that is, by 1 followed by 7 zeros. The 7 would be termed the "exponent" of 10.

The key point here is that the scheme used to store a floating-point number is different from the one used to store an integer. Floating-point representation involves breaking up a number into a fractional part and an exponent part and storing the parts separately. Thus, the 7.00 in this list would not be stored in the same manner as the integer 7, even though both have the same value. The decimal analogy would be to write "7.0" as "0.7E1". Here "0.7" is the fractional part, and the "1" is the exponent part. A computer, of course, would use binary numbers and powers of two instead of powers of ten for internal storage. You can find more information on this subject in Appendix G. Here, let's concentrate on the practical differences, which are these;

1. Integers are whole numbers, while floating-point numbers can represent both whole and fractional numbers.
2. Floating-point numbers can represent a much larger range of values than integers can. See Table 3.1.
3. For some arithmetic operations, such as subtracting one large number from another, floating-point numbers are subject to greater loss of precision.

4. Floating-point operations normally are slower than integer operations. However, there are now microprocessors specifically developed to handle floating-point operations, and they are quite swift.

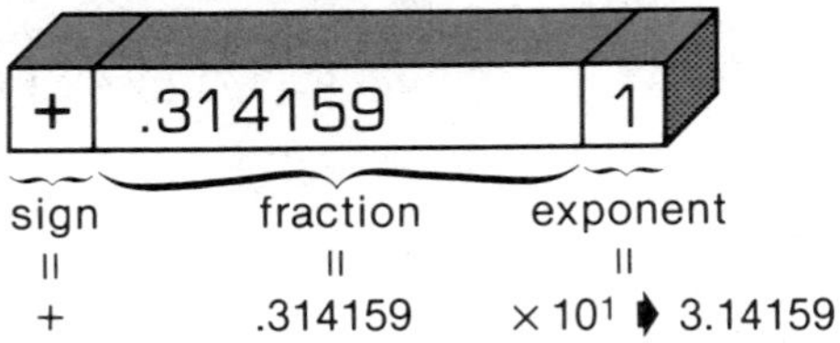

Figure 3.3
Storing the number PI in floating-point (decimal version)

FLOATING-POINT ROUNDOFF ERRORS

Take a number. Add 1 to it, and subtract the original number. What do you get? We get 1. But a floating-point calculation may give another answer:

```
/* floaterror */
main()
{
  float a,b;

  b = 2.0e20 + 1.0;
  a = b - 2.0e20;

  printf("%f \n", a);
}
```

The output:

```
0.000000
```

The reason for this odd result is that the computer doesn't keep track of enough decimal places to do the operation correctly. The number 2.0e20 is 2 followed by 20 zeros, and by adding 1, we are trying to change the 21st digit. To do this correctly, the program would need to be able to store a 21-digit number. But a **float** number is just 6 or 7 digits scaled to bigger or smaller numbers with an exponent. The attempt is doomed. On the other hand, if we used, say, 2.0e4 instead of 2.0e20, we would get the correct answer, for here we are trying to change the 5th digit, and **float** numbers are precise enough for that.

C DATA TYPES

Now let's take a look at the specifics for the basic types used by C. For each type, we will show how to declare a variable, how to represent a constant, and what a typical use would be. Some C compilers do not support all these types, so check your manual to see which ones you have available.

Types *int, short,* and *long*

C offers a variety of integer types so that you can refine a program to meet the requirements of a particular machine or task. If you don't wish to worry about such details, usually you can just stick to type **int** and not fret about the other choices.

The data types **int, short,** and **long** are all "signed integers." This means that the allowed values are whole numbers and can be positive, negative, or zero. C also has "unsigned integers," which are just positive or zero. A bit is used up to indicate the sign of a number, so the biggest signed integer that can fit in a word is smaller than the biggest unsigned integer. For instance, a 16-bit word can hold any unsigned integer from 0 to 65535. The same word could hold any signed integer from −32768 to +32767. Notice that the total range is the same for the two types.

The designers of C give the option of defining three size classes for integers. Type **int** usually is assigned the standard word size for the computer being used. Type **short** is guaranteed to be no longer than **int,** and **long** is guaranteed to be no shorter. For some systems, one or both of these types are the same as **int.** It all depends on what works best for the particular system. The table at the end of this section shows the number of bits and various data types used for a few representative computers and the range of numbers they can represent.

Declaring Integer Types

Just type in the variable type and follow it with a list of the variable names. Here are some possible declarations.

```
int erns;
short stops;
long johns;
int hogs, cows, goats;
```

Use commas to separate variable names, and terminate the list with a semicolon. You can collect like types together in one statement or spread them over several statements. For instance, the declaration

```
int erns, hogs, cows, goats;
```

would have the same effect as the two separate **int** declarations in the preceding example. Or you could use four separate **int** declarations, one for each variable.

You may encounter combinations such as **long int** or **short int.** These are simply the long forms for **long** and **short.**

Integer Constants

C recognizes a number without a decimal point and without an exponent as being an integer. Thus **22** and **−273** are integer constants. But **22.0** isn't, because it contains a decimal point, and **22E3** isn't, because it contains exponent notation. Also, don't use commas when writing an integer. Write 23456 and not 23,456.

If you want to identify a constant as being type **long,** you can do so by tagging an L or a l to the end of the number. Using the capital L is better, for it is less likely to be confused with the digit 1. An example of a **long** constant is **212L.** Obviously the number 212 is not itself very long, but adding the L ensures that it will be stored in the proper number of bytes. This is important for compatibility if the number is to be used with other **long** constants and variables.

Quite possibly that is all you will need to know about writing constants, but C does offer two other options. First, if an integer begins with the digit **0,** it is interpreted as an "octal" number. Octal numbers are "base eight," that is, they are written as combinations of powers of eight. For example, the number **020** represents two times the first power of eight and is the octal equivalent of **16.** A simple **20,** without the leading **0,** is just plain old **20.**

Secondly, an integer beginning with **0x** or **0X** is interpreted as a hexadecimal number, that is, a number in base 16. Thus **0x20** represents 2 times the first power of 16, or **32.**

Octal and hexadecimal numbers are popular with many computer workers. Because 8 and 16 are powers of 2, and 10 isn't, these number systems are more natural for computers. For example, the number 65536, which often pops up in 16-bit machines, is just 10000 in hexadecimal, or hex, as it often is called. If you wish to know more about octal or hexadecimal numbers, you will find them discussed in Appendix G.

Initializing Integer Variables

One common use of constants is to "initialize" a variable. This means to give a variable some value to start with. Here are examples of initializations.

```
erns = 1024;
stops = -3;
johns = 12345678;
```

You can initialize a variable in a declaration statement if you like. Here are some examples.

```
int hogs = 23;
int cows = 32, goats = 14;
short dogs, cats = 92;
```

On the last line just **cats** was initialized. A quick reading might lead one to think that **dogs,** too, is initialized to **92,** so it is better to avoid putting initialized and noninitialized variables in the same declaration statement.

Usage

Which signed integer type should you use? One purpose of having three size classes is to let you match the type to the needs of the problem. For instance, if **int** is one word and **long** is two words, then **long** will let you handle longer numbers. If your problem doesn't use such long numbers, then don't use **long,** for the word juggling involved in using a two-word number rather than a one-word number slows the computer down. Whether you need to use **long** will depend on your system, since **int** on some systems can be larger than **long** on a different system. Again, you usually can get by just using **int.**

INTEGER OVERFLOW

What happens if an integer tries to get too big for its type? Let's set an integer to its largest possible value, add to it, and see what happens.

```
/* toobig */
main()
{
   int i = 32767;

   printf("%d %d %d\n", i, i+1, i+2);
}
```

Here's the result for our system:

```
32767 -32768 -32767
```

The integer **i** is acting like a car's odometer. When it reaches its maximum value, it starts over at the beginning. The main difference is that an odometer begins at 0, while our **int** begins at −32768.

Notice that you are not informed that **i** has exceeded ("overflowed") its maximum value. You would have to include your own programming to keep tabs of that.

The behavior we have described here is not mandated by the rules of C, but it is the typical implementation.

Type *unsigned*

Normally, this type is a modifier of one of the preceding three types. Thus we might use **unsigned int** or **unsigned long** as types. You can use just the keyword **unsigned** to mean **unsigned integer.** Some systems don't support **unsigned long,** and for some microprocessor versions **unsigned** is a separate type, available in just one size.

Unsigned integer constants are written in the same manner as signed integer constants, except that no minus sign is allowed.

Unsigned integer variables are declared and initialized in the same manner as signed integer variables. Here are a few examples.

```
unsigned int students;
unsigned players;
unsigned short ribs = 6;
```

You can use this type to ensure that the value of something is never negative. Also, if you are dealing only with positive numbers, you can use the fact that this type can handle a larger number than can the equivalent signed type. Typical uses would be for memory addresses and for making counts.

Type *char*

This defines an unsigned integer in the range 0 to 255. Usually this integer is stored in a single byte. The computer uses a code to translate numbers to characters and back. Most varieties of computer use the ASCII code described in the appendix. Many IBM computers (but not the IBM PC) use a different code called EBCDIC. We will use ASCII code throughout this book so that we can give definite examples.

Declaring Character Variables

We use the keyword **char** to declare a character variable. The rules regarding declaring more than one variable and initializing a variable are the same as for the other basic types. Thus all the following are legal.

```
char response;
char itable, latan;
char isma = 'S';
```

Character Constants

In C, characters are set off by single quotes. Thus, when we assign a value to the **char** variable **broiled,** we use

```
broiled = 'T'; /* RIGHT */
```

and not

```
broiled = T; /* WRONG */
```

If the single quote marks are omitted, the compiler will think we are using a variable named **T.** It also will think we forgot to declare that variable.

In standard C a **char** variable or constant is restricted to having a single character as its value. Thus the following sequence is not allowed because it tries to assign two characters to the variable **bovine.**

```
char bovine;
bovine = 'ox'; /* NOT VALID */
```

If you look at the ASCII table, you will see that some of the "characters" are "nonprinting." For instance, character number 7 makes the computer terminal beep. How can you write a character that you can't type? C has two ways to accomplish this.

The first way uses the ASCII code itself. You just use the ASCII code number preceded by a backslash. We did this in our program **goldenyou** with the line:

```
beep = '\007';
```

There are two points you must keep in mind. The first is that ASCII code sequence is enclosed by single quotes, just as an ordinary character is. The second is that the code number must be written in Octal. Incidentally, we can omit leading zeros from the code. Thus we could have used **'\07'** or even **'\7'** to represent the beep character. Don't omit trailing zeros, however. The representation **'\020'** can be written as **'\20'** but not as **'\02'.**

When you use ASCII code, note the difference between numbers and number characters. For example, the *character* "4" is represented by ASCII code value 52. This represents the symbol "4" and not the numerical value 4.

Int Family Constants			
member	hex	octal	decimal
char	N.A.	'\034'	N.A.
short	±0X23	±078	±92
unsigned short	±0X23	±078	±92
long	±0X23L	±078L	±92L

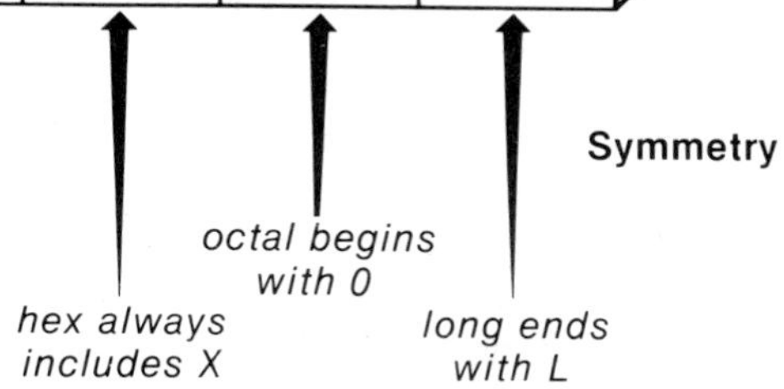

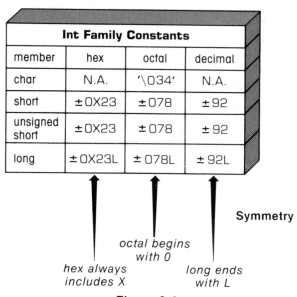

Figure 3.4
Writing constants within the *int* family

The second method C uses to represent awkward characters is to use special symbol sequences. They are called "escape sequences" and are as follows:

```
\n          newline
\t          tab
\b          backspace
\r          carriage return
\f          form feed
\\          backslash(\)
\'          single quote(')
\"          double quote(")
```

These, too, would be enclosed in single quotes when assigned to a character variable. For example, we could make the statement

```
nerf = '\n';
```

and then print the variable **nerf** to advance the printer or screen one line.

The first five escape sequences are common printer control characters. A newline starts a new line. A tab moves the cursor or printhead over a fixed amount, often 5 or 8 spaces. A backspace moves back one space. A carriage return moves to the beginning of a line. A form feed advances printer paper one page. The last three let you use \, ', and " as character constants. (Because these symbols are used to *define* character constants as part of a **printf( )** command, the situation could get confusing if you use them literally.) If you want to print out the line:

```
Gramps sez, "a \ is a backslash."
```

use:

```
printf("Gramps sez, \"a \\ is a backslash.\"\n");
```

At this point you may have two questions. 1. Why didn't we enclose the escape sequences in single quotes in the last example? 2. When should you use the ASCII code, and when should you use the escape sequences we just showed? (We hope these are your two questions, for they are the ones we are about to answer.)

1. When a character, be it an escape sequence or not, is part of a string of characters enclosed by double quotes, don't enclose it in single quotes. Notice that all the other characters in this example (G,r,a,m,p,s, etc.) also are not marked off by single quotes. A string of characters enclosed in double quotes is called a "character string." We will explore this topic next chapter.
2. If you have a choice between using one of the special escape sequences, say **'\f'**, or an equivalent ASCII code, say **'\016'**, use the **'\f'.** First, the representation is more mnemonic. Secondly, it is more portable. If you have a system that doesn't use ASCII code, the **'\f'** will still work.

A Program

Here is a short program that lets you find what the code number for a character is on your system, even if the code isn't ASCII.

```
main() /* finds code number for a character */
{
  char ch;

  printf("Please enter a character.\n");
```

```
    scanf("%c", &ch);      /* user inputs character */
    printf("The code for %c is %d.\n", ch, ch);
}
```

When you use the program, remember to use the [enter] or [return] key after typing the character. **Scanf( )** then fetches the character you typed, and the ampersand (**&**) sees to it that the character is assigned to the character variable **ch. Printf( )** then prints out the value of **ch** twice, first as a character (prompted by the **%c** code), then as a decimal integer (prompted by the **%d** code).

Types *float* and *double*

The various integer types serve well for most software development projects. However, mathematically oriented programs often make use of "floating-point" numbers. In C, such numbers are called type **float;** they correspond to the **real** types of FORTRAN and Pascal. This approach, as you have seen if you were attentive, allows you to represent a much greater range of numbers, including decimal fractions. Floating-point numbers are analogous to scientific notation, a system used by scientists to inspire awe and to express very large and small numbers. Let's take a look.

In scientific notation, numbers are represented as decimal numbers times powers of ten. Here are some examples.

NUMBER		SCIENTIFIC NOTATION		EXPONENTIAL NOTATION
1,000,000,000	=	1.0×10^9	=	1.0e9
123,000	=	1.23×10^5	=	1.23e5
322.56	=	3.2256×10^2	=	3.2256e2
0.000056	=	5.6×10^{-5}	=	5.6e−5

The first column shows the usual notation, the second column scientific notation, and the third column the way scientific notation is usually written for and by computers, with the "e" followed by the power of ten.

Usually 32 bits are used to store a floating-point number. Eight bits are used to give the exponent its value and sign, and 24 bits are used to represent the nonexponent part. The important things for you to know are that this produces a 6 or 7 decimal digit precision and a range of $\pm(10^{-37}$ to $10^{+38})$. This can come in handy if you like to use numbers like the mass of the sun (2.0e30 kilograms) or the charge of a proton (1.6e−19 coulombs). (We love using these numbers.)

Many systems also support type **double** (for double precision), which uses twice as many bits, typically 64. Some systems use all 32 additional bits for the nonexponent part. This increases the number of significant figures and reduces roundoff errors. Other systems use some of the bits to accommodate a larger exponent; this increases the range of numbers that can be accommodated.

Another way to specify **double** is to use the keyword combination **long float.**

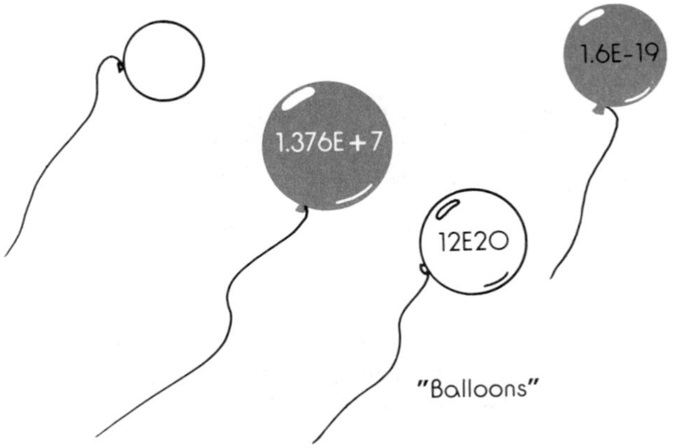

Figure 3.5
Some floating-point numbers

Declaring Floating-Point Variables

Floating-point variables are declared and initialized in the same manner as their integer cousins. Here are some examples.

```
float noah, jonah;
double trouble;
float planck = 6.63e-34;
```

Floating-Point Constants

We have many choices open to us when we write a floating-point constant. The most general form of a floating-point constant is a signed series of digits including a decimal point, then an e or E, then a signed exponent indicating the power of 10 used. Here are two examples:

$-1.56E+12 \qquad 2.87e-3$

You can leave out positive signs. You can do without a decimal point or an exponential part, but not both simultaneously. You can omit a fractional part or an integer part, but not both (that wouldn't leave much!). Here are some more valid floating-point constants:

3.14159 .2 4e16 .8E−5 100.

Don't use spaces in a floating-point constant.

WRONG 1.56 E+12

Floating-point constants are taken to be double precision. Suppose, for example, that **some** is a **float** variable, and that you have the statement

```
some = 4.0 * 2.0;
```

Then the 4.0 and 2.0 are stored as **double**, using (typically) 64 bits for each. The product (8, if you are wondering) is calculated using double precision arithmetic, and only then is the answer trimmed down to regular **float** size. This ensures maximum precision for your calculations.

FLOATING-POINT OVERFLOW AND UNDERFLOW

What happens if you try to make a **float** variable exceed its limits? For example, suppose you multiply 10e38 by 100 (overflow) or divide 10e−37 by 1000 (underflow)? The result depends on the system. On our system, any number that overflows is replaced by the largest legal value, and any number that underflows is replaced by 0. Other systems may issue warnings or balk or offer you a choice of responses. If this is a matter that concerns you, you'll have to check out the rules on your system. If you can't find the information, don't be afraid to try a little trial and error.

SUMMARY: THE BASIC DATA TYPES

Keywords:
The basic data types are set up using the following 7 keywords: **int, long, short, unsigned, char, float, double.**

Signed Integers:
These can have positive or negative values.
int : the basic integer type for a given system
long or **long int** : can hold an integer at least as large as the largest **int** and possibly larger
short or **short int** : the largest **short** integer is no larger than the largest **int** and may be smaller Typically, **long** will be bigger than **short,** and **int** will be the same as one of the two. For example, IBM PC Lattice C has 16-bit **short** and **int,** and 32-bit **long.** It all depends on the system.

Unsigned Integers:
These have zero or positive values only. This extends the range of the largest possible positive number. Use the keyword **unsigned** before the desired type: **unsigned int, unsigned long, unsigned short.**
A lone **unsigned** is the same as **unsigned int.**
Characters: These are typographic symbols such as A, &, and +. Typically just one byte of memory is used.
char : the keyword for this type

Floating Point:
These can have positive or negative values.
float : the basic floating-point size for the system
double or **long float** : a (possibly) larger unit for holding floating-point numbers. It may allow more significant figures and perhaps larger exponents.

SUMMARY: HOW TO DECLARE A SIMPLE VARIABLE

1. Choose the type you need.
2. Choose a name for the variable.
3. Use this format for a declaration statement:
   type-specifier variable-name;
   The *type-specifier* is formed from one or more of the type keywords. Here are some examples:
   int erest;
   unsigned short cash;
4. You may declare more than one variable of the same type by separating the variable names by commas:
   char ch, init, ans;
5. You can initialize a variable in a declaration statement:
   float mass = 6.0E24;

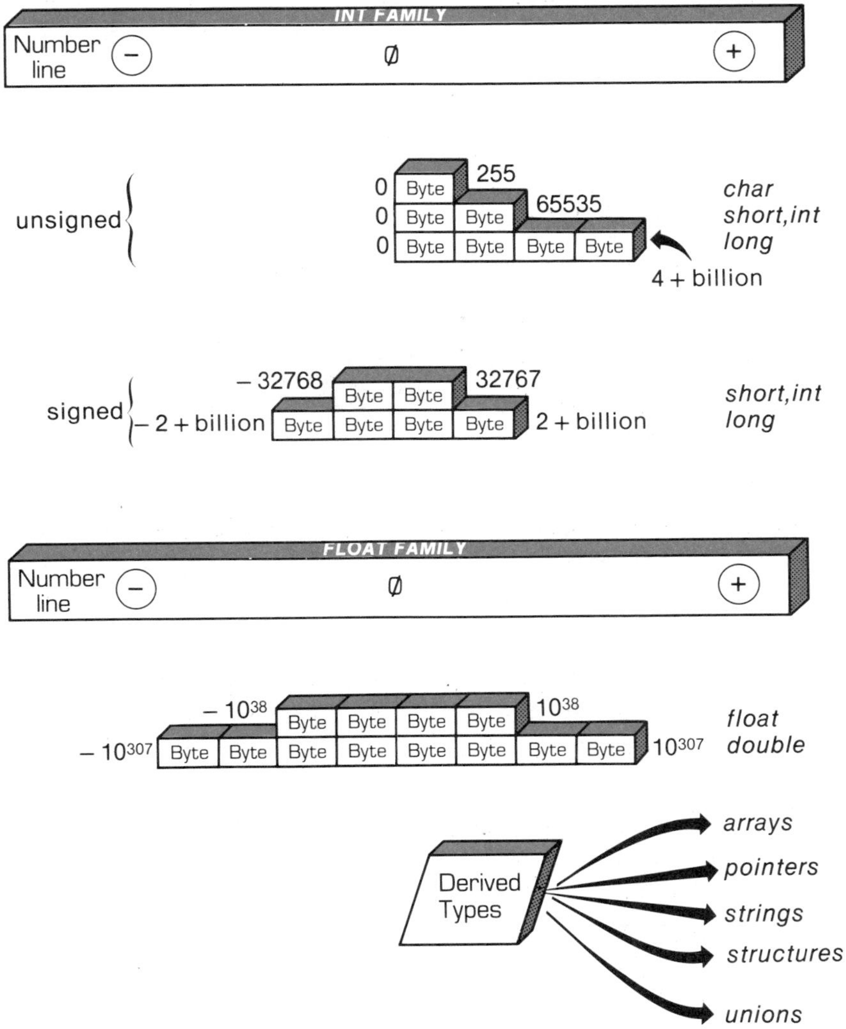

Figure 3.6
C data types for a typical system

Other Types

That finishes our list of fundamental data types. For some of you, that may seem like a lot. Others of you might be thinking that these are not enough. What about a Boolean type or a string type? C doesn't have them, but it still can deal quite well with logical manipulations and with strings. We will take a first look at strings in the next chapter.

C does have other types derived from the basic types. These types include arrays, pointers, structures, and unions. Although these are subject matter for later chapters, we already have smuggled some pointers into this chapter's examples. (Pointers are used by **scanf( )** and are indicated in that case by the & prefix.)

Type Sizes

Here is a table of type sizes for some common C environments.

Table 3-1. Type Facts for Representative Systems

word size	DEC PDP-11 16 bits	DEC VAX 32 bits	Interdata 8/3 32 bits	IBM PC (Lattice C) 16 bits
char	8	8	8	8
int	16	32	32	16
short	16	16	16	16
long	32	32	32	32
float	32	32	32	32
double	64	64	64	64
exponent range **(double)**	±38	±38	±76	−307 to 308

What is your system like? Try running this program to find out.

```
main()
{
  printf("Type int has a size of %d bytes.\n", sizeof(int));
  printf("Type char has a size of %d bytes.\n", sizeof(char));
  printf("Type long has a size of %d bytes.\n", sizeof(long));
  printf("Type double has a size of %d bytes.\n",
sizeof(double));
}
```

C has a built-in operator called **sizeof** that gives the size of things in bytes. Our output from this program was

```
Type int has a size of 2 bytes.
Type char has a size of 1 bytes.
Type long has a size of 4 bytes.
Type double has a size of 8 bytes.
```

We found the size of just four types, but you can easily modify this program to find the size of any other type that interests you.

USING DATA TYPES

When you develop a program, take note of the variables you need and of what type they should be. Most likely you can use **int** or possibly **float** for the numbers and **char** for the characters. Declare them at the beginning of the function that uses them. Choose a name for the variable that suggests its meaning. When you initialize a variable, match the constant type to the variable type.

```
int apples = 3;                    /* RIGHT */
int oranges = 3.0;                 /* WRONG */
```

C is more forgiving about such mismatches than, say, Pascal, but it is best not to develop sloppy habits.

WHAT YOU SHOULD HAVE LEARNED

We covered a goodly amount of material in this chapter. In this summary we will stick to the more practical aspects of what we have covered. As in the previous chapter, we will include short examples as room permits. Here, then, are some things you should know.

What the basic C data types are: **int, short, long, unsigned, char, float, double**

How to declare a variable of any type: **int beancount; float rootbeer;** and so on.

How to write an **int** constant: **256, 023, 0XF5,** etc.

How to write a **char** constant: **'r', 'U', '\007', '?',** etc.

How to write a **float** constant: **14.92, 1.67e−27,** etc.

What words, bytes, and bits are.

When to use different data types.

QUESTIONS AND ANSWERS

Working through these questions should help you digest the material in this chapter.

Questions

1. Which data type would you use for each of the following kinds of data?
   a. The population of Rio Frito
   b. The average weight of a Rembrandt painting
   c. The most common letter in this chapter
   d. The number of times that letter occurs
2. Identify the type and meaning, if any, of each of the following constants.
   a. `'\b'`
   b. `1066`
   c. `99.44`
   d. `0XAA`
   e. `2.0e30`
3. Virgila Ann Xenopod has concocted an error-laden program. Help her find the mistakes.

```
#include <stdio.h>
main
(
  float g; h;
  float tax, rate;

  g = e21;
  tax = rate*g;
)
```

Answers

1. **a.** **int,** possibly **short;** population is a whole number
   b. **float;** it's unlikely the average will be an exact integer
   c. **char**
   d. **int,** possibly **unsigned**
2. **a.** **char,** the backspace character
   b. historic **int**
   c. **float** measure of soap purity
   d. hexadecimal **int;** decimal value is 170
   e. **float** mass of the sun in kg
3. Line 1 is fine.
   Line 2 should have a parentheses pair follow **main,** i.e., **main( )**
   Line 3: use {, not (
   LINE 4: should be a comma, not a semicolon, between **g** and **h**
   LINE 5: fine
   LINE 6: (the blank line) fine
   LINE 7: There should be at least one digit before the **e.**

Either **1e21** or **1.0e21** is okay.
LINE 8: okay
LINE 9: use }, not)
Missing Lines: First, **rate** is never assigned a value. Second, the variable **h** is never used. Also, the program never informs us of the results of its calculation. Neither of these errors will stop the program from running (although you may be given a warning about the unused variable), but they do detract from its already limited usefulness.

4

CHARACTER STRINGS, #define, printf( ), AND scanf( )

In this chapter you will find

- Character Strings—An Introduction
  - String Length—*strlen( )*
- Constants and the C Preprocessor
  - C—A Master of Disguise: Creating Aliases
- Exploring and Exploiting *printf( )* and *scanf( )*
  - Using *prinft( )*
  - *printf( )* Conversion Specification Modifiers
  - Examples
  - Using *printf( )* To Make Conversions
  - Using *scanf( )*
- Usage Tips
- What You Should Have Learned
- Questions and Answers

4. CHARACTER STRINGS, #define, printf( ), AND scanf( )

CONCEPTS

Character strings
The C preprocessor
Formatted output

In this chapter we continue our data dalliance by delving into matters beyond basic data types and looking at the character string. We'll first take a look at an important C facility, the C preprocessor, and learn how to define and use symbolic constants. Then we will look again at ways to communicate data to and from a program, this time exploring the features of **printf( )** and **scanf( )** more fully. By now you probably expect a sample program at the beginning of the chapter, and we won't disappoint you.

```
/* talkback */
#define DENSITY 62.4 /* human density in lbs per cu ft */
main() /* nosy, informative program */
{
  float weight, volume;
  int size, letters;
  char name[40]; /* or try "static char name[40];" */

  printf("Hi! What's your first name?\n");
  scanf("%s", name);
  printf("%s, what's your weight in pounds?\n", name);
  scanf("%f", &weight);
  size = sizeof name;
  letters = strlen(name);
  volume = weight/DENSITY;
  printf("Well, %s, your volume is %2.2f cubic feet.\n",
       name, volume);
```

```
    printf("Also, your first name has %d letters,\n",
         letters);
    printf("and we have %d bytes to store it in.\n", size);
}
```

Running **talkback** produces results such as the following:

```
Hi! What's your first name?
Angelica
Angelica, what's your weight in pounds?
102.5
Well, Angelica, your volume is 1.64 cubic feet.
Also, your first name has 8 letters,
and we have 40 bytes to store it in.
```

Here are the main new features of this program.

1. We have used an "array" to hold a "character string," in this case, someone's name.
2. We used the %s "conversion specification" to handle the input and output of the string.
3. We used the C preprocessor to define the symbolic constant **DENSITY.**
4. We used the C function **strlen( )** to find the length of a string.

The C approach may seem a little complex compared to the input/output modes of, say, BASIC. However, this complexity buys a finer control of I/O and a greater program efficiency. And it is not all that difficult once you get into it.

Let's flesh out these new ideas.

CHARACTER STRINGS—AN INTRODUCTION

A "character string" is a series of one or more characters. An example of a string is:

```
"Zing went the strings of my heart!"
```

The double quotes are not part of the string. They are there to mark off the string, just as single quotes are used to mark off a character.

C has no special variable type for strings. Instead, strings are stored in an "array" of **char** type. This means you can think of the characters in a string as being stored in adjacent memory cells, one character per cell. See Fig. 4.1.

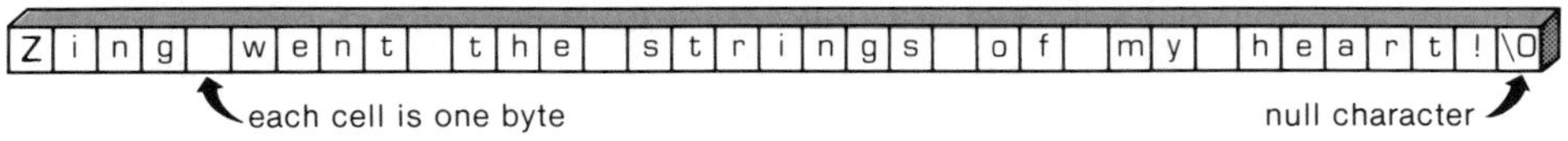

Figure 4.1
A string in an array

Note in the figure that we show the character **\0** in the last array position. This is the "null character," and C uses it to mark the end of a string. The null character is not the digit zero; it is the nonprinting character whose ASCII code number is 0. The presence of the null character means that the array must have at least one more cell than the number of characters to be stored.

Now just what is an array? We can think of an array as several memory cells in a row. Or, if you prefer more formal and exact language, an array is an ordered sequence of data elements of one type. In our example, we created an array of 40 memory cells, each of which can store one **char**-type value. We accomplished this with the declaration:

```
char name [40];
```

The brackets identify **name** as an array, the 40 indicates the number of elements, and the **char** identifies the type of each element.

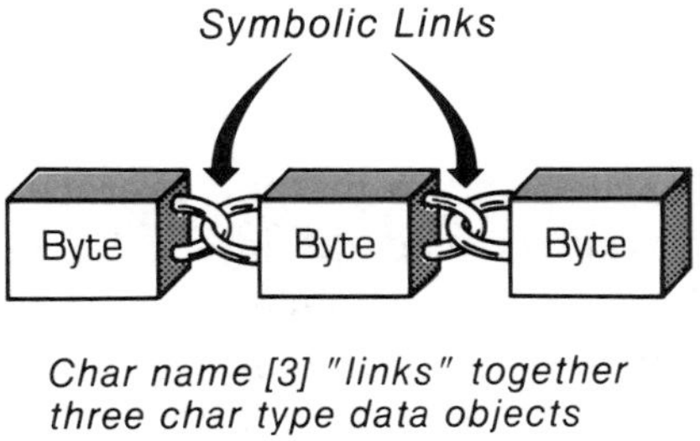

Figure 4.2
Declaring an array name of type *char*

(In a comment we noted that you may wish to use the more elaborate declaration:

```
static char name[40];
```

Due to a peculiarity of **scanf( )** in our system, we have to use this second form, but most likely you won't have to. If you find that the first form gives you problems with our examples, try the second. Indeed, the second should work on all systems, but we don't talk about **static** until we discuss storage classes in Chapter 10.)

This is beginning to sound complicated; you have to create an array, pack in the characters of a string one by one, and remember to add a **\0** at the end! Fortunately for us, the computer can take care of most of the details itself.

Try this program to see how easily it works in practice.

```
/* praise1 */
#define PRAISE "My sakes, that's a grand name!"
main()
{
  char name[50];

  printf("What's your name?\n");
  scanf("%s", name);
  printf("Hello, %s. %s\n", name, PRAISE);
}
```

The %s tells **printf( )** to print a string. Running **praise1** should produce an output similar to this:

```
What's your name?
Elmo Blunk
Hello, Elmo. My sakes, that's a grand name!
```

We did not have to put in the null character ourselves. That task was done for us when **scanf( )** read the input. **PRAISE** is a "character string constant." We'll get to the **#define** statement soon; for now, you should know that the double quotation marks which enclose the phrase following **PRAISE** identify it as a string and take care of putting in the null character.

Note (and this is important) that **scanf( )** just reads Elmo Blunk's first name. When **scanf( )** reads input, it stops at the first "white space" (blank, tab, or newline) it encounters. Thus it stops scanning for **name** when it reaches the blank between "Elmo" and "Blunk." In general, **scanf( )** reads just single words, not whole phrases as a string. C has other input-reading functions, such as **gets( ),** for handling general strings. We will explore strings much more fully in later chapters.

The string **"x"** is not the same as the character **'x'.** One difference is that **'x'** is a basic type **(char)**, while **"x"** is a derived type, an array of **char.** A second difference is that **"x"** really consists of two characters, **'x'** and the null character.

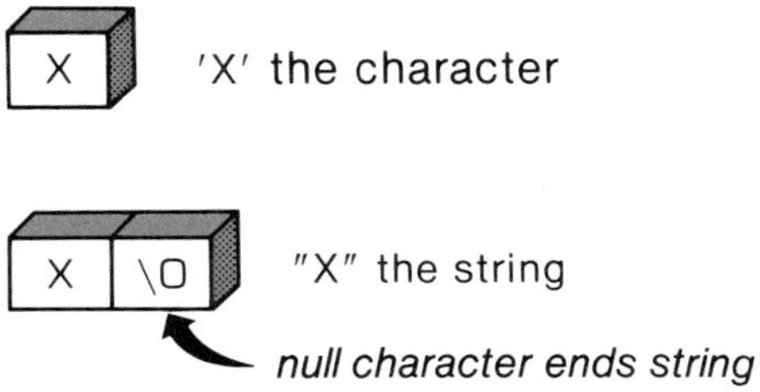

Figure 4.3
'x' and "x"

String Length—*strlen( )*

Last chapter we unleashed the **sizeof** operator, which gave us the size of things in bytes. The **strlen( )** function gives us the length of a string in characters. Since it takes one byte to hold one character, you might suppose both would give the same result when applied to a string, but they don't. Let's add a few lines to our example and see why.

```
/* praise2 */
#define PRAISE "My sakes, that's a grand name!"
main()
{
  char name[50];

  printf("What's your name?\n");
  scanf("%s", name);
  printf("Hello, %s. %s\n", name, PRAISE);
  printf("Your name of %d letters occupies %d memory cells.\n",
         strlen(name), sizeof name);
  printf("The phrase of praise has %d letters ", strlen(PRAISE));
  printf("and occupies %d memory cells.\n", sizeof PRAISE);
}
```

Notice, incidentally, that we have used two methods to handle long **printf( )** statements. We spread one print statement over two lines. We can break a line between arguments but not in the middle of a string. Then we used two **printf( )** statements to print just one line. We did this by using the newline character (**\n**) only in the second statement. Running the program could produce this interchange:

```
What's your name?
Perky
Hello, Perky. My sakes, that's a grand name!
Your name of 5 letters occupies 50 memory cells.
The phrase of praise has 30 letters and occupies 31 memory cells.
```

See what happens. The array **name** has 50 memory cells, and that is what **sizeof** reports to us. But only the first five cells are needed to hold **Perky,** and that is what **strlen( )** reports to us. The sixth cell in the array **name** contains the null character, and its presence tells **strlen( )** when to stop counting.

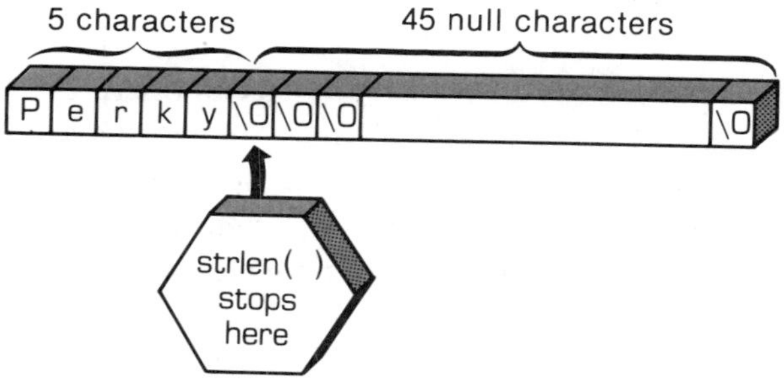

Figure 4.4
***strlen( )* knows when to stop**

When we get to **PRAISE,** we find that **strlen( )** again gives us the exact number of characters (including spaces and punctuation) in the string. The **sizeof** operator gives us a number one larger, for it also counts the invisible null character used to end the string. We didn't tell the computer how much memory to set aside to store the phrase. It had to count the number of characters between the double quotes itself.

One other point: in the preceding chapter we used **sizeof** with parentheses, and this chapter we didn't. Whether you use parentheses or not depends on whether you want the size of a type class or the size of a particular quantity. That is, you would use **sizeof(char)** or **sizeof(float),** but **sizeof name** or **sizeof 6.28.**

We have just used **strlen( )** and **sizeof** to satisfy our curiosity, but they are important programming tools. **Strlen( ),** for example, is useful in all sorts of character-string programs, as we'll see in Chapter 13.

Let's move on to the **#define** statement.

CONSTANTS AND THE C PREPROCESSOR

Sometimes we need to use a constant in a program. For example, we could give the circumference of a circle as

```
circ = 3.14 * diameter;.
```

Here we used the constant 3.14 to represent the famous constant pi. To use a constant, we can just type in the actual value, as we did there. There are good reasons to use a "symbolic constant" instead, however. That is, we could use a statement like

```
circ = pi * diameter;
```

and have the computer substitute in the actual value later.

Why is this good? First, a name tells us more than a number does. Compare these two statements:

```
owed = 0.015 * housevl;
owed = taxrate * housevl;
```

If we are reading through a long program, the meaning of the second version is plainer.

Secondly, suppose we have used a constant in several places, and it becomes necessary to change its value. After all, tax rates do change, and a state legislature once passed a law stating that the value of pi would henceforth be a simple 3 1/7. (Presumably many a circle became a fugitive from justice.) Then we need merely alter the definition of the symbolic constant rather than find and change every occurrence of the constant in the program.

Okay, how do we set up a symbolic constant? One way is to declare a variable and set it equal to the desired constant. We could do this:

```
float taxrate;
taxrate = 0.015;
```

This is okay for a small program, but it is a little wasteful, because the computer has to go peek into the **taxrate** memory location every time it is used. This is an example of "execution time" substitution, for the substitutions take place while the program is running. Fortunately, C has a better idea.

The better idea is the C preprocessor. We've already seen in Chapter 2 how the preprocessor uses **#include** to include information from another file. The preprocessor also lets us define constants. Just add a line like this at the top of the file containing your program:

```
#define TAXRATE 0.015
```

When your program is compiled, the value 0.015 will be substituted everywhere you have used **TAXRATE.** This is called a "compile time" substitution. By the time you run the program, all the substitutions already have been made.

Note the format. First comes **#define.** It should be all the way to the left. Then comes the symbolic name for the constant, then the value for the constant. No semicolon is used, since this is not a C statement. Why is **TAXRATE** capitalized? It is a sensible C tradition to type constants in upper case. Then, when you come across one in the depths of a program, you will know at once that it is a constant and not a variable. It is just another example of trying to make programs readable. Your programs will still work if you don't capitalize the constants, but you should feel a little guilty about it.

Here is a simple example:

```
/* pizza */
#define PI 3.14159
main()     /* learning about your pizza */
{
  float area, circum, radius;

  printf("What is the radius of your pizza?\n");
  scanf("%f", &radius);
  area = PI * radius * radius;
  circum = 2.0 * PI *radius;
  printf("Your basic pizza parameters are as follows:\n");
  printf("circumference = %1.2f, area = %1.2f\n", circum, area);
}
```

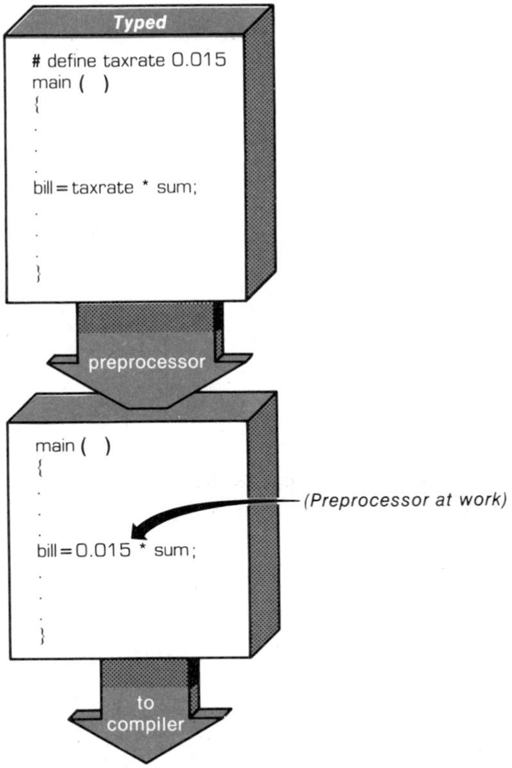

Figure 4.5
What you type vs. what gets compiled

The **%1.2f** in the **printf( )** statement causes the printout to be rounded to two decimal places. Of course, this program may not reflect your major pizza concerns, but it does serve to fill a small niche in the world of pizza programs. Here is a sample run.

```
What is the radius of your pizza?
6.0
Your basic pizza parameters are as follows:
circumference = 37.70, area = 113.10
```

The **#define** statement can be used for character and string constants, too. Just use single quotation marks for the former and double quotes for the latter. Thus, the following examples are valid:

```
#define BEEP '\007'
```

```
#define ESS 'S'
#define NULL '\0'
#define OOPS "Now you have done it!"
```

Now we have a special treat for the lazy. Suppose you develop a whole packet of programs that use the same set of constants. You can do the following.

1. Collect all your **#define** statements in one file; call it, say, **const.h.**
2. At the head of each file of programs, include the statement **#include "const.h".**

Then, when you run the program, the preprocessor will read the file **const.h** and use all the **#define** statements there for your program. Incidentally, the **.h** at the end of the file name is a reminder to you that the file is a "header," i.e., full of information to go at the head of your program. The preprocessor itself doesn't care if you use a **.h** in the name or not.

C—A Master of Disguise: Creating Aliases

The capabilities of **#define** go beyond the symbolic representation of constants. Consider, for instance, the following program.

```
#include "alias.h"
program
  begin
    whole yours, mine then
    spitout("Give me an integer, please.\n ") then
    takein("%d", &yours) then
    mine = yours times TWO then
    spitout("%d is twice your number!\n ", mine) then
  end
```

Hmm, this looks vaguely familiar, a little like Pascal, but it doesn't seem to be C. The secret, of course, is in the file **alias.h.** What's in it? Read on.

```
alias.h
#define program main()
#define begin   {
#define end     }
#define then    ;
```

```
#define takein  scanf
#define spitout printf
#define TWO     2
#define times   *
#define whole   int
```

This example illustrates how the preprocessor works. Your program is searched for items defined by **#define** statements. Finds are then replaced literally. In our example, all **thens** are rendered into semicolons, etc., at compilation. The resulting program is identical to what we would have gotten by typing in the usual C terms in the first place.

This powerful ability can be used to define a "macro," which is sort of a poor man's function. We will return to this topic in Chapter 11.

There are some limitations. For example, parts of a program within double quotes are immune to substitution. For instance, this combination wouldn't work:

```
#define MN "minimifidianism"
printf("He was a strong believer in MN.\n");
```

The printout would just read

```
He was a strong believer in MN.
```

However, the statement

```
printf("He was a strong believer in %s.\n", MN);
```

would produce

```
He was a strong believer in minimifidianism.
```

In this case, the **MN** was outside the double quotes, so it was replaced by its definition.

The C preprocessor is a useful, helpful tool, so take advantage of it when you can. We'll show you more applications as we move along.

EXPLORING AND EXPLOITING *printf( )* AND *scanf( )*

The functions **printf( )** and **scanf( )** let us communicate with a program. We call them input/output functions, or I/O functions for short. These are not the only I/O functions we can use with C, but they are the most versatile. These functions are *not* part of the definition of C. Indeed, C leaves the implementation of I/O up to the compiler writers; this makes it possible to better match I/O to specific machines. However, in the interests of compatibility, various systems all come with versions of **scanf( )** and **printf( ).** What we say here should be mostly true for most systems, but don't be astonished if you find your version to be different in some small fashion.

Generally, **printf( )** and **scanf( )** work much the same, each using a "control string" and a list of "arguments." We will first show how these work with **printf( ),** then with **scanf( ).**

The instructions we give **printf( )** when we ask it to print a variable depend on what type the variable is. For instance, we have used the **%d** notation when printing an integer and the **%c** notation when printing a character. Let's list all the identifiers the **printf( )** function uses, and then show how to use them. First, here are the identifiers and the type of output they cause to be printed. The first five serve most needs, but the other four are available if you desire them.

IDENTIFIER	OUTPUT
%d	decimal integer
%c	a single character
%s	character string
%e	floating-point number, e-notation
%f	floating-point number, decimal notation
%g	use %f or %e, whichever is shorter
%u	unsigned decimal integer
%o	unsigned octal integer
%x	unsigned hexadecimal integer

Now let's see how they are used.

Using *printf( )*

Here is a program that uses some of the examples we will discuss:

```
/* printstuff */
#define PI 3.14159
main()
{
  int number = 5;
```

```
float ouzo = 13.5;
int cost = 31000;

printf("The %d women drank %f glasses of ouzo.\n",number,ouzo);
printf("The value of pi is %f.\n", PI);
printf("Farewell! thou art too dear for my possessing,\n");
printf("%c%d\n", '$', cost);
}
```

The output, of course, is

```
The 5 women drank 13.500000 glasses of ouzo.
The value of pi is 3.14159.
Farewell! thou art too dear for my possessing,
$31000
```

The format for using **printf( )** is this:

```
printf(Control, item1, item2, . . . );
```

Item1, item2, and so on, are the items to be printed. They can be variables or constants, or even expressions that are evaluated first before the value is printed. **Control** is a character string describing how the items are to be printed. For example, in the statement

```
printf("The %d women drank %f glasses of ouzo.\n", number, ouzo);
```

control would be the phrase in double quotes (after all, it is a character string), and **number** and **ouzo** would be the items, or in this case, the values of two variables.

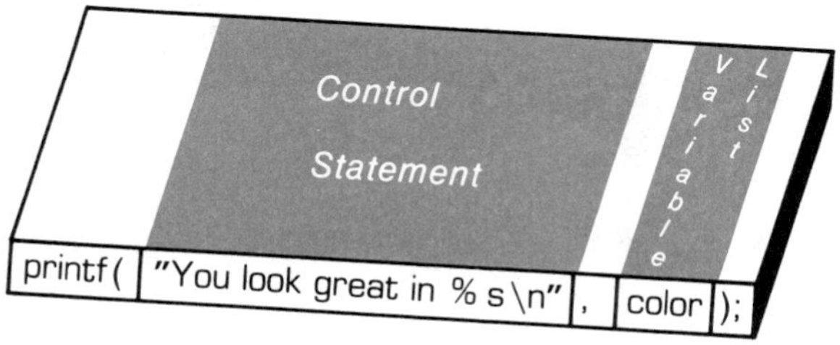

Figure 4.6
Arguments for *printf( )*

Here is a second example.

```
printf("The value of pi is %f.\n", PI);
```

This time, the list of items has just one member—the symbolic constant PI.

We see that **Control** contains two distinct forms of information:

1. characters that are printed literally, and
2. the data identifiers, also called "conversion specifications."

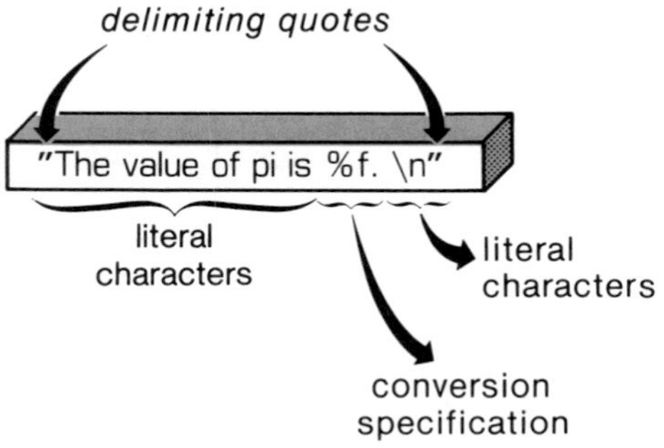

Figure 4.7
Anatomy of a control string

There should be one conversion specification for each item in the list following **Control.** Woe (or is it whoa?) unto you should you forget this basic requirement! Don't do this:

```
printf("The score was Squids %d, Slugs %d.\n", score1);
```

Here there is no value for the second **%d.** The result of this faux pas will depend on your system, but at best you will get nonsense.

If you just want to print a phrase, you don't need any conversion specifications, and if you just want to print data, you can dispense with the running commentary. Thus each of the following statements is quite acceptable.

```
printf("Farewell! thou art too dear for my possessing,\n");
printf("%c%d\n", '$', cost);
```

Note that in the second example, the first item on the print list was a character constant rather than a variable.

Since the **printf( )** function uses the % symbol to identify the conversion specifications, there is a slight problem if you wish to print the % sign itself. If you just use a lone % sign, the compiler will think you have bungled a conversion specification. The way out is simple: just use two % symbols:

```
pc = 2*6;
printf("Only %d%% of Sally's gribbles were edible.\n", pc);
```

would produce the following output.

```
Only 12% of Sally's gribbles were edible.
```

printf( ) Conversion Specification Modifiers

We can modify a basic conversion specification by inserting modifiers between the % and the defining conversion character. Here is a list of the symbols you can place there legally. If you use more than one modifier, they should be in the order they appear in this table. Not all combinations are possible.

Modifier	**Meaning**
−	The item will be printed beginning at the left of its field width (as defined below). Normally the item is printed so that it ends at the right of its field. Example: **%−10d**
digit string	The minimum field width. A wider field will be used if the printed number or string won't fit in the field. Example: **%4d**
.digit string	Precision. For floating types, the number of digits to be printed to the right of the decimal. For character strings, the maximum number of characters to be printed. Example: **%4.2f** (2 decimal places in a field 4 characters wide)
l	The corresponding data item is **long** rather than **int.** Example: **%ld**

Examples

Let's put these modifiers to work. We'll begin by looking at the effect of the field width modifier on printing an integer. Consider the following program.

```
main()
{
  printf("/%d/\n", 336);
  printf("/%2d/\n", 336);
  printf("/%10d/\n", 336);
  printf("/%-10d/\n", 336);
}
```

This program prints the same quantity 4 times, but using 4 different conversion specifications. We used **/'s** to let you see where each field begins and ends. The output looks like this:

```
/336/
/336/
/       336/
/336       /
```

The first conversion specification is **%d** with no modifiers. We see that it uses a field with the same width as the integer. This is the so-called "default" option, i.e., what gets done if you don't give further instructions. The second conversion specification is **%2d.** This should produce a field with a width of 2, but since the integer is three digits long, the field is expanded automatically to fit the number. The next conversion specification is **%10d.** This produces a field ten spaces wide, and, indeed, there are 7 blanks and 3 digits between the **/'s,** with the number tucked into the right end of the field. The final specification is **%−10d.** It also produces a field 10 spaces wide, and the − puts the number at the left end, just as advertised. Once you get used to it, this system is easy to use and gives you nice control over the appearance of your output.

Okay, let's look at some floating-point formats. Let the program look like this:

```
main()
{
  printf("/%f/\n", 1234.56);
```

```
    printf("/%e/\n", 1234.56);
    printf("/%4.2f/\n", 1234.56);
    printf("/%3.1f/\n", 1234.56);
    printf("/%10.3f/\n", 1234.56);
    printf("/%10.3e/\n", 1234.56);
}
```

This time we get this output:

```
/1234.560059/
/1.234560E+03/
/1234.56/
/1234.6/
/  1234.560/
/ 1.234E+03/
```

Again we begin with the default version, **%f.** In this case there are two defaults: field width, and digits to the right of the decimal. The second default is 6 digits, and the field width is whatever it takes to hold the number. Notice that the printed number is slightly different from the one we started with. This is because we are printing a total of 10 digits, and floating-point numbers on our system store no more than about 6 or 7 digits accurately.

Next is the default for **%e.** We see it prints one digit to the left of the decimal point and 6 places to the right. We seem to be getting a lot of digits! The cure is to specify the number of decimal places to the right of the decimal, and the last four examples in this segment do that. Notice how the fourth and the sixth examples cause the output to be rounded off.

Now let's examine some of the string options. Consider this example:

```
#define BLURB "Outstanding acting!"
main()
{
   printf("/%2s/\n", BLURB);
   printf("/%22s/\n", BLURB);
   printf("/%22.5s/\n", BLURB);
   printf("/%-22.5s/\n", BLURB);
}
```

Here's the output:

```
/Outstanding acting!/
/ Outstanding acting!/
/                Outst/
/Outst                /
```

Notice how the field is expanded to contain all the specified characters. Also notice how the precision specification limits the number of characters printed. The .5 in the format specifier tells **printf( )** to print just 5 characters.

Okay, you've seen some examples. Now how would you set up a statement to print something of the following form?

```
The NAME family just may be $XXX.XX dollars richer!
```

Here NAME and XXX.XX represent values that will be supplied by variables in the program, say, **name[40]** and **cash.**

Here is one solution:

```
printf("The %s family just may be $%.2f richer!\n",name,cash);
```

So far we have played it safe and matched the conversion specification to the variable type, **%f** for type **float,** and so on. But, as we saw in our program to find the ASCII code for a character, we can also use **printf( )** to make type conversions! But we have to keep reasonable and stay within the family of integer types.

Using *printf( )* To Make Conversions

Once again, we will print an integer. Since we know about fields now, we won't bother using /'s to mark them.

```
main()
{
   printf("%d\n", 336);
   printf("%o\n", 336);
   printf("%x\n", 336);
   printf("%d\n", -336);
   printf("%u\n", -336);
}
```

Our system produces the following results:

```
336
520
150
-336
65200
```

First, as you would expect, the **%d** specification gives us the number 336, just as it did a few lines ago. But look what happens when you ask the program to print this decimal integer as an octal integer. It prints 520, which is the octal equivalent of 336. $(5 \times 64 + 2 \times 8 + 0 \times 1 = 336)$. Similarly, 150 is the hex equivalent to 336.

Thus we can use the **printf( )** conversion specifications to convert decimal to octal or hexadecimal, and vice versa. Just ask for the number to be printed in the form you want; use **%d** to get decimal, **%o** to get octal, or **%x** to get hex. It doesn't matter in what form the number originally appeared in the program.

But there is more to the output. Printing −336 using **%d** produces no surprise. But the **%u** (unsigned) version came out as 65200, not as the 336 you might have expected. This results from the way negative numbers are represented on our reference system. It uses a method called the "two's complement." In this method, the numbers 0 to 32767 represent themselves, and the numbers 32768 to 65535 represent negative numbers, with

65535 being −1, 65534 being −2, etc. Thus **−366** is represented by **65536 − 336** or 65200. Not all systems use this method to represent negative integers. Nonetheless, there is a moral: don't expect a **%u** conversion simply to strip the sign from a number.

Now we come to an interesting example that we have used already—using **printf( )** to find the ASCII code of a character. For instance,

```
printf ("%c %d\n", 'A', 'A');
```

produces

```
A 65
```

for output. **A** is the letter, of course, and **65** is the decimal ASCII code for the character **A.** We could use **%o** if we want the octal ASCII code.

This gives us an easy way to find the ASCII code for various characters and vice versa. Of course, you may prefer to look them up in Appendix G.

What happens if you try to convert a number bigger than 255 to a character? The following program line and its output give the answer.

```
 printf("%d %c\n", 336, 336);
336 P
```

The ASCII decimal code for **P** is 80, and 336 is just 256+80. Apparently the number is interpreted modulo 256. (That's math talk meaning the remainder when the number is divided by 256.) In other words, whenever the computer reaches a multiple of 256, it starts counting over again, and 256 is considered to be 0, 257 is 1, 511 is 255, 512 is 0, 513 is 1, etc.

Finally, we try printing an integer (65616) that's larger than the maximum **int (32767)** allowed on our system:

```
printf("%ld %d \n", 65616, 65616);
```

The result is

```
65616 80
```

Again, the computer does its modulo thing. This time the counting is done in groups of 65536. A number between 32767 and 65536 would be printed out as a negative number because of the way negative numbers are stored.

Systems with different integer sizes would have the same general behavior, but with different numerical values.

We haven't exhausted all possible combinations of data and conversion specifications, so feel free to try some yourself. Better yet, see if you can predict in advance what the result will be when a certain item is printed using the conversion specification of your choice.

Using *scanf( )*

We will make just rudimentary use of **scanf( )** for the while, so we will only highlight its use here.

Like **printf( )**, **scanf( )** uses a control string followed by a list of arguments. The chief difference is in the argument list. **Printf( )** uses variable names, constants, and expressions. **Scanf( )** uses pointers to variables. Fortunately, we don't have to know anything about pointers to use the function. Just remember these two rules:

1. If you wish to read in a value for one of the basic variable types, precede the variable name with an &.
2. If you wish to read in a value for a string variable, don't use an &.

This is a valid program:

```
main()
{
    int age;
    float assets;
    char pet[30];

    printf("Enter your age, assets, and favorite pet.\n");
    scanf("%d %f", &age, &assets);
    scanf("%s", pet); /* no & for char array */
    printf("%d $%.0f %s\n ", age, assets, pet);
}
```

And here is a sample exchange:

```
Enter your age, assets, and favorite pet.
82
8345245.19 rhino
82 $8345245 rhino
```

Scanf( ) uses white space (blanks, tabs, and spaces) to decide how to divide the input into separate fields. It matches up consecutive conversion specification to consecutive fields, skipping over the white space in between. Note how we spread our input over two lines. We could just as well have used one or five lines, as long as we had at least one newline, space, or tab between each entry. The only exception to this is the **%c** specification, which reads the very next character, even if it is white space.

The **scanf( )** function uses pretty much the same set of conversion-specification characters as **printf( )** does. The main differences for **scanf( )** are these:

1. There is no **%g** option.
2. The **%f** and the **%e** options are equivalent. Both accept an optional sign, a string of digits with or without a decimal point, and an optional exponent field.
3. There is a **%h** option for reading **short** integers.

Scanf( ) is not the most commonly used input function in C. We have featured it here because of its versatility (it can read all the different data types), but C has several other input functions, such as **getchar( )** and **gets( )** that are better suited for specific tasks, such as reading single characters or reading strings containing spaces. We will cover some of these functions in Chapters 6, 13, and 15.

USAGE TIPS

Specifying fixed field widths is useful when you want to print columns of data. Since the default field width is just the width of the number, the repeated use of, say,

```
printf("%d %d %d\n", val1, val2, val3);
```

would produce ragged columns if the numbers in a column had different sizes. For example, the output could look like this:

```
12 234 1222
4 5 23
22334 2322 10001
```

(This assumes that the value of the variables has been changed between print statements.)

The output can be cleaned up using a sufficiently large fixed field width. Using

```
printf("%9d %9d %9d\n", val1, val2, val3);
```

would yield

```
       12        234       1222
        4          5         23
    22334       2322      10001
```

Leaving a blank between one conversion specification and the next ensures that one number will never run into the next, even if it overflows its own field. This is so because the regular characters in the control string, including spaces, are printed out.

On the other hand, if a number is to be embedded in a phrase, it often is convenient to specify a field as small or smaller than the expected number width. This makes the number fit in without unnecessary blanks. For example,

```
printf("Count Beppo ran %.2f miles in 3 hours.\n",
    distance);
```

might produce

```
Count Beppo ran 10.22 miles in 3 hours.
```

while changing the conversion specification to %10.2f would give

```
Count Beppo ran      10.22 miles in 3 hours.
```

WHAT YOU SHOULD HAVE LEARNED

What a character string is: some characters in a row
How to write a character string: **"some characters in a row"**
How a string is stored: **"some characters in a row\0"**

Where to store a string: **char phrase[25]** or **static char phrase[25]**
How to find the length of a string: **strlen(phrase)**
How to print out a string: **printf("%s", phrase)**
How to read in a one-word string: **scanf("%s," name)**
How to define a numerical constant: **#define TWO 2**
How to define a character constant: **#define WOW '!'**
How to define a string constant: **#define WARN "Don't do that!"**
I/O conversion specifications: **%d %f %e %g %c %s %u %o %x**
How to fine-tune output format: **%-10d %3.2f**
How to make conversions:**printf("%d %o %c\n", WOW, WOW, WOW);**

QUESTIONS AND ANSWERS

Questions

1. Run the opening program again, but this time give your first and last name when it asks you for your first name. What happens? Why?
2. What would each of the following program fragments cause to be printed, assuming they are part of a complete program?
   a. `printf("He sold the painting for $%2.2f.\n", 2.345e2);`
   b. `printf("%c%c%c\n", 'H', 105, '\41');`
   c. `#define Q "His Hamlet was funny without being vulgar."`
   `printf("%s\nhas %d characters.\n", Q, strlen(Q));`
   d. `printf("Is %2.2e the same as %2.2f?\n", 1201.0, 1201.0);`
3. In Question 2c, what changes could we make so that string Q is printed out enclosed in quotes?
4. It's find the error time!

```
define B booboo
define X 10
main()
{
    int age;
    char name;

    printf("Please enter your first name.");
    scanf("%s", name);
    printf("All right, %c, what's your age?\n", name);
```

```
    scanf("%f", age);
    xp = age + X;
    printf("That's a %s! You must be at least %d.\n", B, xp);
}
```

Answers

1. The program bombs. The first **scanf( )** statement reads just your first name, leaving your last name untouched, but still stored in the input "buffer." (This buffer is just a temporary storage area used to store the input.) When the next **scanf( )** statement comes along looking for your weight, it picks up where the last reading attempt ended, and reads your last name as your weight. This produces garbage. On the other hand, if you respond to the name request with something like "Lasha 144," it will use 144 as your weight even though you typed it before your weight was requested.
2. **a.** `He sold the painting for $234.50.`

   b. `Hi!`

   Note: the first character is a character constant, the second is a decimal integer converted to a character, and the third is ASCII representation of a character constant.

   c. `His Hamlet was funny without being vulgar.`
   `has 41 characters.`

   d. `Is 1.20E+03 the same as 1201.00?`
3. Remember the escape sequences of Chapter 3 and try
   `printf("\"%s\"\nhas %d characters.\n", Q, strlen(Q));`
4. Line 1: the # was omitted. **booboo** should be **"booboo"**.
   Line 2: the # was omitted.
   Line 6: **name** should be an array; **char name[25]** would serve.
   Line 8: There should be **\n** in the control string.
   Line 10: The **%c** should be **%s.**
   Line 11: Since **age** is integer, use **%d,** not **%f.** Also, use **&age,** not **age.**
   Line 12: xp never was declared
   Line 13: okay, but will be messed up by improperly defined B.
   Also, the program is guilty of poor manners.

5

OPERATORS, EXPRESSIONS, AND STATEMENTS

In this chapter you will find

5. OPERATORS, EXPRESSIONS, AND STATEMENTS

CONCEPTS

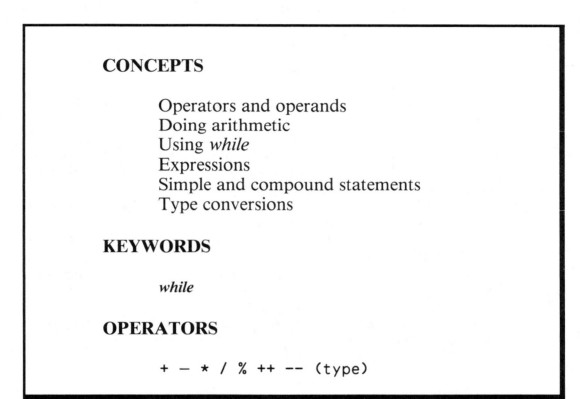

Operators and operands
Doing arithmetic
Using *while*
Expressions
Simple and compound statements
Type conversions

KEYWORDS

while

OPERATORS

```
+ - * / % ++ -- (type)
```

INTRODUCTION

In Chapters 3 and 4 we talked about the kinds of data C recognizes. Now we look at ways to do things to the data. C offers many possibilities. We will start with basic arithmetic: addition, subtraction, multiplication and division. To make our programs more interesting and useful, we will take a first look at loops in the chapter. Meanwhile, to get you into the proper frame of mind, here is a sample program that does a little arithmetic.

```
/* shoesize1 */
#define OFFSET 7.64
#define SCALE 0.325
main()
{
 /* this program converts shoe size to foot size in inches */
  float shoe, foot;

  size = 9.0;
  foot = SCALE*shoe + OFFSET;
  printf("Shoe size (men's)    foot length\n");
  printf("%10.1f %13.2f inches\n", shoe, foot);
}
```

Wow! Here is a program with multiplication *and* addition. It takes your shoe size (if you wear a size 9) and tells you how long your foot is in inches. But you say you could solve this problem by hand more quickly than you could type the program? That's a good point. It is a waste of time and effort to produce a one-shot program that does just one shoe size. We could make it more useful by writing it as an interactive program, but that still barely taps the potential of a computer.

What we need is some way to have a computer do repetitive calculations. After all, that is one of the main reasons for using a computer to do arithmetic. C offers several methods to accomplish repetitive calculations, and we will outline one here. This approach, called a "**while** loop," will enable us to make a more interesting exploration of operators. Here, then, is our improved shoe sizing program.

```
/* shoesize2 */
#define OFFSET 7.64
#define SCALE 0.325
main()
{
 /* this program converts shoe size to foot size in inches */
  float shoe, foot;

  printf("Shoe size (men's)    foot length\n");
  size = 9.0;
  while (shoe < 18.5) {
     foot = SCALE*shoe + OFFSET;
     printf("%10.1f %15.2f inches\n", shoe, foot);
     shoe = shoe + 1.0;
```

```
    }
    printf("If the shoe fits, wear it.\n");
}
```

Here is a condensed version of **shoesize2**'s output:

```
Shoe size (men's)    foot length
       3.0           8.61 inches
       4.0           8.94 inches
     . . .             . . .
     . . .             . . .
      17.0          13.16 inches
      18.0          13.49 inches
If the shoe fits, wear it.
```

(Incidentally, the constants for this conversion were obtained during an incognito visit to a shoe store. The only shoe-sizer left lying around was for men's sizes only. Those of you interested in women's sizes will have to make your own visit to a shoe store.)

This is how the **while** loop works. When the program first reaches the **while** statement, it checks to see if the condition in parentheses is true or not. In this case the expression is

```
shoe < 18.5
```

where the < symbol means "less than." Well, **shoe** was initialized to **3.0,** which certainly is less than **18.5.** Thus the condition is true. In this case the program proceeds to the next statement, which converts the size to inches. Then it prints out the results. The next statement,

```
shoe = shoe + 1.0;
```

increases **shoe** by 1.0, making it 4.0. At this point the program returns to the **while** portion to check the condition. Why at this point? Because the next line is a closing brace (}), and we have used a set of braces ({ }) to mark the extent of the **while** loop. The statements between the two braces are the ones that may be repeated. Now back to our program. Is **4** less than **18.5?** Yup. So the whole cycle of embraced commands following the **while** is repeated. (In computerese, the program is said to "loop" through these statements.) This continues until **shoe** reaches a value of **19.0.** At this point the condition

```
shoe < 18.5
```

becomes false, since **19.0** is not less than **18.5.** When this happens, control passes to the next statement following the **while** loop. In our case, that is the final **printf( )** statement.

You easily can modify this program to do other conversions. For example, change **SCALE** to **1.8** and **OFFSET** to **32.0,** and you have a program that converts Centigrade to Fahrenheit. Or change **SCALE** to **0.6214** and **OFFSET** to **0,** and you convert kilometers to miles. If you make these changes, you probably should change the printed messages, too, to lessen confusion.

The **while** loop gives us a convenient, flexible means of controlling a program. Now let us turn to the fundamental operators that we can use in programs.

FUNDAMENTAL OPERATORS

C uses "operators" to represent arithmetic operations. For example, the + operator causes the two values flanking it to be added together. If the name "operator" seems odd to you, please reflect that they had to call those things something. "Operator" does seem to be a better choice than, say, "those things" or "arithmetical transactors." We'll look now at =, +, −, *, and /. (C does not have an exponentiating operator. In a later chapter we will present a function to accomplish this task.)

Assignment Operator: =

In C, the equals sign does not mean "equals." Instead, it is a value-assigning operator. The statement

```
bmw = 2002;
```

assigns the value 2002 to the variable named **bmw.** That is, the item to the left of the = sign is the *name* of a variable, and the item on the right is the *value* of the variable. We call the = symbol an "assignment operator." Again, don't think of the line as saying, "**bmw** equals 2002." Instead, read it as "assign the value 2002 to the variable **bmw.**" The action goes from right to left for this operator.

Perhaps this distinction between the name of a variable and the value of a variable seems like hair-splitting, but consider the following very common type of computer statement:

```
i = i + 1;
```

As mathematics, it makes no sense. If you add one to a finite number, the result isn't equal to the number you started with. But as a computer assignment statement, it is perfectly reasonable. It means, in long-winded English, "find the value of the variable whose name is **i**. To that value, add 1, then assign this new value to the variable whose name is **i**."

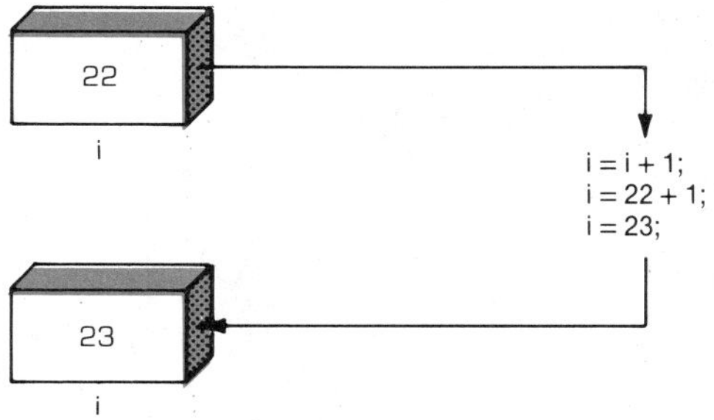

Figure 5.1
i = i + 1;

A statement such as

```
2002 = bmw;
```

makes no sense in C because **2002** is just a number. You can't assign a value to a constant; it already *is* its value. So when you sit down at the keyboard, remember that the item to the left of = sign must be the name of a variable.

For those of you who like to get the names of things right, the proper term for what we have called "items" is "operands." Operands are what operators operate upon. For example, you can describe eating a hamburger as applying the "eat" operator to the "hamburger" operand.

The basic C assignment operator is a little flashier than most. Try this short program.

```
 /* golf tournament score card */
main()
{
  int jane, tarzan, cheeta;

  cheeta = tarzan = jane = 68;
  printf(" cheeta    tarzan    jane\n");
  printf("First round score %4d %8d %8d\n",cheeta,tarzan,jane);
}
```

Many languages would boggle at the triple assignment made in this program, but C accepts it routinely. The assignments are made right to left;

first **jane** gets the value 68, then **tarzan** does, and finally **cheeta** does. Thus the output is

```
                    cheeta    tarzan    jane
First round score    68        68        68
```

C has several other assignment operators that work differently from the one described here, and we promise to tell you about them in a later chapter.

Addition Operator: +

The addition operator causes the two values on either side of it to be added together. For example, the statement

```
printf("%d", 4 + 20);
```

causes the number **24** to be printed and not the expression

```
4 + 20.
```

The operands can be variables as well as constants. Thus the statement

```
income = salary + bribes;
```

will cause the computer to look up the values of the two variables on the right, add them up, and assign this total to the variable **income.**

The + operator is termed a "binary" or "dyadic" operator, meaning that it takes *two* operands.

Subtraction Operator: −

The subtraction operator causes the number after the − sign to be subtracted from the number before the sign. The statement

```
takehome = 224.00 - 24.00;
```

assigns the value 200.0 to **takehome.**

Sign Operator: −

The minus sign also is used to indicate or to change the algebraic sign of a value. For instance, the sequence

```
rocky = -12;
smokey = -rocky;
```

gives **smokey** the value **12.**

When the minus sign is used this way, it is called a "unary" operator, meaning that it takes just one operand.

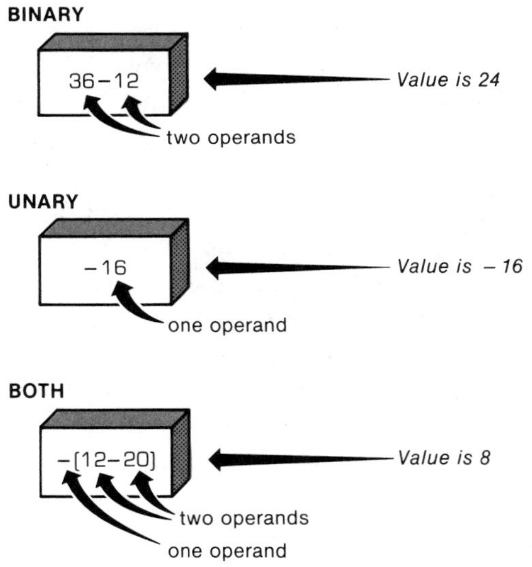

Figure 5.2
Unary and binary operators

Multiplication Operator: *

Multiplication is indicated by the * symbol. The statement

```
cm = 2.54 * in;
```

multiplies the variable **in** by 2.54 and assigns the answer to **cm.**

By any chance do you want a table of squares? C doesn't have a squaring function, but we can use multiplication.

```
 /* squares */
main () /* produces table of squares */
{
   int num = 1;

   while ( num < 21) {
   printf("%10d %10d\n", num, num*num);
   num = num + 1;
   }
}
```

This program prints out the first 20 integers and their squares, as you can verify for yourself.

Let's look at a more interesting example.

You probably have heard the story of the powerful ruler who seeks to reward a scholar who has done him a great service. When the scholar is asked what he would like, he points to a chessboard and says, just one grain of wheat on the first square, two on the second, four on the third, eight on the next, and so on. The ruler, lacking mathematical erudition, is astounded at the modesty of this request, for he had been prepared to offer great riches. The joke, of course, is on the ruler, as this next program shows. It calculates how many grains go on each square and keeps a running total. Since you may not be up to date on wheat crops, we also compare the running total to a rough estimate of the annual wheat crop in the U.S.

```
 /* wheat */
#define SQUARES 64 /* squares on a checkerboard */
#define CROP 7E14 /* US wheat crop in grains */
main()
{
   double current, total;
   int count = 1;

   printf("square   grains added   total grains    ");
   printf("fraction of \n");
   printf("                                        ");
    printf("   US total");
    total = current = 1.0; /*start with one grain */
   printf("%4d %15.2e %13.2e %12.2e\n", count, current,
     total, total/CROP);
   while ( count < SQUARES )
      {
```

```
        count = count + 1;
        current = 2.0 * current; /*double grains on next square*/
        total = total + current; /* update total */
        printf("%4d %15.2e %13.2e %12.2e\n", count, current,
             total, total/CROP);
      }
}
```

The output begins innocuously enough:

```
square   grains added  total grains   fraction of
                                        US total
   1        1.00E+00      1.00E+00      1.43E-15
   2        2.00E+00      3.00E+00      4.29E-15
   3        4.00E+00      7.00E+00      1.00E-14
   4        8.00E+00      1.50E+01      2.14E-14
   5        1.60E+01      3.10E+01      4.43E-14
   6        3.20E+01      6.30E+01      9.00E-14
   7        6.40E+01      1.27E+02      1.81E-13
   8        1.28E+02      2.55E+02      3.64E-13
   9        2.56E+02      5.11E+02      7.30E-13
  10        5.12E+02      1.02E+03      1.46E-12
```

After 10 squares, the scholar has acquired just a little over a thousand grains of wheat. But look what has happened by square 50!

The haul has exceeded the total US annual output! If you want to see what happens by the 64th square, you will have to run the program yourself.

This example illustrates the phenomenon of exponential growth. The world population growth and our use of energy resources have followed the same pattern.

Division Operator: /

C uses the / symbol to represent division. The value to the left of the / is divided by the value to the right. For example,

```
four = 12.0/3.0;
```

gives **four** the value of 4.0. Division works differently for integer types than it does for floating types. Floating-type division gives a floating-point answer, but integer division yields an integer answer. An integer has to be a whole number, which makes dividing 5 by 3 awkward since the answer isn't a whole number. In C, any fraction resulting from integer division is discarded. This process is called "truncation."

Try this program to see how truncation works and how integer division differs from floating-point division.

```
 /* divisions we have known */
main()
{

   printf ("integer division:  5/4   is %d \n", 5/4);
   printf ("integer division:  6/3   is %d \n", 6/3);
   printf ("integer division:  7/4   is %d \n", 7/4);
   printf ("floating division: 7./4. is %1.2f \n", 7./4.);
   printf ("mixed division:    7./4  is %1.2f \n", 7./4);
}
```

We also included a case of "mixed types" by having a real number divided by an integer. C is a more forgiving language than some and will let you get away with this, but normally you should avoid mixing types. Now for the results:

```
integer division:  5/4   is 1
integer division:  6/3   is 2
integer division:  7/4   is 1
floating division: 7./4. is 1.75
mixed division:    7./4  is 1.75
```

Note how integer division does not round to the nearest integer, but always rounds down. And when we mixed integers with floating point, the answer came out the same as floating point. When a calculation like this has both types, the integer is converted to floating point before division.

The properties of integer division turn out to be quite handy for some problems. We will give an example fairly soon. First, there is another important matter to raise, namely, what happens when you combine more than one operation into one statement? That is our next topic.

Operator Precedence

Consider the line

```
butter = 25.0 + 60.0*n/SCALE;
```

This statement has an addition, a multiplication, and a division. Which operation takes place first? Is 25.0 added to 60.0, the result of 85.0 then multiplied by n, and that result then divided by **SCALE?** Or is 60.0 multiplied by n, the result added to 25.0, and that answer then divided by **SCALE?** Or is it some other order? Let's take **n** to be 6.0 and **SCALE** to be 2.0. If you work through using these values, you will find that the first approach yields a value of 255. The second approach gives 192.5. A C program must have some other order in mind, for it would give a value of 205.0 for **butter.**

Clearly the order of executing the various operations can make a difference, so C needs unambiguous rules for choosing what to do first. C does this by setting up an operator pecking order. Each operator is assigned a precedence level. Multiplication and division have a higher precedence than addition and subtraction, so they are performed first. What if two operators have the same precedence? Then they are executed according to the order in which they occur in the statement. For most operators the order is from left to right. (The = operator was an exception to this.) Therefore, in the statement

```
butter = 25.0 + 60.0*n/SCALE;
```

the order of operations is

60.0*n —the first * or / in the statement then (assuming n = 6 so that 60.0*n =360.0)

360.0/SCALE —the second * or / in the statement and finally (since SCALE = 2.0)

25.0 + 180 —the first + or − in the statement to yield 205.0. Many people like to represent the order of evaluation with a type of diagram called an "expression tree." Figure 5.3 is an example of such a diagram.

The diagram shows how the original expression is reduced by steps to a single value.

But what if you want, say, an addition to take place before a division. Then you can do as we do in this line:

```
flour = (25.0 + 60.0*n)/SCALE;
```

Whatever is enclosed in parentheses gets done first. Within the parentheses, the usual rules hold. For this example, first the multiplication takes place, then the addition. That takes care of what was in the parentheses. Only then is the result divided by **SCALE.**

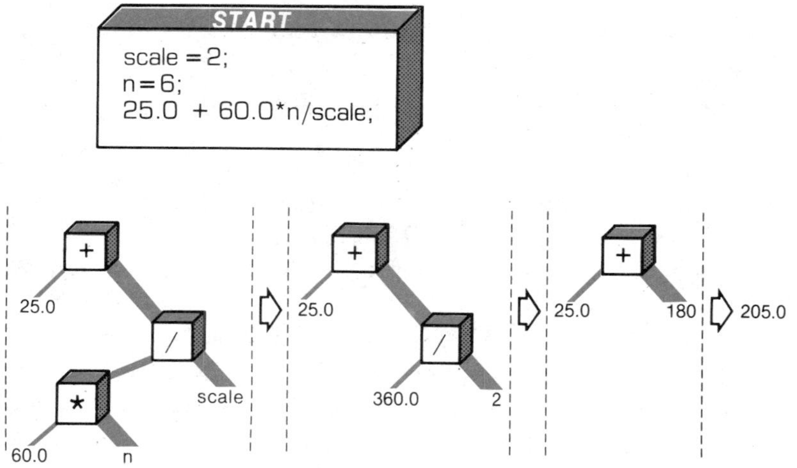

Figure 5.3
Expression trees showing operators, operands, and order of evaluation.

We can make a table to summarize our rules for the operators we've used so far. (Appendix C contains a table covering all operators.)

Table 5-1. Operators in Order of Decreasing Precedence

OPERATORS	*ASSOCIATIVITY*
( )	left to right
− (unary)	left to right
* /	left to right
+ − (subtraction)	left to right
=	right to left

Notice that the two uses of the minus sign have different priorities. The associativity column tells us how an operator associates with its operands. For example, the unary minus sign associates with the quantity to its right, and in division the left operand is divided by the right.

Let's try these rules out on a more complex example.

```
 /* precedence test */
main()
{
int top, score;
```

```
    top = score = -(2 + 5)*6 + (4 + 3*(2 + 3));
    printf("top = %d \n", top);
}
```

What value will this program print out? Figure it out, then run the program or read the following description to check your answer. (We think you probably will get it right.)

Okay, parentheses are the highest priority. Going from left to right, the first pair of parentheses is **(2+5),** so we evaluate the contents, getting

```
top = score = -7*6 + (4 + 3*(2 + 3))
```

The next pair of parentheses is **(4 + 3*(2 +3)),** so we evaluate its contents, that is, the expression **4 + 3*(2 + 3).** Aha! More parentheses! So the first step here is to find 2 + 3. The expression becomes

```
top = score = -7*6 + (4 + 3*5)
```

We still have to finish up what is in the parentheses. Since * has priority over +, the expression becomes

```
top = score = -7*6 + (4 + 15)
```

and then

```
top = score = -7*6 + 19
```

What's next? If you guessed **7*6,** you're wrong. Notice that unary − (sign change) has a higher priority than *. So first, the **7** is changed to **−7,** then **−7** is multiplied by **6.** The line becomes

```
top = score = -42 + 19
```

then addition makes it

```
top = score = -23
```

Then **score** is assigned the value **−23,** and, finally, **top** gets the value **−23.** Remember that the = operator associates from right to left.

SOME ADDITIONAL OPERATORS

C has about 40 operators, but some are used much more than others. The ones we just covered are the most common, and we would like to add three additional useful operators to the list.

Modulus Operator: %

The modulus operator is used in integer arithmetic. It gives the remainder that results when the integer to its left is divided by the integer to its right. For example, **13 % 5** (read as "13 modulo 5") has the value 3, since 5 goes into 13 twice, with a remainder of 3.

Don't bother trying to use this operator with floating-point numbers; it just won't work.

At first glance, this operator may strike you as an esoteric tool for mathematicians, but actually it is rather practical and helpful. One common use is to help you control the flow of a program. Suppose, for example, you are working on a bill-preparing program that is supposed to add in an extra charge every third month. Just have the program evaluate the month number modulo 3 (i.e., **month % 3**) and check to see if the result is 0. If so, add in the extra charge. Once we get to "if statements" you'll see better how this works.

Here's an example using %.

```
 /* sectomin */
 /* converting seconds to minutes and seconds */
#define SM 60 /* seconds in a minute */
main()
{
   int sec, min, left;

   printf("Convert seconds to minutes and seconds!\n");
   printf("Enter the number of seconds you wish to convert.\n");
   scanf("%d", &sec);  /* number of seconds is read in */
   min = sec/SM;     /* truncated number of minutes  */
   left = sec % SM; /* number of seconds left over  */
   printf("%d seconds is %d minutes, %d seconds.\n", sec, min,
          left);
}
```

Here is a sample output:

```
Convert seconds to minutes and seconds!
Enter the number of seconds you wish to convert.
234
234 seconds is 3 minutes, 54 seconds.
```

One problem with this interactive program is that it processes just one input value. Can you come up with a way to have the program prompt you repeatedly for new input values? We will return to that problem in this chapter's question section, but if you work out your own solution first, we will be pleased.

The Increment and Decrement Operators: ++ and --

The increment operator performs a simple task; it increments (increases) the value of its operand by one. The operator comes in two varieties. The first variety has the ++ come before the affected variable; this is the "prefix" mode. The second variety has the ++ come after the affected variable; this is the "postfix" model. The two modes differ with regard to the precise time the incrementing takes place. We'll look at the similarities first and then return to that difference. This short example shows how the increment operators work.

```
 /* addone */
main() /*incrementing: prefix and postfix */
{   int ultra = 0, super = 0;

    while (super < 6) {
       super++;
       ++ultra;
       printf("super = %d, ultra = %d \n", super, ultra);
    }
}
```

Running **addone** produces

```
super = 1, ultra = 1
super = 2, ultra = 2
super = 3, ultra = 3
super = 4, ultra = 4
super = 5, ultra = 5
```

Gosh, we've counted to 5! Twice! Simultaneously! (If you have a need to count further, just change the limit in the **while** statement.)

We confess we could have achieved exactly the same results by replacing the two increment statements by

```
super = super + 1;
ultra = ultra + 1;
```

There are simple enough statements. Why bother creating one, let alone two, abbreviations?

First, the compact form makes your programs neater and easier to follow. These operators give your programs an elegant gloss that cannot fail to please the eye.

For instance, we can rewrite part of **shoesize2** this way:

```
size = 3.0;
 while (size < 18.5) {
    foot = SCALE*size + OFFSET;
    printf("%10.1f %20.2f inches\n", size, foot);
    ++size;
}
```

But we still haven't taken full advantage of the increment operator. We can shorten the fragment this way:

```
size = 2.0;
 while (++size < 18.5) {
   foot = SCALE*size + OFFSET;
   printf("%10.1f %20.2f inches\n", size, foot);
 }
```

Here we have combined the incrementing process and the **while** comparison into one expression. This type of construction is so common in C that it merits a closer look. First, how does it work? Simply. The value of **size** is increased by one, then compared to **18.5.** If it is less, the statements between the braces are executed once. Then **size** is increased by one again, and the cycle is repeated until the **size** gets too big. We changed the initial value of **size** from **3.0** to **2.0** to compensate for **size** being incremented before the first evaluation of **foot.**

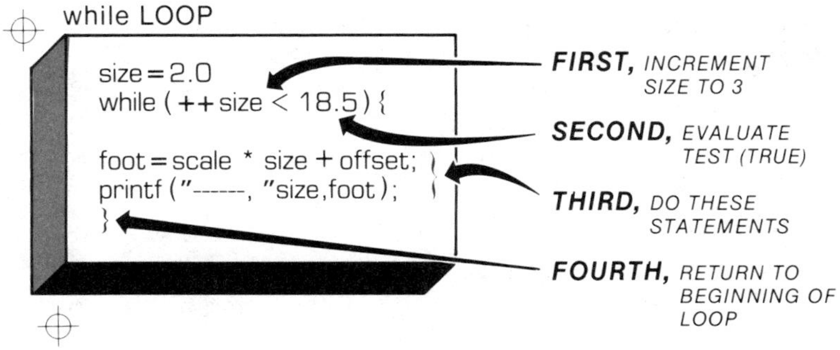

Figure 5.4
Through the loop once

Secondly, what's so good about this approach? It is more compact. More importantly, it gathers in one place the two processes that control the loop. The first process is the test: do we continue or not? In this case, the test is checking to see if the shoe size is less than 18.5. The second process changes an element of the test; in this case, the shoe size is increased. Suppose we forgot to change the shoe size. Then **size** would *always* be less than **18.5,** and the loop would never end. The computer would churn out line after identical line, caught in a dreaded "infinite loop." Eventually, you would lose interest in the output and have to kill the program somehow. Having the loop test and the loop change at one place instead of at separate locations makes it easier to remember to include a loop change.

Another advantage of the increment operator is that it usually produces slightly more efficient machine language code, since it is similar to actual machine language instructions.

Finally, these operators have an additional feature that can be of use in certain delicate situations. To learn what this feature is, try running the next program.

```
main()
{
    int a = 1, b = 1;
    int aplus, plusb;

    aplus = a++;         /* postfix */
    plusb = ++b;         /* prefix  */
    printf("a aplus b plusb \n");
    printf("%3d %5d %5d %5d\n", a, aplus, b, plusb);
}
```

If you do this correctly and if we remember correctly, you should get this as the result.

```
 a   aplus   b   plusb
 2     1     2     2
```

Both **a** and **b** were increased by 1, as promised. However, **aplus** has the value of **a** before **a** changed, while **plusb** has the value of **b** after **b** changed. This is the difference between the prefix form and the postfix form.

`aplus = a++` postfix: **a** changed *after* its value is used
`plusb = ++b` prefix: **b** changed *before* its value is used

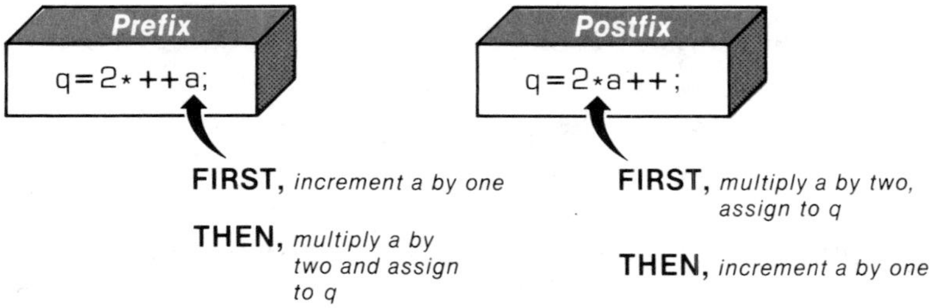

Figure 5.5
Prefix and Postfix.

When one of these increment operators is used by itself, as in a solitary **ego++;** statement, it doesn't matter which form you use. The choice does matter, however, when the operator and its operand are part of a larger expression, as in the assignment statements we just saw. In this kind of situation you must give some thought to the result you want. For instance, recall our use of

```
while (++size < 18.5)
```

This gave us a table up to size 18. But if we had used **size++** instead, the table would have gone to size 19, since **size** would be increased after the comparison instead of before.

Of course, you could fall back on the less subtle

```
size = size + 1;
```

form, but then no one will believe you are a true C programmer.

We suggest you pay attention to our examples of increment operators as you read through your book. Ask yourself if we could have used either one or if circumstances dictate a particular choice. Speaking of examples, here comes another one.

Do computers ever sleep? Of course they do, but they usually don't tell us. This program reveals what really goes on.

```
 /* sheep */
#define MAX 40
main()
{
   int count = 0;

   printf("I count sheep to go to sleep.\n");
   while (++count < Max )
     printf("%d million sheep and still not asleep . . . \n",
             count);
   printf("%d million sheep and zzzzzz . . . . \n",count);
}
```

Try it and see if it does what you think it will. Of course the value of **MAX** may be different for your computer. (Incidentally, what would be the effect of replacing the prefix form of the increment operator with the postfix form?)

Decrementing: −−

For each increment operator, there is a corresponding decrement operator. Instead of ++, we use −−.

```
-- count;    /* prefix form of decrement operator */
count --;    /* postfix form of decrement operator */
```

Here is an example illustrating that computers can be accomplished lyricists:

```
 /* bottles */
#define MAX 100
main()
{
  int count = MAX + 1;

  while( --count > 0) {
  printf("%d bottles of beer on the wall, %d bottles of beer!\n",
             count, count);
  printf("Take one down and pass it around,\n");
  printf("%d bottles of beer!\n\n", count-1);
}
 }
```

The output starts like this:

```
100 bottles of beer on the wall, 100 bottles of beer!
Take one down and pass it around,
99 bottles of beer!
99 bottles of beer on the wall, 99 bottles of beer!

Take one down and pass it around,
98 bottles of beer!
```

It goes on a bit and ends this way:

```
1 bottles of beer on the wall, 1 bottles of beer!
Take one down and pass it around,
0 bottles of beer!
```

Apparently our accomplished lyricist has a problem with plurals, but that could be fixed up using the conditional operators of Chapter 7.

Incidentally, the > operator stands for "greater than." Like <, it is a "relational operator." We will take a longer look at relational operators in Chapter 7.

Precedence

The increment and decrement operators have a very high precedence of association; only parentheses are higher. Thus, **x*y++** means **(x)*(y++)** and not **(x*y)++**, which is fortunate, since the latter is meaningless. (The increment and decrement operators affect a *variable,* and the combination **x*y** is not itself a variable, although its parts are.)

Don't confuse precedence of these two operators with the order of evaluation. Suppose we have

```
y = 2;
n = 3;
nextnum = (y + n++)*6;
```

What values does **nextnum** get? Well, by substituting in values,

```
nextnum = (2 + 3)*6 = 5*6 = 30
```

Only after the whole expression is evaluated is **n** increased to **4.** Precedence tells us that the ++ is attached only to the **n.** It also tells us when the value of **n** is used for evaluating the expression, but the nature of the increment operator determines when the value of **n** is changed.

Don't Be Too Clever

You can get fooled if you try to do too much at once with the increment operators. For example, you might think that you could improve on our program to print integers and their squares by replacing our **while** loop with this one.

```
while ( num < 21) {
    printf("%10d %10d\n", num, num*num++);
    }
```

This looks reasonable. We print the number **num,** we multiply it by itself to get the square, and then we increase **num** by one. In fact, this program may even work on some systems. But not all. The problem is that when **printf( )** goes to get the values for printing, it may evaluate the last argument first and increment **num** before getting to the other argument. Thus, instead of printing, say,

```
5          25
```

it will print

```
6          25
```

C gives the compiler freedom to choose which arguments in a function to evaluate first; this increases compiler efficiency but can cause trouble if you use an increment operator on an argument.

Another possible source of trouble is a statement like

```
ans = num/2 + 5*(1 + num++);
```

Again, the problem is that the compiler may not do things in the same order you have in mind. You would think that it would find **num/2** first, then move on. But it might do the last term first, increase **num**, and use the new value in **num/2**. There is just no guarantee.

It is easy enough to avoid these problems.

1. Don't use increment or decrement operators on a variable that is part of more than one argument of a function.
2. Don't use increment or decrement operators on a variable that appears more than once in an expression.

EXPRESSIONS AND STATEMENTS

We have been using the terms "expression" and "statement" throughout these first few chapters, and now the time has come to study their meanings more closely. Statements form the basic program steps of C, and most statements are constructed from expressions. This suggests we look at expressions first, and we will.

Expressions

An expression consists of a combination of operators and operands. (An operand, recall, is what an operator operates on.) The simplest expression is a lone operand, and you can build in complexity from there. Here are some expressions:

```
4
-6
4+21
a*(b + c/d)/20
q = 5*2
x = ++q % 3
q > 3
```

As you can see, the operands can be constants, variables, or combinations of the two. Some expressions are combinations of smaller expressions, which we can call subexpressions. For instance, **c/d** is a subexpression of our fourth example.

An important property of C is that every C expression has a value. To find the value, we perform the operations in the order dictated by operator precedence. The value of the first few expressions is clear, but what about the ones with = signs? Those expressions simply have the same value that the variable to the left of the = sign gets. And the expression **q > 0?** Such relational expressions have the value **1** if true and **0** if false. Here are some expressions and their values:

Expression	Value
`-4+6`	2
`c = 3 + 8`	11
`5 > 3`	1
`6 +(c = 3 + 8)`	17

That last one looks strange! But it is perfectly legal in C, for it is just the sum of two subexpressions, each of which has a value.

Statements

Statements are the primary building blocks of a program. A program is just a series of statements with a little punctuation thrown in. A statement is a complete instruction to the computer. In C, statements are indicated by a semicolon at the end. Thus

```
legs = 4
```

is just an expression (which could be part of a larger expression), but

```
legs = 4;
```

is a statement.

What makes an instruction complete? It has to complete an action. The expression

```
2 + 2
```

is not a complete instruction. It tells the computer to add 2 and 2, but it fails to tell the computer what to do with the answer. If we say

```
kids = 2 + 2;
```

however, we tell the computer to store the answer (4) in the memory location labeled **kids.** With the number **4** thus disposed, the computer can then move on to the next task.

So far we have encountered four kinds of statements. Here is a short sample that uses all four.

```
 /* addemup */
main()                     /*finds sum of first 20 integers */
{
  int count, sum;                /* declaration statement */

  count = 0;                     /* assignment statement  */
  sum = 0;                       /*       ditto           */
  while ( count++ < 20 )         /*       while           */
     sum = sum + count;          /*     statement         */
  printf("sum = %d\n", sum);     /* function statement    */
}
```

Let's discuss that example. By now you must be pretty familiar with the declaration statement. Nonetheless, we will remind you that it establishes the names and type of variables and causes memory locations to be set aside for them.

The assignment statement is the workhorse of most programs; it assigns a value to a variable. It consists of a variable name followed by the assignment operator (=) followed by an expression followed by a semicolon. Note that the **while** statement includes an assignment statement within it.

A function statement causes the function to do whatever it does. In our example, the **printf( )** function is invoked to print out some results.

A **while** statement has three distinct parts. First is the keyword **while.** Then, in parentheses, comes a test condition. Finally comes the statement that is performed if the test is met. Only one statement is included in the loop. It can be a simple statement, as in this example, in which case no braces are needed to mark it off. Or the statement can be a compound statement, like some of our earlier examples, in which case braces are required. Read about compound statements just ahead.

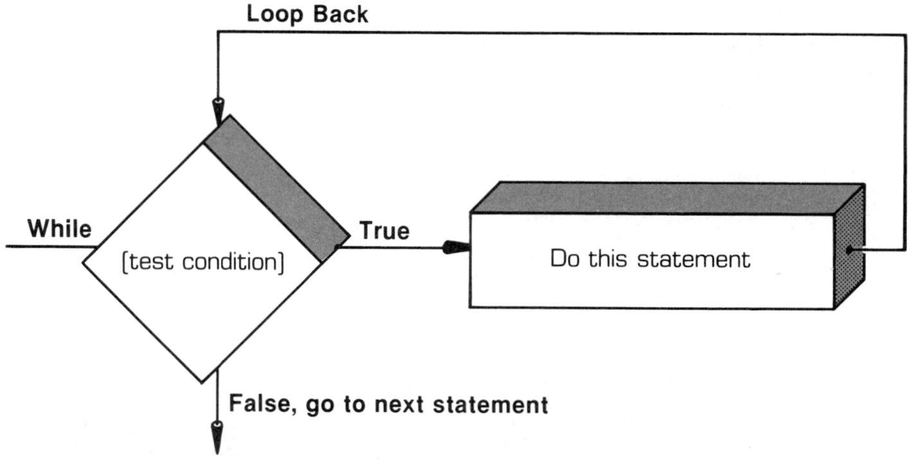

Figure 5.6
Structure of a simple "while" loop.

The **while** statement belongs to a class of statements sometimes called "structured statements" because they possess a structure more complex than that of a simple assignment statement. In later chapters we will encounter many other kinds of structured statements.

Compound Statements (Blocks)

A "compound statement" is two or more statements grouped together by enclosing them in braces; it also is called a "block." We used one in our

shoesize2 program in order to let the **while** statement encompass several statements. Compare the following program fragments:

```
 /* fragment 1 */
index = 0;
while (index++ < 10 )
  sam = 10*index + 2;
printf ("sam = %d\n", sam);

 /* fragment 2 */
index = 0;
while (index++ < 10 ) {
  sam = 10*index + 2;
  printf ("sam = %d\n", sam);
  }
```

In fragment 1, only the assignment statement is included in the **while** loop. (In the absence of braces, a **while** statement runs from the **while** to the next semicolon.) The printout will occur just once, after the loop has been completed.

In fragment 2, the braces ensure that both statements are part of the **while** loop, and we get a printout each time the loop is executed. The entire compound statement is considered to be the single statement in terms of the structure of a **while** statement.

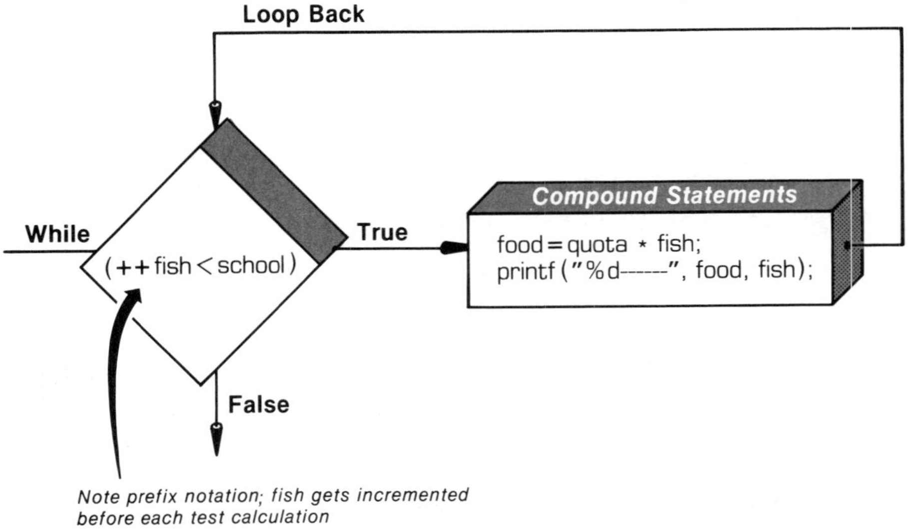

Figure 5.7
While loop with a compound statement.

STYLE TIPS

Look again at the two **while** fragments and notice how we have used indentation to mark off the body of the **while** loops. The indentation makes no difference whatsoever to the compiler; it uses the braces and its knowledge of the structure of **while** loops to decide how to interpret our instructions. The indentation is there for us, so that we can see at a glance how the program is organized.

We have shown one popular style for positioning the braces for a block, or compound statement. Another very common style is this:

```
while (index++ < 10)
  {
  sam = 10*index + 2;
  printf("sam = %d \n", sam);
  }
```

This style emphasizes that the statements form a block, while the other style highlights the attachment of the block to the **while.** Again, as far as the compiler is concerned, both forms are identical.

To sum up, use indentation as a tool to point out the structure of a program.

SUMMARY: EXPRESSIONS AND STATEMENTS

Expressions:
An expression is a combination of operators and operands. The simplest expression is just a constant or a variable with no operator, such as **22** or **beebop.** More complex examples are **55 + 22** and **vap = 2*(vip + (vup = 4)).**

Statements:
A statement is a command to the computer. There are simple statements and compound statements.
Simple statements terminate in a semicolon. Examples are

1. declaration statements `int toes;`
2. assignment statements: `toes = 12;`
3. function call statements: `printf("%d\n", toes);`

4. control statements:
```
while ( toes < 20 )
          toes = toes + 2;
```

5. the null statement:
```
;
```

Compound statements, or *blocks,* consist of one or more statements (which themselves can be compound) enclosed in braces. The following **while** statement contains an example:

```
while ( years < 100 )
     {
     wisdom = wisdom + 1;
     printf("%d %d\n", years, wisdom);
     years = years + 1
      }
```

TYPE CONVERSIONS

Statements and expressions normally should use variables and constants of just one type. If, however, you mix types, C doesn't stop dead in its tracks the way, say, Pascal does. Instead, it uses a set of rules to make type conversions automatically. This can be a convenience, but it also can be a danger, especially if you are mixing types inadvertently. (The **lint** program, found on many UNIX systems, checks for type "clashes.") It is a good idea to have at least some knowledge of the type conversion rules.

The basic rules are these:

1. In any operation involving two types, both values are converted to the "higher" ranking of the two types. This process is called "promotion."
2. The ranking of types, from highest to lowest, is **double, float, long, int, short,** and **char.** Also, **unsigned** outranks the corresponding signed type.
3. In an assignment statement, the final result of the calculations is converted to the type of the variable that is being assigned a value. This process can result in promotion, as described above, or "demotion," in which a value is converted to a lower-ranking type.

Promotion usually is a smooth, uneventful process, but demotion can

lead to real trouble. The reason is simple: the lower ranking type may not be big enough to hold the complete number. A **char** variable can hold the integer **101** but not the integer **22334.**
This sample illustrates the working of these rules.

```
 /* conversions */
main()
{
   char ch;
   int i;
   float fl;

   fl = i = ch = 'A';     /* line 8 */
   printf("ch = %c, i = %d, fl = %2.2f\n", ch, i, fl);
   ch = ch + 1;           /* line 10 */
   i = fl + 2*ch;         /* line 11 */
   fl = 2.0*ch + i;       /* line 12 */
   printf("ch = %c, i = %d, fl = %2.2f\n", ch, i, fl);
   ch = 2.0e30;           /* line 14 */
   printf("Now ch = %c\n", ch);
}
```

This is what running **conversions** produces:

```
ch = A, i = 65, fl = 65.00
ch = B, i = 197, fl = 329.00
Now ch =
```

This is what happened.
Lines 8 and 9: The character 'A' is stored as a character by **ch.** The integer variable **i** receives the integer conversion of 'A', which is 65. Finally, **fl** receives the floating conversion of **65,** which is **65.00.**
Lines 10 and 13: The character variable 'A' is converted to the integer **65,** which then is added to the **1.** The resulting integer **66** then is converted to the character **B** and stored in **ch.**
Lines 11 and 13: The value of **ch** is converted to an integer **(66)** for the multiplication by **2.** The resulting integer **(132)** is converted to floating point in order to be added to **fl.** The result **(197.00)** is converted to int and stored in **i.**
Lines 12 and 13: The value of **ch ('B')** is converted to floating point for multiplication by **2.0.** The value of **i (197)** is converted to floating point for the addition, and the result **(329.00)** is stored in **fl.**

Lines 14 and 15: Here we try a case of demotion, setting **ch** equal to a rather large number. The results are poor. Whatever cramming and truncating took place resulted in producing code for some nonprinting character on our system.

Actually, there is one other kind of conversion that took place. In order to preserve numerical accuracy, *all* **float** values are converted to **double** when arithmetic calculations are done. This greatly reduces roundoff error. The final answer, of course, is converted back to **float** if that is the declared type. This conversion you needn't worry about, but it is nice to know that the compiler is looking after your best interests.

Cast Operator

Usually it is best to steer clear of type conversions, especially of demotions. But sometimes it is convenient to make conversions, providing you exercise care in what you do. The type conversions we've discussed so far are done automatically. It also is possible for you to demand the precise type conversion you want. The method is called a "cast" and consists of preceding the quantity with the name of the desired type in parentheses. The parentheses and type name together constitute a "cast operator." The general form of a cast operator is

```
(type)
```

where the actual type desired is substituted for the word "type."

Consider these two lines, in which **mice** is an **int** variable. The second line contains two casts to type **int.**

```
mice = 1.6 + 1.7;
mice = (int) 1.6 + (int) 1.7;
```

The first example uses automatic conversion. First **1.6** and **1.7** are added to yield **3.3.** This number is then converted through truncation to the integer **3** in order to match the **int** variable. In the second example, **1.6** is converted to an integer **(1)** before addition, as is **1.7,** so that **mice** is assigned the value **1+1,** or **2.**

Normally, you shouldn't mix types; that's why some languages don't allow it. But there are occasions when it is useful. The C philosophy is to avoid putting barriers in your way and to give you the responsibility of not abusing that freedom.

SUMMARY: OPERATING IN C

Here's what the operators we have discussed so far do.

I. Assignment Operator

=	Assigns value at its right to the variable at its left

II. Arithmetic Operators

+	Adds value at its right to the value at its left
−	Subtracts value at its right from the value at its left
−	As a unary operator, changes the sign of the value at its right
*	Multiplies value at its right by the value at its left
/	Divides value at its left by the value at its right. Answer is truncated if both operands are integers
%	Yields the remainder when the value at its left is divided by the value to its right (integers only)
++	Adds 1 to the value of the variable to its right (prefix mode) or of the variable to its left (postfix mode)
−−	Like ++, but subtracts 1

III. Miscellaneous

`sizeof` Yields the size, in bytes, of the operand to its right. The operand can be a type-specifier in parentheses, as in **sizeof (float)**, or it can be the name of a particular variable or array, etc., as in **sizeof foo.**

(type) Cast operator: converts following value to the type specified by the enclosed keyword(s). For example, (**float**) 9 converts the integer **9** to the floating-point number **9.0.**

AN EXAMPLE PROGRAM

In Figure 5.8 we've put together a useful program (if you're a runner or know one) that just happens to illustrate several of the ideas in this chapter. It looks long, but all the calculations are done in six lines near the end. The bulk of the program relays information between the computer and user. We've tried using enough comments to make it nearly self-explanatory, so read it through, and when you are done, we'll clear up a few other points.

```
 /* running */
#define SM      60 /* seconds in a minute   */
#define SH    3600 /* seconds in an hour    */
#define MK 0.62137 /* miles in a kilometer */
main()
{
  float distk, distm; /* distance run in km and in miles  */
  float rate;         /* average speed in mph             */
  int min, sec;       /* minutes and seconds of running time*/
  int time;           /* running time in seconds only     */
  float mtime;        /* time in seconds for one mile     */
  int mmin, msec;     /* minutes and seconds for one mile*/

  printf("This program converts your time for a metric race\n");
  printf("to a time for running a mile and to your average\n");
  printf("speed in miles per hour.\n");
  printf("Please enter, in kilometers, the distance run.\n");
  scanf("%f", &distk);
  printf("Next enter the time in minutes and seconds.\n");
  printf("Begin by entering the minutes.\n");
  scanf("%d", &min);
```

```
    printf("Now enter the seconds.\n");
    scanf("%d", &sec);
    time = SM*min + sec;         /* converts time to pure seconds */
    distm = MK*distk;             /* converts kilometers to miles */
    rate = distm/time*SH; /* miles per sec × sec per hour = mph */
    mtime =(float) time/distm; /* time/distance = time per mile */
    mmin = (int) mtime / SM;                  /* find whole minutes */
    msec = (int) mtime % SM;              /* find remaining seconds */
    printf("You ran %1.2f km (%1.2f miles) in %d min, %d sec.\n",
            distk, distm, min, sec);
    printf("That pace corresponds to running a mile in %d min,",
             mmin);
    printf("%d sec.\nYour average speed was %1.2f mph.\n",msec,
            rate);
}
```

Figure 5.8
A useful runner program

We utilized the same approach we used in **sectomin** to convert the final time to minutes and seconds, but we also had to make type conversions. Why? Because we need integer arguments for the seconds-to-minutes part of the program, but the metric to mile conversion involves floating-point numbers. We have used the cast operator to make these conversions explicit.

To tell the truth, it should be possible to write the program using just automatic conversions. In fact we did so, using **mtime** of type **int** to force the time calculation to be converted to integer form. However, that version only ran on one of our two reference systems. Using casts not only makes your intent clearer to the reader, it also may make it clearer to the compiler.

Here's a sample output.

```
This program converts your time for a metric race
to a time for running a mile and to your average
speed in miles per hour.
Please enter, in kilometers, the distance run.
10.0
Next enter the time in minutes and seconds.
Begin by entering the minutes.
36
Now enter the seconds.
23
```

```
You ran 10.00 km (6.21 miles) in 36 min, 23 sec.
That pace corresponds to running a mile in 5 min, 51 sec.
Your average speed was 10.25 mph.
```

WHAT YOU SHOULD HAVE LEARNED

How to use several operators: +, −, *, /, %, ++, −−, **(type)**
What an operand is: That which an operator acts upon.
What an expression is: a combination of operators and operands.
How to evaluate an expression: follow the order of precedence.
How to recognize a statement: by its semicolon.
Several kinds of statements: declaration, assignment, **while,** compound.
How to form a compound statement: enclose a series of statements within braces { }.
How to form a **while** statement: **while (test)** statement;
What happens in expressions of mixed types: automatic conversion.

QUESTIONS AND ANSWERS

Questions

1. Assume all variables are of type **int.** Find the value of each of the following variables.

   a. `x = (2 + 3) * 6;`
   b. `x = (12 + 6)/2*3;`
   c. `y = x = (2 + 3)/4;`
   d. `y = 3 + 2*(x = 7/2);`
   e. `x = (int) 3.8 + 3.3;`

2. We suspect that there are some errors in the next program. Can you help us find them?

```
main()
{
  int i = 1,
```

```
    float n;
    printf("Watch out! Here come a bunch of fractions!\n");
    while (i < 30)
      n = 1/i;
      printf(" %f", n);
    printf("That's all, folks!\n");
}
```

3. Here's a first attempt at making sectomin interactive. The program is not satisfactory; why not? How can it be improved?

```
#define SM 60
main()
{
    int sec, min, left;

    printf("This program converts seconds to minutes and");
    printf("seconds.\n");
    printf("Just enter the number of seconds.\n");
    printf("Enter 0 to end the program.\n");
    while ( sec > 0 ) {
      scanf("%d", &sec);
      min = sec/SM;
      left = sec % SM;
      printf("%d sec is %d min, %d sec. \n", sec, min, left);
      printf("Next input?\n");
      }
    printf("Bye!\n");
}
```

Answers

1. **a.** 30
   b. 27 (not 3). (12 + 6)/(2*3) would give 3
   c. x = 1, y = 1 (integer division)
   d. x =3 (integer division) and y = 9
   e. x = 6, for (int) 3.8 = 3; 3 + 3.3 = 6.3, which becomes 6, since x is **int**
2. Line 3 should end in a semicolon, not a comma.
   Line 7: the **while** statement sets up an infinite loop, for the value of **i** remains 1 and is always less than 30. Presumably we meant to write **while(i++ < 30).**
   Lines 7-9: The indentation implies we wanted lines 8 and 9 to form a block, but the lack of braces means the **while** loop includes only line 8. Braces should be added.
   Line 8: Since **1** and **i** both are integers, the result of the division will be **1** when **i** is **1**, and

0 for all larger values. Using **n = 1.0/i;** would cause **i** to be converted to floating-point before division and yield nonzero answers.
Line 9: We omitted a newline character (**n**) in the control statement; this will cause the numbers to be printed on one line, if possible.

3. The main problem lies in the relationship between the test statement (is **sec** greater than 0?) and the **scanf( )** statement that fetches the value of **sec.** In particular, the first time the test is made, the program hasn't had a chance to even get a value for **sec,** and the comparison will be made to some garbage value that happens to be at that memory location. One solution, albeit an inelegant one, is to initialize **sec** to, say, **1** so that the test is passed the first time through. This uncovers a second problem. When we finally type **0** to halt the program, **sec** doesn't get checked until after the loop gets finished, and we get the results for **0** seconds printed out. What we really want is to have a **scanf( )** statement just before the **while** test is made. We can accomplish that by altering the central part of the program to read this way:

```
scanf("%d", &sec);
while ( sec > 0 ) {
  min = sec/SM;
  left = sec % SM;
  printf("%d sec is %d min, %d sec. \n", sec, min, left);
  printf("Next input?\n");
  scanf("%d", &sec);
  }
```

The first time through the **scanf( )** outside the loop is used. Thereafter, the **scanf( )** at the end of the loop (and hence just before the loop begins again) is used. This is a common method for handling problems of this sort.

EXERCISES

These are problems for which we don't provide answers. The way to tell if you are right is to see if your answer works when you run it as a program.

1. Change our program **addemup** that found the sum of the first 20 integers. (If you prefer, you can think of it as a program that calculates how much money you get in 20 days if you receive $1 the first day, $2 the second day, $3 the third day, and so on.) Modify the program so that you can tell it interactively how far the calculation should go; that is, replace the **20** with a variable that is read in.
2. Now modify the program so that it computes the sum of the squares of the integers. (Or, if you prefer, how much money you get if you get $1 the first day, $4 the second day, $9 the third day, and so on. This looks like a much better deal!) C doesn't have a squaring function, but you can use the fact that the square of n is just n*n.

3. Now modify the program so that it when it finishes a calculation, it asks you for a new limit so that it can repeat the process. Have the program terminate when you enter a **0.** (Hint: use a loop within a loop. Also, see Problem 3 and its answer.)

6

INPUT/OUTPUT FUNCTIONS AND REDIRECTION

In this chapter you will find

6. INPUT/OUTPUT FUNCTIONS AND REDIRECTION

CONCEPTS

Input and output (I/O)
getchar( ) and *putchar( )*
End-of-File (EOF)
Redirection: < and >
System-dependent I/O
Time-delay loops

The words "input" and "output" have more than one use in computing. We can talk about input and output *devices,* such as keyboards, disk drives, dot matrix printers, and the like. Or we can talk about the *data* that are used for input and output. And we can talk about the *functions* that perform input and output. Our main intent in this chapter is to discuss functions used for input and output (I/O for short), but we also will touch on the other meanings of I/O.

By I/O functions we mean functions that transport data to and from your program. We've used two such functions already: **printf( )** and **scanf( ).** Now we will look at some of the other options that C gives.

Input/output functions are not part of the definition of C; their development is left to the implementers of C. If you are putting together a C compiler, you can create whatever input/output functions you like. If the system you are designing for has some special feature, such as the 8086 microprocessor port I/O approach, you can build in special I/O functions which use that feature. We will look at an example of this at the end of this chapter On the other hand, everyone benefits if there are standard I/O functions available on all systems. This allows you to write "portable" programs that can be moved easily from one system to another. C has many I/O functions of this type, such as **printf( )** and **scanf( ).** Now we will look at **getchar( )** and **putchar( ).**

These two functions perform input and output one character at a time. That may strike you at first as a rather silly way of doing things. After all, you and I easily read groupings larger than a single character. But this method does suit the ability of a computer. Furthermore, this approach is the heart of most programs that deal with text, that is, with ordinary words. We'll see how to parlay these two simple functions into programs that count characters, read files, and copy files. En route, we will learn about buffers, echoes, and redirection.

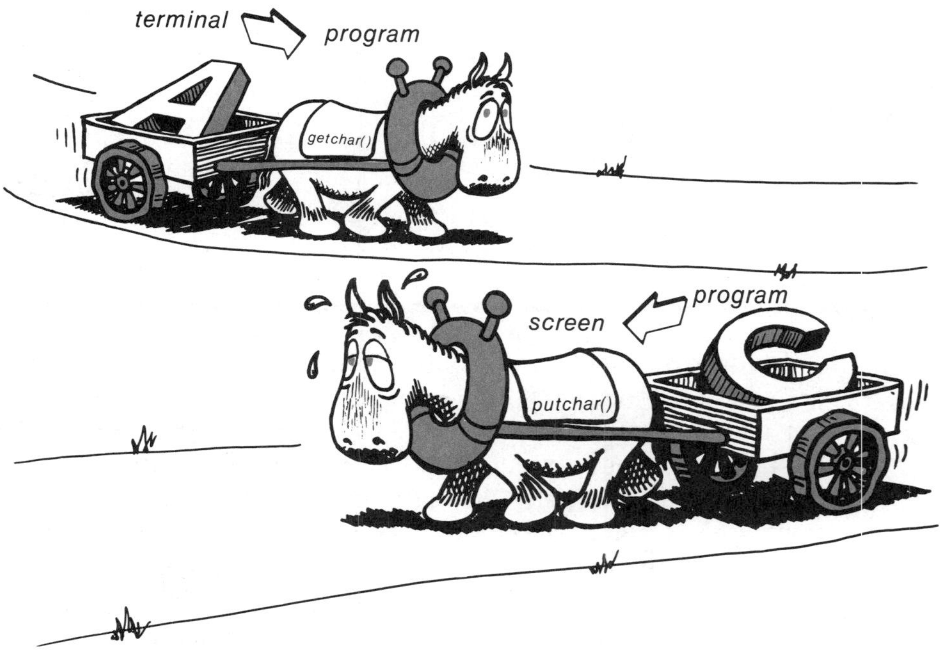

Figure 6.1
***getchar( )* and *putchar( ):* word-processing workhorses**

SINGLE-CHARACTER I/O: *getchar( )* and *putchar( )*

The **getchar( )** function gets one character (hence the name) from your keyboard and delivers it to an executing program. The **putchar( )** function gets one character from an executing program and puts it on your screen. Here is a very simple example. All it does is fetch one character from the keyboard and print it on the screen. We will modify this program step by step until it acquires a variety of useful abilities. You'll have to read on to find what they are, but first look at our humble beginning version.

```
/* getput1 */
#include <stdio.h>
main()
{
  char ch;

  ch = getchar();     /* line 1 */
  putchar(ch);        /* line 2 */
}
```

On most systems the definitions of **getchar** and **putchar** are found in the system file **stdio.h,** and that is why we have included that file in the program. Using this program produces exchanges like this:

```
g [enter]
g
```

or possibly like this:

```
gg
```

The **[enter]** is our way of indicating that you hit the [enter] key. In each case you type the first g and the computer produces the second g.

The result depends on whether or not your system has "buffered" input. If you had to hit the [enter] key before getting a response, then your system is buffered. Let's finish looking at **getchar( )** and **putchar( )** before we dive into buffers.

The **getchar( )** function has no argument (i.e., nothing within the parentheses). It simply fetches the next character and gives itself the value of that character. That is, if it fetches the letter Q, the function itself takes the value Q. Line 1 then assigns **getchar( )**'s value to the variable **ch.**

The **putchar( )** function takes an argument. You must place between the parentheses whatever single character you wish printed. The argument can be a single character (including the escape sequences of Chapter 3) or a variable or function whose value is a single character. These all are valid uses of **putchar( );**

```
putchar('S');     /* note that single quotes are          */
putchar('\n');    /* used for character constants         */
putchar('\007');
putchar(ch);      /* where ch is type char variable       */
putchar(getchar());
```

We can use the last form to rewrite our program as

```
#include <stdio.h>
main()
{
 putchar(getchar());
}
```

This is compact and uses no variables. It is more efficient than the first form, but perhaps less clear.

Now that we see how these two functions work, we can turn to the subject of buffers.

BUFFERS

When you run this program (either version) on some systems, the letter you input is repeated ("echoed") immediately. On other systems, nothing happens until you hit the [enter] key. The first case is an instance of "unbuffered" (or "direct") input, meaning that the character you type is immediately made available to the waiting program. The second case is one of "buffered" input, in which the characters you type are collected and stored in an area of temporary storage called a "buffer." Hitting the [enter] key then causes the block of characters (or single character, if that is all you typed) to be made available to your program. For our program, only the first character would be used, since there is just one use of **getchar( )**. For example, a buffered system would cause our program to work like this:

```
Here is a long line of input. [enter]
H
```

The unbuffered system, on the other hand, would return the **H** as soon as you typed it. The input-output might look like this:

```
HHere is a long line of input.
```

The second H came from the program butting in immediately. In either case only one character is processed by the program, since **getchar( )** is invoked but once.

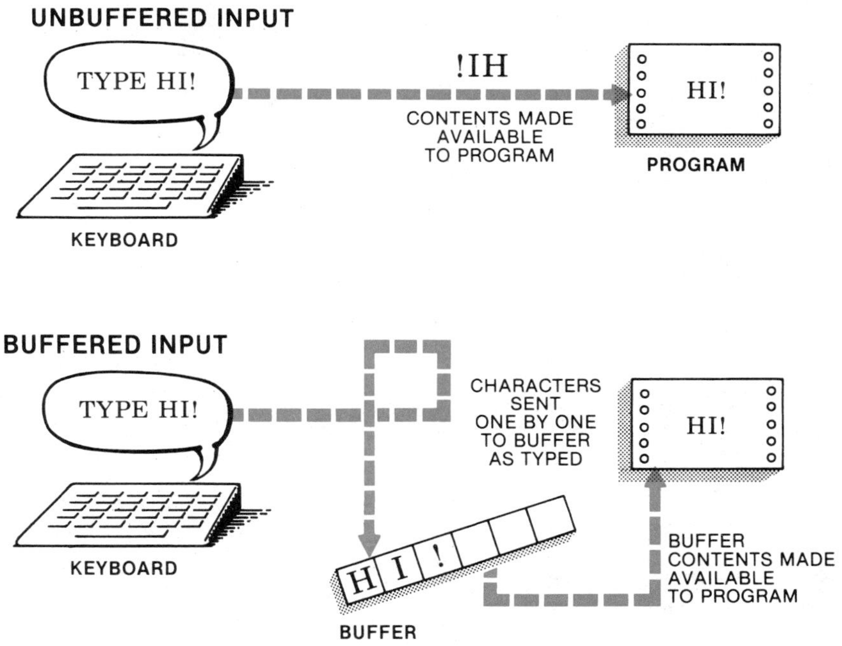

Figure 6.2
Buffered vs. unbuffered input

Why have buffers? First, it is much less time-consuming to transmit several characters as a block than one by one. Secondly, if you mistype, you can use your keyboard correction facilities to fix your mistake. When you finally hit [enter], the corrected version can be transmitted.

Unbuffered input, on the other hand, may be desired for some interactive programs. In a word processor, for instance, you would like each command to take place as soon as you hit a key. So both buffered and unbuffered output have their uses.

Which do you have? You can find out by running our program and seeing which behavior results. Some C compilers give you your choice. On our microcomputer system, for example, **getchar( )** provides buffered input while **getch( )** gives direct input.

ONWARD

Let's tackle something a little more ambitious than reading and printing just one character. Let's take on lots of characters. We would like the program to stop eventually, so let's design it to stop when some particular character, say an asterisk (*), is typed. We can do this with a **while** loop.

```
 /* getput2 */
/*this program fetches and prints characters until stopped*/
#include <stdio.h>
#define STOP '*' /* give the * character the symbolic name STOP */
main()
{
  char ch;

  ch = getchar();               /* line 9  */
  while ( ch != STOP) {         /* line 10 */
     putchar(ch);               /* line 11 */
     ch = getchar();            /* line 12 */
 }
}
```

Here we've used the program structure we discussed in Question 3, Chapter 5. The first time through, **putchar( )** gets its argument from line 9; after that it gets it from line 12 until the loop terminates. We've introduced a new relational operator, **!=**, which stands for "not equal to." Thus the **while** statement means to keep printing and reading characters until the program runs across a **STOP** character. We could have omitted the **#define** statement and just used an * in the **while** statement, but our choice makes the intent more obvious.

Before you rush to get this marvelous program on your machine, look at our next version. It will do the same job but is more C-like in its style.

```
 /* getput3 */
#include <stdio.h>
#define STOP '*'
main()
{
   char ch;

   while ((ch = getchar()) != STOP) /* line 8 */
      putchar(ch);
}
```

Line 8 of this marvel replaces lines 9, 10, and 12 of **getput2.** How does it work? Start with the contents of the inner parentheses:

```
ch = getchar()
```

This is an expression. Its effect is to activate **getchar( )** and to assign its value to **ch.** That takes care of what **getput2** did in lines 9 and 12. Next, recall that an expression has a value and that an assignment expression has the same value as a whole that the variable to the left of the = sign has. Thus the value of **(ch = getchar( ))** is just the value of **ch,** so

```
(ch = getchar()) != STOP
```

has the same effect as

```
ch != STOP
```

This takes care of what **getput2** did in line 10. This sort of construction (combining an assignment with a comparison) is very common in C.

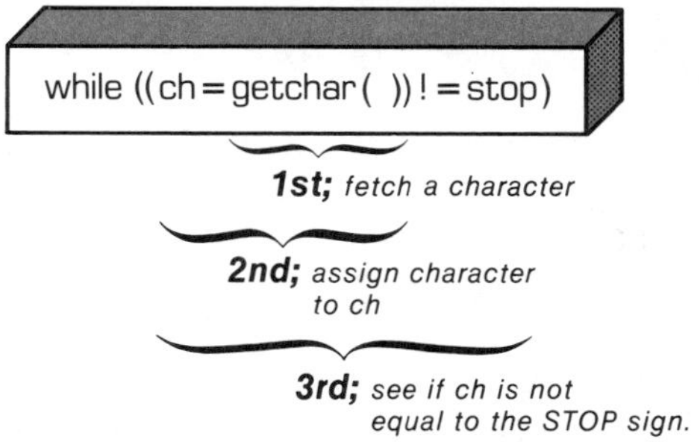

Figure 6.3
Evaluating the *while* loop condition.

Like our earlier example using **while (++size < 18.5),** this form has the advantage of putting the loop test and the action that changes the test together in one place. The structure closely resembles the way we might think of the process: "I want to read a character, look at it, and decide what to do next."

Now let's return to our program and try it out. If you are using an unbuffered system, the result might look like this:

```
II  wwoonnddeerr  iiff  tthhiiss  wwoorrkkss..*I guess it did.
```

All the characters up to the STOP signal (the asterisk) are echoed back as you type. Even the spaces are doubled. Once you type in the STOP signal, however, the program stops and what you type appears on the screen without an echo.

Now let's switch to a buffered system. This time nothing happens until we hit the [enter] key. Here is a possible exchange:

```
I wonder if this works.*Hmm, I can't tell.[enter]
I wonder if this works.
```

The whole first line was sent to the program. The program read it one character at a time and printed out one character at a time until it found the asterisk *.

Now let's make the program a little more useful. We'll have it count the characters it reads. We need to make only a few changes.

```
/* charcount1 */
#define STOP '*'
main()
{
  char ch;
  int count = 0;     /* initialize character counter to 0 */

  while ((ch = getchar()) ! = STOP) {
        putchar(ch);
        count++;                          /* add one to the count */
        }
 printf("\nA grand total of %d characters were read.\n",
      count);
}
```

We can omit the **putchar( )** line if we want just to count without echoing the characters. This little program counts characters, and it is only a few small steps away from a program that can count lines and words. The next chapter will provide the tools we need to do that.

Reading a Single Line

Meanwhile, let's see what other improvements we can make with just the tools at hand. One thing we can change easily is the stop signal. Can we come up with a better choice than the asterisk *? One possibility is to use the newline (\n) character. All we need to do is redefine **STOP.**

```
#define STOP '\n'
```

What effect will this have? Well, a newline character is transmitted when you hit the [enter] key, so this will cause our program to operate on one line of input. For example, suppose we make this change in **charcount1** and then type the following input.

```
Oh to be in Fresno now that summer's here,[enter]
```

The response would be

```
Oh to be in Fresno now that summer's here,
A grand total of 42 characters were read.
```

(If we had left out the initial \n in the final **printf( )** statement, the counting message would have been tacked on right after the comma after **here.** We elected to avoid such tacky tacking on.)

The count of 42 does not include the [enter] key, for the counting is done inside the loop.

We now have a program that reads in one line. Depending on what statements we leave inside the **while** loop, the program can echo the line, count the characters in the line, or both. This looks potentially useful, perhaps as part of some larger program. But it would be nice to be able to read larger chunks of data, perhaps even a file of data. It can be done with the proper choice for **STOP.**

Reading a File

What would the ideal **STOP** character be? It should be one that does not normally show up in text. That way it won't pop up accidentally in the middle of some input, stopping the program before we want it to stop.

This kind of problem is not new, and, fortunately for us, it already has been solved by the people who design computer systems. Actually, their problem was slightly different, but we still can use their answer. Their problem concerned "files." A file is just a block of memory in which information is stored. Normally a file would be kept in some sort of permanent memory, such as on a floppy disk, a hard disk, or tape. To keep track of where one file ends and another begins, it would be useful to have a special character to mark the end of the file. It should be a character that you wouldn't expect to find in the middle of a file, just as we want a character that wouldn't show up in the middle of input. The answer is to have a character called the End-Of-File character, or the "EOF" character for short. The exact choice of the EOF character depends on the system; it may even consist of more than one character. But such a character will exist, and your C compiler will know what it is for your system.

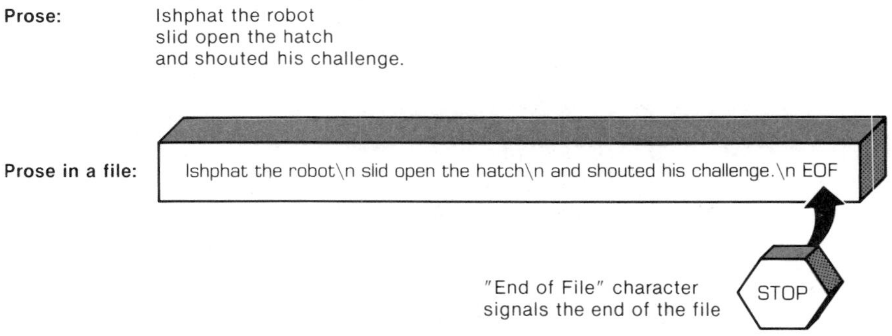

Figure 6.4
A file with an EOF.

How can you use the EOF character? Normally, it is defined in the <**stdio.h**> file. A common choice is

```
#define EOF (-1)
```

This lets you use expressions such as

```
while((ch = getchar()) != EOF)
```

in your programs. So we can rewrite our basic read and echo program this way:

```
 /* getput4 */
#include <stdio.h>
main()
{
   int ch;

   while ((ch = getchar()) != EOF)
      putchar(ch);
}
```

Note these points:

1. We don't have to define EOF, for **stdio.h** takes care of that.
2. We don't have to worry about the actual value of the EOF character, for the **#define** statement in **stdio.h** lets us use the symbolic representation EOF.
3. We've changed **ch** from type **char** to type **int.** We did this because **char** variables are represented by unsigned integers in the range 0 to 255, but the EOF "character' may have the numerical value −1. That is an impossible value for a **char** variable, but not for **int.** Fortunately, **getchar( )** is actually of type **int** itself, so it can read the EOF character.
4. The fact that **ch** is an integer doesn't faze **putchar( ).** It still prints out the character equivalent.
5. To use this program on keyboard input, we need a way to type the EOF character. No, you can't just type the letters E-O-F, and you can't just type −1. (The −1 is the equivalent to ASCII code for the character and is not the character itself.) Instead, you have to find out what the system uses. Most UNIX systems, for example, will interpret [control−d] (holding down the [control] key while you hit the [d] key) as the EOF character. Many microcomputers use [control−z] for the same purpose.

Here is a buffered example of running **getput4.**

```
She walks in beauty, like the night
She walks in beauty, like the night
  Of cloudless climes and starry skies . . .
  Of cloudless climes and starry skies . . .
                      Lord Byron
                      Lord Byron
[control-z]
```

Each time we hit [enter], the characters stored in the buffer are processed, and a copy of the line is printed out. This continues until we type the EOF character.

Let's stop for a moment and think about the possibilities for **getput4.** It copies onto the screen whatever input we feed it. Suppose we could somehow feed a file to it. Then it would print the contents of the file onto the screen, stopping when it reaches the end of the file, for it will find an EOF character there. Or suppose instead that we could find a way to direct the program's output to a file. Then we could type stuff on the keyboard and use **getput4** to store what we type. Or suppose we could do both simultaneously; suppose we could direct input from one file into **getput4** and send the output to another file. Then we could use **getput4** to copy files. Thus our little program has the potential to look at the contents of files, to create new files, and to make copies of files—pretty good for such a short program! The key is to control the flow of input and output, and that is our next topic.

REDIRECTION AND FILES

Input and output involve functions, data, and devices. Consider, for instance, our **getput4** program. It uses the input function **getchar( ).** The input device (we have assumed) is a keyboard and the input data are individual characters. We would like to keep the same input function and the same kind of data, but to change where the program looks for data. A good question to ask (and to answer) is "how does a program know where to look for its input?"

By default, a C program looks to the "standard input" as a source for input. This "standard input" is whatever has been set up as the usual way for reading data into the computer. It could be magnetic tape, punched cards, a teletype, or (as we will continue to assume) a video terminal. A modern computer is a suggestible tool, however, and we can influence it to look elsewhere for input. In particular, we can tell a program to seek its input from a file instead of from a keyboard.

There are a couple ways to get a program to work with files. One way is to explicitly use special functions that open files, close files, read files, write in files, and so forth. We don't want to get that involved yet. The second way is to use a program designed to work with keyboard and screen, but to "redirect" input and output along different channels, to and from files, for example. This approach is more limited in some respects than the first, but is much simpler to use. We will study redirection of this section.

Redirection is a feature of the UNIX operating system, not of C itself. But it is such a useful aid that when people transported C to other systems, they often brought along a form of redirection with it. Furthermore, many of the newer operating systems, including MS-DOS 2, have included redirection. So even if you are not on a UNIX system, there is a good chance that you have some form of redirection available. We will discuss UNIX redirection first, then non-UNIX redirection.

UNIX

Redirecting Output

Suppose you have compiled our **getput4** program and placed the executable version in a file called **getput4.** Then to run the program, you just type the file name

```
getput4
```

and the program runs as we described earlier, taking its input from what you type at the keyboard. Now suppose that you wish to use the program on the "text file" called **words.** (A text file is one containing text, that is, data stored as characters. It could be an essay or a program in C, for example. A file containing machine language instructions, such as the file holding the executable version of a program is *not* a text file. Since our program works with characters, it should be used with text files.) All you need do is to enter this command instead of the previous one:

```
getput4 <words
```

The < symbol is a UNIX redirection operator. It causes the contents of the **words** file to be channelled into **getput4.** The **getput4** program itself doesn't know (or care) that the input is coming from a file instead of the keyboard. All that it knows is that a stream of characters is being fed to it, so it reads them and prints them one character at a time until an EOF shows up. UNIX puts files and I/O devices on the same footing, so the file is now the I/O "device." Try it!

```
getput4 <words
To see a World in a grain of sand,
And a Heaven in a wild flower,
Hold Infinity in the palm of your hand,
And Eternity in an hour.
```

Of course we cannot guarantee that William Blake will turn up in the file you choose.

Redirecting Input

Now suppose (assuming your supposer is still working) that you wish to have the words you type sent to a file called **mywords.** Then you can enter

```
getput4 >mywords
```

and begin typing. The > is a second UNIX redirection operator. It causes a new file called **mywords** to be created for your use, and then redirects the output of **getput4** (that output is a copy of the characters you type) to that file. If you already have a file with the name **mywords,** it would normally be erased and then replaced by the new one. (Some UNIX systems give you the option of protecting existing files, however.) All that appears on the screen are the letters you type, and the copies go to the file instead. To end the program, type the EOF character, usually a [control−d] on UNIX systems. Try it. If you can't think of anything to type, just imitate this example. Here we show the UNIX prompt, which we take to be a %. Remember to end each line with a [return] so as to send the buffer contents to the program.

```
% getput4 >mywords
  You should have no problem recalling which redirection
operator does what. Just remember that each operator points
in the direction the information flows. Think of it as a
funnel.  [control-d]
%
```

Once the [control−d] is processed, the program terminates and returns control to the UNIX operating system, as is indicated by the return of the UNIX prompt. Did the program work? The UNIX **ls** command, which lists file names, should show you that the file **mywords** now exists. You can use the UNIX **cat** command to check the contents, or you can use **getput4** again, this time redirecting the file *to* the program.

```
% getput4 <mywords
  You should have no problem recalling which redirection
operator does what. Just remember that each operator points
in the direction the information flows. Think of it as a
funnel.
%
```

Combined Redirection

Now crank up your supposer one more time and suppose you want to make a copy of the file **mywords** and call it **savewords.** Just issue the command

```
getput4 <mywords >savewords
```

and the deed is done. The command

```
getput4 >savewords <mywords
```

would have served as well, since the order of redirection operations doesn't matter.

Don't use the same file for both input and output in one command.

```
getput 4 <mywords >mywords WRONG
```

The reason not to do this is that the >**mywords** causes the original **mywords** to be erased before it ever gets used as input.

Figure 6.5
Combined redirection.

Perhaps we now should summarize the rules governing the use of the two redirection operators < and >.

1. A redirection operator connects an *executable* program (including standard UNIX commands) with a file. It cannot be used to connect one file to another or one program to another.
2. Input cannot be taken from more than one file, nor can output be directed to more than one file using these operators.
3. Normally the spaces between the names and operators are optional, except occasionally when some characters with special meaning to the UNIX shell are used. We could, for example, have used **getput4<words** or the more attractive **getput4 < words.**

We already have given several proper examples. Here are some wrong examples, with **addup** and **count** as executable programs and **fish** and **stars** as text files.

`fish > stars`	Violates Rule 1
`addup < count`	Violates Rule 1
`addup < fish < stars`	Violates Rule 2
`count > stars fish`	Violates Rule 2

Unix also features a >> operator, which lets you add data to the end of an existing file, and the pipe operator (¦) which lets you connect the output of one program to the input of a second program. See a UNIX book (UNIX PRIMER PLUS comes to mind) for more information on all these operators.

Let's try one more example and construct a very simple cypher program. We'll alter **getput** slightly and obtain

```
 /* simplecode */
/* this program replaces each text character by the next */
/* in the ASCII sequence */
#include <stdio.h>
main()
{
  int ch;

  while ((ch = getchar()) != EOF)
     putchar(ch + 1);
}
```

The **putchar( )** function converts the integer **"ch + 1"** to the appropriate character.

Now compile the program and store the executable version in a file called **simplecode.** Next, put the following into a file called **original.** (You can use your system editor, or you can use **getput4** as we showed earlier.)

```
Good spelling is an aid
to clear writing.
```

Now give the command

```
simplecode <original
```

The result should be something like this:

```
Hppe!tqfmmjoh!jt!bo!bje^Kup!dmfbs!xsjujoh/^K
```

The **G** is changed to an **H,** the **o** to a **p,** and so on. You may have a couple of surprises. Notice that the spaces become exclamation marks. This reminds us that a space is a character on the same footing as other characters. Secondly, two lines were compressed into one. Why? Because **original** contains a newline character at the end of the first line; that's how the computer knows to start the next word on a new line. But that character also got changed. On our system it was changed to **^K,** which is another way to write [control−k], and so no new line was started. If we want an encyphering program that preserves the original line structure, we need a way to change all the characters *except* the newline character. The next chapter will give us the tools to do that.

Non-UNIX

We'll deal mainly with the differences from UNIX, so if you skipped over the part, go back and read it (it's pretty easy going). There are two varieties in this category:

1. Other operating systems with redirection, and
2. C compilers with redirection.

We can't cover all possible operating systems, so we will give just one example, but of one that is in widespread use. That system is MS-DOS 2. MS-DOS began as an offshoot of CP/M, but now is evolving towards XENIX, a UNIX-like system. Version 2 of MS-DOS has instituted redirection operators < and > which work just as we described in the previous section.

We also can't cover all possible C compilers. However, five out of the six microcomputer versions of C compilers we've looked at use the < and > symbols for redirection. Compiler-generated redirection differs in two respects from UNIX redirection:

1. It works only with C programs, while UNIX redirection works for any executable program.
2. There must be a space between the program name and the operator, and there must be no space between the operator and the file name. Here is an example of the proper form.

```
getput4 <words
```

Comment

Redirection is a simple yet potent tool. With it we can make our tiny **getput4** program into a file producer, a file reader, and a file copier. The approach exemplifies the C (and UNIX) philosophy of creating simple tools which can be combined in a variety of ways to perform a variety of tasks.

SUMMARY: HOW TO REDIRECT INPUT AND OUTPUT

With most C systems you can use redirection, either for all programs through the operating system, or else just for C programs, courtesy of the C compiler. In the following, let **prog** be the name of the executable program and let **file1** and **file2** be names of files.

Redirecting Output to a File: >

```
prog >file1
```

Redirecting Input from a File: <

```
prog <file2
```

Combined Redirection

```
prog <file2 >file1 or
prog >file1 <file2
```

Both forms use **file2** for input and **file1** for output.

Spacing
Some systems (C compilers, especially) require a space to the left of the redirection operator and no space to the right. Other systems (UNIX, for example) will accept either spaces or no spaces on either side.

A GRAPHIC EXAMPLE

We can use **getchar( )** and **putchar( )** to produce geometric patterns using characters. Here is a program that does that. It reads a character and then prints it a number of times that depends on the ASCII value. It also prints a sufficient number of spaces to center each line.

```
  /* patterns */
/* produces a symmetric pattern of characters */
#include <stdio.h>
main()
{
  int ch;  /* read character */
  int index;
  int chnum;

  while ((ch = getchar()) != '\n') {
     chnum = ch % 26; /* produces a number from 0 to 25 */
     index = 0;
     while (index++ < (30 - chnum))
         putchar(' '); /* spaces to center pattern */
     index = 0;
     while (index++ < (2*chnum + 1))
          putchar(ch); /* print ch several times */
     putchar('\n');
     }
}
```

The only new technical point is that we have used subexpressions, such as **(30 - chnum)** in the **while** loop conditions. One **while** loop controls the printing of the initial spaces, and the second controls the printing of the characters.

What you get depends on the data you input. If, for example, you type

```
What's up?
```

then the response is

```
                WWWWWWWWWWWWWWWWWWW
                         h
       aaaaaaaaaaaaaaaaaaaaaaaaaaaaaaaaaaaaaaa
             ttttttttttttttttttttttttt
             '''''''''''''''''''''''''''
              sssssssssssssssssssssss

             uuuuuuuuuuuuuuuuuuuuuuuuuuu
                 ppppppppppppppppp
              ???????????????????????
```

What can you do with this program? You can ignore it. You can tinker with it to change the kinds of patterns it makes. You can try to find combinations of input characters that produce a pretty pattern. For example, the input

```
hijklmnopqrstuiii
```

produces

```
                         h
                        iii
                       jjjjj
                      kkkkkkk
                     lllllllll
                    mmmmmmmmmmm
                   nnnnnnnnnnnnn
                  ooooooooooooooo
                 ppppppppppppppppp
                qqqqqqqqqqqqqqqqqqq
               rrrrrrrrrrrrrrrrrrrrr
              sssssssssssssssssssssss
             ttttttttttttttttttttttttt
            uuuuuuuuuuuuuuuuuuuuuuuuuuu
                        iii
                        iii
                        iii
```

SYSTEM-DEPENDENT I/O: 8086/8088 I/O PORTS

Let's take a look at a different sort of I/O device as we turn now to an example of fitting C to the requirements of a specific system. Many of the new generation of microcomputers are based on the Intel's 8086 and 8088 microprocessor chip. The best known example is the IBM PC, which uses the 8088. We will discuss a particular example for the IBM PC, but the principles involved apply to other users for the 8086/8088 family.

A computer like the IBM has more to it than just the 8088 chip. It has a keyboard, a speaker, perhaps a cassette drive or a disk drive, a monitor, built-in memory, timers, and other microprocessors to control the flow of data. The central processing unit (incorporated into the 8088 chip) needs a way to communicate with the other parts of the computer. Some of this is done by using memory addresses, and some is done by using input/output "ports." The 8088 chip has 65536 ports that it can use for communication. Each device is assigned its own particular port or ports to use for communicating with the 8088. (Not all 65536 are used!) For example, ports 992, 993, and 1000 to 1004 are used to communicate with the color/graphics adapter. The speaker is controlled using port 97. That sounds a bit simpler than the color/graphics adapter, so we will use the speaker to illustrate the use of I/O ports.

Port 97 doesn't control the speaker directly. The device that does is something called an 8255 Programmable Parallel Interface Controller. This microprocessor has three "registers" (small, easily accessed memory units), each of which holds a number. The numbers in the registers control what the device does. Each register is connected with the 8088 through a port, and port 97 is connected to the register that controls the speaker. We program the control by using the port to change the number in the register. The right number will cause the speaker to sound a tone. The wrong number can cause problems. Thus we need to know what number to send and how to send it. In particular, we need to know how to use C to send the number.

First, let's look into what numbers to send. The first thing to know is that an 8255 register accepts an 8-bit number, which is stored as a binary number, such as 01011011. Each of the eight storage bits is regarded as an on-off switch for some device or action. The presence of a 0 or 1 in a particular bit position determines whether or not the device is on. For example, bit 3 (the bits are numbered from 0 to 7 going from right to left) determines if the cassette motor is on, and bit 7 enables and disenables the keyboard. Notice the need for caution. If we turn the speaker on and neglect the other bits, we might accidentally turn the keyboard off! So let's take a look at

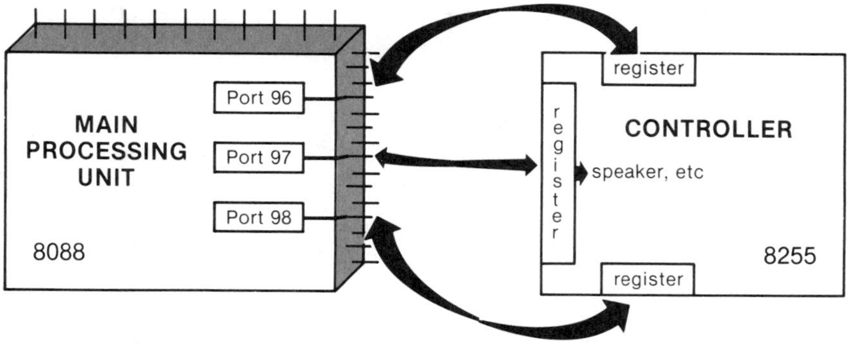

Figure 6.6
The 8088-8255 connection.

what each bit does by looking at the next figure. (The information is from IBM's Technical Reference Manual, and we don't have to know what most of it means.)

```
bit 0 + timer 2 gate speaker
bit 1 + speaker data
bit 2 + (read read/write memory size or (read spare key)
bit 3 + cassette motor off
bit 4 - enable read/write memory
bit 5 - enable i/o ch ck
bit 6 - hold kbd clk low
bit 7 - (enable kbd) or + (clr kbd & enable sense sw's)
```

Figure 6.7
Port 97: what each bit controls.

Note the little plus and minus signs in the figure. A plus sign indicates that a 1 means the condition holds, while a minus indicates that a 0 means the condition holds. Thus a 1 in the bit-3 position means the cassette motor is off, and a 0 in the bit-4 position means the read/write memory is enabled.

How do we turn the speaker on? It turns out that for the speaker to be on, both the "timer 2 gate speaker" bit (bit 0) and the "speaker data" bit (bit 1) should be on. This means we can turn the speaker on by sending the binary number 11 (or decimal number 3) through port 97. But before you rush off to do that, note that this has some side effects, such as setting bit 4 to off, which may not be what we want to happen. Preventing you from making such a hasty error is one reason we haven't yet told you how to use the ports!

To be safe, we should check first to see what the register reads normally. Fortunately, that is not too difficult (we'll show you in a moment), and the answer is that the register usually holds "76" or "77." Let's translate that to binary. (You may wish to check the appendix on binary numbers at this point.) Table 6-1 shows the conversion for some numbers:

Table 6-1. Binary Conversions of Some Decimal Numbers

decimal	bit number	7	6	5	4	3	2	1	0
76		0	1	0	0	1	1	0	0
77		0	1	0	0	1	1	0	1
78		0	1	0	0	1	1	1	0
79		0	1	0	0	1	1	1	1

Without going into what "hold keyboard clock low" might mean, it is clear that the safest course of action is to leave all the bit positions other than 0 and 1 unchanged. This corresponds to sending binary number 01001111, or decimal 79, to the register. As an added precaution, we should read the original value in the register and then restore the register to that value when we are done sounding the speaker. (The bitwise operators discussed in the appendix offer another approach for setting the register.)

Okay, we are ready now to sound the speaker. What do we do next?

Using a Port

There are two things you can do with a port. You can send information from the 8088 to the attached device, or you can read information from the attached device to the 8088. In assembly language these tasks are accomplished using the OUT and the IN instructions. In C the method depends on the compiler. Some compilers offer an analogous C function. Lattice C and Supersoft C, for example, use **outp( )** and **inp( ).** Other compilers may use slightly different names. If you are using a compiler that doesn't offer this function, most likely you can either use assembly language to define such a function or else simply insert the assembly code (which is very simple) directly into your program. Check your compiler documentation. Meanwhile, we will assume that you have access to the **outp( )** and **inp( )** functions.

Here, then, is a first pass at beeping your beeper.

```
 /* beep1 */
/* a program to make the speaker beep */
main()
{
  int store;

  store = inp(97); /* store the initial port 97 reading */
  printf("port 97 = %d\n", store); /* check results */
  outp(97,79);    /* send 79 to port 97; turns speaker on */
  outp(97,store);         /* restore to initial condition */
  }
```

You probably can tell what the **inp( )** and **outp( )** functions do, but here is a formal description.

`inp(portnumber)` This function returns an 8-bit integer value (which is converted to a 16-bit **int** by adding zeros to the left) from input port **portnumber.** It does not alter whatever the port is connected to.

`outp(portnumber, value)` This function sends the 8-bit integer `value` to output port **portnumber.**

Note that a port can be both an input and an output port, depending on how it is used.

Now run the program. You may not be very satisfied, for it doesn't take very long for the computer to turn the speaker off after turning it on. It would be much more satisfactory if we could get the computer to wait a bit before turning the speaker off. Can that be done? Yes, we just have to give the computer something to do in the meantime. That can be arranged, as the next program shows.

```
 /* beep2 */
/* a longer beep */
#define LIMIT 10000
main()
```

```
{
    int store;
    int count = 0; /* something for the computer to count with */

    store = inp(97);
    outp(97,79);
    while(count++ < LIMIT)
        ; /* whiling away time doing nothing */
    outp(97,store);
}
```

Notice that all the **while** statement does is increase **count** until it reaches **LIMIT.** The semicolon following the **while** statement is the "null" statement, one that does nothing. Thus, **beep2** turns the speaker on, counts to 10000, then turns the speaker off. You can adjust the size of **LIMIT** to control how long the sound continues. Or you can replace **LIMIT** with a variable and use **scanf( )** to read in a value controlling the duration.

It would be nice if we could control the pitch, too. Well, we can. After we study functions more fully, you can check the appendix for a program that makes the terminal keyboard into a musical keyboard.

Summary

Once again we have dealt with I/O devices, I/O data, and I/O functions. The devices were the 8255 controller and the speaker, the data were the numbers communicated to and from one of the 8255 registers, and the functions were **inp( )** and **outp( ).** Using these functions or their assembly code equivalents is necessary if we want to use the 8086/8088 I/O ports, and C compilers give you one or both options.

TAPPING THE HIDDEN HORSEPOWER OF YOUR COMPUTER

Want to unlock the awesome number-crunching potential of the beast? We have created an amazing program (revealed in Fig. 6.8) that does just that. It is a program that you must run to appreciate fully. Warning: for proper effect you should choose a LIMIT value appropriate for your system. More on that in a moment, but first, here is the program.

```
 /* hans */
#include <stdio.h>
#define LIMIT 8000L
main()
{
  int num1, num2;
  long delay = 0;
  int count = 0;

  printf("Hans the computer horse will add two very ");
  printf("small integers for your pleasure.\n");
  printf("Please enter the first small integer.\n");
scanf("%d", &num1);
  printf("Thank you. Now enter the second integer.\n");
scanf("%d", &num2);
  printf("Okay, Hans, how much is that?\n");
  while( delay++ < LIMIT);
  while( count++ < (num1 + num2 -1))
    {
    putchar('\007');
    delay = 0;
    while( delay++ < LIMIT);
    putchar('\n');
    }
  printf("Yes?\n");
  delay = 0;
  while( delay++ <  3*LIMIT);
  putchar('\007');
  printf("Very good, Hans!\n");
}
```

Figure 6.8
A number-crunching program

Technical notes: The **while** statements containing **delay** do nothing but mark time. The semicolon at the end of the line indicates that the **while** loop ends there and does not include any of the following lines. The use of a **while** loop within another **while** loop is called "nesting." We find that 8000 is a good value for **LIMIT** on the IBM PC. For a VAX 11/750 we prefer a value around 50000, but the time-sharing load on the system can affect that choice. We set **LIMIT** equal to a **long** constant (that's what the terminal **L** does) to avoid problems with the maximum **int** size. (This wasn't really necessary for the value of **8000,** but even changing the value to 12000 on an IBM would have made it necessary, for then the expression **3*LIMIT** would be 36000, which is larger than the maximum **int** on that system.)

If your system doesn't have a speaker or a bell, perhaps you could replace **putchar('\007')** with **printf("CLOP").**

This program will impress your friends and probably soothe those who fear computers.

We think this program can form the core of a "C Calculator," but we leave the development of the concept to our readers.

WHAT YOU SHOULD HAVE LEARNED

What **getchar( )** does: fetches a character from the keyboard
What **putchar(ch)** does: sends the character **ch** to the screen
What **!=** means: not equal to
What **EOF** is: a special character indicating the end of a file
How to redirect input from a file: **program < file**
How to redirect output to a file: **program > file**
What ports are: I/O accesses to attached devices
How to use ports: **inp( )** and **outp( )**

QUESTIONS AND ANSWERS

Questions

1. **putchar(getchar( ))** is a valid expression. Is **getchar(putchar( ))** also valid?
2. What would each of the following statements accomplish?
   a. `putchar('H');`
   b. `putchar('\007');`
   c. `putchar('\n');`
   d. `putchar('\b');`
3. Suppose you have a program **count** that counts the characters in a file. Devise a command that counts the number of characters in the file **essay** and stores the result in a file named **essayct.**
4. Given the program and files of question 3, which of the following are valid commands?
   a. `essayct <essay`
   b. `count essay`

   c. `essay >count`

5. What does the statement **outp(212,23)** do?

Answers

1. No. **getchar( )** doesn't use an argument, and **putchar( )** needs one.
2. **a.** print the letter H
   b. output the character '\007' which produces a beep
   c. start a new line
   d. backspace one space
3. **count** <**essay** >**essayct** or else **count** >**essayct** <**essay**
4. **a.** invalid, for **essayct** is not an executable program
   b. invalid, for the redirection operator was omitted.
   (However, you later will learn to write programs that don't need the redirection operator.)
   c. invalid; the executable program name must come first.
5. It sends the number 23 out through port number 212.

EXERCISES

1. Produce the program described in Question 3. That is, devise a program that counts the number of characters in a file.
2. Modify **count** so that it beeps each time it counts a character. Insert a short counting loop to separate one beep from the next.
3. Modify **beep2** so that you can input the counting loop limit when the program runs.

7

CHOOSING ALTERNATIVES

In this chapter you will find

7. CHOOSING ALTERNATIVES

CONCEPTS

Making decisions
True and false in C
Making comparisons
Logic in C

KEYWORDS

if, else, switch, break, case, default

OPERATORS

`> >= <= < == != && || / :?`

Do you want to create powerful, intelligent, versatile, and useful programs? Then you need a language that provides the three basic forms of program "flow" control. According to computer science (which is the science of computers and not science by computers—yet) a good language should provide these three forms of program flow:

1. Executing a series of statements.
2. Repeating a sequence of statements until some condition is met.
3. Using a test to decide between alternative actions.

The first form we know well; all our programs have consisted of a sequence of statements. The **while** loop is one example of the second form, and we will pick up other methods in Chapter 8. The final form, choosing between different possible courses of action, makes a program much more "intelligent" and increases enormously the usefulness of a computer. We will explore that topic in this chapter.

THE *if* STATEMENT

Let's start with a very simple example. We already have seen how to write a program that counts the number of characters in a file. Suppose we want to count lines, instead. We can do that by counting the number of newline characters in a file. Here's how.

```
 /* linecounter */
#include <stdio.h>
main()
{
  int ch;
  int linecount = 0;

  while ( (ch = getchar()) != EOF)
       if (ch == '\n')
           linecount++;
  printf("I counted %d lines.\n", linecount);
}
```

The core of this program is the statement

```
if (ch == '\n')
    linecount++;
```

This "if statement" instructs the computer to increase **linecount** by 1 *if* the character just read (**ch**) is the newline character. The == is not a misprint; it means "is equal to." Don't confuse this operator with the assignment operator (=).

What happens if **ch** is not equal to a newline character? Nothing happens, and the **while** loop moves on to read the next character.

The **if** statement we just used counts as a single statement, running from the initial **if** to the closing semicolon. That is why we didn't have to use braces to mark the limits of the **while** loop.

It is a simple matter to make the program count both characters and lines, so let's do it.

```
 /*line and character counter */
#include <stdio.h>
main()
```

```
{
  int ch;
  int linecount = 0;
  int charcount = 0;

  while ( (ch = getchar()) != EOF)
       {
       charcount++;
       if (ch == '\n')
           linecount++;
       }
  printf("I counted %d characters and %d lines.\n",
       charcount, linecount);
}
```

Now the **while** loop encompasses two statements, so we use braces to mark off the body of the loop.

We will call the compiled program **lcc** and use redirection to count the characters and lines in a file called **chow.**

```
lcc <chow
I counted 8539 characters and 233 lines.
```

The next step in developing this program will be to have it count words. That's only a little harder than what we've done so far, but we need to learn a little more about using **if** statements first.

ADDING *else* TO THE *if* STATEMENT

The simplest form of an **if** statement is the one we just used:

```
if(expression)
     statement
```

Normally the expression is a relational expression; that is, it compares the magnitude of two quantities (**x** > **y** or **c** == **6,** for example). If the expression is true (**x** is greater than **y,** or **c** does equal **6**), then the statement is executed. Otherwise it is ignored. More generally, any expression can be used, and an expression with a 0 value is taken to be false—more on that a little later.

The statement portion can be a simple statement, as in our example, or it can be a compound statement or block, marked off by braces:

```
if ( score > big)
    printf("Jackpot!\n"); /* simple statement */

if ( joe > ron)
    {
    joecash++;
    printf("You lose, Ron.\n");
    }                         /* compound statement */
```

The simple form of an 'if' statement gives you the choice of executing a statement (possibly compound) or skipping it. C also lets us choose between two statements by using the **if-else** structure.

Choice: ***if-else***

In the last chapter we presented a very simple cypher program that converted each character to the next one in the ASCII sequence. Unfortunately, it even converted the newline character, causing several lines to combine. We can eliminate that problem by creating a program that makes a simple choice: if the character is a newline, leave it alone; otherwise, convert it. Here is how this can be done in C:

```
 /* code1 */
#include <stdio.h>
main()
{
  char ch;

  while ((ch = getchar()) != EOF) {
       if (ch == '\n')        /*  leave the newline      */
           putchar(ch);       /*  character unchanged    */
       else
           putchar(ch + 1);   /* change other characters */
       }
}
```

Last time we used a file containing the following text.

```
Good spelling is an aid
to good writing.
```

Using the same text with our new program gives this result:

```
Hppe!tqfmmjoh!jt!bo!bje
up!hppe!xsjujoh/
```

Gosh! It works. Incidentally, we can make the decoding program very simply. Just duplicate **code1,** but replace **(ch + 1)** with **(ch − 1).**

Did you note the general form of the **if-else** statement? It's

```
if(expression)
     statement
 else
     statement
```

If the expression is true, the first statement is executed. If the expression is false, the statement following the **else** is executed. The statements can be simple or compound. The indentation is not required by C, but it is the standard style. It shows at a glance those statements whose execution depends on a test.

The **if** lets us choose whether or not to do one action. The **if-else** lets us choose between two actions. What if we need more choices than that?

Multiple Choice: *else-if*

Often life offers us more than two choices. We can extend the **if-else** structure with **else-if** to accommodate this fact. Let's look at a particular example. Utility companies often have charges that depend on the amount of energy you use. Here are the rates we are charged for electricity:

first 240 kw-hrs:	$0.05418 per kw-hr
next 300 kw-hrs:	$0.07047 per kw-hr
over 540 kw-hrs:	$0.09164 per kw-hr

If you worry about your energy management, you might wish to prepare a program to calculate your energy costs. Here is a first step in that direction.

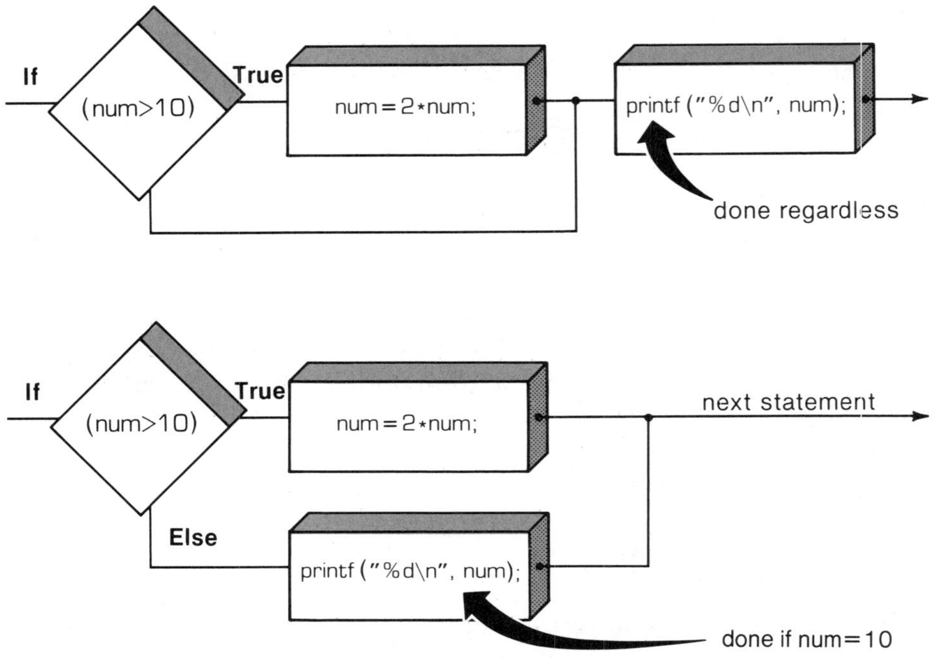

Figure 7.1
If* vs. *if-else.

```
 /* electbill */
/* calculates electric bill   */
#define RATE1 0.05418      /* rate for first 240 kw-hrs */
#define RATE2 0.07047      /* rate for next 300 kw-hrs  */
#define RATE3 0.09164      /* rate for over 540 kw-hrs  */
#define BASE1 13.00        /* total cost first 240 kw-hrs */
#define BASE2 34.14        /* total cost first 540 kw-hrs */
#define BREAK1 240.0       /* first breakpoint for rates  */
#define BREAK2 540.0       /* second breakpoint for rates */
main()
{
  float kwh;    /* kilowatt-hours used */
  float bill;   /* charges */

  printf("Please enter the kw-hrs used.\n");
  scanf("%f", &kwh);
  if (kwh <= BREAK1)
      bill = RATE1 * kwh;
```

```
    else if (kwh <= BREAK2)       /* kwh between 240 and 540 */
        bill = BASE1 + RATE2 * (kwh -240);
    else                          /* kwh above 540 */
        bill = BASE2 + RATE3 * (kwh -540);
    printf("The charge for %.1f kw-hrs is $%1.2f.\n", kwh, bill);
}
```

We have used symbolic constants for the rates. This way our constants are gathered in one place. If the power company changes its rates (and this can happen), having the rates in one place makes it less likely that we will fail to update a rate. We also expressed the rate breakpoints symbolically. They, too, are subject to change. The flow of the program is straightforward, with the program selecting one of three formulas, depending on the value of **kwh.** Figure 7.2 illustrates the flow. We should point out that the only way the program can reach the first **else** is if **kwh** is equal to or greater than **240.** Thus the **else if (kwh < BREAK2)** line really is equivalent to demanding that **kwh** is between **240** and **540,** as we noted in the program comment. Similarly, the final **else** can be reached only if **kwh** equals or exceeds **540.** Finally, note that **BASE1** and **BASE2** represent the total charges for the first 240 and 540 kw-hrs, respectively. Thus we only need to add on the additional charges for electricity in excess of those amounts.

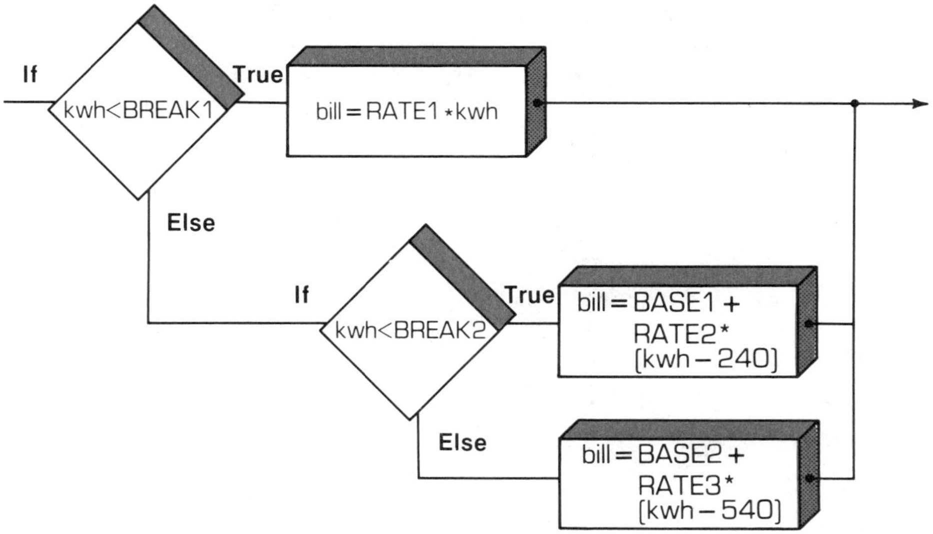

Figure 7.2
Program flow for electbill.

Actually, the **else-if** is just a variation on what we already knew. For example, the core of our program is just another way of writing

```
if ( kwh < BREAK1 )
     bill = RATE1 * kwh;
 else
    if ( kwh < BREAK2 )
        bill = BASE1 + RATE2 * (kwh -240);
    else
        bill = BASE2 + RATE3 * (kwh -540);
```

That is, the program consists of an **if-else** statement for which the statement part of the **else** is another **if-else** statement. The second **if-else** statement is said to be "nested" in the first. (Incidentally, the entire **if-else** structure counts as a single statement, which is why we didn't have to enclose the nested **if-else** in braces.)

These two forms are perfectly equivalent. The only differences are in where we put spaces and newlines, and these are ignored by the compiler. Nonetheless, the first form is preferred, for it shows more clearly that we are making a three-way choice. This form makes it easier to scan through the program and check what the choices are. Save the nested forms for when they are needed, for instance, when you must test two separate quantities. An example would be if there were a 10% surcharge for kw-hrs in excess of 540 for summer only.

You may string together as many **else-ifs** as you need, as illustrated by this fragment:

```
if (score < 1000)
     bonus = 0;
else if (score < 1500)
     bonus = 1;
else if (score < 2000)
     bonus = 2;
else if (score < 2500)
     bonus = 4;
else
     bonus = 6;
```

(This could be part of a game program, where **bonus** represents how many additional photon bombs or food pellets you get for the next round.)

Pairing *else's* with *if's*

When you have a lot of **ifs** and **elses,** how does the computer decide which **if** goes with which **else?** For example, consider the program fragment

```
if ( number > 6 )
    if ( number < 12 )
       printf("You're close!\n");
else
    printf("Sorry, you lose a turn!\n");
```

When does "Sorry, you lose a turn!" get printed, when **number** is less than or equal to **6,** or when **number** is greater than **12?** In other words, does the **else** go with the first **if** or the second?

The answer is, it goes with the second **if.** That is, you would get these responses:

Number	Response
5	none
10	`You're close!`
15	`Sorry, you lose a turn!`

The rule is that an **else** goes with the most recent **if** unless braces indicate otherwise. We indented our example to make it look as if the **else** goes with the first **if,** but remember that the compiler ignores indentation. If we really want the **else** to go with the first **if,** we can write the fragment this way.

```
if ( number > 6 )
     {
     if (number < 12 )
         printf("You're close!\n");
     }
else
   printf("Sorry, you lose a turn!\n");
```

Now we would get these responses:

Number	Response
5	`Sorry, you lose a turn!`
10	`You're close!`
15	none

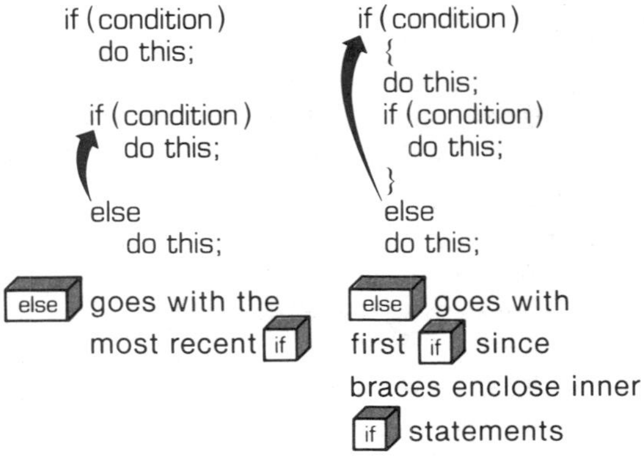

Figure 7.3
***if-else* pairings**

SUMMARY: USING *if* STATEMENTS FOR MAKING CHOICES

Keywords: ***if, else***
General Comments:
In each of the following forms, the *statement* can be either a simple statement or a compound statement. A "true" expression, more generally, means one with a nonzero value.

Form 1:

```
if ( expression )
    statement
```

The *statement* is executed if the *expression* is true.

Form 2:

```
if ( expression )
    statement1
  else
    statement2
```

If the *expression* is true, *statement1* is executed. Otherwise *statement2* is executed.

Form 3:

```
if ( expression1 )
    statement1
else if ( expression2 )
    statement2
else
    statement3
```

If *expression1* is true, then *statement1* is executed. If *expression1* is false but *expression2* is true, *statement2* is executed. Otherwise, if both expressions are false, *statement3* is executed.

Example

```
if (legs == 4)
    printf("It might be a horse.\n");
 else if (legs > 4)
     printf("It is not a horse.\n");
 else     /* case of legs < 4 */
     {
     legs++;
     printf("Now it has one more leg.\n")
     }
```

WHICH IS BIGGER: RELATIONAL OPERATORS AND EXPRESSIONS

Relational operators are used to make comparisons. We have used several already, and now we will show you the complete list of C relational operators.

OPERATOR	MEANING
<	is less than
<=	is less than or equal to
==	is equal to
>=	is greater than or equal to
>	is greater than
!=	is not equal to

That pretty much covers all the possibilities for numerical relationships. (Numbers, even complex ones, are less complex than humans.) The main caution we offer is to not use = for ==. Some computer languages (BASIC, for example) do use the same symbol for the assignment operator as for the relational equality operator, but the two operations are quite different. The assignment operator *assigns* a value to the left-hand variable. The relational equality operator, however, checks to see if the left-hand and right-hand sides are already equal. It doesn't change the value of the left-hand variable, if one is present.

`canoes = 3` assigns the value **3** to **canoes**
`canoes == 5` checks to see if **canoes** has the value **5**

Some care is needed, for a compiler will let you use the wrong form in some cases, yielding results other than what you expect. We will show an example shortly.

Table 7-1. Assignment and Relation Equality Operators in Some Common Languages

Language	Assignment	Relational Equality
BASIC	=	=
FORTRAN	=	.EQ.
C	=	==
Pascal	:=	=
PL/I	=	=
Logo	make	=

The relational operators are used to form the relational expressions used in **if** and **while** statements. These statements check to see if the expression is true or false. Here are four unrelated statements containing examples of relational expressions; the meaning, we hope, is clear.

```
if ( number < 6)
    printf("Your number is too small.\n");

while ( ch != '$')
     count++;

if ( total == 100)
    printf("You have hit the jackpot!\n");
```

```
if ( ch > 'M' )
     printf ("Send this person to another line.\n");
```

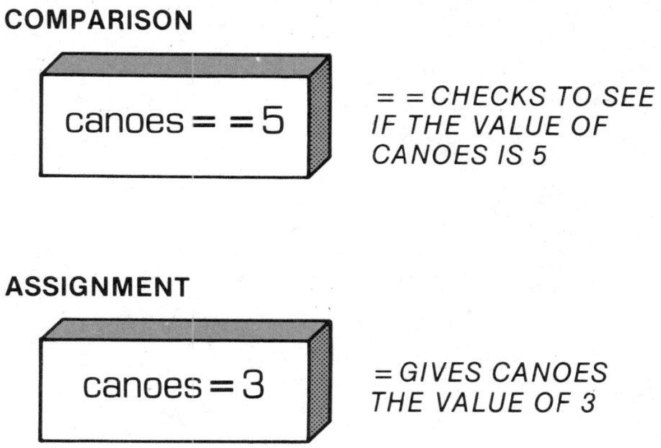

Figure 7.4
== and =.

Note that the relational expressions can be used with characters, too. The machine code (which we have been assuming to be ASCII) is used for the comparison. However, you can't use the relational operators to compare strings; in Chapter 13 we will show you what to use for strings.

The relational operators can be used with floating-point numbers, too. However, you should limit yourself to using only < and > in floating-point comparisons. The reason is that roundoff errors can prevent two numbers from being equal even though logically they should be. Consider, for example, this decimal system analogue. Certainly the product of 3 and 1/3 is 1.0, but if we express 1/3 as a 6-place decimal fraction, the product is .999999, which is not quite equal to 1.

Each relational expression is judged to be "true" or "false." This raises an interesting question.

What Is Truth?

We can answer this age-old question, at least as far as C is concerned. First, recall that an expression in C always has a value. This is so even for relational expressions, as this next example shows. In it we find the values of two relational expressions, one true and one false.

```
 /* trueandfalse */
main()
{
  int true, false;

  true = ( 10 > 2);    /* value of a true relationship  */
  false = ( 10 == 2); /* value of a false relationship */
  printf("true = %d; false = %d \n", true, false);
}
```

Here we have assigned the values of two relational expressions to two variables. Being straightforward, we assigned **true** the value of a true expression, and **false** the value of a false expression. Running the program produces the following simple output:

```
true = 1; false = 0
```

Aha! For C, truth is **1** and falsity is **0.** We can check that easily enough by running the next program.

```
 /* truthcheck */
main()
{
  if (1)
       printf("1 means true.\n");
  else
       printf("1 doesn't mean true.\n");
  if (0)
       printf("0 doesn't mean false.\n");
  else
       printf("0 means false.\n");
}
```

We say that the **1** should evaluate as a true statement, and the **0** should evaluate as a false statement. If what we say is accurate, then the first **if** statement should take its first branch (the **if** branch), and the second **if** statement should take its second branch (the **else** branch). Try it out and see if we are right.

So What Else Is True?

If we can use a **1** or a **0** as an **if** statement test expression, can we use other numbers? If so, what happens? Let's experiment.

FOUR OF THE GREATEST INVENTIONS IN HUMAN HISTORY....
THE WHEEL
THE LIGHT BULB
THE MICRO COMPUTER
MICRO COMPUTER MANUAL AND RESOURCE BOOK AUTHORS


```
/* iftest */
main()
{
   if(200)
     printf("200 is true.\n");
   if (-33)
     printf("-33 is true.\n");
}
```

The results:

```
200 is true.
-33 is true.
```

Apparently C regards **200** and **−33** as "true," also. Indeed, all nonzero values are regarded as "true," and only **0** is recognized as "false." C has a very tolerant notion of truth!

Many programmers make use of this definition of truth. For example, the phrase

```
if(goats != 0)
```

can be replaced by

```
if(goats)
```

since the expression **(goats != 0)** and the expression **(goats)** both become **0** or false only when **goats** has the value **0.** We think the second form is not as clear in meaning as the first. However, it is more efficient, for it requires fewer processing operations for the computer when the program runs.

Troubles with Truth

C's tolerant notion of truth can lead to trouble. Consider the following program.

```
 /* employment */
main()
{
  int age = 20;

  while (age++ <= 65)
    {
       if (( age % 20) == 0) /* is age divisible by 20? */
         printf("You are %d. Here is a raise.\n", age);
       if (age = 65)
         printf("You are %d. Here is your gold watch.\n",
                age);
    }
  }
```

At first glance you might think the output of this program would be

```
You are 40. Here is a raise.
You are 60. Here is a raise.
You are 65. Here is your gold watch.
```

The actual output, however, is

```
You are 65. Here is your gold watch.
You are 65. Here is your gold watch.
You are 65. Here is your gold watch.
You are 65. Here is your gold watch.
You are 65. Here is your gold watch.
          . . .
```

and so on indefinitely

What has happened! Not only did we design the program poorly, but we ignored our own cautionary remarks and used

```
if (age = 65)
```

instead of

```
if (age == 65)
```

The effect is disastrous. When the program reaches that line, it looks at the expression **(age = 65).** An assignment expression, which this is, has the value the variable gets, **65** in this case. Since **65** is nonzero, the expression is evaluated as "true" and the following print instruction is executed. Then, when the program returns to the **while** test, **age** is **65,** which is less than or equal to 65. The test is met, **age** is then increased to **66** (because of the postfix increment operator **++**), and the loop is traversed again. Will it stop next time? It should, because **age** is now greater than **65.** But when the program reaches our faulty **if** statement again, **age** gets set back to **65** again! So the message is printed out once more, and the loop is repeated again, ad infinitum. (Unless, of course, you eventually decide to abort the program.)

To sum up, the relational operators are used to form relational expressions. Relational expressions have the value "1" if true and "0" if false. Statements (such as **while** and **if**) that normally use relational expressions as tests can use any expression as a test, with nonzero values recognized as "true" and zero values as "false."

Priority of Relational Operators

The priority of the relational operators is less than that of + and − and greater than that of assignment. This means, for example, that

```
x > y + 2
```

means the same as

```
x > (y + 2)
```

It also means that

```
ch = getchar() != EOF
```

is the same as

```
ch = (getchar() != EOF)
```

since the higher priority of **!=** means that operation is done before assignment. Thus **ch** would receive either **1** or **0** for a value, for **(getchar( ) != EOF)** is a relational expression whose value is assigned to **ch.** Since our program examples up to now have wanted **ch** to get the value of **getchar( ),** we have used parentheses to get the correct grouping:

```
(ch = getchar()) != EOF
```

The relational operators are themselves organized into two different priorities.

higher priority group: < <= >= >
lower priority group: == !=

Like most other operators, the relational operators associate from left to right. Thus

```
ex != wye == zee
```

is the same as

```
(ex != wye) == zee
```

Thus first C checks to see if **ex** and **wye** are equal. The resulting value of **1** or **0** (true or false) then is compared to the value of **zee.** We don't anticipate using this sort of construction, but we feel that it is our duty to point out such sidelights.

We remind the reader who wishes to keep her or his priorities straight that Appendix C has a complete priority ranking of all operators.

SUMMARY: RELATIONAL OPERATORS AND EXPRESSIONS

I. Relational Operators:
Each of these operators compares the value at its left to the value at its right.

<	less than
<=	less than or equal to
==	equal to
>=	great than or equal to
>	greater than
!=	unequal to

II. Relational Expressions:
A simple relational expression consists of a relational operator with an operand on each side. If the relation is true, the relational expression has the value 1. If the relation is false, the relational expression has the value 0.

III. Examples
5 > 2 is true and has the value 1
(2+a) == a is false and has the value 0

LET'S GET LOGICAL

Sometimes it is useful to combine two or more relational expressions. For instance, suppose we want a program that counts only non-whitespace characters. That is, we wish to keep track of characters that are not spaces, not newline characters, and not tab characters. We can use "logical" operators to meet this need. Here is a short program illustrating the method.

```
 /* chcount */
/* counts non-whitespace characters */
main()
{
  int ch;
  int charcount = 0;
```

```
    while ((ch = getchar()) != EOF)
        if( ch != ' ' && ch != '\n' && ch != '\t')
            charcount++;
    printf("There are %d non-whitespace characters.\n", charcount);
}
```

The action begins as it often has in past programs: the program reads a character and checks to see if it is the End-Of-File character. Next comes something new, a statement using the logical "and" operator **&&.** We can render the **if** statement thus:

If the character is not a blank **AND** if it is not a newline character **AND** if it is not a tab character, then increase **charcount** by one.

All three conditions must be true if the whole expression is to be true. The logical operators have a lower priority than the relational operators, so it was not necessary to use additional parentheses to group the subexpressions.

There are three logical operators in C:

OPERATOR	MEANING
&&	and
||	or
!	not

Suppose **exp1** and **exp2** are two simple relational expressions like **cat > rat** or **debt == 1000.** Then

1. **exp1 && exp2** is true only if both **exp1** and **exp2** are true.
2. **exp1 || exp2** is true if either or both of **exp1** and **exp2** are true.
3. **!exp1** is true if **exp1** is false and vice versa.

Here are some concrete examples:

`5 > 2 && 4 > 7` is false because only one subexpression is true.

`5 > 2 || 4 > 7` is true because at least one of the subexpressions is true.

`!(4 > 7)` is true because 4 is not greater than 7.

The last expression, incidentally, is equivalent to

```
4 <= 7.
```

If you are unfamiliar or uncomfortable with logical operators, remember that

```
practice && time == perfect
```

Priorities

The **!** operator has a very high priority, higher than multiplication, the same as the increment operators, and just below that of parentheses. The **&&** operator has higher priority than ||, and both rank below the relational operators and above assignment in priority. Thus the expression

```
a > b && b > c || b > d
```

would be interpreted as

```
((a > b) && (b > c)) || (b > d)
```

that is, **b** is between **a** and **b**, or **b** is greater than **d.**

Order of Evaluation

Ordinarily C does not guarantee which parts of a complex expression will be evaluated first. For example, in the statement

```
apples = (5 + 3) * (9 + 6);
```

the expression **5 + 3** might be evaluated before **9 +6** or it might be evaluated afterwards. (However, operator priorities do guarantee that both will be evaluated before the multiplication takes place.) This ambiguity was left in the language to enable compiler designers to make the most efficient choice for a particular system. The exception to this rule (or lack of rule) is the treatment of logical operators. C guarantees that logical expressions are evaluated from left to right. Furthermore, it guarantees that as soon as an element is found which invalidates the expression as a whole, the evaluation stops. These guarantees make it possible to use constructions such as

```
while((c = getchar()) != EOF && c != '\n')
```

The first subexpression gives a value to **c** which then can be used in the second subexpression. Without the order guarantee, the computer might try to test the second expression before finding out what value **c** had.

Another example is

```
if ( number != 0 && 12/number == 2)
     printf("The number is 5 or 6.\n");
```

If **number** has the value **0,** the expression is false, and the relational expression is not evaluated any further. This spares the computer the trauma of trying to divide by zero. Many languages do not have this feature. After seeing that **number** is 0, they still plunge ahead to check the next condition.

SUMMARY: LOGICAL OPERATORS AND EXPRESSIONS

I. Logical Operators

Logical operators normally take relational expressions as operands. The **!** operator takes one operand. The rest take two, one to the left, one to the right.

`&&`	and
`||`	or
`!`	not

II. Logical Expressions

`expression1 && expression2`	is true if and only if both expressions are true
`expression1 || expression2`	is true if either one or both expressions are true
`!expression`	is true if the expression is false, and vice versa

III. Order of Evaluation

Logical expressions are evaluated from left to right; evaluation stops as soon as something is discovered that renders the expression false.

IV. Examples

```
6 > 2 && 3 == 3      is true
! ( 6 > 2 && 3 ==3 )is false
x != 0 && 20/x < 5   The second expression is evaluated only if
                     x is nonzero
```

Now let's apply our understanding in a couple examples. Our first example is a handy one.

A WORD-COUNT PROGRAM

Now we have the tools to make a word-counting program. (We might as well count characters and lines while we are at it.) The key point is to devise a way for the program to recognize a word. We will take a relatively simple approach and define a word as a sequence of characters which contains no white space. Thus, "glymxck" and "r2d2" are words. We will use a variable called **word** to keep track of whether or not we are in a word. When we encounter white space (a blank, tab, or newline), we will know we've reached the end of a word. Then the next nonwhite space character will mark the start of a new word, and we can increment our word count by 1. Here's the program:

```
#include <stdio.h>
#define YES 1
#define NO 0
main()
{
    int ch;             /* read-in character        */
    long nc = 0L;       /* number of characters     */
    int nl = 0;         /* number of lines          */
    int nw = 0;         /* number of words          */
    int word = NO;      /* ==YES if ch is in a word */

    while(( ch = getchar()) != EOF)
       {
       nc++;      /* count characters */
       if (ch == '\n')
       nl++;      /* count lines      */
       if( ch != ' ' && ch != '\n' && ch != '\t' && word == NO)
           {
           word = YES;  /* starting a new word */
           nw++;        /* count word          */
           }
       if(( ch == ' ' || ch == '\n' || ch == '\t') &&
           word == YES)
           word = NO;      /* reached end of word */
     }
```

```
    printf("characters = %ld, words = %d, lines = %d\n",
     nc,nw,nl);
}
```

Since there are three different white space characters, we had to use the logical operators to check for all three possibilities. Consider, for example, the line

```
if( ch != ' ' && ch != '\n' && ch != '\t' && word == NO)
```

It says, "if **ch** is *not* a space and *not* a newline and *not* a tab, and if we are not in a word." (The first three conditions together ask if **ch** is not white space.) If all four conditions are met, then we must be starting a new word, and **nw** is incremented. If we are in the middle of a word, then the first three conditions hold, but **word** will be **YES**, and **nw** is not incremented. When we reach the next white space character, we set **word** equal to **NO** again.

Check the coding to see whether or not the program gets confused if there are several spaces between one word and the next.

To use this program on a file, use redirection.

CHARACTER SKETCHES

Now let's look at something less utilitarian and more decorative. Our plan is to create a program with which you can draw rough, filled-in figures using characters. Each line of output consists of an unbroken row of characters. We choose the character and the length and position of the row. The program keeps reading our choices until it reads an EOF character. Fig. 7-5 presents the program.

Suppose we call the executable program **sketcher.** To run the program, we type its name. Then we enter a character and two numbers. The program responds, then we enter another set of data, and the program responds again until we provide an EOF character. On a UNIX system an exchange could look like this:

```
% sketcher
B 10 20
         BBBBBBBBBBB
Y 12 18
           YYYYYYY
[control-d]
%
```

```
 /* sketcher */
/* this program makes solid figures */
#include <stdio.h>
#define MAXLENGTH 80
main()
{
  int ch;               /* character to be printed */
  int start, stop;      /* starting and stopping points */
  int count ;           /* position counter */

  while((ch = getchar()) != EOF) /* read in character */
    {
    if (ch != '\n')  /* pass over newline character */
      {
      scanf("%d %d", &start, &stop); /* read limits */
      if( start  > stop||start < 1||stop > MAXLENGTH)
        printf("Inappropriate limits were entered.\n");
      else
        {
        count = 0;
        while (++count < start)
           putchar(' '); /* print blanks to starting point */
        while ( count++ <= stop)
           putchar(ch);  /* print char to stopping point */
        putchar('\n');   /* end line and start a new one  */
        }   /* end of else */
      }    /* end of ch if */
    }     /* end of while loop */
}        /* end of main */
```

Figure 7.5
Character sketch program.

The program printed out the character **B** in columns 10 to 20, and it printed **Y** in columns 12 to 18. Unfortunately, when we use the program interactively, our commands are interspersed with the output. A much more satisfactory way to use the program is to create a file containing suitable data and then to use redirection to feed the file to the program. Suppose, for example, the file **fig** contains the following data:

```
_ 30 50
| 30 50
```

```
| 30 50
| 30 50
| 30 50
| 30 50
= 20 60
: 31 49
: 30 49
: 29 49
: 27 49
: 25 49
: 30 49
: 30 49
/ 30 49
: 35 48
: 35 48
```

Then the command **sketcher** <**fig** produces the output shown in Fig. 7.6.

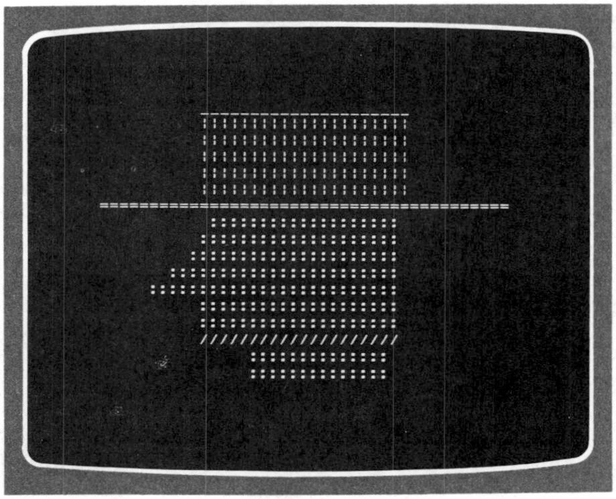

Figure 7.6
Output of character sketch program

(Note: printers and screens have different values for the vertical-to-horizontal ratio for characters, and this causes figures of this sort to look more compressed vertically when printed than when displayed on a screen.)

Analyzing the Program

This program is short, but it is more involved than the examples we have given before. Let's look at some of its elements.

Line Length

We limited the program to print no further than the 80th column, since 80 characters is the standard width of many video monitors and of normal-width paper. However, you can redefine the value of **MAXLENGTH** if you wish to use the program with a device having a different output width.

Program Structure

Our program has three **while** loops, one **if** statement, and one **if-else** statement. Let's see what each does.

```
while((ch = getchar()) != EOF)
```

The purpose of the first **while** loop is to allow us to read in several data sets. (Each data set consists of a character and of the two integers that indicate where the character is to be printed.) By reading the character first, we were able to combine reading the character with testing for End-of-File. If the EOF character is read, then the program stops without trying to read values for **start** and **stop.** Otherwise, values for **start** and **stop** are read using **scanf( ),** and then the program processes them. That completes the loop. Then a new character is read, and the procedure is repeated.

Note that we used two statements, not one, to read in the data. Why didn't we just use a single statement?

```
scanf("%c %d %d", &ch, &start, &stop);
```

Suppose we had. Consider what happens when the program finishes reading the last line of data from a file. When the loop begins again, the only thing left in the file is the EOF character. The **scanf( )** function reads the EOF and assigns it to **ch.** Then it tries to read a value for **start,** but there is nothing left in the file to read! The computer belches forth a complaint, and your program dies ignominiously. By separating the character read from the rest, we gave the computer a chance to test for EOF *before* attempting to read further.

```
if (ch != '\n')
```

The purpose of the first **if** statement is to make it easier to enter data. We explain how this works in the section following this one.

```
if ( start > stop || start < 1 || stop > MAXLENGTH)
     printf("Inappropriate limits were entered.\n");
else
```

The purpose of the **if-else** statement is to let the program skirt around values of **start** and **stop** that would lead to trouble. This, too, we will discuss later. Note, however, how we have used logical and relational operators to check for any one of three dangers.

The main body of the program consists of the compound statement that follows the **else.**

```
count = 0;
```

First, a counter called **count** is set to zero.

```
while (++count < start)
    putchar(' ');
```

Then a **while** loop starts printing blanks until the **start** position is reached. If **start** is, say, 10, then 9 spaces are printed. Thus the character printing will start in the 10th column. Note how using the prefix form of the increment operator with the < operator acts to yield this result. If we had used **count++ < start,** the comparison would have taken place before **count** was incremented, and one additional space would have been permitted.

```
while ( count++ <= stop)
    putchar(ch);
```

The second **while** loop in this block performs the task of printing the character from the **start** column to the **stop** column. This time we used the postfix form and the <= operator. This combination produces the desired result of printing the character up to and including the stop position. You can use logic or trial-and-error to verify this.

```
putchar('\n');
```

Finally, we use **putchar('\n')** to finish the line and start a new one.

Data Form

When we write a program, we need to understand how it is going to interact with the input data, so we will look into that now.

The data used for input should be in a form compatible with the input functions used by the program. Here the burden is on the user to get the data in the right form. A more sophisticated program would shift more of that burden to the program itself. The clearest form for entering data is:

```
H 10 40
I 9 41
```

with the character followed by its starting column position and its stopping column position. But our program also accepts this form:

```
H
10
40
I
9
41
```

or this form:

```
H10 40I 9 41
```

but not this!

```
H 10 40 I 9 41
```

Why are some spaces optional and some spaces required? Why can there be a newline character but no space between the last integer of one data set and the first character of the next? These questions raise points which are relevant to more than just this program. Let's review how **getchar( )** and **scanf( )** work and find the answer to these questions.

The **getchar( )** function reads the first character it finds, be it alphabetic, a space, a newline, or whatever. The **scanf( )** function does the same if reading in the **%c** (character) format. But when **scanf( )** reads in the **%d** (integer) format, it skips over spaces and newlines. Thus any spaces or newlines between the character read by **getchar( )** and the next integer read by **scanf( )** are ignored. Then **scanf( )** reads in digits until it runs into a nondigit, such as a space, newline, or alphabetic character. Hence we need a space or newline between the first and second integer so that **scanf( )** can tell when one ends and the next begins.

That explains why we can have a space or newline between a character and the following integer and why we must have a space or newline between the two integers. But why can't we have a space between the final integer of a data set and the next character? Well, the next time through the **while** loop, **getchar( )** picks up where **scanf( )** stopped. Thus it reads the very next character after the previous integer, be it a space, a newline, or whatever.

If we were completely subservient to the demands of **getchar( )**, we would have to structure the data this way:

```
w10 50a20 60y10 30
```

with nothing separating the final integer from the next character. But this is awkward, and it makes the **50** look like it goes with the **a** and not the **w.** So we put in the line

```
if (ch != '\n')
```

to make the program skip over the case of **ch** being a newline. Thus we can use

```
w10 50
a20 60
y10 30
```

instead, with a newline character between the **50** and the **a.** The program reads the newline character, does nothing with it, then goes on to read the next character.

Error Checking

The problem of getting the user to input data that the computer can use properly is a pervasive one. One technique is to use "error checking." This means having the computer check the data to see if it is okay before using it. We have included a beginning effort at error checking in this program with the lines

```
if ( start > stop || start < 1 || stop > MAXLENGTH)
printf("Inappropriate limits were entered.\n");
```

This was part of an **if-else** structure which indicated that the main part of the program took place only if none of **if** tests were true.

What were we protecting against? First, it makes no sense for the starting position to come after the final position; terminals normally print from left to right, not vice versa. So the expression **start > stop** checks for that possible error. Secondly, the first column on a screen is column 1; we can't write to the left of the left margin. The **start < 1** expression guards against making an error there. Finally, the expression **stop > MAXLENGTH** checks to see that we don't try to print past the right margin.

Are there any other erroneous values we could give to **start** and **stop?** Well, we could try to make **start** greater than **MAXLENGTH.** Would that pass our test? No. It is true that we don't check for this error directly. However, suppose **start** is greater than **MAXLENGTH.** Then either **stop** is also greater then **MAXLENGTH**—in which case that error is caught—or else stop isn't greater than **MAXLENGTH.** But if **stop** is less than **MAXLENGTH** it must also be less than **start,** so this case gets caught by the first test. Another possible error is that **stop** is less than 1. We leave it to you to check that this error doesn't sneak through, either.

We kept the test pretty simple. If you design a program for serious use, you should put more effort than we did into this part of the program. For instance, you could put in error messages to identify which values are wrong and why. And you could inject more personality into the messages. Here are some possibilities:

```
Your value of 897654 for stop exceeds the screen width.
Oh my! Your START is bigger than your STOP. Please try again.
THE START VALUE SHOULD BE BIGGER THAN 0, TURKEY.
```

The personality you inject, of course, is up to you.

THE CONDITIONAL OPERATOR: ?:

C offers a shorthand way to express one form of the **if-else** statement. It is called a "conditional expression" and uses the conditional operator **?:**. This is a two-part operator that has three operands. Here is an example which yields the absolute value of a number:

```
x = ( y < 0 ) ? -y : y;
```

Everything between the = and the semicolon is the conditional expression. The meaning of the statement is this: If **y** is less than zero, then **x = −y;** otherwise, **x = y.** In **if-else** terms

```
if (y < 0)
    x = -y;
 else
     x = y;
```

The general form of the conditional expression is
expression1 ? *expression 2* : *expression 3*
If expression1 is true (nonzero), then the whole conditional expression has the same value as expression2. If expression1 is false (0), the whole conditional expression has the same value as expression3.

You can use the conditional expression when you have a variable to which could be assigned two possible values. A typical example is setting a variable equal to the maximum of two values:

```
max = (a > b) ? a : b;
```

Conditional expressions are not necessary, since **if-else** statements can accomplish the same end. They are, however, more compact, and they usually lead to more compact machine language code.

SUMMARY: THE CONDITIONAL OPERATOR

I. The Conditional Operator: ?:

This operator takes three operands, each of which is an expression. They are arranged this way: *expression1* ? *expression2* : *expression3* The value of the whole expression equals the value of *expression2* if *expression1* is true, and equals the value of *expression3* otherwise.

II. Examples:

```
( 5 > 3 ) ? 1 : 2
( 3 > 5 ) ? 1 : 2
( a > b) ? a : b
```

- `( 5 > 3 ) ? 1 : 2` has the value 1
- `( 3 > 5 ) ? 1 : 2` has the value 2
- `( a > b) ? a : b` has the value of the larger of a or b

MULTIPLE CHOICE: *switch* AND *break*

The conditional operator and the *if-else* construction make it easy to write programs that choose between *two* alternatives. Sometimes, however, a program needs to choose one of *several* alternatives. We can do this using **if-else if— . . . —else,** but in many cases it is more convenient to use the C **switch** statement. Here is an example showing how it works. This program reads in a letter, then responds by printing an animal name which begins with that letter.

```
 /* animals */
main()
{
  char ch;

  printf("Give me a letter of the alphabet, and I will give ");
  printf("an animal name\nbeginning with that letter.\n");
  printf("Please type in a letter; type a # to end my act.\n");
```

```
    while((ch = getchar()) != '#')
     {
     if (ch != '\n') /* skip over newline */
       {
       if ( ch >= 'a' && ch <= 'z') /* lower case only */
         switch (ch)
         {
         case 'a' :
              printf("argali, a wild sheep of Asia\n");
              break;
         case 'b' :
              printf("babirusa, a wild pig of Malay\n");
              break;
         case 'c' :
              printf("coati, racoonlike mammal\n");
              break;
         case 'd' :
              printf("desman, aquatic, molelike critter\n");
              break;
         case 'e' :
              printf("echidna, the spiny anteater\n");
              break;
         default :
              printf("That's a stumper!\n");
         }
     else
         printf("I only recognize lower-case letters.\n");
     printf("Please enter another letter or a #.\n");
     } /* end of skip newline if */
   } /* while loop end */
  }
```

Figure 7.7
Animal names program.

We got a little lazy and stopped at "e." Let's look at a sample run before explaining the program further.

```
Give me a letter of the alphabet, and I will give an animal name
beginning with that letter.
```

```
Please type in a letter; type a # to end my act.
a [return]
argali, a wild sheep of Asia
Please enter another letter or a #.
d [return]
desman, aquatic, molelike critter
Please enter another letter or a #.
r [return]
That's a stumper!
Please enter another letter or a #.
Q [return]
I only recognize lower-case letters.
Please enter another letter or a #.
# [return]
```

This is how the **switch** statement works. The expression in the parentheses following the word **switch** is evaluated. In this case it has whatever value we last entered for **ch.** Then the program scans the list of "labels" **(case 'a' :, case 'b' :,** etc., in this instance) until it finds one that matches that value. The program then jumps to that line. What if there is no match? If there is a line labeled **default :,** the program jumps there. Otherwise the program proceeds to the statement following the **switch.**

What about the **break** statement? It causes the program to break out of the **switch** and skip to the next statement after the switch. (See the next figure.) Without the **break** statement, every statement from the matched label to the end of the **switch** would be processed. For example, if we removed all the **break** statements from our program, then ran the program using the letter **d,** we would get this interchange.

```
Give me a letter of the alphabet, and I will give an animal name
beginning with that letter.
Please type in a letter; type a # to end my act.
d [return]
desman, aquatic, molelike critter
echidna, the spiny anteater
That's a stumper!
Please enter another letter or a #.
# [return]
```

All the statements from **case 'd' :** to the end of the **switch** were executed.

If you are familiar with Pascal, you will recognize the **switch** statement as being similar to the Pascal **case** statement. The most important difference is that the **switch** statement requires the use of a **break** if you want only the labeled statement to be processed.

The **switch** labels must be integer-type (including **char**) constants or constant expressions (expression containing only constants). You can't use a variable for a label. The expression in the parentheses should be one with an integer value (again, including type **char**). This, then, is the structure of a **switch:**

```
switch(integer expression)
     {
     case constant1 :
              statements; (optional)
     case constant2 :
              statements; (optional)
          . . .
     default : (optional)
              statements; (optional)
     }
```

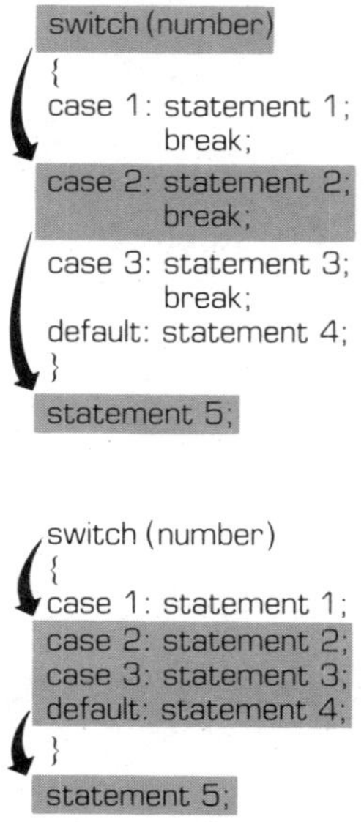

In each case
number has the value 2.

Figure 7.8
Program flow in switches with and without breaks.

We can use labels without statements when we want several labels to have the same result. For instance, the fragment

```
case 'F' :
case 'f' :
     printf(ferret, a weasellike mammal.\n);
     break;
```

would cause either **F** or **f** to trigger the printing of the ferret message. If **F** is entered, for example, the program jumps to that line. There are no statements there, so the program moves on until it reaches the **break.**

Our program has two other small features we wish to mention. First, since it is intended to be used interactively, we decided to use # instead of EOF as a stop signal. A computer innocent might feel baffled if asked to enter an EOF character or even a control character, but a # is pretty straightforward. Since this makes it unnecessary for the program to read an EOF, we don't have to declare **ch** to be type **int.** Secondly, we installed an **if** statement which causes the program to ignore newline characters when reading in characters. This, too, is a concession to the interactiveness of the program. Without this **if** statement, each time we hit the [return] key, it would be processed as a character.

When should you use a **switch** and when should you use the **else-if** construction? Often you don't have a choice. You can't use a **switch** if your choice is based on evaluating a **float** variable or expression. Nor can you conveniently use a **switch** if a variable must fall into a certain range. It is simple to write

```
if (integer < 1000 && integer > 2 )
```

but covering this possibility with a **switch** would involve setting up case labels for each integer from 3 to 999. However, if you can use a **switch,** your program will run more efficiently.

SUMMARY: MULTIPLE CHOICE WITH *switch*

I. Keyword: *switch*

II. General Comments:

Program control jumps to the statement bearing the value of *expression* as a label. Program flow then proceeds through the remaining statements unless redirected again. Both *expression* and labels must have integer values (type **char** is included), and the labels must be constants or expressions formed solely from constants. If no label matches the expression value, control goes to the statement labeled **default,** if present. Otherwise control passes to the next statement following the **switch** statement.

III. Form:

```
switch ( expression )
    {
    case label1 : statement1
    case label2 : statement2
    default     : statement3
    }
```

There can be more than 2 labeled statements, and the **default** case is optional.

IV. Example:

```
 switch ( letter )
     {
     case 'a' :
     case 'e' : printf("%d is a vowel\n", letter);
     case 'c' :
     case 'n' : printf("%d is in \"cane\"\n", letter);
     default  : printf("Have a nice day.\n");
     }
```

If **letter** has the value **'a'** or **'e'**, all three messages are printed; **'c'** and **'n'** cause the last two to be printed. Other values print just the last message.

The material here will let you tackle much more powerful and ambitious programs than before. Just compare some of the examples in this chapter to those of the earlier chapters, and you will see the truth of that claim. But there still is more to learn, and that's why there still are a few more pages for you to mosey through.

WHAT YOU SHOULD HAVE LEARNED

How to choose between executing a statement or not: **if**
How to choose between two alternatives: **if-else**

How to choose among multiple alternatives: **else-if, switch**
The relational operators: > >= == <= < !=
The logical operators; **&&** || **!**
The conditional operator: **? :**

QUESTIONS AND ANSWERS

Questions

1. Determine which expressions are true and which are false.
   a. `100 > 3`
   b. `'a' > 'c'`
   c. `100 > 3 && 'a' > 'c'`
   d. `100 > 3 || 'a' > 'c'`
   e. `!(100 > 3)`
2. Construct an expression to express the following conditions.
   a. **number** is equal to or greater than 1 but smaller than 9.
   b. **ch** is not a **q** or a **k**
   c. **number** is between 1 and 9 but is not a 5.
   d. **number** is not between 1 and 9.
3. The following program has unnecessarily complex relational expressions as well as some outright errors. Simplify and correct it.

```
main()                                                    /* 1 */
{                                                          /* 2 */
  int weight, height; /*weight in lbs, height in inches */
                                                           /* 4 */
  scanf("%d, weight, height);                              /* 5 */
  if ( weight < 100)                                       /* 6 */
     if ( height >= 72 )                                   /* 7 */
        printf("You are very tall for your weight.\n");
     else if ( height < 72 && > 64)                        /* 9 */
        printf( "You are tall for your weight.\n");
  else if ( weight > 300 && !(weight <= 300) )            /* 11 */
    if ( !(height >= 48)                                  /* 12 */
         printf( " You are quite short for your weight.\n");
  else                                                    /* 14 */
     printf("Your weight is ideal.\n");                 /* 15 */
                                                         /* 16 */
}
```

Answers

1. true: a,d
2. a. **number >= 1 && number < 9**
   b. **ch != 'q' && ch != 'k'**
   note: ch != 'q' || ch != 'k' would always be true, for if **ch** was a **q** then it couldn't be **k,** so the second alternative would be true, making the whole "or" combination true.
   c. **number > 1 && number < 9 && number != 5**
   d. **!(number > 1 && number < 9)**
   or
   number <= 1 || number >= 9
   note: saying that a number ISN'T between 1 and 9 is the same as saying that it IS equal to or less than 1 OR equal to or greater than 9. The second form is more awkward as words but slightly simpler as an expression.
3. Line 5 should be **scanf("%d %d", &weight, &height);** Don't forget those **&**s for **scanf( ).** Also this line should be preceded by a line prompting input.
   Line 9: what is meant is **(height < 72 && height > 64).** However, the first part of the expression is unnecessary, since **height** must be less than **72** for the **else-if** to be reached in the first place. Thus a simple **(height > 64)** will serve.
   Line 11: the condition is redundant; the second subexpression (**weight** not less than or equal to 300) means the same as the first. A simple **(weight > 300)** is all that is needed. But there is more trouble. Line 11 gets attached to the wrong **if!** Clearly this **else** is meant to go along with line 6. By the most recent **if not** rule, however, it will be associated with the **if** of line 9. Thus line 11 is reached when **weight** is less than 100 and **height** is 64 or under. This makes it impossible for **weight** to exceed 300 when this statement is reached.
   Lines 7 through 9 should be enclosed in braces. Then line 11 will become an alternative to line 6, not to line 9.
   Line 12: simplify the expression to (**height < 48**)
   Line 14: this **else** associates with the last **if,** the one on line 12. Enclose lines 12 and 13 in braces to force this **else** to associate with the **if** of line 11. Note that the final message is printed only for those weighing between 100 and 300 pounds.

8

LOOPS AND OTHER CONTROL AIDS

In this chapter you will find

- The *while* Loop
    - Terminating a *while* Loop
- Algorithms and Pseudocode
- The *for* Loop
    - *for* For Flexibility!
    - The Comma Operator
    - Zeno Meets the *for* Loop
- An Exit-Condition Loop: *do* while
- Which Loop?
- Nested Loops
- Other Control Statements: *break, continue, goto*
    - Avoiding the *goto*
- Arrays
- A Question of Input
- Summary
- What You Should Have Learned
- Questions and Answers
- Exercises

8. LOOPS AND OTHER CONTROL AIDS

CONCEPTS

Looping
Nested loops
Making program jumps
Using loops with arrays

KEYWORDS

while, do, for, break, continue, goto

OPERATORS

`+= -= *= /= %= ,`

As you tackle more complex tasks, the flow of your programs becomes more involved. You need structures and statements to control and organize the workings of these programs. C provides you with valuable tools to meet this need. Already we have seen how useful the **while** loop is when we need to repeat an action several times. C provides two more loop structures: the **for** loop and the **do . . . while** loop. In this chapter we will explore the workings of these control structures and see how to make the best use of each. We will discuss **break, continue, goto,** and the comma operator, all of which can be used to control the flow of a program. Also, we will talk a bit more about arrays, which are often used with loops.

THE *while* LOOP

We have used this form extensively, but let us review it with a simple, perhaps simple-minded, program to guess a number.

```
  /* numguess1 */
/* an inefficient number-guesser */
#include <stdio.h>
main()
{
  int guess = 1;
  char response;

  printf("Pick an integer from 1 to 100. I will try to guess ");
  printf("it.\nRespond with a y if my guess is right and");
  printf("\nwith an n if it is wrong.\n");
  printf("Uh . . . is your number %d?\n", guess);
  while((response = getchar()) != 'y')          /* get response */
     if( response != '\n')          /* ignore newline character */
         printf("Well, then, is it %d?\n", ++guess);
  printf("I knew I could do it!\n");
}
```

Note the logic. If you respond with a **y**, the program quits the loop and goes to the final print statement. The program asks you to respond with an **n** if the guess is wrong, but in fact any response other than **y** sends the program through the loop. However, if the character is a newline character, the effect of the loop is to do nothing. Any other character causes the next larger integer to be guessed. (What would happen if we had used **guess++** instead of **++guess**?)

The **if(response != '\n')** portion tells the program to ignore the extraneous newline character that is transmitted when you use the [enter] key.

This **while** loop did not require braces because the two-line **if** statement counts as a single statement.

You probably noticed that this is a rather dumb program. It is written in proper C and gets the job done, but its approach is very inefficient. This example illustrates that correctness is not the only criterion by which to judge a program. Efficiency, too, is important. We'll come back to this program later and try to spiff it up a bit.

The general form of the **while** loop is

```
while(expression)
      statement
```

Our examples have used relational expressions for the expression part, but the expression can be of any sort. The statement part can be a simple statement with a terminating semicolon or it can be a compound statement enclosed in braces. If the expression is true (or, more generally, nonzero), the statement is executed once, and then the expression is tested again. This cycle of test and execution is repeated until the expression becomes false (or, more generally, zero). Each cycle is called an "iteration." The structure is very similar to that of an **if** statement. The chief difference is that in an **if** statement, the test and (possibly) the execution are done just once; but in the **while** loop, the test and execution may be repeated several times.

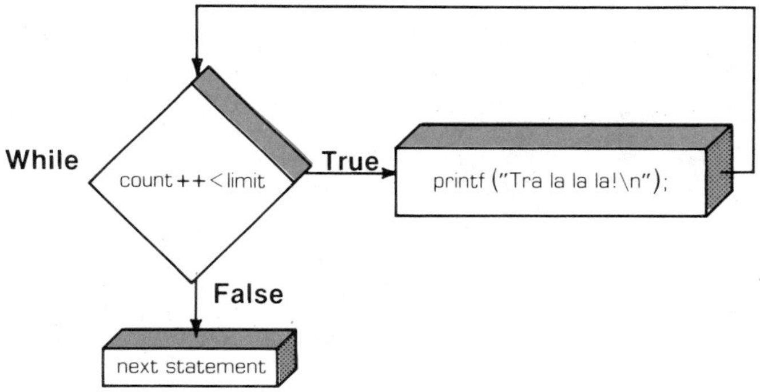

Figure 8.1
Structure of the *while* loop.

Terminating a *while* Loop

Here is a CRUCIAL point about **while** loops. When you construct a **while** loop, it must include something that changes the value of the test expression so that the expression eventually becomes false. Otherwise the loop will never terminate. Consider this example:

```
index = 1;
 while ( index < 5 )
   printf("Good morning!\n");
```

This fragment prints its cheerful message indefinitely, for nothing in the loop changes the value of **index** from its initial value of 1.

```
index = 1;
 while ( --index < 5 )
   printf("How are the old atoms vibrating!\n");
```

This fragment isn't much better. It changes the value of **index,** but in the wrong direction! At least this version will terminate eventually when **index** drops below the most negative number the system can handle.

The **while** loop is a "conditional" loop using an "entry condition." It is called conditional because the execution of the statement portion depends on the condition we describe through the expression portion. Is **index** less than 5? Is the last character read the EOF character? The expression forms an *entry* condition because the condition must be met *before* the body of the loop is entered. In a situation like the following, the body of the loop is never entered because the condition is false to begin with.

```
index = 10;
   while ( index++ < 5)
      printf("Have a fair day or better.\n");
```

Change the first line to

```
index = 3;
```

and you have a working program.

ALGORITHMS AND PSEUDOCODE

Okay, let's return to our dim-witted number-guessing program. The fault with this program is not in the programming per se, but in the "algorithm"—that is, the method used to guess the number. We can represent the method this way:

ask user to choose a number
computer guesses 1
while guess is wrong, increase guess by 1

This, incidentally, is an example of "pseudocode," which is the art of expressing a program in simple English that parallels the forms of a computer language. Pseudocode is useful for working out the logic of a program. Once the logic seems right, you then can attend to the details of translating the pseuducode to the actual programming code. The advantage of pseudocode is that it lets you concentrate on the logic and organization of a program while sparing you the effort of simultaneously worrying how to express the ideas in a computer language.

If we want to improve the program, we need to improve the algorithm. One method is to choose a number halfway between 1 and 100 (50 is close enough) and to have the user reply whether the guess is high, low, or correct. If the use replies that the guess is too high, that immediately eliminates all the numbers from 50 to 100. The program's next guess would be a number halfway between 1 and 49. Again, a high or low answer would eliminate half the remaining choices, and by continuing the process, the program rapidly narrows the choices down until the correct number is guessed. Let's put that into pseudocode. We'll let **highest** stand for the highest possible value the number could have and **lowest** stand for the lowest possible value. Initially these will be 100 and 1, respectively, so we can start there.

```
set highest to 100
set lowest to 1
ask user to choose a number
guess (highest + lowest)/2
while guess is wrong do the following:
   { if guess is high, set highest to old guess minus 1
     if guess is low, set lowest to old guess plus 1
     new guess is (highest + lowest)/2 }
```

Note the logic: if the first guess of 50 is high, then the highest possible value the number could have is 49. If 50 is too low, then the lowest the number could be is 51.

Now we will convert this approach to C. Fig. 8.2 presents the program.

```
  /* numguess2 */
/* a better number-guesser */
#include <stdio.h>
#define HIGH 100
#define LOW  1
main()
{
  int guess = (HIGH + LOW)/2;
  int highest = HIGH;
  int lowest = LOW;
  char response;

  printf("Pick an integer from %d to %d.  I will try ",LOW,HIGH);
  printf("to guess it.\nRespond with a y if my guess is right,");
  printf("with an h if it\nis high, and with an l if my");
```

```
        printf("guess is low.\n");
        printf("Uh . . . is your number %d?\n", guess);
        while((response = getchar()) != 'y')
           {
           if ( response != '\n')
                {
                if (response == 'h')
                 {  /* reduce upper limit if guess is too high */
                highest = guess - 1;
                guess = (highest + lowest)/2;
                printf("Too high, huh. Is your number %d?\n", guess);
                }
           else if (response == 'l')
                { /* increase lower limit if guess is too low */
                lowest = guess + 1;
                guess = (highest + lowest)/2;
                printf("Too low, huh. Is your number %d?\n", guess);
                }
           else
                {  /* guide user to correct response   */
                printf("I don't understand; please type a y, h,");
                printf("or l.\n");
               }
           }
         }
        printf("I knew I could do it!\n");
     }
```

Figure 8.2
Number-guessing program.

The final **else** gives the user another chance to reply whenever she makes a nonstandard response. Also, notice that we used symbolic constants to make it simple to change the range.

Does the program work? Here is a sample run. Our number is 71.

```
Pick an integer from 1 to 100.  I will try to guess it.
Respond with a y if my guess is right, with an h if it
is high, and with an l if my guess is low.
Uh . . . is your number 50?
n
I don't understand; please type a y, h, or l.
l
```

```
Too low, huh. Is your number 75?
h
Too high, huh. Is your number 62?
l
Too low, huh. Is your number 68?
l
Too low, huh. Is your number 71?
y
I knew I could do it!
```

Can anything go wrong with this program? We've protected it against people typing unwanted characters, so that shouldn't be a problem. The one thing that can mess it up is someone typing an **h** when he means **l,** or vice versa. Unfortunately there is no way to make the user truthful and error-free. However, there are some steps you can take if you are sufficiently interested. (You may, for example, desire to distract your 6-year-old niece.) First, notice that our approach needs at most seven guesses to get any number. (Each guess cuts the possibilities in half. Seven guesses cover 2^7-1, or 127, possibilities, enough to handle the hundred numbers.) You can alter the program so that it counts the number of guesses. If the count exceeds 7, you can print out a complaining message, then reset **highest, lowest,** and the count to their original values. Other changes you could make are to modify the **if** statements so they accept both upper- and lower-case letters.

SUMMARY: The *while* STATEMENT

I. Keyword: ***while***

II. General Comments:

The **while** statement creates a loop that repeats until the test *expression* becomes false, or zero. The **while** statement is an *entry-condition* loop; the decision to go through one more pass of the loop is made *before* the loop is traversed. Thus it is possible that the loop is never traversed. The *statement* part of the form can be a simple statement or a compound statement.

III. Form:

```
while ( expression )
        statement
```

The *statement* portion is repeated until the *expression* becomes false or zero.

IV. Examples:

```
while ( n++ < 100 )
      printf(" %d %d\n",n, 2*n+1 );

while ( fargo < 1000 )
      {
      fargo = fargo + step;
      step = 2 * step;
      }
```

Our last example of a **while** loop uses an indefinite condition; we don't know in advance how many times the loop will be executed before the expression becomes false. Many of our examples, however, have used **while** loops to count out a definite number of repetitions. Here is a short example of a **while** counting loop.

```
count = 1;                              /* initialization */
  while ( count <= NUMBER )             /* test           */
     {
     printf("Be my Valentine!\n");      /* action         */
     count++;                           /* increment count */
 }
```

Although this form works fine, it is not the best form for this type of situation since the actions which define the loop are not all gathered together. Let's elaborate on that point.

Three actions are involved in setting up a loop which is to be repeated a fixed number of times. A counter must be initialized, compared with some limiting number, and incremented each time the loop is traversed. The **while** loop condition takes care of the comparison. The increment operator takes care of the incrementation. As we have done elsewhere, we can combine these two actions into one expression by using **count++ <= NUMBER.** But the initialization of the counter is done outside the loop, as in our statement **count = 1;.** This makes it possible to forget to initialize a counter, and what *might* happen *will* happen eventually. Let's look at a control statement that avoids these problems.

THE *for* LOOP

The **for** loop gathers all three actions into one place. By using a **for** loop, we can replace the preceding fragment by one statement:

```
for( count = 1; count <= NUMBER; count++)
     printf("Be my Valentine!\n");
```

The parentheses contain three expressions separated by semicolons. The first expression is an initialization. It is done just once, when the **for** loop first starts. The second expression is a test condition; it is evaluated before each potential execution of a loop. When the expression is false (when count is greater than number), the loop is terminated. The third expression is evaluated at the end of each loop. We have used it to increment the value of **count,** but it needn't be restricted to that use. The **for** statement is completed by following it with a simple or compound statement. Fig. 8.3 summarizes the structure of a **for** loop.

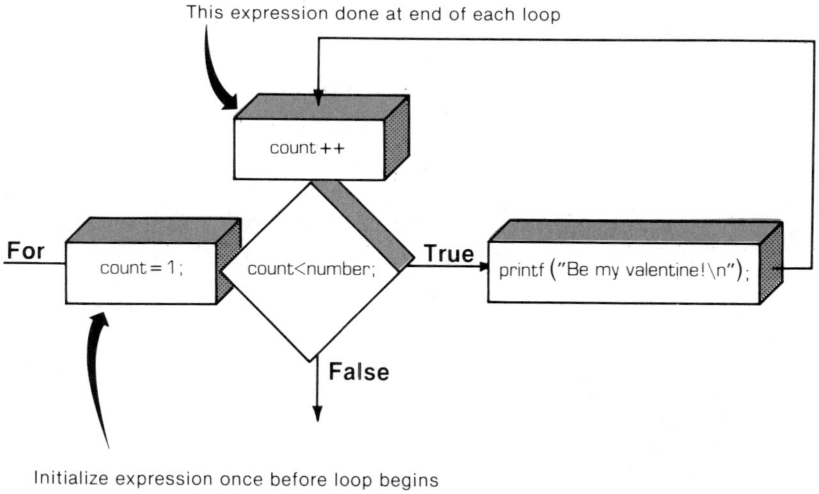

Figure 8.3
Structure of a *for* loop.

Here we use a **for** loop in a program that prints a table of cubes:

```
/* forcubed */
main()
{
  int num;
```

```
    printf("  n    n cubed\n");
    for ( num = 1; num <= 6; num++)
     printf("%5d %5d\n", num, num*num*num);
}
```

This prints the integers 1 through 6 and their cubes:

```
n   n cubed
1     1
2     8
3    27
4    64
5   125
6   216
```

Looking at the first line of the **for** loop tells us immediately all the information about the loop parameters: the starting value of **num,** the final value of **num,** and by how much **num** increases each looping.

One common use of a **for** loop is to have the computer mark time, slowing its responses down to human levels.

```
for( n = 1; n <= 10000; n++)
      ;
```

This loop has the computer count to 10000. The lone semicolon on the second line tells us that nothing else is done in the loop. We can think of a solitary semicolon as a ''null'' statement, a statement that does nothing.

for For Flexibility!

Although the **for** loop looks similar to the FORTRAN DO loop, the Pascal FOR loop, and the BASIC FOR . . . NEXT loop, it is much more flexible than any of these. This flexibility stems from how the three expressions in a **for** specification can be used. So far we have used the first expression to initialize a counter, the second expression to express the limit for the counter, and the third expression to increase the counter by 1. When used this way, the C **for** statement is very much like the others we have mentioned. But there are many other possibilities, and here we will show you nine variations.

1. You can use the decrement operator to count down instead of to count up.

```
for ( n = 10; n > 0; n--)
       printf("%d seconds!\n", n);
 printf("We have ignition!\n");
```

2. You can count by twos, tens, etc., if you want.

```
for ( n = 2;  n < 60; n = n + 13)
     printf(  "%d \n", n);
```

This would increase **n** by 13 each cycle, printing the digits 2, 15, 28, 41, and 54.

Incidentally, C offers a short-hand notation for incrementing a variable by a fixed amount. Instead of

```
n = n + 13
```

we can use

```
n += 13
```

The += is the "additive assignment operator," and it adds whatever is to its right to the variable name on the left. See the box up ahead for more details.

3. You can count by characters instead of by numbers.

```
for ( ch = 'a'; ch <= 'z'; ch++)
   printf("The ASCII value for %c is %d.\n", ch, ch);
```

This will print out the letters **a** through **z** along with their ASCII values. This works because characters are stored as integers, so this fragment really counts by integers anyway.

4. You can test some condition other than the number of iterations. In our **forcubed** program we can replace

```
for ( num = 1; num <= 6; num++)
```

by

```
for (num = 1; num*num*num <= 216; num++)
```

We would do this if we were more concerned with limiting the size of the cube than in limiting the number of iterations.

5. You can let a quantity increase geometrically instead of arithmetically; that is, instead of adding a fixed amount each time, you can multiply by a fixed amount.

```
for ( debt = 100.0; debt < 150.0; debt = debt*1.1 )
    printf("Your debt is now $%.2f.\n", debt);
```

This program fragment multiplies **debt** by 1.1 each cycle, increasing it by 10%. The output looks like this.

```
Your debt is now $100.00.
Your debt is now $110.00.
Your debt is now $121.00.
Your debt is now $133.10.
Your debt is now $146.41.
```

As you may have guessed, there is a shorthand notation for multiplying **debt** by 1.1. We could have used the expression

```
debt *= 1.1
```

to accomplish that multiplication. The *= operator is the "multiplicative assignment operator," and it multiplies the variable to its left by whatever is to its right. (See the box below.)

6. You can use any legal expression you want for the third expression. Whatever you put in will be updated each iteration.

```
y = 55;
for ( x = 1; y <= 75; y = ++x*5 +50)
      printf("%10d %10d\n", x, y);
```

This fragment prints out the values of **x** and of the algebraic expression **5*x+ 50.** The output would look like this:

```
         1         55
         2         60
         3         65
         4         70
         5         75
```

Notice that the test involved **y** and not **x.** Each of the three expressions in the **for** loop control can use different variables.

Although this example is valid, it does not show good style. The program would be clearer if we didn't mix the updating process with an algebraic calculation.

7. You can even leave one or more expressions blank (but don't omit the semicolons). Just be sure to include within the loop itself some statement which will eventually cause the loop to terminate.

```
ans = 2;
for (n = 3; ans <= 25; )
    ans = ans*n;
```

This loop will keep the value of **n** at 3. The variable **ans** will start with the value 2, then increase to 6, 18, and obtain a final value of 54. (The value 18 is less than 25, so the **for** loop goes through one more iteration, multiplying 18 by 3 to get 54.)

The loop

```
for( ; ; )
     printf("I want some action\n");
```

goes on forever, since an empty test is considered to be true.

8. The first expression need not initialize a variable. It could, instead, be a **printf( )** statement of some sort. Just remember that the first expression is evaluated or executed just once, before any other parts of the loop are executed.

```
for ( printf("Keep entering numbers!\n"); num == 6;  )
          scanf("%d", num);
printf("That's the one I want!\n");
```

This fragment prints the first message once, then keeps accepting numbers until you enter a 6.

9. The parameters of the loop expressions can be altered by actions within the loop. For example, suppose you have the loop set up like this:

```
for(n = 1; n < 10000; n += delta)
```

If after a few iterations your program decided **delta** was too small or large, an **if** statement inside the loop could change the size of **delta.** In an interactive program, **delta** could be changed by the user as the loop was working.

In short, the freedom you have in selecting the expressions that control a **for** loop makes this loop able to do much more than just perform a fixed number of iterations. The power of the **for** loop is enhanced further by the operators we will discuss shortly.

SUMMARY: THE *for* STATEMENT

I. Keyword: *for*

II. General Comments:

The **for** statement uses three control expressions, separated by semicolons, to control a looping process. The *initialize* expression is executed once, before any of the loop statements are executed. If the **test** expression is true (or nonzero), the loop is cycled through once. Then the **update** expression is evaluated, and it is time to check the **test** expression again. The **for** statement is an *entry-condition* loop; the decision to go through one more pass of the loop is made *before* the loop is traversed. Thus it is possible that the loop is never traversed. The *statement* part of the form can be a simple statement or a compound statement.

III. Form:

for (*initialize* ; *test* ; *update*)
    statement

The loop is repeated until *test* becomes false or zero.

IV. Example:

```
for ( n = 0;  n < 10 ; n++ )
        printf(" %d %d\n", n, 2*n+1 );
```

MORE ASSIGNMENT OPERATORS: +=, −=, *=, /=, %=

Some time ago we mentioned that C had several assignment operators. The most basic one, of course, is =, which simply assigns the value of the expression at its right to the variable at its left. The other assignment operators update variables. Each is used with a variable name at its left and an expression at its right. The variable is assigned a new value equal to its old value adjusted by the value of the expression at the right. The exact adjustment depends on the operator. For example:

```
scores += 20   is the same as  scores = scores + 20
dimes -= 2     is the same as  dimes = dimes - 2
bunnies *= 2   is the same as  bunnies = bunnies * 2
time /= 2.73   is the same as  time = time / 2.73
reduce %= 3    is the same as  reduce = reduce % 3
```

We used simple numbers on the right, but we could have used more elaborate expressions:

```
x *= 3*y + 12 is the same as x = x * (3*y + 12)
```

These assignment operators have the same low priority that = does, i.e., less than that of + or *. This is reflected in the last example.

You are not required to use these forms. They are, however, more compact, and they usually produce more efficient machine code than the longer form. They are particularly useful if you are trying to squeeze something into a **for** loop specification.

The Comma Operator

The comma operator extends the flexibility of the **for** loop by allowing you to include more than one initialization or update in a **for** loop specification. For example, here is a program that prints out first class postage rates. (At the time of this writing, the rate is 20 cents the first ounce and 17 cents for each additional ounce.)

```
 /* postalrates */
#define FIRST 20
#define NEXT  17
main()
{
   int ounces, cost;

   printf(" ounces  cost\n");
   for(ounces=1, cost=FIRST; ounces<= 16; ounces++, cost += NEXT)
      printf("%5d %7d\n", ounces, cost);
}
```

The first four lines of output look like this:

```
ounces  cost
   1     20
   2     37
   3     54
```

We used the comma operator in the first and the third expressions. Its presence in the first expression causes **ounces** *and* **cost** to be initialized. Its second occurrence causes **ounces** to be increased by 1 and **cost** to be increased by 17 (the value of **NEXT**) each iteration. All the calculations are done in the **for** loop specifications.

The comma operator is not restricted to **for** loops, but that is where it is most often used. The operator has one further property: it guarantees that the expressions it separates will be evaluated in a left-to-right order. Thus **ounces** is initialized before **cost.** That is not important for this example, but it would be important if the expression for **cost** contained **ounces.**

The comma also is used as a separator. Thus the commas in

```
char ch, date;
```

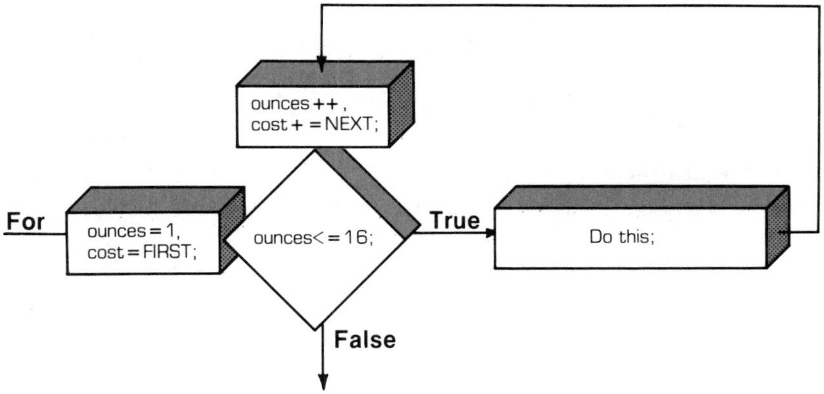

Figure 8.4
The comma operator and the *for* loop

or

```
printf("%d %d\n", chimps, chumps);
```

are separators, not comma operators.

SUMMARY: OUR NEW OPERATORS

I. Assignment Operators:

Each of these operators updates the variable at its left by the value at its right, using the indicated operation. We use r-h for right-hand, and l-h for left-hand.

`+=`	adds the r-h quantity to the l-h variable
`-=`	subtracts the r-h quantity from the l-h variable
`*=`	multiplies the l-h variable by the r-h quantity
`/=`	divides the l-h variable by the r-h quantity
`%=`	gives the remainder from dividing the l-h variable by the r-h quantity.

Example:

`rabbits *= 1.6;` is the same as `rabbits = rabbits * 1.6;`

II. Miscellaneous: The Comma Operator

The comma operator links two expressions into one and guarantees that the left-most expression is evaluated first. It is typically used to include more information in a **for** loop control expression.

Example:

```
for ( step = 2, fargo = 0; fargo < 1000; step *= 2)
       fargo += step;
```

Zeno Meets the *for* Loop

Let's see how the comma operator can solve an old paradox. The Greek philosopher Zeno once argued that an arrow will never reach its target. First, he said, the arrow covers half the distance to the target. Then it has to cover half of the remaining distance. Then it still has half of what's left to cover, ad infinitum. Since the journey has an infinite number of parts, it would take arrow an infinite amount of time to reach its journey's end. However, we doubt that Zeno would have volunteered to be a target just on the strength of this argument.

Let's take a quantitative approach and suppose it takes the arrow one second to travel the first half. Then it would take 1/2 a second to travel half of what was left, 1/4 a second to travel half of what was left next, etc. We can represent the total time by the infinite series 1+1/2+1/4+1/8+1/16+ . . . We can write a short program to find the sum of the first few terms.

```
 /* zeno */
#define LIMIT 15
main()
{
 int count;
 float sum, x;

 for(sum=0.0, x=1.0, count=1; count <= LIMIT; count++, x *= 2.0)
    {
    sum += 1.0/x;
    printf("sum = %f when count = %d.\n", sum, count);
    }
}
```

This gives the sum of the first 15 terms:

```
sum = 1.000000 when count = 1.
sum = 1.500000 when count = 2.
sum = 1.750000 when count = 3.
sum = 1.875000 when count = 4.
sum = 1.937500 when count = 5.
sum = 1.968750 when count = 6.
sum = 1.984375 when count = 7.
sum = 1.992188 when count = 8.
sum = 1.996094 when count = 9.
sum = 1.998047 when count = 10.
sum = 1.999023 when count = 11.
sum = 1.999512 when count = 12.
sum = 1.999756 when count = 13.
sum = 1.999878 when count = 14.
sum = 1.999939 when count = 15.
```

We can see that although we keep adding more terms, the total seems to level out. Indeed, mathematicians have proven that the total approaches 2.0 as the number of terms approaches infinity, just as our program suggests. Thank heavens, for if Zeno were right, motion would be impossible. (But if motion were impossible, there would be no Zeno.)

What about the program itself? It shows that we can use more than one comma operator in an expression. We initialized **sum, x,** and **count.** Once we set up the conditions for the loop, the program itself is extremely brief.

AN EXIT-CONDITION LOOP: *do while*

The **while** loop and the **for** loop are both entry-condition loops. The test condition is checked before each iteration of the loop. C also has an "exit-condition" loop in which the condition is checked after each iteration of the loop. This variety is a do while loop and looks like this:

```
do
    {
    ch = getchar();
    putchar(ch);
    } while (ch != '\n');
```

How does this differ from, say,

```
while ((ch = getchar()) != '\n')
    putchar(ch);
```

The difference comes when the newline character is read. The **while** loop prints out all the characters *up to* the first newline character, and the **do while** loop prints out all the characters *up to and including* the newline character. Only after it has printed the newline character does the loop check to see if a newline character has shown up. In a **do while** loop that action comes before the test condition.

The general form of the **do while** loop is

```
do
    statement
       while (expression);
```

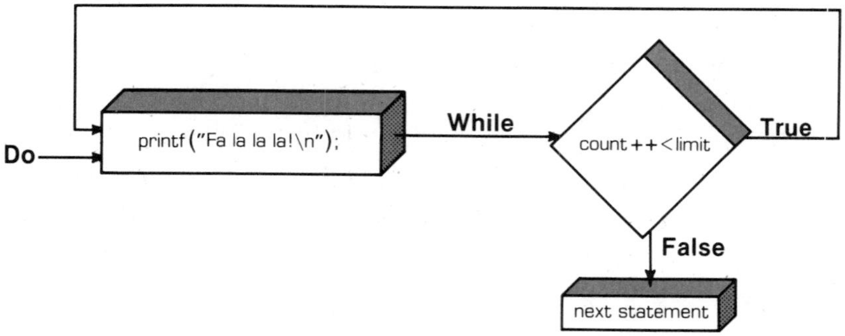

Figure 8.5
Structure of a *do while* loop

The statement can be simple or compound.

A **do while** loop always is executed at least once, since the test is made after the body of the loop is executed. A **for** loop or a **while** loop, on the other hand, may be executed zero times, since the test is made before execution. You should restrict the use of **do while** loops to cases which require at least one iteration. For instance, we could have used a **do while** loop for our number guessing programs. In pseudocode we could structure the program this way:

```
do
   {
   make a guess
   get a response of y, h, or l
   } while ( response isn't y)
```

You should avoid a **do while** structure of the type shown in the following pseudocode.

```
ask user if he wants to continue
do
   some clever stuff
   while ( answer is yes)
```

Here, after the user answers "no," some clever stuff gets done anyway because the test comes too late.

SUMMARY: THE *do while* STATEMENT

I. Keywords: ***do, while***

II. General Comments:

The **do while** statement creates a loop that repeats until the test *expression* becomes false or zero. The **do while** statement is an *exit-condition* loop; the decision to go through one more pass of the loop is made *after* the loop is traversed. Thus the loop must be executed at least once. The *statement* part of the form can be a simple statement or a compound statement.

III. Form:

```
do
     statement
          while ( expression );
```

The *statement* portion is repeated until the *expression* becomes false or zero.

IV. Example:

```
do
     scanf("%d", &number)
        while( number != 20 );
```

WHICH LOOP?

Once you decide you need a loop, which one should you use? First, decide whether you need an entry-condition loop or an exit-condition loop. Your answer should usually be an entry-condition loop. Kernighan and Ritchie estimate that the exit-condition loop (**do while**) is needed for about 5% of loops. There are several reasons why computer scientists consider an entry-condition loop superior. One is the general principle that it is better to look before you leap (or loop) than after. A second point is that a program is easier to read if the loop test is found at the beginning of the loop. Finally, in many uses, it is important that the loop be skipped entirely if the test is not initially met.

Assume you need an entry-condition loop. Should it be a **for** or a **while?** This is partly a matter of taste, since what you can do with one, you can do with the other. To make a **for** like a **while,** you can omit the first and third expressions:

```
    for ( ;test; )
```

is the same as

```
while(test)
```

To make a **while** like **for,** preface it with an initialization and include update statements:

```
initialize;
while (test)
  {
  body;
  update;
  }
```

is the same as

```
for (initialize; test; update)
   body;
```

In terms of style, it seems appropriate to use a **for** loop when the loop involves initializing and updating a variable and to use a **while** loop when the conditions are otherwise. Thus, **while** is natural for the

```
while((ch = getchar()) !=EOF)
```

idiom we have used. The **for** loop is a more natural choice for loops involving counting with an index:

```
for ( count = 1; count <= 100; count++)
```

NESTED LOOPS

A nested loop is a loop that is inside another loop. Here is a problem which uses nested loops to find all the prime numbers up to a given limit. A prime number is one that can be divided evenly only by two distinct numbers, 1 and itself. The first primes are 2, 3, 5, 7, and 11.

A straightforward approach to find out if a number is prime is to divide it by all the numbers between 1 and itself. If it can be divided by any of them evenly, then the number is not prime. We can use the modulus operator (%) to check if the division is even. (You remember the modulus operator, don't you? It yields the remainder when the first operand is divided by the second. If a number can be divided evenly, then the modulus operator yields a 0.) Once we find a divisor, there is no point in checking further, so we will want to terminate the process as soon as a divisor is found.

We'll start by checking a single number. This will use just one loop.

```
 /* prime1 */
main()
{
  int number, divisor;

  printf("Which number do you wish to test for primeness?\n");
  scanf("%d", &number);                     /* get response */
  while (number < 2)                            /* no go */
     {
     printf("Sorry, we don't accept numbers less than 2.\n");
     printf("Please try again.\n");
     scanf("%d", &number);
     {
 for ( divisor = 2; number % divisor != 0; divisor++)
   ; /* prime test made inside loop specifications */
 if (divisor == number) /* executed after loop terminates*/
```

```
        printf("%d is prime.\n", number);
    else
        printf("d is not prime.\n", number);
    }
```

We used a **while** structure to steer clear of input values that would crash the program.

Notice that all the calculation is done inside the **for** loop specification section. The quantity **number** is divided by progressively larger divisors until one goes in evenly (i.e., **number % divisor** becomes 0). If the first divisor to go in evenly is the number itself, then **number** is prime. Otherwise it will have a smaller divisor and that will terminate the loop earlier.

To find all the primes up to a certain value, we need to enclose our **for** loop in another loop. In pseudocode,

for number = 1 to limit
    check if number is prime

The second line represents our preceding program. Translating to C, we get

```
 /* prime2 */
main()
{
  int number, divisor, limit;
  int count = 0;

  printf("Please enter the upper limit for the prime search.\n");
  printf("The limit should be 2 or larger.\n");
  scanf("%d", &limit);
  while ( limit < 2)  /* second chance if entry error */
     {
     printf("You weren't paying attention! Try again.\n");
     scanf("%d", &limit);
     }
  printf("Here come the primes!\n");
  for ( number = 2; number <= limit; number++)  /* outer loop */
     {
     for (divisor =2; number % divisor != 0; divisor++)
       ;
     if(divisor == number)
          {
          printf("%5d ", number);
          if ( ++count % 10 == 0)
```

```
            printf("\n");    /* start new line every 10 primes */
          }
      }
   printf("\nThat's all!\n");
}
```

The outer loop selects each number in turn from 2 to **limit** for testing. The inner loop performs the testing. We used **count** to keep track of the number of primes. Every tenth prime we start a new line. Here is a sample output:

```
Please enter the upper limit for the prime search.
The limit should be 2 or larger.
250
Here come the primes!

   2      3      5      7     11     13     17     19     23     29
  31     37     41     43     47     53     59     61     67     71
  73     79     83     89     97    101    103    107    109    113
 127    131    137    139    149    151    157    163    167    173
 179    181    191    193    197    199    211    223    227    229
 233    239    241
 That's all!
```

This approach is quite straightforward but is not the ultimate in efficiency. For example, if you are testing to see if 121 is prime, there is no need to check divisors past 11. If any divisor bigger than 11 went in evenly, the result of the division would be a number smaller than 11, and that divisor would have been found earlier. Thus we only need to check divisors up to the square root of the number, but the programming for that is a bit trickier. We leave it as an exercise for the clever reader. (Hint: rather than compare the divisor to the square root of the number, compare the square of the divisor to the number itself.)

OTHER CONTROL STATEMENTS: *break, continue, goto*

The looping statements we have just discussed and the conditional statements (**if, if-else,** and **switch**) are the most important control mechanisms in C. They should be used to provide the overall structure of a program. The three statements we discuss below should be used more sparingly. Using them excessively will make a program harder to follow, more error prone, and harder to modify.

break:

The most important of these three control statements is **break,** which we already encountered when studying **switch.** It can be used with **switch**, where often it is necessary, and also with any of the three loop structures. When encountered, it causes the program to break free of the **switch, for, while,** or **do while** that encloses it, and to proceed to the next stage of the program. If the **break** statement is inside nested structures, it affects only the innermost structure containing it.

Sometimes **break** is used to leave a loop when there are two separate reasons to leave. Here's an echo loop that stops when it reads either an EOF character or a newline character:

```
while ( ( ch = getchar()) != EOF )
      {
      if (ch == '\n')
            break;
      putchar(ch);
      }
```

We can make the logic clearer if we put both tests in one place:

```
while ( ( ch = getchar()  ) != EOF && ch != '\n' )
      putchar(ch);
```

If you find that you have used a **break** as a part of an **if** statement, see if you can re-express the condition (as we did above) so that the need for the **break** is ended.

continue:

This statement can be used in the three loop forms, but not in a **switch.** Like **break,** it interrupts the flow of a program. Instead of terminating the whole loop, however, **continue** causes the rest of an iteration to be skipped and the next iteration to be started. Let's replace the **break** in the last fragment with a **continue:**

```
while ( ( ch = getchar()  ) != EOF  )
      {
      if ( ch == '\n' )
          continue;
      putchar(ch);
      }
```

The **break** version quits the loop entirely when a newline character is encountered. The **continue** version merely skips over the newlines and quits only when an EOF character is encountered.

Of course, this fragment could have been expressed more economically as

```
while ( ( ch = getchar() ) != EOF )
      if ( ch != '\n')
           putchar(ch);
```

Often, as in this case, reversing an **if** test will eliminate the need for a continue.

On the other hand, the **continue** statement can shorten some programs, particularly if they involve nested **if else** statements.

goto:

The **goto** statement, bulwark of BASIC and FORTRAN, is available in C. However, C, unlike those two languages, can get along quite well without it. Kernighan and Ritchie refer to the **goto** statement as "infinitely abusable" and suggest that it "be used sparingly, if at all."

First we will show you how to use it, then we will show why you don't need to.

The **goto** statement has two parts: the **goto** and a label name. The label is named following the same conventions used in naming a variable. An example is

```
goto part2;
```

For this statement to work, there must be another statement bearing the **part2** label. This is done by beginning a statement with the label name followed by a colon.

```
part2: printf("Refined analysis:\n");
```

Avoiding the *goto*

In principle, you never need to use the **goto** in a C program. But if you have a background in FORTRAN or BASIC, both of which require its use, you may have developed programming habits that depend on using the **goto.**

To help you get over that dependence, we will outline some familiar **goto** situations and then show you a more C-like approach.

1. Handling an **if** situation that requires more than one statement:

```
if ( size > 12)
    goto a;
goto b;
a: cost = cost * 1.05;
   flag = 2;
b: bill = cost * flag;
```

(In standard BASIC and FORTRAN only the single statement immediately following the **if** condition is attached to the **if.** We have translated that pattern into the equivalent C.)
The standard C approach of using a compound statement or block is much easier to follow:

```
if (size > 12)
     {
     cost = cost * 1.05;
     flag = 2;
     }
bill = cost * flag;
```

2. Choosing from two alternatives:

```
if ( ibex > 14)
   goto a;
sheds = 2;
goto b;
a: sheds = 3;
b: help = 2 * sheds;
```

Having the **if-else** structure available allows C to express this choice much more cleanly:

```
if ( ibex > 14)
     sheds = 3;
else
     sheds = 2;
help = 2 * sheds;
```

3. Setting up an indefinite loop:

```
readin: scanf("%d", &score);
if( score < 0)
   goto stage2;
lots of statements;
goto readin;
stage2: more stuff;
```

Use a **while** loop instead:

```
scanf("%d", &score);
while( score >= 0)
     {
     lots of statements;
     scanf("%d", &score);
     }
more stuff;
```

4. Skipping to the end of a loop: use **continue** instead.

5. Leaving a loop: use **break** instead. Actually, **break** and **continue** are specialized forms of a **goto.** The advantages of using them are that their names tell you what they are supposed to do and that since they don't use labels, there is no danger of putting a label in the wrong place.

6. Leaping madly about to different parts of a program: don't!

There is one use of **goto** that is tolerated by some C practitioners, and that is to get out of a nested set of loops if trouble shows up. (A single **break** just gets you out of the innermost loop.)

```
while ( funct > 0 )
     {
     for (i = 1, i <= 100; i++)
          {
          for ( j= 1; j <= 50; j++)
               {
               statements galore;
               if ( big trouble)
                    goto help;
```

```
                statements;
                }
            more statements;
            }
        yet more statements;
        }
    and more statements;
    help : bail out;
```

As you can see from our examples, the alternative forms are clearer than the **goto** forms. This difference grows even greater when you mix several of these situations together. Which **gotos** are helping **ifs,** which are simulating **if-elses,** which are controlling loops, which are just there because the programmer programmed himself into a corner? A gung-ho **goto** approach lets you create a labyrinth of program flow. If you aren't familiar with **gotos,** keep it that way. If you are used to using them, try to train yourself not to. Ironically, C, which doesn't need a **goto,** has a better **goto** than most languages, because it lets you use descriptive words for labels instead of numbers.

SUMMARY: PROGRAM JUMPS

I. Keywords: ***break, continue, goto***

II. General Comments:

These three instructions cause program flow to jump from one location of a program to another location.

III. break

The **break** command can be used with any of the three loop forms and with the **switch** statement. It causes program control to skip over the rest of the loop or **switch** containing it and to resume with the next command following the loop or **switch.**

Example:

```
switch (number )
     {
     case  4:  printf("That's a good choice.\n");
               break;
     case  5:  printf("That's a fair choice.\n");
               break;
```

```
    default:  printf("That's a poor choice.\n");

    }
```

IV. continue

The **continue** command can be used with any of the three loop forms but not with a **switch.** It causes program control to skip the remaining statements in a loop. For a **while** or **for** loop, the next loop cycle is started. For a **do while** loop, the exit condition is tested and then, if necessary, the next loop cycle is started.

Example:

```
    while ( (ch = getchar())  != EOF)
         {
         if ( ch == ' ' )
              continue;
         putchar(ch);
         chcount++;
         }
```

This fragment echoes and counts nonspace characters.

V. goto

A **goto** statement causes program control to jump to a statement bearing the indicated label. A colon is used to separate a labeled statement from its label. Label names follow the rules for variable names. The labeled statement can come either before or after the **goto.**

Form:

```
    goto label;
        . . .
    label : statement
```

Example:

```
      top : ch = getchar();
              . . .
      if ( ch != 'y' )
             goto top;
```

ARRAYS

Arrays are important features in many programs. They let you store lots of related information in a convenient fashion. We will devote a whole chapter to arrays later, but because arrays often hang around loops, we want to start using them now.

An array is a series of variables which share the same basic name and are distinguished from one another by a numerical tag. For instance, the declaration

```
float debts[20];
```

announces that **debts** is an array with twenty members or "elements." The first element of the array is called **debts[0],** the second element is called **debts[1],** etc., up to **debts[19].** Note that the numbering of array elements starts with 0 and not 1. Because we declared the array to be type **float**, each element can be assigned a **float** value. For example, we can have

```
debts[5] = 32.54;
debts[6] = 1.2e+21;
```

An array can be of any data type:

```
int nannies[22];       /* an array to hold 22 integers    */
char alpha[26];        /* an array to hold 26 characters  */
long big[500];      /* an array to hold 500 long integers  */
```

Earlier, for example, we talked about strings, which are a special case of **char** arrays. (A **char** array in general is one whose elements are assigned **char** values. A string is a **char** array in which the null character, **'\0',** is used to mark the end of the string.)

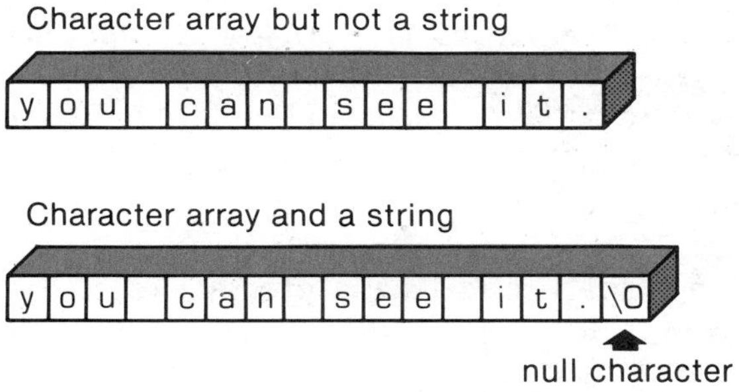

Figure 8.6
Character arrays and strings.

The numbers used to identify the array elements are called "subscripts" or "indices." The subscripts must be integers, and, as we mentioned, the subscripting begins with 0. The array elements are stored next to each other in memory, as shown in Fig. 8.6.

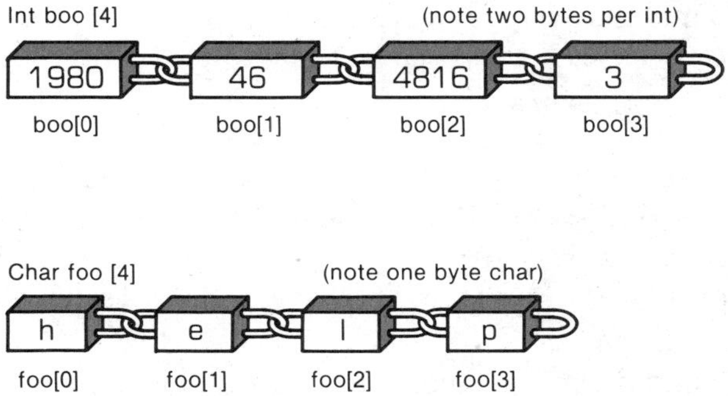

Figure 8.7
"char" and "int" arrays in memory.

There are many, many uses for arrays. Here is a relatively simple one. Suppose you want a program that reads in 10 scores, which will be processed later on. By using an array, you can avoid inventing 10 different variable names, one for each score. Also, you can use a **for** loop to do the reading.

```
 /* scoreread */
main()
{
  int i, score[10];

  for (i = 0; i <= 9; i++)
      scanf("%d", &score[i]);  /* read in the ten scores   */
  printf("The scores read in are as follows:\n");
  for (i=0; i < = 9; i++)
      printf("%5d", score[i]);  /* verify input */
  printf("\n");
}
```

It is good practice to have a program repeat or "echo" the values it has just read in. It helps ensure that the program is processing the data you think it is.

Our approach here is much more convenient than using 10 separate **scanf( )** statements and 10 separate **printf( )** statements to read in and verify the ten scores. The **for** loop provides a very simple and direct way to utilize the array subscripts.

What sort of operations might we perform on these scores? We could find the average, we could find the standard deviation (yes, we know how), we could find the highest score, we could sort the scores. Let's tackle the two easiest parts: finding the average and finding the highest score.

To find the average, we can add this to the program:

```
int sum, average;

for (i = 0, sum = 0; i <=9; i++)  /* two initializations */
     sum += a[i];   /* add up the array elements */
average = sum/10;     /* time-honored method of averaging */
printf("The average of these scores is %d.\n", average);
```

To find the highest score, we can add this to the program:

```
int highest;
```

```
for (highest = a[0], i = 1; i <= 9; i++)
     if ( a[i] > highest)
          highest = a[i];
printf("The highest score is %d.\n", highest);
```

Here we begin by setting **highest** equal to **a[0].** Then we compare **highest** to each element of the array. Whenever we find a value higher than the current value of **highest,** we set **highest** equal to the new, higher value.

Now put the parts together. In pseudocode,

read in scores
echo scores back
find and print average
find and print highest score

While we are at it, we will generalize slightly.

```
 /* scores */
#define NUM 10
main()
{
 int i, sum, average, highest, score[NUM];

 printf("Enter the %d scores now.\n,NUM);
 for (i = 0; i < NUM; i++)
      scanf("%d", &score[i]);  /* read in the ten scores  */
 printf("The scores read in are as follows:\n");
 for (i = 0; i < NUM; i++)
     printf("%5d", score[i]);  /* verify input */
 printf("\n");
 for (i = 0, sum = 0; i < NUM; i++)
      sum += score[i];  /* add up the array elements  */
 average = sum/NUM;      /* time-honored method of averaging */
 printf("The average of these scores is %d.\n", average);
 for (highest = score[0], i = 1; i < NUM; i++)
      if ( score[i] > highest) /* see which is bigger */
         highest = score[i];
 printf("The highest score is %d.\n", highest);
}
```

We replaced **10** with a symbolic constant, and we used the fact that **i <= (NUM −1)** is the same as **i < NUM.**

Let's check to see if it works, then we can make a few comments.

```
Enter the 10 scores now.
76 85 62 48 98 71 66 89 70 77
The scores read in are as follows:
   76   85   62   48   98   71  66  89  70  77
The average of these scores is 74.
The highest score is 98.
```

One point to note is that we used four separate **for** loops. You may wonder if this was really necessary. Could we have combined some of the operations in one loop? The answer is that we could have done so. That would have made the program more compact. However, we were swayed (impressionable folk that we are) by the principle of modularity. The idea behind this phrase is that a program should be broken into separate units or "modules," with each module having one task to perform. (Our pseudocode reflects the four modules to this program.) This makes it easier to read a program. Perhaps even more importantly, it makes it much easier to update or modify a program if different parts of it are not intermingled. Just pop out the offending module, replace it with a new one, and leave the rest of the program unchanged.

The second point to note is that it is rather unsatisfying to have a program that processes exactly 10 numbers. What if someone drops out and only 9 scores are available? True, by using a symbolic constant for 10, we made it simple to change the program, but still you would have to recompile it. Are there other choices? We will look at that next.

A QUESTION OF INPUT

There are several approaches to reading in a series, say, of numbers. We will outline some here, going from least convenient to more convenient.

In general, the least convenient approach is the one we just used—writing a program to accept a fixed number of input items. (However, the approach is fine for situations in which the number of input items never changes.) If the number of input items changes, then the program must be recompiled.

The next step up is to ask the user how many items will be read in. Since the size of the array is fixed by the program, the program should check to see that the user's answer is no larger than the array size. Then the user can input the data. We can remake the beginning of our program into the following:

```
printf("How many data items will you be entering?\n");
scanf("%d", &nbr);
while ( nbr > NUM)
```

```
    {
    printf("I can handle only up to %d items; please enter  a");
    printf("smaller value.\n", NUM);
    scanf("%d", &nbr);
    } /* ensures that nbr <= NUM, the maximum array size */
for ( i = 0; i < nbr ; i++)
      scanf("%d", &score[i]);
```

We would continue by replacing every **NUM** in the program (except in the **#define** statement and in the array declaration) by **nbr.** This makes the various operations affect only those elements of the array which are filled with data.

The problem with this approach is that it relies on the user to count correctly, and relying on the user to do things right leads to fragile programs.

This leads to the next approach, which is to let the computer count the number of numbers entered. After all, computers do have some aptitude in that direction. The main problem here is how to let the computer know when you are done entering numbers. One method is to have the user give a special signal to announce the end. This signal has to be of the *same data type* as the rest of the data in order to be read by the same program statement. But is must also be *distinct* from ordinary data. For instance, if we were reading in scores for a test on which a person could score from 0 to 100 points, we wouldn't choose 74 as a signal, because that could be a legitimate test score. A number like 999 or −3, on the other hand, would make a suitable stop signal, since it isn't a legitimate score. Here is an implementation of this approach:

```
#define STOP 999 /* signal to stop reading input */
#define NUM 50
main()
{
  int i, count, temp, score[NUM];

  printf("Begin entering score values.  Enter 999 to signify\n");
  printf("the end of data. The maximum number of scores you\n");
  printf("can enter is %d.\n", NUM);
  count = 0;
  scanf("%d", &temp); /* read in a value */
  while( temp != STOP && count <= NUM)  /* check for STOP sign */
       {                      /* and check to see if room is left */
       score[count++] = temp; /* store value and update count  */
```

```
        if (count < NUM + 1)
            scanf("%d", &temp);    /* read in next value  */
        else
            print("I ain't takin' no mo' data.\n");
        }
printf("You entered %d scores, as follows:\n", count);
for (i = 0; i < count; i++)
     printf("%5d\n", score[i]);
}
```

We read input into a temporary variable **temp** and assign the value to the array only if the value is not the stop signal. It's not really necessary to do it this way; we just thought it might make the testing process a bit clearer.

Notice that we check for two things: first, to see if the stop signal has been read and second, to see if there is room in the array for another number. If we fill the array before getting a stop signal, the program politely informs us so and quits reading in data.

Note, too, that we use the postfix form of the increment operator. Thus when **count** is 0, **score[0]** is assigned the value of **temp,** and then **count** is increased to 1. After each iteration of the **while** loop, **count** is one larger than the last subscript used for the array. This is what we want, since **score[0]** is the first element, **score[20]** is the 21st element, and so on. When the program finally leaves the loop, **count** equals the total number of data numbers read. We then use **count** as the upper limit for the following **for** loops.

This scheme works wells as long as we have a fund of numbers that would never be entered as data. But what if we want a program to accept *any* number of the proper data type as data? Then that would leave no number to use as a stop signal.

We faced a problem like that before when we sought an End-of-File character. The solution then was to have a character-fetching function **(getchar())** that was actually a type **int.** This enabled the function to read a "character" (EOF) that really wasn't an ordinary character. What would be useful for our current example is a function that fetches an integer but is also capable of reading a noninteger which can be used as a stop symbol.

The good news is that this is possible. The bad news is that we need to know a little more about how functions work, so we will postpone developing this idea until Chapter 10.

SUMMARY

Our main topic was program control. C offers many aids for structuring your programs. The **while** and the **for** statements provide entry-condition loops. The latter are particularly suited for loops that involve initialization and updating. The comma operator lets you initialize and update more than one variable in a **for** loop. For the rare occasion when an exit-condition loop is needed, C provides the **do while** statement. The **break, continue,** and **goto** statements provide further means of controlling the flow of a program.

We also discussed arrays further. Arrays are declared in the same fashion as ordinary variables, but have a number in brackets to indicate the number of elements. The first element of an array is numbered 0, the second is numbered 1, etc. The subscripts used to number arrays can be manipulated conveniently by using loops.

WHAT YOU SHOULD HAVE LEARNED

C's three loop forms: **while, for,** and **do while**
The difference between entry-condition and exit-condition loops
Why entry-condition loops are used much more often than exit-condition loops
The other assignment operators: += -= *= /= %=
How to use the comma operator
When to use **break** and **continue:** sparingly
When to use **goto:** when you want clumsy, hard-to-follow programs
How to use a **while** to protect a program from faulty input
What an array is and how to declare one: **long arms[8]**

QUESTIONS AND ANSWERS

Questions

1. Find the value of quack after each line.

```
int quack = 2;
quack += 5;
quack *= 10;
quack -= 6;
quack /= 8;
quack %= 3;
```

2. What output would the following loop produce?

```
for ( value = 36; value > 0; value /= 2)
        printf("%3d", value);
```

3. How can you modify the **if** statements in **numguess2** to accept both upper- and lower-case letters?
4. We suspect the following program is not perfect. What errors can you find?

```
 main()                                          /* line 1 */
{                                                /* line 2 */
  int i, j, list(10);                            /* line 3 */

  for (i = 1, i <= 10,  i++)                     /* line 5 */
      {                                          /* line 6 */
      list[i] = 2*i + 3;                         /* line 7 */
      for (j = 1, j > = i, j++)                  /* line 8 */
          printf("%d\n", list[j]);               /* line 9 */
      }                                              /*  line 10 */
```

5. Used nested loops to write a program that produces this pattern:

```
$$$$$$$$
$$$$$$$$
$$$$$$$$
$$$$$$$$
```

6. Write a program that creates an array with 26 elements and stores the 26 lower-case letters in it.

Answers

1. 2, 7, 70, 64, 8, 2
2. **36 18 9 4 2 1** Recall how integer division works. 1 divided by 2 is 0, so the loop terminates after value equals 1.
3. `if ( response == 'h' || response == 'H')`
4. line 3: should be **list[10]**
   line 5: commas should be semicolons
   line 5: range for i should be from 0 to 9, not 1 to 10
   line 8: commas should be semicolons
   line 8: >= should be <=. Otherwise, when i is 1, the loop never ends.
   line 10: There should be another closing brace between lines 9 and 10. One brace closes the compound statement, and one closes the program.

5.
```
main()
{
int i,j;

for(i = 1; i <= 4; i++)
    {
    for(j = 1; j <= 8; j++)
          printf("$");
    printf("\n");
    }
}
```

6.
```
main()
 {
 int i;
 char ch, alpha[26];

 for ( i = 0, ch = 'a'; i < 26; i++, ch++)
      alpha[i] = ch;
 }
```

EXERCISES

1. Modify **numguess2** along the lines we suggested to improve the program.
2. Implement our suggestion to improve the efficiency of the prime number program.
3. Use nested loops to produce the following pattern:

```
$
$$
$$$
$$$$
$$$$$
```

BUT YOU SAID YOU WERE LOOKING FOR A HOME COMPUTER

9

HOW TO FUNCTION PROPERLY

In this chapter you will find

9. HOW TO FUNCTION PROPERLY

CONCEPTS

Functions
Program building blocks
Communicating between functions: arguments, pointers, return
Function types

KEYWORDS

return

The design philosophy of C is based on using functions. Already we have used several functions to help our programming: **printf( )**, **scanf( )**, **getchar( )**, **putchar( )**, and **strlen( )**. These functions come with the system, but we also created several functions of our own, all called **main( )**. Programs always start by executing the instructions in **main( )**; after that, **main( )** can call other functions, like **getchar( )**, into action. Now we will learn how to create our own functions and make them available to **main( )** and to each other.

First, what is a function? A function is a self-contained unit of program code designed to accomplish a particular task. A function in C plays the same role that functions, subroutines, and procedures play in other languages, although the details may be different. Some functions cause action to take place. For example, **printf( )** causes data to be printed on your screen. Some functions find a value for the program to use. For instance, **strlen( )** tells a program how long a certain string is. In general, a function can both produce actions and provide values.

Why do we use functions? For one thing, they save us from repetitious programming. If we have to do a certain task several times in a program, we write an appropriate function once, then have the program use that function wherever needed. Or we can use the same function in different programs, just as we use **putchar( )** in many programs. Even if we do a task just once in just one program, it is worthwhile to use a function, because functions make a program more modular, hence easier to read and easier to change or fix. Suppose, for example, we want to write a program that does the following:

read in a list of numbers
sort the numbers
find their average
print out a bar graph

We could use this program.

```
main()
{
  float list[50];

  readlist(list);
  sort(list);
  average(list);
  bargraph(list);
}
```

Of course, we would also have to write the four functions **readlist( ), sort( ), average( ),** and **bargraph** . . . mere details. By using descriptive function names, we have made it quite clear what the program does and how it is organized. We then can fiddle with each function separately until it does its job right. An added benefit is that if we make the functions general enough, they can prove useful in other programs.

Many programmers like to think of a function as a "black box" defined in terms of the information that goes in (its input) and of what it produces (its output). What goes on inside the black box is not our concern, unless we are the ones who have to write the function. For example, when we use **printf( ),** we know we have to give it a control string and, perhaps, some arguments. We also know what output **printf( )** should produce. We never had to think about the programming that went into creating **printf( ).** Thinking of functions in this manner helps us concentrate on the overall design of the program rather than on the details.

What do we need to learn about functions? We need to know how to define them properly, how to call them up for use, and how to set up communications between a function and the program that invokes it. To learn these things we will begin with a very simple example and then bring in more features until we have the full story.

CREATING AND USING A SIMPLE FUNCTION

Our modest first goal is to create a function that types 65 asterisks in a row. To give our function a context, we will include it in a program that prints a simple letterhead. Here is the complete program. It consists of the functions **main( )** and **starbar( ).**

```
 /* letterhead1 */
#define NAME "MEGATHINK, INC."
#define ADDRESS "10 Megabuck Plaza"
#define PLACE "Megapolis, CA 94904"
main()
{
  starbar();
  printf("%s\n", NAME);
  printf("%s\n", ADDRESS);
  printf("%s\n", PLACE);
  starbar();
}
/* now comes the starbar() function */
#include <stdio.h>
#define LIMIT 65
starbar()
{
  int count;

  for ( count = 1; count <= LIMIT; count++)
      putchar('*');
  putchar('\n');
}
```

Here is the output:

```
*****************************************************************
MEGATHINK, INC.
10 Megabuck Plaza
Megapolis, CA 94904
*****************************************************************
```

And here are the major points to note about this program:

1. We called (invoked, summoned) the function **starbar( )** from **main( )** by using just its name. It is a bit like summoning a demon, but instead of inscribing a pentagon, we just follow the name with a semicolon, creating a statement:

```
starbar();
```

This is one form for calling up a function, but it isn't the only one. Whenever the computer reaches a **starbar( )** statement, it looks for the **starbar( )** function and follows the instructions there. When finished, it returns to the next line of the "calling program," **main( )**, in this case.

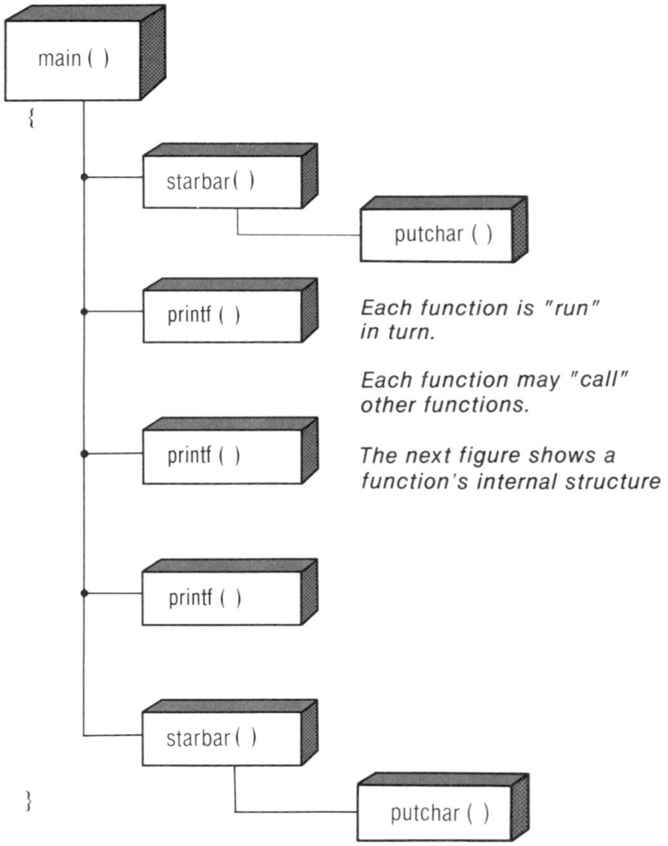

Figure 9.1
Control flow for letterhead 1

2. We followed the same form in writing **starbar( )** as we did in **main( ).** First came the name, then the opening brace, then a declaration of variables used, then the defining statements of the function, then the closing brace. We even preceded the function with **#define** and **#include** statements needed by it and not by **main( ).**

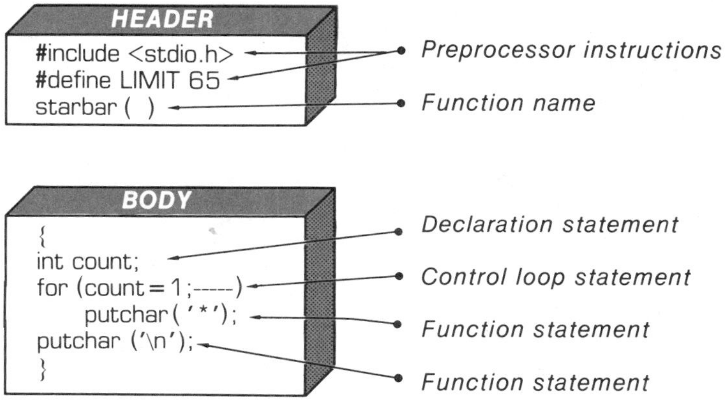

Figure 9.2
Structure of a simple function

3. We included **starbar( )** and **main( )** in the same file. We could have used two separate files. The single-file form is slightly easier to compile. Two separate files make it simpler to use the same function in different programs. We will discuss using two or more files later. For now, we will keep all our functions in one basket. The closing brace of **main( )** tells the compiler where that function ends. The parentheses in **starbar( )** tell the compiler that **starbar( )** is a function. Note that this instance of **starbar( )** is not followed by a semicolon; this lack of a semicolon tells the compiler that we are *defining* **starbar( )** rather than using it.

If we think of **starbar( )** as a black box, its output is the line of stars that is printed. It doesn't have any input because it doesn't need to use any information from the calling program. This function doesn't require any communication with the calling program.

Let's create a case where communication *is* needed.

FUNCTION ARGUMENTS

The letterhead would look a little nicer if the text were centered. We can center the text by printing the right number of spaces before the rest of the line is printed. Let's use a function to print spaces. Our **space( )** function (let's call it that) will be a lot like our **starbar( )** function, except this time there has to be communication from **main( )** to the function telling it how many spaces to print.

Let's get more specific. Our bar of stars is 65 spaces wide, and MEGATHINK, INC. is 15 spaces wide. Thus in our first version, there were 50 spaces following the heading. To center it, we should lead off with 25 spaces, which will result in 25 spaces on either side of the phrase. Therefore we want to be able to communicate the value "25" to the spacing function. We will use the same method we use to communicate the value '*' to **putchar( ):** use an argument. Then **space(25)** will mean to skip 25 spaces. The **25** is the argument. We will call **space( )** three times, once for each line of the address. Here is how it looks:

```
 /* letterhead2 */
#define NAME "MEGATHINK, INC."
#define ADDRESS "10 Megabuck Plaza"
#define PLACE "Megapolis, CA 94904"
main()
{
  int spaces;

  starbar();
  space(25);         /*   space () using a constant as argument */
  printf("%s\n", NAME);
  spaces = (65 - strlen(ADDRESS))/2;
      /* we let the program calculate how many spaces to skip */
  space(spaces);                   /* a variable as argument   */
  printf("%s\n", ADDRESS);
  space((65-strlen(PLACE))/2); /* an expression as argument */
  printf("%s\n", PLACE);
  starbar();
}
/* here is starbar() */
#include <stdio.h>
#define LIMIT 65
starbar()
{
  int count;

  for ( count = 1; count <= LIMIT: count++)
      putchar('*');
```

```
  putchar('\n');
}
/* and here is the space() function */
space(number)
int number;     /* declare argument before brace */
{
  int count;    /* declare other variable after brace */

  for ( count = 1; count <= number; count++)
       putchar(' ');
}
```

Figure 9.3
Letterhead program

Notice that we experimented by expressing the argument in three different ways. Did they all work? Yes, and here is the proof.

```
*****************************************************************
                        MEGATHINK, INC.
                      10 Megabuck Plaza
                     Megapolis, CA 94904
*****************************************************************
```

First, let's look at how to set up a function with an argument. After that, we'll look at how it is used.

Defining a Function with an Argument: Formal Arguments

Our function definition begins with two lines:

```
space(number)
   int number;
```

The first line informs the compiler that **space( )** uses an argument, and that the argument will be called **number.** The second line is a declaration informing the compiler that **number** is of type **int.** Note that the argument is declared *before* the brace that marks the start of the body of the function. Incidentally, you can condense these two lines to one:

```
space (int number;)
```

With either form, the variable **number** is called a "formal" argument. It is, in fact, a new variable, and the computer must set aside a memory location for it.

Now let's see how we use this function.

Calling a Function with an Argument: Actual Arguments

The trick is to assign a value to the formal argument, **number,** in this case. Once that variable has a value, then the program does its task. We give **number** a value by using an "actual argument" in the function call. Consider our first use of **space( )**

```
space(25);
```

The actual argument is 25, and this *value* is assigned to the formal argument, the variable **number.** That is, the function call has this effect:

```
number = 25;
```

In short, the formal argument is a variable in the called program, and the actual argument is the particular value assigned to that variable by the calling program. As we showed in our example, the actual argument can be a constant, a variable, or an even more elaborate expression. Regardless of which it is, the actual argument is evaluated, and it is the value (in this case, an integer) that is sent to the function. For instance, consider our final use of **space( )**

```
space((65-strlen(PLACE))/2);
```

First, that long expression forming the actual argument was evaluated to 23. Then the value 23 is assigned to the variable **number.** The function neither knows nor cares whether that number came from a constant, a variable, or a more general expression. Again, the actual argument is a specific value which is assigned to the variable known as the formal argument.

The Black Box Viewpoint

In the black box view of **space( )**, the input is the number of spaces to be skipped, and the output is the skipping of the spaces. The input is commu-

```
.
.
.
space(number)        "Formal" argument = name
int number;          created by function definition
{
  ---
  ---
  ---
}

main( )
{
  ---                "Actual" argument = value = 25
  ---                initialized by main ( )
space(25);
  ---
}
```

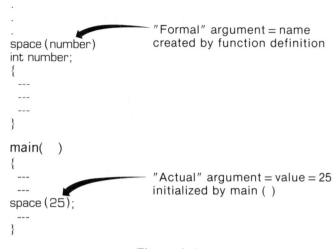

Figure 9.4
Actual arguments and formal arguments

nicated to the function via an argument. The argument provides a communication link between **main( )** and **space( ).** The variable **count,** on the other hand, is declared inside the body of the function, and other functions know nothing about **count.** It is part of the mechanism hidden within the black box. It is not the same variable as the **count** in **starbar( ).**

Multiple Arguments

If more than one argument is needed, you can provide an argument list, with the arguments separated by commas, as shown below.

```
printnum( i,j)
int i, j;
{
   printf("New points = %d.  Total points = %d.\n", i, j);
}
```

We have seen how to communicate information from the calling program to the called function. How can we send information the other way? That is our next topic.

RETURNING A VALUE FROM A FUNCTION: *return*

Let's construct an absolute value function. The absolute value of a number is its value when the sign is ignored. Hence the absolute value of 5 is 5 and the absolute value of −3 is 3. We'll call the function **abs( ).** The input to **abs( )** will be whatever number for which we want the absolute value. The output of the function will be the number shorn of any negative signs. We can handle the input with an argument. The output, as you shall see, is handled using the C keyword **return.** Since **abs( )** has to be called by another function, we will create a simple **main( )** whose sole purpose is to check to see if **abs( )** works. A program designed to test functions this way is called a "driver." The driver takes a function for a spin. If the function pans out, then it can be installed in a more noteworthy program. (The term driver also is used for programs that run devices.) Here is our driver and our absolute value function:

```
 /* abs.driver */
main()
{
   int a = 10, b = 0, c = -22;
   int d, e, f;

   d = abs(a);
   e = abs(b);
   f = abs(c);
   printf ("%d %d %d\n", d, e, f);
}
   /* absolute value function */
abs(x)
int x;
{
   int y;

   y = (x < 0) ? -x : x; /* remember the ?: operator */
   return (y);     /* returns the value of y to calling program */
}
```

Here is the output:

```
10 0 22
```

First, let's refresh our memory about **?:**, the conditional operator. The conditional operator in **abs( )** works this way: if **x** is less than **0, y** is set to **−x;** otherwise **y** is set to **x.** This is what we want, for if **x** is **−5,** then **y** is **−(−5)** or just **5.**

The keyword **return** causes the value of whatever expression is in the parentheses to be assigned to the function containing the **return.** Thus, when **abs( )** is first called by our driver, **abs(a)** acquires the value 10, which then can be assigned to the variable **d.**

The variable **y** is private to **abs( ),** but the value of **y** is communicated back to the calling program with **return.** The effect of

```
d = abs(a);
```

is as if we could say

```
abs(a);
d = y;
```

Can we actually say the latter? No, for the calling program doesn't even know that **y** exists.

The returned value can be assigned to a variable, as in our example, or it can be used as part of an expression. You can do this, for example:

```
answer = 2*abs(z) + 25;
printf("%d\n", abs(-32 + answer);
```

Using **return** has one other effect. It terminates the function and returns control to the next statement in the calling function. This occurs even if the **return** statement is not the last in the function. Thus we could have written **abs( )** this way:

```
 /* absolute value function, second version */
abs(x)
int x;
{
   if ( x < 0)
        return (-x);
   else
         return(x);
}
```

This version is clearer, and it doesn't use the additional variable **y.** To the user, however, both versions are the same, since both take the same input and produce the same output. Just the innards are different. Even this version works the same:

```
 /* absolute value function, third version */
abs(x)
int x;
{
   if ( x < 0)
       return(-x);
   else
       return(x);
    printf("Professor Fleppard is a fopdoodle.\n")
}
```

The **return** statements prevent the **printf( )** statement from ever being reached. Professor Fleppard can use the compiled version of this function in his own programs and never learn the true feelings of his student programmer.

You can use a statement like this, too:

```
return;
```

It causes the containing function to terminate and return control to the calling function. Because no expression is included in parentheses, no value is given to the function.

LOCAL VARIABLES

Several times we have remarked about how the variables in a function are private to it and not known to the calling function. Similarly, the variables of the calling function are not known to the called function. That is why we use arguments and **return** to communicate values back and forth. Variables known only to the one function that contains them are called "local" variables. So far these are the only kind of variables we have used, but C does provide for variables that are known to several functions. These nonlocal variables are termed "global" variables, and we will return to them later. Meanwhile, we want to emphasize that local variables are truly local. Even if we use the same name for variables in two different functions, the computer distinguishes between them. We can show this using the **&** operator (not to be confused with the **&&** operator).

FINDING ADDRESSES: THE & OPERATOR

The **&** operator gives us the address at which a variable is stored. If **pooh** is the name of a variable, then **&pooh** is the address of the variable. We can think of the address as a location in memory, but we also can think of it as the label the computer uses to identify a variable. Suppose we have the statement

```
pooh = 24;
```

And suppose that the address where **pooh** is stored is 12126. Then the statement

```
printf("%d %d\n", pooh, &pooh);
```

would produce

```
24 12126
```

Furthermore, the machine code for the first statement would be something along the lines of "Store 24 in location 12126."

Let's use this operator to check where variables of the same name, but in different functions, are kept.

```
 /* locationcheck */
main()
{
  int pooh = 2, bah = 5;

  printf("In main(), pooh = %d and &pooh = %u\n", pooh, &pooh);
  printf("In main(), bah = %d and &bah = %u\n", bah, &bah);
  mikado(pooh);
}
mikado(bah)
int bah;
{
  int pooh = 10;

  printf("In mikado(), pooh = %d and &pooh = %u\n", pooh, &pooh);
  printf("In mikado(), bah = %d and &bah = %u\n", bah, &bah);
}
```

We used the **%u** (unsigned integer) format for printing the addresses in case they turn out to be larger than the maximum **int** size. On our system, the output of this little exercise is

```
In main(), pooh = 2 and &pooh = 56002
In main(), bah = 5 and &bah = 56004
In mikado(), pooh = 10 and &pooh = 55994
In mikado(), bah = 2 and &bah = 56000
```

What does this show? First, the two **pooh**es have different addresses. The same is true of the two **bah**es. Thus, as promised, the computer considers these to be four separate variables. Secondly, the call **mikado(pooh)** did convey the value (2) of the actual argument (**pooh** of **main( )**) to the formal argument (**bah** of **mikado( )**). Note that just the value was transferred. The two variables involved (**pooh** of **main( )** and **bah** of **mikado( )**) retain their distinct identities.

We raise the second point because it is not true for all languages. In a FORTRAN subroutine, for example, the subroutine uses the variables in the calling program. The subroutine may call the variables by different names, but the addresses are the same. C doesn't do this. Each function uses its own variables. This is preferable, for it means that the original variables won't get altered mysteriously by some side effect of the called function. But it can make for some difficulties, too, as our next section shows.

ALTERING VARIABLES IN THE CALLING PROGRAM

Sometimes we want one function to make changes in the variables of a different function. For example, a common task in sorting problems is interchanging the values of two variables. Suppose we have two variables called **x** and **y** and that we wish to swap values. The simple sequence

```
x = y;
 y = x;
```

does not work, for by the time the second line is reached, the original value of **x** has been lost. We have to put in an additional line to save the original value of **x:**

```
temp = x;
x = y;
y = temp;
```

Now that we have a working method, let's put it into a function and construct a driver to test it. To make clear which variables belong to **main( )** and which belong to the **interchange( )** function, we will use **x** and **y** for the first, and **u** and **v** for the second.

```
 /* switch1 */
main()
{
   int x = 5, y = 10;

   printf("Originally x = %d and y = %d.\n", x , y);
   interchange(x,y);
   printf("Now x = %d and y = %d.\n", x, y);
}
interchange(u,v)
int u,v;
{
  int temp;

  temp = u;
  u = v;
  v = temp;
}
```

Next, we run the program.

```
Originally x = 5 and y = 10.
Now x = 5 and y = 10.
```

Oops! They didn't get switched! Let's put some printing statements in **interchange( )** to see what has gone wrong.

```
 /* switch2 */
main()
{
   int x = 5, y = 10;

   printf("Originally x = %d and y = %d.\n", x , y);
   interchange(x,y);
   printf("Now x = %d and y = %d.\n", x, y);
}
interchange(u,v)
int u,v;
{
   int temp;

   printf("Originally u = %d and v = %d.\n", u , v);
   temp = u;
   u = v;
   v = temp;
   printf("Now u = %d and v = %d.\n", u, v);
}
```

Here is the new output:

```
Originally x = 5 and y = 10.
Originally u = 5 and v = 10.
Now u = 10 and v = 5.
Now x = 5 and y = 10.
```

Well, nothing is wrong with **interchange( );** it does swap the values of **u** and **v.** The problem is communicating the results back to **main( ).** As we pointed out, **interchange( )** uses different variables from **main( ),** so interchanging the values of **u** and **v** have no effect on **x** and **y!** Can we use **return** somehow? Well, we could finish **interchange( )** with the line

```
return(u);
```

and change the call in **main( )** to

```
x = interchange(x,y);
```

This will give **x** its new value, but it leaves **y** in the cold.

With **return** *you can send just one value back to the calling program.* But we need to communicate *two* values. It can be done! All we have to do is use "pointers."

Pointers: A First Look

Pointers? What are they? Basically, a pointer is a symbolic representation of an address. For example, earlier we used the address operator to find the address of the variable **pooh.** Then **&pooh** is a "pointer to **pooh**." The actual address is a number (56002, in our case), and the symbolic representation **&pooh** is a pointer *constant.* After all, the variable **pooh** is not going to change addresses while the program is running.

C also has pointer *variables.* Just as a **char** variable has a character as a value and an **int** variable has an integer as a value, the pointer variable has an address as a value. If we give a particular pointer the name **ptr,** then we can have statements like

```
ptr = &pooh;  /* assigns pooh's address to ptr */
```

We say that **ptr** "points to" **pooh.** The difference between **ptr** and **&pooh** is that **ptr** is a variable while **&pooh** is a constant. If we want, we can make **ptr** point elsewhere:

```
ptr = &bah;  /* make ptr point to bah instead of to pooh */
```

Now **ptr's** value is the address of **bah.**

The Indirection Operator: *

Suppose we know that **ptr** points to **bah.** Then we can use the indirection operator * to find the value stored in **bah.** (Don't confuse this *unary* indirection operator with the *binary* * operator of multiplication.)

```
val = *ptr;  /* finding the value prt points to  */
```

The last two C statements, taken together, amount to

```
val = bah;
```

Using the address and indirection operators is a rather indirect way of accomplishing this result, hence the name "indirection operator."

SUMMARY: POINTER-RELATED OPERATORS

I. The Address Operator:

& When followed by a variable name, gives the address of that variable

Example:

`&nurse` is the address of the variable **nurse**

II. The Indirection Operator

* When followed by a pointer, gives the value stored at the pointed-to address

Example:

```
nurse = 22;
ptr = &nurse;  /* pointer to nurse */
val = *ptr;
```

The net effect is to assign the value 22 to val.

Declaring Pointers

We know how to declare **int** variables and the like. How do we declare a pointer variable? You might guess like this:

```
pointer ptr;     /* not the way to declare a pointer  */
```

Why not? Because it is not enough to say that a variable is a pointer. We also have to say what kind of variable the pointer points to! The reason for this is that different variable types take up different amounts of storage, and some pointer operations require knowledge of the storage size. Here's how pointers are declared:

```
int *pi;          /* pointer to an integer variable  */
char *pc;         /* pointer to a character variable */
float *pf,*pg;    /* pointers to float variables     */
```

The type specification identifies the type of variable pointed to, and the asterisk (*) identifies the variable itself as a pointer. The declaration **int *pi;** says that **pi** is a pointer and that ***pi** is type **int.**

Similarly, the value (***pc**) of what **pc** points to is of type **char.** What of **pc** itself? We describe it as being of type "pointer to **char**". Its value, being an address, is an unsigned integer, so we would use the **%u** format to print **pc's** value.

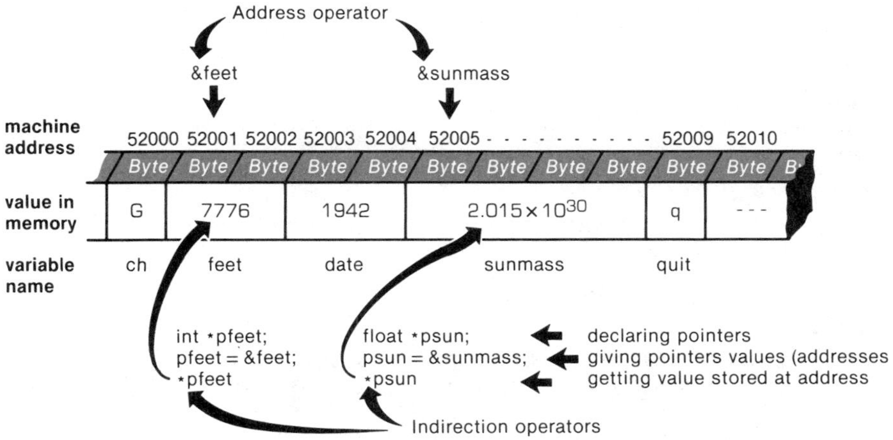

Figure 9.5
Declaring and using pointers.

Using Pointers To Communicate Between Functions

We have touched only the surface of the rich and fascinating world of pointers, but our concern here is using pointers to solve our communication problem. Here's a program that uses pointers to make the interchange function work. Let's look at it, run it, and then try to understand its workings.

```
 /* switch3 */
main()
{
    int x = 5, y = 10;

    printf("Originally x = %d and y = %d.\n", x, y);
    interchange(&x,&y);  /* send addresses to function */
    printf("Now x = %d and y = %d.\n", x, y);
}
interchange(u,v)
int *u, *v;  /* u and v are pointers  */
{
    int temp;

    temp = *u;  /* temp gets value that u points to */
    *u = *v;
    *v = temp;
}
```

After all this trouble, does it really work?

```
Originally x = 5 and y = 10.
Now x = 10 and y = 5.
```

Yes, it works.

Now, lets see how it works. First, our function call looks like this:

```
interchange(&x,&y);
```

Instead of transmitting the *values* of **x** and **y**, we are transmitting their *addresses*. This means that the formal arguments **u** and **v** appearing in

```
interchange(u,v)
```

will have addresses as values, hence they should be declared as pointers. Since **x** and **y**, are integers, **u** and **v** are pointers to integers, so we declare

```
int *u, *v;
```

Next, in the body of the function, we declare

```
int temp;
```

to provide the temporary storage we need. We want to store the value of **x** in **temp,** so we say

```
temp = *u;
```

Remember, **u** has the value **&x,** so **u** points to **x.** This means that ***u** gives us the value of **x,** which is what we want. We *don't* want to write

```
temp = u;   /* NO */
```

for that would store the *address* of **x** rather than its *value;* and we are trying to interchange values, not addresses.

Similarly, to assign y's *value* to x, we use

```
*u = *v;
```

which translates to

```
x = y;
```

Let's summarize what we did. We wanted a function that would alter the values **x** and **y.** By telling the function the addresses of **x** and **y,** we gave the function access to those variables. Using pointers and the * operator, the function could examine the values stored at those locations and change them.

More generally, we can communicate two kinds of information about a variable to a function. If we use a call of the form

```
function1(x);
```

we transmit the *value* of **x.** If we use a call of the form

```
function2(&x);
```

we transmit the *address* of **x.** The first form requires that the function definition include a formal argument of the same type as **x:**

```
function1(num)
int num;
```

The second form requires that the function definition include a formal argument that is a pointer to the right type:

```
function2(ptr)
int *ptr;
```

Use the first form if the function needs a value for some calculation or action. Use the second form if the function needs to alter variables in the calling program. We have been doing this all along with the **scanf( )** function. When we want to read in a value for a variable **num,** we use **scanf("%d", &num).** That function reads a value, then uses the address we give it when it stores the value.

Pointers let us get around the fact that the variables of **interchange( )** were local. They let our function reach out into **main( )** and alter what was stored there.

Pascal users may recognize the first form as being similar to Pascal's value parameter and the second form as being similar to Pascal's variable parameter. BASIC users may find the whole setup a bit unsettling. If this section does seem strange to you, be assured that a little practice will make it seem simple, normal, and convenient.

VARIABLES: NAMES, ADDRESSES, AND VALUES

Our discussion of pointers hinges on the relationships between the names, addresses, and values of variables, so let's discuss these matters further.

When we write a program we think of a variable as having two attributes: a name and a value. (There are other attributes, including type, but that's another matter.) After the program has been compiled and loaded, the computer also thinks of the same variable as having two attributes: an address and a value. An address is the computer's version of a name.

In many languages, the address is the computer's business, concealed from the programmer. In C, however, we can learn and use the address through the **&** operator:

&barn is the address of the variable **barn**

We can get the value from the name just by using the name:

printf("%d\n", barn) prints the value of **barn**

We can get the value from the address by using the * operator:

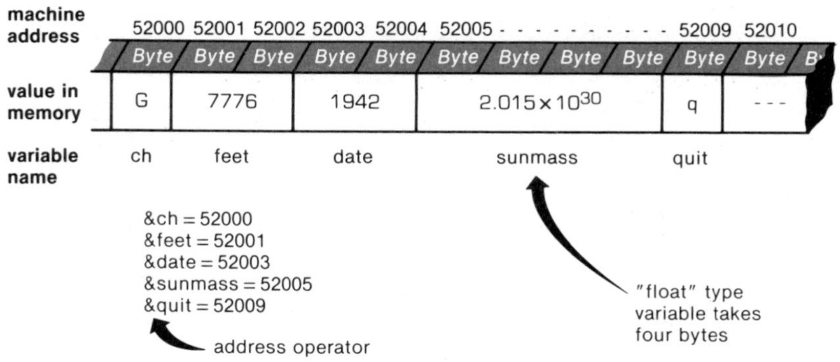

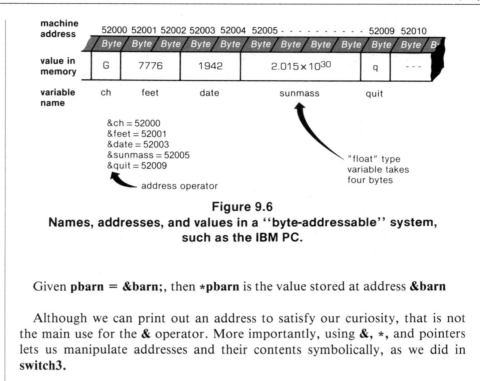

Figure 9.6
Names, addresses, and values in a ''byte-addressable'' system, such as the IBM PC.

Given **pbarn = &barn;**, then ***pbarn** is the value stored at address **&barn**

Although we can print out an address to satisfy our curiosity, that is not the main use for the **&** operator. More importantly, using **&**, *****, and pointers lets us manipulate addresses and their contents symbolically, as we did in **switch3.**

PUTTING OUR KNOWLEDGE OF FUNCTIONS TO WORK

Now that we know a bit about functions, let's put together some useful examples. Let's see, what should we do?

How about a power function, one that lets you raise 2 to the 5th power or 3 to the 3rd, etc? First, we must decide on what input the program needs. That's clear; it needs to know the number and the exponent. We can handle that with two arguments:

```
power(base, exp)
int base, exp;
```

(At this point we have limited ourselves to integers and relatively small answers.)

Next, we need to decide on the output. That, too, is obvious. There should be one number for output, the answer. That we can do with

```
return(answer);
```

Now we decide on an algorithm for calculating the answer.

set answer equal to 1
multiply answer by the base as many times as exp says

Perhaps it's not clear how to perform the second step, so let's break it down further:

Multiply answer by base and decrease exp by 1.
Stop when exp reaches 0.

If exp is, say, 3, then this results in 3 multiplications, so this approach seems sound.

Okay, now put it in code.

```
 /* finds base to the exp power */
power(base, exp)
int base, exp;
{
   int answer;

   for (answer = 1; exp > 0; exp--)
          answer = answer * base;
   return(answer);
}
```

Now test it with a driver.

```
 /* powertest */
main()
{
   int x;

   x = power(2,3);
   printf("%d\n", x);
   x = power(-3,3);
   printf("%d\n", x);
   x = power (4,-2);
   printf("%d\n", x);
   x = power (5,10);
   printf("%d\n", x);
}
```

Put the two functions together, compile and run them. We get this output:

```
8
-27
1
761
```

Well, 2 to the 3rd power is 8, and −3 to 3rd power is −27. So far, so good. But 4 to the −2 power is 1/16, not 1. And 5 to the 10th power is 9,765,625—if memory serves us well.

What went wrong? First, the program is not designed to handle negative powers, so it bombs out on that problem. Secondly, type **int** on our system can't handle numbers beyond 65,535.

We can fix the program by including processing for negative powers and by using floating-point numbers for the base and answer. We need to keep the exponent an integer because that is the number of times we multiply; we can't perform 2.31 multiplications.

```
 /* finds base to the exp power */
double power(base, exp)
double base;
int exp;
{
   double answer;

   if ( exp > 0)
       {
       for (answer = 1.0; exp > 0; exp--)
            answer *= base;
       return(answer);
       }
   else if (base != 0)
       {
       for (answer = 1.0; exp < 0; exp++)
            answer /= base;
       return(answer);
       }
   else  /* base = 0 and exp <= 0  */
       {
       printf("0 to the %d power is not allowed!\n", exp);
       return(0);
       }
}
```

There are some points to note here. Foremost is that we have to declare the function type! Since **answer** is type **double, power( )** itself must be double, because **power** is assigned the value returned by **return.** Why, you ask, did we not declare functions before? The answer is that C functions are assumed to be type **int** (and most are) unless otherwise declared.

Also, we wanted to show you that we haven't forgotten those new assignment operators we introduced in Chapter 8.

Third, we converted negative powers into division, as permitted by the laws of algebra. This brought up a disturbing possibility, division by zero, so we headed that off with an error message. We returned the value of 0 so that the program needn't stop.

We can use the same driver, providing we also declare **power( )**'s type there, too.

```
 /* powertest */
main()
{
   double x;
   double power();  /* this is how to declare a function */

   x = power(2.0,3);
   printf("%.0f\n", x);
   x = power(-3.0,3);
   printf("%.0f\n", x);
   x = power (4.0,-2);
   printf("%d.4f\n", x);
   x = power (5.0,10);
   printf("%.0f\n", x);
}
```

This time the output is satisfactory.

```
8
-27
0.0625
9765625
```

This example suggests we include the next short section.

SPECIFYING FUNCTION TYPES

The type of a function is determined by the type of value it returns, not by the type of its arguments. Functions are assumed to be type **int** unless otherwise declared. If a function is not type **int**, you need to announce its type in two places:

1. Declare the function type in its definition:

```
char pun( ch, n)  /* a function that returns a character */
int n;
char ch;

float raft(num)  /* a function that returns type float */
int num;
```

2. Declare the function type in the calling function also. It can be declared along with the variable declarations; just include the parentheses (no arguments) to identify it as a function.

```
main()
{
char rch, pun();
float raft();
```

Don't forget now. If a function returns a non-**int** value, declare the function type where it is defined and where it is used.

SUMMARY: FUNCTIONS

I. Form:

A typical function definition has this form:

name(argument list)
argument declarations
function body

The presence of the argument list and declarations is optional. Variables other than the arguments are declared within the body, which is bounded by braces.

Example:

```
diff(x,y)      /* function name and argument list */
int x,y;       /* declare arguments */
```

```
{               /* begin function body */
  int z;        /* declare local variable */

  z = x - y;
  return(z);
}               /* end function body */
```

II. Communicating Values:

Arguments are used to convey values from the calling program to the function. If variables **a** and **b** have the values 5 and 2, then the call

```
c = diff(a,b);
```

transmits 5 and 2 to the variables **x** and **y.** The values 5 and 2 are called actual arguments, and the **diff( )** variables **x** and **y** are called formal arguments.

The keyword **return** communicates one value from the function to the calling program. In our example, **c** receives the value of **z,** which is 3.

A function ordinarily has no effect upon the variables in a calling program. Use pointers as arguments to directly affect variables in the calling program. This may be necessary if you wish to communicate more than one value back to the calling program.

III. Function Type:

Functions must have the same type as the value they return. Functions are assumed to be of type **int.** If a function is of another type, it must be declared so in the calling program and in the function definition.

Example:

```
main()
{
  float q, x, duff();  /* declare in calling program */
  int n;
  . . .
  q = duff(x,n);
  . . .
}
float duff( u, k )   /* declare in function definition */
float u;
int k;
{
  float tor;
  . . .
  return(tor);   /* returns a float value */
}
```

ALL C FUNCTIONS ARE CREATED EQUAL

Each C function in a program is on equal footing with the others. Each can call any other function or be called by any other function. This makes the C function somewhat different from Pascal procedures, for Pascal procedures can be nested within other procedures. Procedures in one nest will be ignorant of procedures in another nest.

Isn't the function **main( )** special? Yes, it is a little special in that when a program of several functions is put together, execution starts with the first statement in **main( )**. But that is the limit of its preference. Even **main( )** can be called by other functions, as this example shows.

```
 /* use.main */
#include <stdio.h>
main()
{
  char ch;

  printf("Enter any character you want. A Q will end things.\n");
  ch = getchar();
  printf("Aha! That was a %c!\n", ch);
  if (ch != 'Q')
     more();
}
more()
{
  main();
}
```

The function **main( )** calls **more( )**, and **more( )** calls **main( )!** When **main( )** is called, it starts at the beginning, so we have made a sneaky loop.

Indeed, a function can even call itself. We can simplify the last example to this:

```
 /* main.main */
#include <stdio.h>
main()
{
  char ch;

  printf("Enter any character you want. A Q will end things.\n");
```

```
    ch = getchar();
    printf("Aha! That was a %c!\n", ch);
    if (ch != 'Q')
       main();
}
```

Here's some sample output to show that it works. Note how it even processes the newline character that gets transmitted when we used the [enter] key.

```
Enter any character you want. A Q will end things.
I
Aha! That was a I!
Enter any character you want. A Q will end things.
!
Aha! That was a !!
Enter any character you want. A Q will end things.
Q
Aha! That was a Q!
```

The act of a function calling itself is termed "recursion." The loop we set up using recursion doesn't work the same as a **while** or **do while** loop. When **main( )** calls itself, it doesn't go to its own beginning. Instead, a whole new set of **main( )** variables is created. If you print out the address of a variable in an ordinary loop, the address doesn't change from iteration to iteration. With the loop we have here, the address does change, for a new **ch** is created each loop. If the program loops 20 times, there will 20 different variables created, each called **ch,** but each with its own address.

COMPILING PROGRAMS WITH TWO OR MORE FUNCTIONS

The simplest approach to using several functions is to place them in the same file. Then just compile that file as you would a single-function file.

A second approach is to use the **#include** directive. If one function is a **file1.c** and a second function is in **file2.c,** place this directive in **file1.c:**

```
#include "file2.c"
```

See Chapter 11 for more information about #include.

Other approaches are more system dependent. Here are some:

UNIX

Suppose **file1.c** and **file2.c** are two files containing C functions. Then the command

```
cc file1.c file2.c
```

will compile both files and produce an executable file called **a.out.** In addition, two "object" files called **file1.o** and **file2.o** are produced. If you later change **file1.c** and not **file2.c,** you can compile the first and combine it with the object code version of the second file using the command

```
cc file1.c file2.o
```

Lattice C and Microsoft C

Compile **file1.c** and **file2.c** separately, producing two object code files **file1.obj** and **file2.obj.** Use the linker to combine them with each other and with the standard object module **c.obj:**

```
link c file1 file2
```

Assembly-Code-Based Systems

Some allow you to compile several files at once à la UNIX:

```
cc file1.c file2.c
```

or equivalent. Or in some cases you can produce separate assembly-code modules and then combine those in the assembly process.

SUMMARY

You should use functions as building blocks for larger programs. Each function should have a single, well-defined purpose. Use arguments to communicate values to a function, and use the keyword **return** to communicate a value back to the calling program. If the function returns a value not of type **int,** then you must specify the function type in the function definition and in the declaration section of the calling program. If you want the function to affect variables in the calling program, you should use addresses and pointers.

WHAT YOU SHOULD HAVE LEARNED

How to define a function.

How to communicate information to a function: use arguments.

The difference between a formal argument and actual argument:
one's a variable used by the function, one's a value from the calling function.

Where to declare arguments: after the function name and before the first brace

Where to declare other local variables: after the first brace

When and how to use **return.**

When and how to use addresses and pointers for communication.

QUESTIONS AND ANSWERS

Questions

1. Devise a function that returns the sum of two integers.
2. What changes, if any, would you need to make in order to have the function of Question 1 add two **float** numbers instead?
3. Devise a function **alter( )** that takes two **int** variables **x** and **y** and changes their values to their sum and their difference, respectively.
4. Anything wrong with this function definition?

```
salami(num)
{
   int num, count;

   for(count = 1; count <= num; num++)
       printf(" O salami mio!\n");
}
```

Answers

1. **sum(j,k)**
   int j, k;
   {
   return (j + k);
   }
2. **float sum(j,k)**
   float j, k;
   Also, declare **float sum( )** in the calling program.
3. Since we want to alter two variables in the calling program, we can use addresses and pointers. The call would be **alter(&x,&y)**

   A possible solution is

```
alter(px,py)
int *px, *py;    /* pointers to x and y */
{
  int sum, diff;

  sum = *px + *py;  /* add contents of two addresses */
  diff = *px - *py;
  *px = sum;
  *py = diff;
}
```

4. Yes; **num** should be declared before the first brace, not after. Also, it should be **count++**, not **num++**.

EXERCISES

1. Devise a function **max(x,y)** that returns the larger of two values.
2. Devise a function **chline(ch,i,j)** that prints the requested character in columns **i** to column **j.** See **sketcher** in Chapter 7.

10

STORAGE CLASSES AND PROGRAM DEVELOPMENT

In this chapter you will find

10. STORAGE CLASSES AND PROGRAM DEVELOPMENT

CONCEPTS

Local and global variables
Storage classes
Random number function
Error checking
Modular programming
Sorting

KEYWORDS

auto, extern, static, register

One of C's strengths is that it lets you control the fine points of a program. C's storage classes are an example of that control, because they allow you to determine which functions know which variables and how long a variable persists in a program. Storage classes form the first topic of this chapter.

Secondly, there is more to programming than just knowing the rules of the language, just as there is more to writing a novel (or even a letter) than knowing the rules of English. In this chapter we will develop several useful functions. As we do so, we will try to demonstrate some of the considerations that go into the designing of a function. In particular, we will emphasize the value of a modular approach, breaking down jobs into manageable tasks.

But first, we will discuss storage classes.

STORAGE CLASSES AND SCOPE

We mentioned earlier that local variables are known only to the functions containing them. C also offers the possibility of global variables known to several functions. Suppose, for example, we want both **main( )** and **critic( )** to have access to the variable **units.** We can do this by assigning **units** to the "external" storage class, as shown below:

```
 /* global.units */
int units;    /* an external variable */
main()
{
   extern int units;

   printf("How many pounds to a firkin of butter?\n");
   scanf("%d", &units);
   while ( units != 56)
       critic();
   printf("You must have looked it up!\n");
}
critic()
{
   extern int units;

   printf("No luck, chummy.  Try again.\n");
   scanf"%d", &units);
}
```

Here is a sample output:

```
How many pounds to a firkin of butter?
14
No luck, chummy.  Try again.
56
You must have looked it up!
```

(We did.)

Note how the second value for **units** was read by the **critic( )** function, yet **main( )** also knew the new value when it quit the **while** loop.

We made **units** an external variable by defining it outside of (external to) any function definition. Then, inside the functions that use the variable, we declare the variable by preceding the variable type with the keyword **extern.** The **extern** informs the computer to look for the definition of this variable outside the function. If we had omitted the keyword "extern" in, say, **critic( ),** the computer would have set up a separate variable private to

critic( ), but also named **units.** Then the other **units** (the one in **main( )**) would never have its value reset.

Each variable, we know, has a type. In addition, each variable has a storage class. There are four keywords used to describe storage classes: **extern** (for external), **auto** (for automatic), **static,** and **register.** You haven't noticed storage classes before because variables declared within a function are considered to be class **auto** unless declared otherwise. (They are automatically automatic.)

The storage class of a variable is determined by where it is defined and by what keyword, if any, is used.

The storage class determines two things. First, it controls which functions have access to a variable. The extent to which a variable is available is called its "scope." Secondly, the storage class determines how long the variable persists in memory. Let's go over the properties of each type.

Automatic Variables

By default, variables declared in a function are automatic. You can, however, make your intentions perfectly clear by explicitly using the keyword **auto:**

```
main()
{
  auto int plox;
```

You might do this, for example, to show that you intentionally are overriding an external function definition.

An automatic variable has local scope. Only the function in which the variable is defined knows the variable. (Of course, arguments can be used to communicate the value and the address of the variable to another function, but that is partial and indirect knowledge.) Other functions can use variables with the same name, but they will be independent variables stored in different memory locations.

An automatic variable comes into existence when the function which contains it is called. When the function finishes its task and returns control to its caller, the automatic variable disappears. The memory location can now be used for something else.

One more point about the scope of an automatic variable: the scope is confined to the block (paired braces) in which the variable is declared. We have always declared our variables at the beginning of the function block, so the scope is the whole function. But in principle one could declare a variable within a sub-block. Then that variable would be known only to that subsection of the function. Normally, you wouldn't use this feature when designing a program. However, sometimes harried programmers use this option when trying to make a quick fix.

External Variables

A variable defined outside a function is external. An external variable also should be declared in a function that uses it by using the **extern** keyword. Declarations look like this:

```
int errupt;  /* 3 externally defined variables */
char coal;
double up;
main()
{
  extern int errupt;  /* declaring that 3 variables are */
  extern char coal;   /*      defined externally        */
  extern double up;
```

The group of **extern** declarations may be omitted entirely if the original definitions occur in the same file and before the function that uses them. Including the **extern** keyword allows a function to use an external variable even if it is defined later in a file or in a different file. (Both files, of course, have to be compiled, linked, or assembled at the same time.)

If just the **extern** is omitted from the declaration in a function, then a separate, automatic variable is set up by that name. You may want to label this second variable "auto" to show that this is a matter of intention and not of oversight.

These three examples show the four possible combinations:

```
 /* Example 1 */
int hocus;
main()
{
   extern int hocus;  /* hocus declared external */
    . . .
}
magic()
```

```
{
   extern int hocus;
    . . .
}
```

Here there is one external variable **hocus,** and it is known to both **main( )** and **magic( ).**

```
 /*Example 2 */
int hocus;
main()
{
   extern int hocus;  /* hocus declared external */
    . . .
}
magic()
{
  /* hocus not declared at all */
    . . .
}
```

Again, there is one external variable **hocus** known to both functions. This time, **magic( )** knows it by default.

```
 /* Example 3 */
int hocus;
main()
{
  int hocus; /* hocus declared, is auto by default */
    . . .
}
magic()
{
   auto int hocus; /* hocus declared automatic */
    . . .
}
```

In this case, three separate variables are created. The **hocus** in **main( )** is automatic by default and is local to **main.** The **hocus** in **magic( )** is automatic explicitly and is known only to **magic( ).** The external **hocus** is not known to **main( )** or **magic( ),** but would be known to any other function in the file that did not have its own local **hocus.**

These examples illustrate the scope of external variables. They persist as long as the program runs, and since they aren't confined to any one function, they don't fade away when a particular function ends its task.

Static Variables

The name sounds like a contradiction, like a variable that can't vary. Actually, the "static" means the variable stays put. These variables have the same scope as automatic variables, but they don't vanish when the containing function ends its job. The computer remembers their values from one function call to the next. The next example illustrates this point and shows how to declare a static variable.

```
 /* static variable */
main()
{
   int count;

   for (count = 1; count <= 3; count++)
       {
       printf("Here comes iteration %d:\n", count);
       trystat();
       }
}
trystat()
{
  int fade = 1;
  static int stay = 1;

  printf("fade = %d and stay = %d\n", fade++, stay++);
}
```

Note that **trystat( )** increments each variable after printing its value. Running this program gives this output:

```
Here comes iteration 1:
fade = 1 and stay = 1
Here comes iteration 2:
fade = 1 and stay = 2
Here comes iteration 3:
fade = 1 and stay = 3
```

The static variable **stay** remembers that its value was increased by 1, while the **fade** variable starts anew each time. This points out a difference in initialization: **fade** is initialized each time **trystat( )** is called, while **stay** is initialized just once, when **trystat( )** is compiled.

External Static Functions

You can also declare a **static** variable outside any function. This act creates an "external static" function. The difference between an ordinary external variable and an external static variable is the scope. The ordinary external variable can be used by functions in any file, while the external static variable can be used only by functions in the same file and below the variable definition. You set up an external static variable by placing the definition outside any function:

```
static randx = 1;
rand()
{
```

In just a bit we will show you an example for which you need this sort of variable.

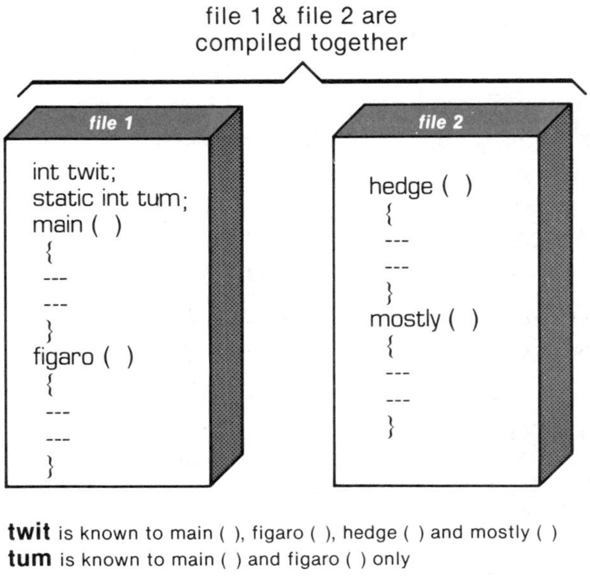
file 1 & file 2 are
compiled together
file 1
int twit;
static int tum;
main ( )
{

}
figaro ( )
{

}
file 2
hedge ( )
{

}
mostly ( )
{

}
twit is known to main ( ), figaro ( ), hedge ( ) and mostly ( )
tum is known to main ( ) and figaro ( ) only

Figure 10.1
External vs external static

Register Variables

Variables normally are stored in computer memory. With luck, register variables are stored in the CPU registers, where they can be accessed and manipulated more rapidly than in memory. In other respects, register variables are the same as automatic variables. They are set up this way:

```
main()
{
    register int quick;
```

We say "with luck," for declaring a variable as register class is more a request than a direct order. The compiler has to weigh your demands against the number of registers that are available, so you may not get your wish. In that case, the variable becomes an ordinary automatic variable.

Which Storage Class?

The answer to that question almost always is "automatic." After all, why else was it selected as the default? Yes, we know that at first glance external storage is quite alluring. Just make all your variables external, and you'll never have to worry about using arguments and pointers to communicate back and forth between functions. Unfortunately, you will have to worry about function A sneakily altering variables in function C although that was not your intention at all. The unquestionable evidence of untold years of collective computer experience is that the latter danger far outweighs the superficial charms of using external storage extensively.

One of the golden rules of protective programming is to observe the "need to know" principle. Keep the workings of each function as private as possible, sharing values only as they are needed.

Since there are times when the other classes are useful, they are available. But ask yourself if it is necessary to use one before doing so.

SUMMARY: STORAGE CLASSES

I. Keywords: ***auto, external, static, register***

II. General Comments:

The storage class of a variable determines its scope and how long the variable persists. Storage class is determined by where the variable is defined and by the associated keyword. Variables defined outside a function are external and have global scope. Variables declared inside a function are automatic and local unless one of the other keywords is used. External variables defined above a function are known to it even if not declared internally.

III. Properties:

STORAGE CLASS	KEYWORD	DURATION	SCOPE
automatic	`auto`	temporary	local
register	`register`	temporary	local
static	`static`	persistent	local
external	`extern`	persistent	global (all files)
external static	`static`	persistent	global (one file)

Those above the dotted line are declared inside a function.
Those below the line are defined outside a function.

Now let's look at a function that makes use of an external static variable.

A RANDOM NUMBER FUNCTION

You should not be without a random number function. When someone demands a number of you, you can turn to this powerful resource instead of stammering a plea for more time. Less practically, you can use it in many computer games.

Actually, we will show you a "pseudo-random number generator." This means that the actual sequence of numbers is predictable (computers are not known for their spontaneity) but that they are spread pretty uniformly over the possible range of values.

The scheme starts with a number called the "seed." It uses the seed to produce a new number, which becomes the new seed. Then the new seed can be used to produce a newer seed, and so on. For this scheme to work, the random number function must remember the seed it used last time it was called. Aha! This calls for a static variable.

Here is version 1. (Yes, version 2 comes soon.)

```
 /* rand1 */
rand()
```

```
{
  static int randx = 1;

  randx = (randx * 25173 + 13849) % 65536; /* magic formula */
  return( randx);
}
```

The static variable **randx** starts out with the value 1 and is altered by the magic formula each time the function is called. The result on our system is a number somewhere in the range of −32768 to 32767. Systems with a different **int** size will produce different results.

Let's try it with this simple driver:

```
 /* randdrive1 */
main()
{
   int count;

   for(count = 1; count <= 5; count++)
        printf("%d\n", rand());
}
```

Here's the output:

```
-26514
-4449
20196
-20531
3882
```

Well, that looks random enough. Let's run it again. This time the result is

```
-26514
-4449
20196
-20531
3882
```

Hmmm, that looks familiar; this is the "pseudo" aspect. Each time the main program is run, we start off with the same seed of 1. We can get around this problem by introducing a second function **srand( )** that lets you reset the seed. The trick is to make **randx** an external static variable known only to **rand( )** and **srand( ).** Keep these two functions in their own file and compile that file separately. Here is the modification:

```
 /* file for rand() and srand() */
static int randx = 1;
rand()
{
  randx = (randx *25173 + 13849) % 65536;
  return( randx);
}
srand(x)
unsigned x;
{
   randx = x;
}
```

Use this driver:

```
 /* randdrive2 */
main()
{
   int count;
   int seed;

   printf("Please enter your choice for seed.\n");
   scanf("%d", &seed);
   srand(seed);    /* reset seed */
   for(count = 1; count <= 5; count++)
        printf("%d\n", rand());
}
```

Run the program once:

```
Please enter your choice for seed.
1
-26514
-4449
20196
-20531
3882
```

Using a value of 1 for **seed** yields the same values as before. Now let's try a value of 2:

```
Please enter your choice for seed.
2
23832
20241
-1858
-30417
-16204
```

Very good! We get a different set of numbers. Now let's develop a use for this set of functions.

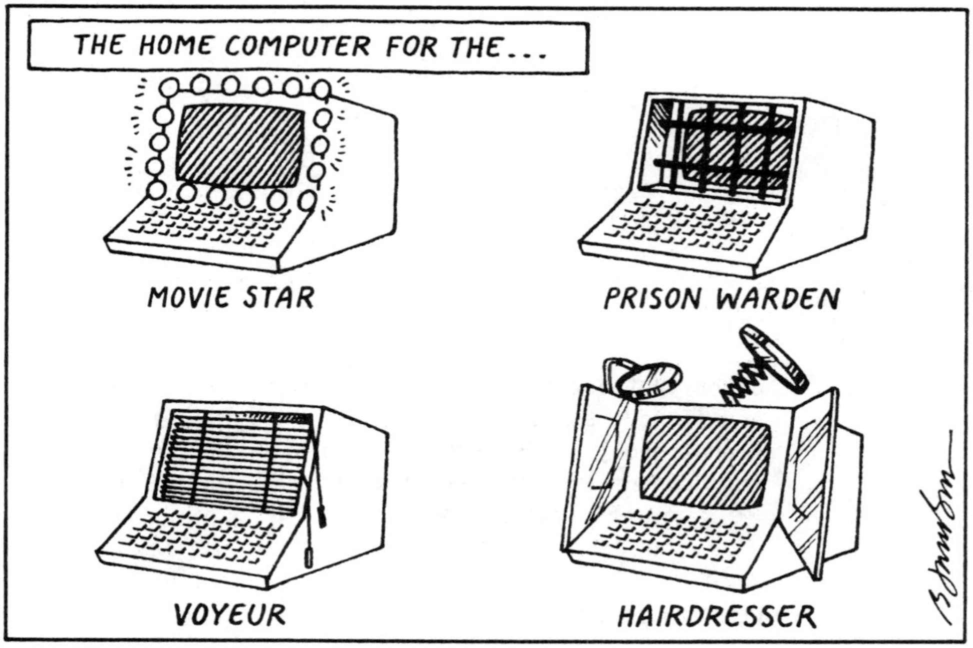

ROLL 'EM

We are going to simulate that very popular random activity, dice-rolling. The most popular form of dice rolling uses two six-sided dice. But there are other possibilities. Many adventure-fantasy game players use all of the five geometrically possible dice: 4 sides, 6 sides, 8 sides, 12 sides, and 20 sides. (Those clever ancient Greeks proved that there are but 5 regular solids having all faces the same shape and size, and these solids are the bases for the dice varieties. One could make dice with other numbers of sides, but the faces would not all be the same, so they wouldn't all have equal odds of turning up.)

Computer calculations aren't limited by these geometric considerations, and we will devise an electronic die that can have any number of side we want. Let's start with 6 sides, then generalize. We want a random number from 1 to 6, but *rand( )* produces the range −32768 to 32767, so we have some adjustments to make. Here's one approach.

1. Divide the random number by 32768. This results in a number x in the range $-1 <= x < 1$. (We'll have to convert to type *float* so that we can have decimal fractions.)
2. Add 1. Our new number satisfies the relationship $0 <= x < 2$.
3. Divide by 2. Now $0 <= x < 1$.
4. Multiply by 6. Now $0 <= x < 6$. (Close, but 0 is not a possible value.)
5. Add 1: $1 <= x < 7$. (Note: these are still decimal fractions.)
6. Truncate to an integer. Now we have an integer in the range of 1 to 6.
7. To generalize, just replace 6 in step 4 by the number of sides.

Here is a function that does these steps:

```
 /* dice roller */
#define SCALE 32768.0
rollem(sides)
float sides;
{
   float roll;

   roll = ( (float) rand()/SCALE + 1.0) * sides / 2.0 + 1.0;
   return ( (int) roll);
}
```

We included two explicit type casts to emphasize where type conversions take place.

Now for a program that uses these tools:

```
 /* multiple dice roll */
main()
```

```
{
  int dice, count, roll, seed;
  float sides;

  printf("Enter a seed value.\n");
  scanf("%d", &seed);
  srand(seed);
  printf("Enter the number of sides per die, 0 to stop.\n");
  scanf("%f", &sides);
  while (sides > 0)
      {
      printf("How many dice?\n");
      scanf("%d", &dice);
      for ( roll = 0, count = 1; count <= dice; count ++)
          roll += rollem(sides); /* running total of dice pips */
      printf("You have rolled a %d using %d %.0f-sided dice.\n",
                   roll, dice, sides);
      printf("How many sides? Enter 0 to stop.\n");
      scanf("%f", &sides);
      }
  printf("GOOD FORTUNE TO YOU!\n");
}
```

Now let's use it:

```
Enter a seed value.
1
Enter the number of sides per die, 0 to stop.
6
How many dice?
2
You have rolled a 4 using 2 6-sided dice.
How many sides? Enter 0 to stop.
6
How many dice?
2
You have rolled a 7 using 2 6-sided dice.
How many sides? Enter 0 to stop.
0
GOOD FORTUNE TO YOU!
```

Thanks.

You can use **rollem( )** many ways. With **sides** equal to two, the function simulates a coin toss with "heads" = 2 and "tails" = 1 (or vice versa if you really prefer it). You can easily modify the program to show the individual results as well as the total. Or you can construct a craps simulator. If you require a large number of rolls (a dread Dungeon Master rolling character attributes) you can easily modify our program to produce output like this:

```
Enter a seed value.
10
Enter the number of sets; enter 0 to stop.
18
How many sides and how many dice?
6 3
Here are 18 sets of 3 6-sided throws.
  7    5    9    7   12   10    7   12   10   14
  9    8   13    9   10    7   16   10
How many sets? Enter 0 to stop.
0
```

Another use of **rand( )** (but not of **rollem( )**) would be to modify our number-guessing program so that the computer chooses and you guess instead of vice versa.

Now let's develop some more functions. Our first project will be to design a function that reads integers.

AN INTEGER-FETCHING FUNCTION : *getint( )*

Perhaps this strikes you as a rather simple project. After all, we can just use **scanf( )** with the **%d** format if we want to read in an integer. But this lazy approach has one big drawback. If you mistakenly type, say, a T instead of a 6, **scanf( )** will try to interpret the T as an integer. We want to design a function that looks at the input and warns you if it is not an integer. Now, perhaps, our project seems less simple. Don't fret, however, because we are off to a good start: we have a name for our new function. We will call it **getint( )**.

A Plan

Fortunately, we also have a strategy in mind. First, we note that any input can be read in as a string of characters. The integer 324, for example, can be read in as a string of three characters: the character **'3'**, the character **'2'**, and the character **'4'**. This suggests the following plan:

1. Read the input in as a character string.
2. See if the string consists just of digit characters, preceded, perhaps, by a plus or minus sign.
3. If so, convert it to the correct numerical value.
4. If not, issue a warning.

This plan is so clever, it should work. (The fact that it is a standard approach that has been around for years also gives us some confidence.) But before we plunge into writing the code, we should think more about what our function will do.

In particular, before we start fussing about the innards of **getint( ),** we should decide exactly how the function should interact with its environment: what the information flow will be. What information should it get from the calling program? What information should it give back? In what form should this information be? Once again we are looking at the function as a black box. Our first concern is what goes in and what goes out; after that we worry about what is inside. This approach helps produce a much smoother interaction between different parts of a program. Otherwise, you might find yourself in the position of trying to install a Volvo transmission in a Toyota. The general function is correct, but the interface is a problem.

Information Flow for getint( )

What output should our function have? It should surely give the value of the number it reads. Of course, **scanf( )** already does that. Secondly—and this is why we are taking the time to create this function—it should provide a status report. It should tell us whether or not it found an integer. To make the function really useful, it should also tell us if it finds an EOF character. Then we could use **getint( )** in a **while** loop that keeps reading integers until it finds an EOF character. In short, we want **getint( )** to return two values: the integer and the status.

Since we want two items of information, we can't use just a **return.** We could use two pointers. However, the common solution for this sort of problem is to use pointers to do the main work of the function and to use **return** to send back some sort of status code. Indeed, **scanf( )** does just this. It returns the numbers of items it has found, and it returns the EOF character if that's what it found. We just haven't used that feature, but we could by using a call of this form:

```
status = scanf("%d", &number);
```

We will follow that model. Our function call would look like this:

```
status = getint(&number);
```

The right-hand side uses the address of **number** to get a value to **number,** and **return** is used to get a value to **status.**

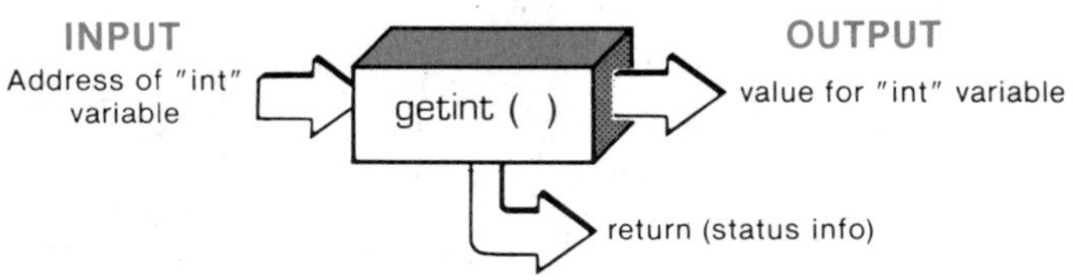

Figure 10.2
Designing the *getint( )* function

We have to decide on a code for the status report. Since undeclared functions are assumed to be type **int,** our code should consist of integers. Let's use this code for the status report:

−1 means an EOF character was found
1 means a string containing nondigits was found
0 means a digit string was found

In short, our **getint( )** function has one input, the address of the integer variable whose value is being read. It has two outputs. First, the value of the read integer is provided through a pointer. (Thus, the pointer argument is a two-way channel for information.) Second, a status code is provided by using **return.** This tells us the skeleton of our function should look like this:

```
getint(ptint)
int *ptint;     /* pointer to integer */
{
   int status;
    . . .
   return(status);
}
```

Great! Now we just have to fill in the interior of the function.

Inside *getint( )*

Our general plan, in rough pseudocode, for **getint( )** is this:

```
read in the input as characters
while no EOF is encountered, place the characters
   into a character string
if EOF is encountered, set status to STOP
else
   check string, covert to integer if possible, and
   report status (YESNUM or NONUM)
```

Here we use STOP, YESNUM, and NONUM as symbolic constants representing the −1, 0, and 1 described above.

We still have some design decisions to make. How does the function decide when it reaches the end of the input string? Should we put a limit on how long the string should be?

We enter a region where we have to decide between the convenience of the programmer and the convenience of the user. The simplest thing would be to have the user terminate a string by using the [enter] key. This would mean one entry per line. On the other hand, it would be nice for the user if she could place several numbers on the same line:

```
2   34   4542   2   98
```

We decided to give the user a break. The function will consider a string to begin with a nonblank, nonnewline character and to end when the next blank or newline is encountered. Thus input can be on one line or several lines.

We'll limit the input string to 80 characters. Since strings are terminated with a null character, we will need an array of 81 characters to include the null. This is stupendously generous, since we only need 6 characters for a 16-bit integer and sign. You can enter longer numbers, but they will be cut down to size.

To make the program more modular, we'll delegate the actual conversion to another function, which we will call **stoi( )** for "string to integer." We also will have **stoi( )** return the proper status code to **getint( )**, and **getint( )** then can relay the status to its calling program. The function **stoi( )** will perform the last two lines of our pseudocode plan.

Fig. 10.3 presents the code for **getint( ); stoi( )** will follow later:

```
/*  getint()  */
#include <stdio.h>
#define LEN 81     /* maximum length of string  */
#define STOP -1  /* status codes */
#define NONUM 1
#define YESNUM 0
getint(ptint)
int *ptint;        /* pointer to integer output */
{
   char intarr[LEN]; /* store input string */
   int  ch;
   int ind = 0; /* array index */

   while ((ch = getchar()) == '\n' || ch == ' ' || ch == '\t');
          /* skip over initial newlines, blanks, and tabs */
   while ( ch != EOF && ch != '\n' && ch != ' ' && ind < LEN)
        {
        intarr[ind++] = ch;  /* put character into array  */
        ch = getchar();      /* get next character */
        }
   intarr[ind] = '\0';  /* end array with null character */
   if (ch == EOF)
     return(STOP);
   else
      return ( stoi(intarr, ptint) );  /* does conversion */
}
```

Figure 10.3
Code for *getint ( )*

We get a character **ch.** If it is a blank or newline or a tab, we get the next character until we get one that isn't. Then, if it isn't an EOF, we put it in an array. We keep getting more characters and putting them in until we find a forbidden character or until we reach the size limit. Then we place a null character (**'\0'**) in the next position of the array to mark the end of the string. This puts the array into standard character string form. If an EOF was the last character read, return **STOP;** otherwise go and try convert the string. Here we invoke the new function **stoi( )** to do the job. What does **stoi( )** do? As input it takes a character string and a pointer to an integer variable. It will use the pointer to assign a value to the variable itself. It will use **return** to send a status report back, which **getint( )** then relays to **getarray( ).** Wow! a double play.

A less compact way to represent the use of **stoi( )** is this:

```
status = stoi(intarr, ptint);
 return (status);
```

Here **status** would be an **int** variable. The first statement gives a value to whatever **ptint** points to, and it also assigns a value to **status.** The second statement returns the value to the program that called **getint( ).** Our single program line has exactly the same effect, except that no intermediate variable **status** was needed.

Now we need to write **stoi( ),** and we will be done.

String-to-Integer Conversion: *stoi( )*

First, let's describe what input and output this function should have. The input will be a character string, so **stoi( )** will have a character string argument. There will be two output values: the status and the integer conversion. We are using **return** for the status, so we will have to use a pointer to return the other value. Thus there will be a second argument, a pointer-to-integer. Our function skeleton will look like this:

```
stoi(string, intptr)
char string[]; /* input string */
int *intptr; /* pointer to variable getting integer value */
{
   int status;
    . . .
   return(status);
}
```

Okay, what about an algorithm for making the conversion? Let's ignore the sign for a moment and assume the string has only digits in it. Look at the first character and convert it to its numerical equivalent. Suppose the character is **'4'.** This character has the ASCII numeric value 52, and that is how it is stored. If we subtract 48 from it, we get 4; that is,

'4' −48 = 4

But 48 is ASCII code for the character **'0'**, so

'4' − '0' = 4

In fact, this last statement would be true for any code that uses consecutive numbers to represent consecutive digits. So if **num** is the numerical value, and **chn** is a digit character, then

```
num = chn - '0';
```

Okay, we use this technique to convert the first digit to a number. Now we look at the next array member. If it is **'\0'**, then there was only one digit, and we are done. Suppose, though, it is a **'3'**. We convert this to the numerical value 3. But if it is a 3, then the 4 must have been 40, and the total is 43:

```
num = 10 * num + chn - '0';
```

Now just continue this process, multiplying the old value of **num** by 10 every time we find one more digit. Our function will use this technique.

Here is the definition of **stoi( ).** We keep it in the same file as **getint( )** so that it can use the same #**define**'s.

```
  /* converts string to integer and makes status report */
stoi(string, intptr)
char string[];   /* string to be converted to an integer */
int *intptr;       /* value of the integer */
{
   int sign = 1;              /* keep track of + or - */
   int index = 0;

   if ( string[index] == '-' || string[index] == '+' )
       sign = (string[index++] == '-') ? -1 : 1; /* set sign */
   *intptr = 0;  /* initialize value */
   while ( string[index] >= '0' && string[index] <= '9')
       *intptr = 10 * (*intptr) + string[index++] - '0';
   if ( string[index] == '\0')
       {
       *intptr = sign * ( *intptr );
       return(YESNUM);
       }
```

```
        else  /* found a nondigit other than sign or '\0' */
            return(NONUM);
    }
```

The **while** statement jogs along, converting digits to numbers until it reaches a nondigit character. If that character is a **'\0'** character, all is fine, because that marks the end of the string. Any other nondigit sends the program flow to the **else** to report failure.

The standard C library contains a function **atoi( )** (ASCII to integer) very much like **stoi( ).** The main differences are that **stoi( )** checks for nondigital strings, that **atoi( )** uses **return** instead of a pointer to give back the number, and that **atoi( )** does the blank skipping we did in **getint( ).** We could have done all the status checking in **getint( )** and used **atoi( )** instead of **stoi( ),** but we thought it would be more fun to develop our own approach.

Trying It Out

Is our logic as sound as we think? Let's try out our function in a sample program:

```
 /* getint() tryout */
#define STOP -1
#define NONUM 1
#define YESNUM 0
main()
{
  int num, status;

  printf("This program stops reading numbers if EOF is read.\n");
  while ( (status = getint(&num)) != STOP )
       if (status == YESNUM)
          printf("The number %d has been accepted.\n", num);
       else
          printf("That was no integer! Try again.\n");
  printf("That's it.\n");
}
```

Here is a sample run.

```
This program stops reading numbers if EOF is read.
100     -23
```

```
The number 100 has been accepted.
The number -23 has been accepted.
    +892
The number 892 has been accepted.
wonk
That was no integer! Try again.
23skidoo
That was no integer! Try again.
775
The number 775 has been accepted.
[control z]          (sends the EOF character on our system)
 That's it.
```

As you can see, it works. Notice how we were able to set up a loop to read integers indefinitely until an EOF is typed. That is a handy feature.

Are there any bugs? There is at least one. If you follow a number directly with an EOF without an intervening blank or newline character, the input phase stops, ignoring that number:

```
706 EOF        /* 706 is accepted  */
706EOF         /* 706 not accepted */
```

We didn't want to make the example too complicated, so we let this bug pass. Also, this gives us a chance to say that further development is left as an exercise for the reader.

Now that we have a handy function for fetching integers, let's turn to a new project that will use it.

SORTING NUMBERS

One of the most common tests for a computer is sorting. Here we'll develop a program to sort integers. Again, let's take a black box approach and think in terms of input and output. Our overall plan, shown in the Fig. 10.4, is pretty simple.

At this point, the program is still too vaguely defined to code. The next step is to identify the main tasks the program must do to accomplish our goals. We can break down our example to three main tasks:

1. read in the numbers
2. sort them
3. print out the sorted numbers

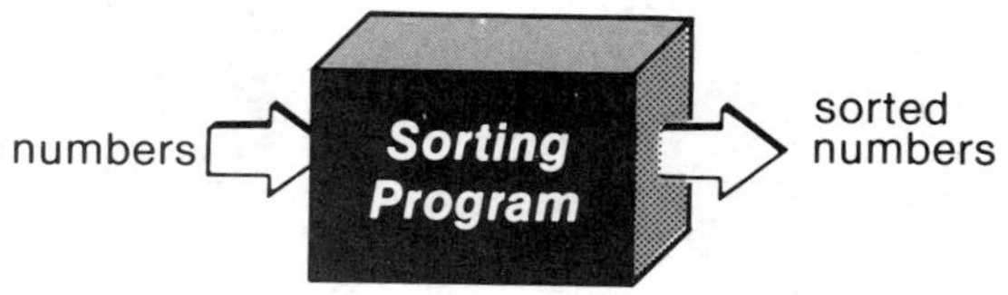

Figure 10.4
Sorting program: a black box view.

The next figure shows this breakdown as we move from this top level of organization down to a more detailed level of organization.

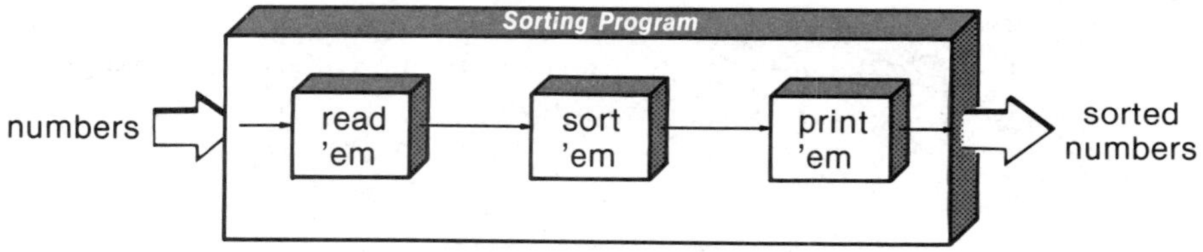

Figure 10.5
Sorting program: peeking inside.

Now we have three black boxes, each with its own input and output. We could assign each part to a different programming team, providing we make sure that the numbers output by "read 'em" are in the same form that "sort 'em" uses for input.

As you can see, we are emphasizing modularity. We have broken the original problem into three smaller, more manageable problems.

What next? Now we apply our efforts to each of the three boxes separately, breaking them down to simpler units until we reach a point at which the code is obvious. As we do this, we pay attention to these important points: data-form choice, error trapping, and information flow.

Let's continue with our example, tackling the reading section first.

Reading In Numeric Data

Many programs involve reading in numbers, so the ideas we develop here will be useful elsewhere. The general form for this part of the program is clear: use a loop to read in numbers until all the numbers are read. But there is more to it than you might think!

Choosing the Data Representation

How do we represent a bunch of numbers? We could use a bunch of variables, one for each number. That is just too much trouble to even think about. We could use an array, one element for each number. That sounds a lot better, so let's use an array.

But what kind of array? Type **int?** Type **double?** We need to know how the program is going to be used. Let's assume it is to be used with integers. (What if it is to be used with both? That's possible, but more work than we want right now.) We will use an array of integers to store the numbers we read.

Ending Input

How will the program know how many numbers to read? In Chapter 8 we discussed several solutions to this problem, most of which were unsatisfactory. Now that we have **getint( ),** however, there is no problem. Here is one approach:

```
read a number
while not EOF
   assign it to an array and
   read the next number if the array isn't full
```

Note that there are two separate conditions that bring this section of the program to a close: an EOF signal or filling the array.

Further Considerations

Before we set this into C code, we still have decisions to make. What will we do about error checking? Should we make this part of the program into a function?

By the first question we mean, what do we do about the possibility of the user entering faulty data, say a letter instead of an integer? Without **getint( ),** we would rely upon the "perfect user theory," which states that the user makes no entry errors. However, we recognize that this theory may not apply to users other than ourselves. Fortunately, we can use **getint( )**'s status report feature to help out here.

The programming that is left can easily be fit into **main( ).** However, it is more modular to use a separate function for each of the three major parts of the program, so that is what we will do. The input to this function will be numbers from the keyboard or a file, and the function output will be an array containing the unsorted numbers. It would be nice if the function let the main program know how many numbers were read, so let's make that part of the output, too. Finally, we should try to make it a little user-friendly, so we will have it print a message indicating its limits, and we will have it echo its input.

main( ) and *getarray( )*

Let's call our reading function **getarray( ).** We have defined the function in terms of input and output, and we have outlined the scheme in pseudocode. Let's write the function now and show how it fits into the main program.

First we give **main( ):**

```
 /* sort1 */
#define MAXSIZE  100  /* limit to number of integers to sort */
main()
{
  int numbers[MAXSIZE]; /* array to hold input */
  int size;             /* number of input items */

  size = getarray(numbers, MAXSIZE); /* put input into array */
  sort(numbers, size);      /* sort the array */
  print(numbers, size);     /* print the sorted array */
}
```

Here we have the overall view of the program. The function **getarray( )** places the input into the array **numbers** and reports back how many values were read in; that value is assigned to **size.** Then **sort( )** and **print( ),** which we have yet to write, sort the array and print the results. Giving them **size** makes their jobs easier and saves them from having to do their own counting. Also, we provide **getarray( )** with **MAXSIZE,** which tells it how big an array it has available for storage.

Now that we are adding **size** to the information flow, we should modify our black box sketch. See Fig. 10.6.

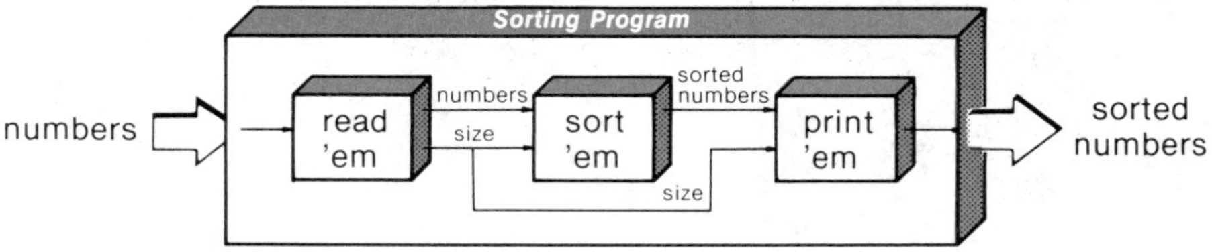

Figure 10.6
Sorting program: adding details.

Now let's look at **getarray( )** in Fig. 10.7:

```
  /* getarray() using getint()  */
#define STOP -1     /* EOF status  */
#define NONUM 1     /* nondigit string status */
#define YESNUM 0    /* digit string status */
getarray( array, limit)
int array[], limit;
{
  int num, status;
  int index = 0;    /* array index */

  printf("This program stops reading numbers after %d values\n",
          limit);
  printf("or if an EOF character is entered.\n");
  while(  index < limit && (status = getint(&num)) != STOP )
     { /* stops reading at size limit or at EOF */
     if ( status == YESNUM)
          {
          array[index++] = num;
          printf("The number %d has been accepted.\n", num);
          }
     else if ( status == NONUM)
          printf("That was no integer! Try again.\n");
     else
          printf("This can't happen! Something's very wrong.\n");
     }
```

```
    if ( index == limit )  /* report if array gets filled */
        printf("All %d elements of the array were filled.\n",
                  limit);
       return(index);
}
```

This is a substantial chunk of program, and we have quite a few points to note.

Explanation

Since it is a little difficult to remember the meaning of, say, a −1 code, we have used mnemonic symbolic constants to represent the status codes.

Using these codes, we set up **getarray( )** to handle each of the possible status values. A **STOP** status causes the reading cycle to end when **getint( )** finds an EOF lurking in its path. A **YESNUM** status results in the number being stored in the awaiting array. Also, the number is "echoed" back to the user to let her know it was accepted. A **NONUM** status sends the user back for another try. (That's being neighborly.)

But there is one more **else** statement. Logically, the only way that statement can be reached is if **getint( )** returns a value other than −1, 0, or 1. But those are the only values that can be returned, so this seems to be a useless statement. Why include it? We include it as an example of "defensive programming," the art of protecting a program from future fiddling. Someday, we, or someone else, may decide to go into **getint( )** and add a few more possible status values to its repertoire. Most likely we will have forgotten, and they may never have known, that **getarray( )** assumes that there are just three possible responses. So we include this final **else** to trap any new responses that show up, and that will make future debugging that much simpler.

The size of the array is established in **main( ).** Therefore we don't give the size of the array when we declare the array argument in **getarray( ).** We do, however, include the brackets in order to point out that the argument is an array.

```
int numbers[MAXSIZE];  /* give size in main */
int array[]; /* no size specification in called function */
```

We'll discuss the use of arrays in functions in Chapter 12.

We decided to use the keyword **return** to communicate back the number of items read. Thus our function call

```
size = getarray(numbers, MAXSIZE);
```

assigns a value to **size** and gives values to the **numbers** array.

You may be wondering why we didn't use pointers in the call

```
size = getarray (numbers, MAXSIZE);
```

After all, we are having the function change the value of something (the array) in the calling program. The answer is, we did use a pointer! In C, the name of an array is also a pointer to the first element of an array, that is:

```
numbers == &numbers[0]
```

When **getarray( )** sets up the array **array,** the address of **array[0]** is the same as the address of **numbers[0],** and so on for the other subscripts. Thus all the manipulations that **getarray( )** does to **array[ ]** actually get done to **numbers[ ].** We will talk more about the relation between pointers and arrays in Chapter 12. The main point we need to know now is that if we use an array as a function argument, the function affects the array in the calling program.

In functions involving counters and limits, like this one, the most likely place to find errors is at the "boundary conditions," where counts reach their limits. Are we going to read a maximum of **MAXSIZE** numbers, or are we going to be off by one? We need to pay attention to details such as **++index** vs. **index++** and < vs <=. We also have to keep in mind that arrays start their subscripting with **0,** not **1.** Check through our coding and see if it works as it should. The easiest thing to do is to imagine that **limit** is **1** and then walk through the procedure step by step.

Often the most difficult part of a program is getting it to interact in a convenient and dependable manner with the user. That is the case with this program. Now that we have gotten through **getarray( ),** we will find **sort( )** to be easier and **print( )** easier yet. Let's move on to **sort( )** now.

Sorting the Data

Let's look at **main( )** again:

Spot Illustration 10.2

```
main()
{
 int numbers[MAXSIZE]; /* array to hold input */
 int size;             /* number of input items */

 size = getarray(numbers, MAXSIZE); /* put input into array */
 sort(numbers, size);     /* sort the array */
 print(numbers, size);  /* print the sorted array */
}
```

We see that the input to **sort( )** is an array of integers to be sorted and a count of the number of elements to be sorted. The output is the array containing the sorted numbers. We still haven't decided how to do the sorting, so we have to refine this description further.

One obvious point to decide is the direction of the sort. Are we going to sort from large to small or vice versa? Again, we'll be arbitrary and say we will sort from large to small. (We could make a program to do either, but then we would have to develop a way to tell the program which choice we want.)

Now let's consider the method we will use to sort. Many sorting algorithms have been developed for computers; we'll use one of the simplest.

Here is our plan in pseudocode:

for n = first to n = next-to-last element find largest remaining number and place it in the nth element

It works like this. First, n = 1. We look through the whole array, find the largest number, and place it in the first element. Then n = 2, and we look through all but the first element of the array, find the largest remaining number, and place it in the second element. We continue this process until we reach the next-to-last element. Now just two elements are left. We compare them and place the larger in the next-to-last position. This leaves the smallest element of all in the final position.

This looks like a **for** loop task, but we still have to describe the "find and place" process in more detail. How do we find the largest remaining number each time? Here is one way. Compare the first and second elements of the remaining array. If the second is larger, switch the two values. Now compare the first element with the third. If the third is larger, switch those two. Each time the larger element floats to the top. Continue this way until you have compared the first with the last element. When you finish, the largest number is now in the first element of the remaining array. In essence, we have sorted the array for the first element, but the rest of the array is in a jumble. In pseudocode:

for n = second element to last element compare nth element with first element; if nth is greater, swap values

This looks like another **for** loop. It will be nested in the first **for** loop. The outer loop indicates which array element is to be filled, and the inner loop finds the value to put there. Putting the two parts of the pseudocode together and translating it into C, we get the following function:

```
 /* sorts an integer array in decreasing order */
sort(array, limit)
int array[], limit;
{
    int top, search;

    for ( top = 0 ; top < limit -1 ; top++)
         for ( search = top + 1; search < limit; search++)
               if ( array[search] > array[top]
                    interchange( &array[search], &array[top] );
}
```

Here we were clever enough to remember that the first element has **0** for a subscript. Also, we recalled that we developed a swapping function in Chapter 9, so we have used it here. Since **interchange( )** works on two elements of an array and not the whole array, we have used the addresses of just the two concerned elements. (While the name **array** is a pointer to the array as a whole, you need to use the **&** operator to point to individual members.)

We used **top** as the subscript for the array element that is to be filled, since it is at the top of the unsorted part of the array. The **search** index roams over the array below the current **top** element. Most texts use **i** and **j** for these indices, but that makes it harder to see what is happening.

This algorithm sometimes is called a "bubble sort" because the larger values slowly percolate to the top.

Now we just have **print( )** to write.

Printing the Data

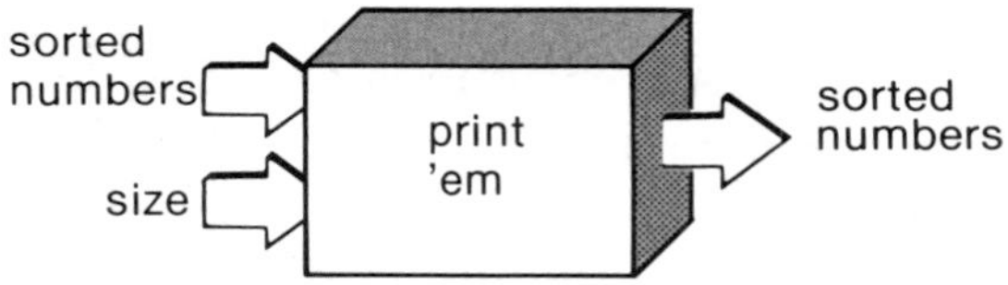

This one is pretty simple:

```
 /* print an array */
print(array, limit)
int array[], limit;
{
   int index;

   for ( index = 0; index <= limit; index++)
       printf("%d\n", array[index]);
}
```

If we want something a little different, such as printing in rows instead of in one column, we can always come back and change this function, leaving the other functions untouched. Similarly, if we found a sorting algorithm we liked better, we could replace that module. That is one of the nice points about a modular program.

Results

Let's compile and test this package. To make checking the boundary conditions simpler, we'll temporarily change **MAXSIZE** to 5.

For our first test, we will feed the program numbers until it refuses to take more.

```
This program stops reading numbers after 5 values
or if an EOF character is entered.
12 34 54 23 67
All 5 elements of the array were filled.
67
54
34
23
12
```

Good, it stopped when 5 numbers were read, and it sorted the results. Now we test to see if it stops when an EOF character is met.

```
This program stops reading numbers after 5 values
or if an EOF character is entered.
 456 928
-23 +16
[control-z]        (transmits EOF on our system)
928
456
16
-23
```

Faster than you can say "oikology is the science of housekeeping," the whole enormous array is sorted.

Success! It wasn't easy, but it wasn't impossible. By breaking the problem down into smaller parts and by thinking about what information should flow into and out of each part, we reduced the problem to manageable proportions. Furthermore, the individual modules we produced could be used as parts of similar programs.

That concludes our examples for this chapter. Now let's step back and look at the lessons of this chapter.

OVERVIEW

What have we accomplished? On the practical side we developed a random-number generator and an integer-sorting program. In the process we developed a **getint( )** function that we can use in other programs. On the educational side we illustrated some general principles and concepts useful in designing programs.

The most fundamental point to note is that programs should be *designed* rather than evolve through some random process of growth, trial, and error. You should think carefully about the form and content of input and output for a program. You should break the program down into well-defined tasks, then program these tasks separately, but with an eye to how they interface with one another. The idea is to achieve modularity. When necessary, break a module into smaller modules. Use functions to enhance the modularity and clarity of the program.

When designing a program, try to anticipate what might go wrong, and then program accordingly. Use error trapping to steer around potential problems or, at least, to alert the user if a problem shows up. It's much better to give the user a second chance to enter data than to send the program crashing in ignominy.

When designing a function, first decide on how it will interact with the calling function. Decide what information flows in and what information flows out. What will the arguments be? Will you use pointers, or **return,** or both? Once you have these design parameters in mind, you can turn your attention to the mechanics of the function.

Put these ideas to use, and your programs will be more reliable and less prone to crashing. You will acquire a body of functions that you can use in other programs. Your programming will take less time. All in all, it seems like a good recipe for healthy programming.

Don't forget about storage classes. Variables can be defined outside of functions, in which case they are called external (or global) variables and are available to more than one function. Variables defined within a function are local to that function and are not known to other functions. When possible, use the automatic variety of local variables. This keeps variables in one function from being contaminated by the actions of other functions.

WHAT YOU SHOULD HAVE LEARNED

How to think of a function: a black box with information flow
What "error-checking" is and why it is good
One algorithm for sorting
How to have a function change an array: **function(array)**
How to convert a digit string to a number
The storage classes: **auto, extern, static,** and **register**
The scope of each storage class.
Which storage class to use: **auto,** mostly.

QUESTIONS AND ANSWERS

Questions

1. What might make our sorting algorithm inefficient?
2. How would you change the sorting routine to make it sort in increasing order instead of decreasing order?
3. Change **print( )** so that it prints 5 numbers per line.

4. How would you change **stoi( )** to handle strings that represent octal numbers?
5. Which functions know each variable in the following? Are there any errors?

```
  /* file 1 */
int daisy;
main()
{
int lily;
}
petal()
{
 extern int daisy, lily;
}
 /* file 2 */
static int lily;
int rose;
stem()
{
   int rose;
}
root()
{
  extern int daisy;
}
```

Answers

1. Suppose you are sorting 20 numbers. The method makes 19 comparisons to find the one largest number. Then it makes 18 comparisons to find the next largest. All the information it got during the first search is forgotten, except for which is largest. The second largest number may have been in the number 1 spot for a while, then got shuffled down to last. A lot of the comparisons made the first time through get repeated the second time through, and the third time, etc.
2. Replace **array[search]** > **array[top]** by

   array[search] < **array[top]**
3.
```
/* print an array */
print(array, limit)
int array[], limit;
{
   int index;

   for ( index = 0; index <= limit; index++)
```

```
        {
        printf("%10d ", array[index]);
        if (index % 5 == 4)
                printf("\n");
         }
    printf("\n");
}
```

4. First, limit the acceptable characters to the digits 0 through 7. Second, multiply by 8 instead of by 10 each time a new digit is detected.
5. **daisy** is known to **main( )** by default, and to **petal( )** and **root( )** because of the **extern** declaration. It is not known to **stem( )** because they are in different files.
   The first **lily** is local to **main:** the reference to **lily** in **petal( )** is an error because there is no external **lily** in either file.
   There is an external static **lily,** but it is known just to functions in the second file.
   The first, external **rose** is known to **root( ),** but **stem( )** has overridden it with its own local **rose.**

EXERCISES

1. Some users might be daunted by being asked to enter an EOF character.
   a. Modify **getarray( )** and its called functions so that a # character is used instead.
   b. Modify them so either an EOF or a # can be used.
2. Create a program that sorts **float** numbers.
3. Create a program that converts text of mixed lower case and upper case to upper case only.
4. Create a program that double spaces single-spaced text.

11

THE C PREPROCESSOR

In this chapter you will find

11. THE C PREPROCESSOR

CONCEPTS

Preprocessor directives
Symbolic constants
Macros and macro "functions"
Macro side effects
File inclusion
Conditional compilation

PREPROCESSOR DIRECTIVES

#define, #include, #undef, #if, #ifdef, #ifndef, #else, #endif

C was developed to meet the needs of working programmers, and working programmers like having a preprocessor. This useful aid looks at your program before it gets to the compiler (hence the term "preprocessor"), and, following your direction, replaces the symbolic abbreviations in your program with the directions they represent. It looks for other files you request. It can also alter the conditions of compilation. These words do not do justice to the true utility and value of the preprocessor, so let's turn to examples. Of course, with **#define** and **#include,** we have provided examples all along but now we can gather what we have learned in one place and add to it.

SYMBOLIC CONSTANTS: *#define*

The **#define** preprocessor directive, like all preprocessor directives, begins with a # symbol in the far left column. It can appear anywhere in the source file, and the definition holds from its place of appearance to the end of the file. We have used it heavily to define symbolic constants in our programs, but it has more range than that, as we will show. Here is an example that illustrates some of the possibilities and properties of the **#define** directive.

```
 /*  simple preprocessor examples */
#define TWO 2    /* you can use comments if you like */
#define MSG "The old grey cat sang a merry \
song."
 /* a backslash continues a definition to the next line */
#define FOUR  TWO*TWO
#define PX printf("X is %d.\n", x)
#define FMT  "X is %d.\n"
main()
{
   int x = TWO;

   PX;
   x = FOUR;
   printf( FMT, x);
   printf("%s\n", MSG);
   printf("TWO: MSG\n");
}
```

Each line has three parts. First comes the **#define** directive. Second comes our chosen abbreviation, known as a "macro" in the computer world. The macro must have no spaces in it. Finally, there is the string (called the "replacement string") that the macro represents. When the preprocessor finds an example of one of your macros within your program, it almost always replaces it with the replacement string. (There is one exception as we will show you in just a moment.) This process of going from a macro to a final replacement string is called "macro expansion." Note that we can insert comments in standard C fashion; they will be ignored by the preprocessor. Also, most systems allow you to use the backslash ('\') to extend a definition over more than one line.

Let's run our example and see how it works.

```
X is 2.
X is 4.
The old grey cat sang a merry song.
TWO: MSG
```

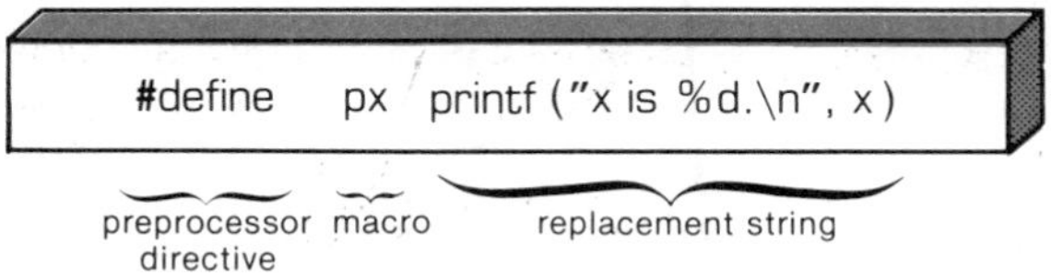

Figure 11.1
Parts of a macro definition.

Here's what happened. The statement

```
int x = TWO;
```
becomes
```
int x = 2;
```

as **2** is substituted for **TWO.** Then the statement

```
PX;
```
becomes
```
printf("X is %d.\n", x);
```

as that wholesale substitution is made. This is a new wrinkle, since up to now we've used macros only to represent constants. Here we see that a macro can express any string, even a whole C expression. Note, though, that this is a constant string; **PX** will print only a variable named **x.**

The next line also represents something new. You might think that **FOUR** is replaced by **4,** but the actual process is this:

```
x = FOUR;
```
becomes
```
x = TWO*TWO;
```
becomes
```
x = 2*2;
```

and ends there. The actual multiplication takes place not while the preprocessor works, but during compilation, for the C compiler evaluates all constant expressions (expressions with just constants). The preprocessor does no calculation; it just makes the suggested substitutions very literally.

Note that a macro definition can include other macros. (Some compilers do not support this "nesting" feature.)

In the next line

```
printf (FMT, x);
```
becomes
```
printf("X is %d.\n",x)
```

as **FMT** is replaced by the corresponding string. This approach could be handy if you had a lengthy control string you had to use several times.

In the next line **MSG** is replaced by the corresponding string. The quotes make the replacement string a character string constant; that is, once the program gets hold of it, it will be stored in an array terminated with a null character. Thus

`#define HAL 'Z'` defines a character constant, but
`#define HAP "Z"` defines a character string: `Z\0`

In general, wherever the preprocessor finds one of your macros in your program, it literally replaces it with the equivalent replacement string. If that string also contains macros, they, too, get replaced. The one exception to replacement is a macro found within double quotes. Thus,

```
printf("TWO: MSG");
```

prints **TWO: MSG** literally instead of printing

```
2: The old grey cat sang a merry song.
```

If you want this last line printed, you could use

```
printf("%d: %s\n", TWO, MSG);
```

for here the macros are outside the quotes.

When should you use symbolic constants? Probably you should use them for most numbers. If the number is some constant used in a calculation, a symbolic name makes its meaning clearer. If the number is an array size, a symbolic number makes it simpler to alter your program to handle a larger array. If the number is a system code for, say, the EOF character, a symbolic representation makes your program much more portable; just change one EOF definition. Mnemonic value, easy alterability, portability: these all make symbolic constants worthwhile.

Easy stuff, eh? Let's get more adventurous and look at the poor man's function, the macro with arguments.

USING ARGUMENTS WITH *#define*

A macro with arguments looks very much like a function since the arguments are enclosed within parentheses. Here are some examples which illustrate how such a "macro function" is defined and used. Some of the examples also point out possible pitfalls, so read them carefully.

```
  /* macros with arguments   */
#define SQUARE(x) x*x
```

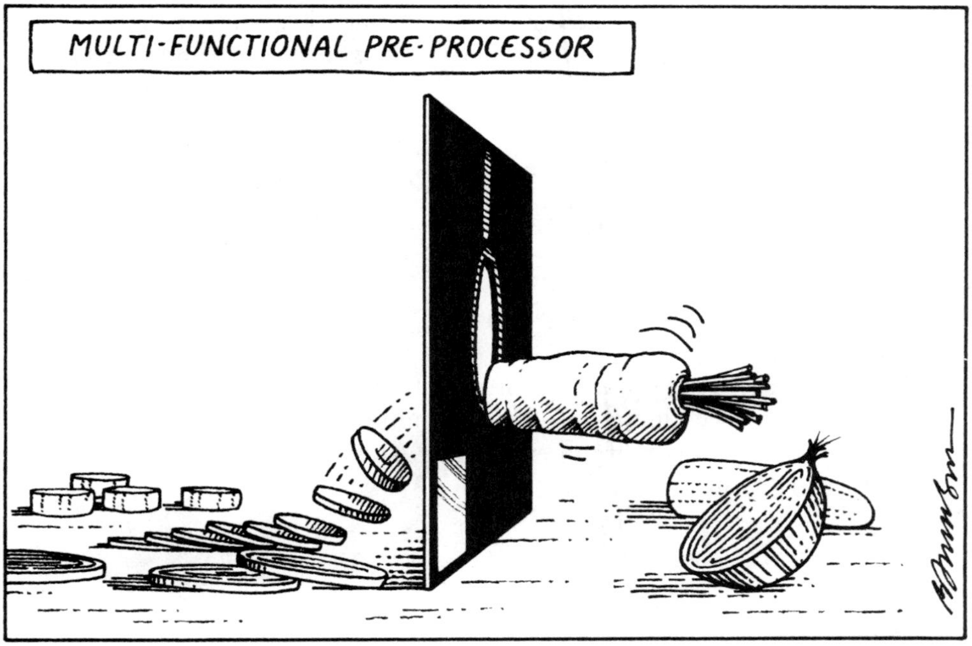


```
#define PR(x)   printf("x is %d.\n", x)
main()
{
     int x = 4;
     int z;

     z = SQUARE(x);
     PR(z);
     z = SQUARE(2);
     PR(z);
     PR(SQUARE(x));
     PR(SQUARE(x+2));
     PR(100/SQUARE(2));
     PR(SQUARE(++x));
}
```

Wherever **SQUARE(x)** appears in your program, it is replaced by **x*x.** What makes the difference from our earlier examples is that we are free to use symbols other than **x** when we use this macro. The **'x'** in the macro definition is replaced by the symbol used in the macro call in the program. Thus **SQUARE(2)** gets replaced by **2*2.** So the **x** really does act as an argument.

However, as we shall soon see, a macro argument does not work exactly like a function argument. Here are the results of running the program. Note that some of the answers are different from what you might expect.

```
z is 16.
z is 4.
SQUARE(x) is 16.
SQUARE(x+2) is 14.
100/SQUARE(2) is 100.
SQUARE(++x) is 30.
```

The first two lines are predictable. Notice, however, that even the **x** inside the double quotes of **PR**'s definition gets replaced by the corresponding argument. ALL arguments in the *definition* get replaced.

The third line is interesting:

```
PR(SQUARE(x));
```

becomes

```
printf("SQUARE(x) is %d.\n", SQUARE(x));
```

after the first stage of macro expansion. The second `SQUARE(x)` is expanded to **x*x,** but the first is left as it is, for it now is inside double quotes in a program statement and thus is immune to further expansion. The final program line is

```
printf("SQUARE(x) is %d.\n", x*x);
```

and that produces the output

```
SQUARE(x) is 16.
```

when the program is run.

Let's run over that double-quote business one more time. If your macro definition includes an argument with double quotes, that argument will be replaced by the string in the macro call. But after that, it is expanded no further, even if the string is another macro. In our example, **x** became **SQUARE(x)** and stayed that way.

Now we get to some peculiar results. Recall that **x** has the value **4.** This might lead you to expect that **SQUARE(x+2)** would be **6*6** or **36.** But the printout says it is **14,** which sure doesn't look like a square to us! The reason for this misleading output is the simple one we already have stated: the preprocessor doesn't make calculations, it just substitutes strings. Wherever our definition shows an **x,** the preprocessor will substitute the string **x+2.** Thus

`x*x` becomes `x+2*x+2.`

The only multiplication is **2*x.** If **x** is **4,** then the value of this expression is

```
4+2*4+2 = 4 + 8 + 2 = 14
```

This example pinpoints a very important difference between a function call and a macro call. A function call passes the *value* of the argument to the function while the program is running. A macro call passes the argument *string* to the program before compilation; it's a different process at a different time.

Can our definition be fixed to make **SQUARE(x+2)** equal to 36? Sure. We simply need more parentheses:

```
#define SQUARE(x)  (x)*(x)
```

Then **SQUARE(x+2)** becomes **(x+2)*(x+2),** and we get our desired multiplication as the parentheses carry over in the replacement string.

This doesn't solve all our problems, however. Consider the events leading to the next output line:

`100/SQUARE(2)` becomes `100/2*2`

By the laws of precedence, this is evaluated from left to right, i.e., as

```
(100/2)*2 or 50*2 or 100.
```

This mix-up can be cured by defining **SQUARE(x)** this way:

```
#define SQUARE(x)  (x*x)
```

This produces

`100/(2*2)` which eventually evaluates to `100/4` or `25.`

To handle both of the last two examples, we need the definition

```
#define SQUARE(x)  ((x)*(x))
```

The lesson here is to use as many parentheses as necessary to ensure that operations and associations are done in the right order.

Even these precautions fail to save the final example from grief:

`SQUARE(++x)` becomes `++x*++x`

and **x** gets incremented twice, once before the multiplication and once afterwards:

```
++x*++x = 5*6 = 30
```

(Because the order of operations is left open, some compilers will render the product **6*5**, but the end result is the same.)

The only remedy for this problem is to not use **++x** as a macro argument. Note that **++x** *would* work as a *function* argument, for it would be evaluated to **5** and then the value **5** would be sent to the function.

MACRO OR FUNCTION?

Many tasks can be done using a macro with arguments or using a function. Which one should you use? There is no hard and fast line, but here are some considerations.

Macros are somewhat trickier to use than regular functions, for they can have odd side effects if you are unwary. Some compilers limit the macro definition to one line, and it is probably best to observe that limit even if your compiler does not.

The macros-vs.-function choice represents a trade-off between time and space. A macro produces "in-line" code, that is, you get a statement in your program. If you use the macro 20 times, then you get 20 lines of code inserted into your program. If you use a function 20 times, you have just one copy of the function statements in your program, so less space is used. On the other hand, program control must shift to where the function is, then return back to the calling program, and this takes longer than in-line code.

Macros have an advantage in that they don't worry about variable types.

(This is because they deal with character strings, not with actual values.) Thus our **SQUARE(x)** macro can be used equally well with **int** or **float.**

Programmers typically use macros for simple functions like the following:

```
#define MAX(X,Y)     ( (X) > (Y) ? (X) : (Y))
#define ABS(X)        ((X) < 0 ? -(X) : (X))
#define ISSIGN(X)    ( (X) == '+' || (X) == '-' ? 1 : 0 )
```

(The last macro has value 1—true—if **x** is an algebraic sign character.) Note these points:

1. There are no spaces in the macro, but spaces can appear in the replacement string. The preprocessor thinks the macro ends at the first space, so anything after that space is lumped into the replacement string.

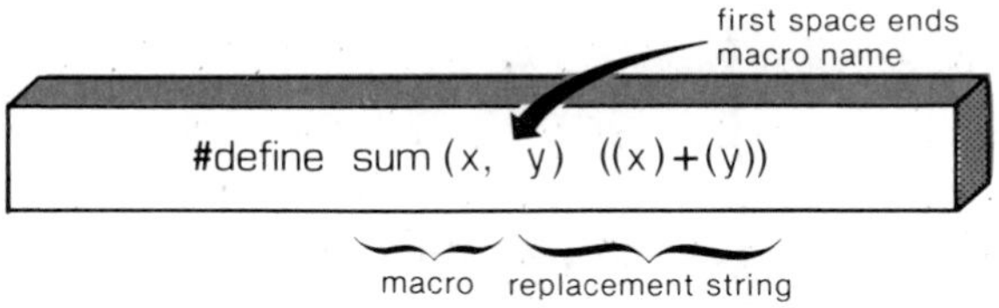

Figure 11.2
Faulty spacing in a macro definition

2. Use parentheses around each argument and around the definition as a whole. This ensures that the terms get grouped properly in an expression like `forks = 2 * MAX(guests + 3, last);`
3. We have used capital letters for macro function names. This convention is not as widespread as that of using capitals for macro constants. One good reason for using it, however, is that it reminds you to be alert to possible macro side effects.

Suppose you have developed some macro functions you like. Do you have to retype them each time you write a new program? Not if you remember the **#include** directive. We will review that now.

FILE INCLUSION : *#include*

When the preprocessor spots an **#include** directive, it looks for the following file name and includes it with the current file. The directive comes in two varieties:

```
#include <stdio.h>            file name in angle brackets
#include "mystuff.h"          file name in double quotes
```

On a UNIX system, the angle brackets tell the preprocessor to look for the file in one or more standard system directories. The quotes tell it to look in your directory (or some other directory, if you specify it in the file name) first, and then to look in the standard places.

```
#include <stdio.h>            searches system directories
#include "hot.h"              searches your current working directory
#include "/usr/biff/p.h"      searches the /usr/biff directory
```

On a typical microprocessor system, the two forms are synonymous, and the preprocessor looks through the indicated disk drive.

```
#include "stdio.h"          searches the default disk drive
#include <stdio.h>          searches the default disk drive
#include "a:stdio.h"        searches disk drive a
```

Why include files? Because they have information you need. The **stdio.h** file, for example, typically includes definitions of **EOF, getchar( ),** and **putchar( ).** The last two are defined as macro functions.

The **.h** suffix conventionally is used for "header" files, files with information to go at the head of your program. Header files usually consist of preprocessor statements. Some, like **stdio.h** come with the system; but you are free to create your own.

Header Files: An Example

Suppose, for instance, that you like using Boolean values. That is, instead of having **1** be true and **0** be false, you would rather use the words **TRUE** and **FALSE.** You could create a file called, say, **bool.h,** which contained these definitions:

```
 /* bool.h file */
#define BOOL int
#define TRUE 1
#define FALSE 0
```

Here is an example of a program using this header:

```
 /* counts whitespace characters */
#include <stdio.h>
#include "bool.h"
main()
{
   int ch;
   int count = 0;
   BOOL whitesp();

   while ( (ch = getchar()  ) != EOF)
          if ( whitesp(ch) )
                 count++;
   printf("There are %d whitespace characters.\n", count);
}

BOOL whitesp(c)
char c;
{
    if ( c == ' ' || c == '\n'  || c == '\t' )
          return(TRUE);
    else
          return(FALSE);
}
```

Program notes:

1. If the two functions in this program (**'main( )** ' and **'whitesp( )** ') were to be compiled separately, you would use the #**include "bool.h"** directive with each.
2. The expression **if (whitesp(ch))** is the same as **if (whitesp(ch) == TRUE),** since **whitesp(ch)** itself has the value **TRUE** or **FALSE.**
3. We have not created a new type **BOOL,** since **BOOL** is just **int.** The purpose of labeling the function **BOOL** is to remind the user that the function is being used for a logical (as opposed to arithmetic) calculation.
4. Using a function for involved logical comparisons can make a program clearer. It also can save effort if the comparison is made more than one place in a program.
5. We could have used a macro instead of a function to define **whitesp( ).**

Many programmers develop their own standard header files to use with their programs. Some files might be for special purposes, others might be used with almost every program. Since included files can include **#include** directives, you can create concise, well-organized header files if you like.

Consider this example:

```
    /* header file mystuff.h */

#include <stdio.n>
#include "bool.h"
#include "funct.h"
#define YES 1
#define NO 0
```

First, we'll remind you that the C preprocessor recognizes the comment marks/* and */so that we can include comments in these files.

Secondly, we have included three files. Presumably the third one contains some macro functions we often use.

Thirdly, we have defined **YES** to be **1**, whereas in **bool.h** we defined **TRUE** to be **1.** There is no conflict here; we can use **YES** and **TRUE** in the same program. Each will be replaced by a **1.**

There would be a conflict if we added the line

```
#define TRUE 2
```

to the file. The second definition would supercede the first, and some preprocessors would warn you that **TRUE** had been redefined.

The **#include** directive is not restricted to header files. If you had stored a needed function in the file **sort.c,** you can use

```
#include "sort.c"
```

to get it compiled along with your current program.

The **#include** and **#define** directives are the most heavily used C preprocessor features. We will treat the other directives much more tersely.

OTHER DIRECTIVES: *#undef, #if, #ifdef, #ifndef, #else,* AND *#endif*

These directives typically are used with larger blocks of programming. They allow one to suspend earlier definitions and to produce files which can be compiled in more than one way.

The **#undef** directive undefines the most recent definition of the named macro.

```
#define BIG 3
#define HUGE 5
#undef BIG              /* BIG now undefined */
#define HUGE 10         /* HUGE redefined as 10 */
#undef HUGE             /* HUGE goes back to 5 */
#undef HUGE             /* HUGE now undefined */
```

Obviously (we hope) you wouldn't put a file together like this. But suppose you had a large standard **#include** file that you want to use, but you need to temporarily change some of its definitions for one function in your program. Rather than monkey with the file, you can just include it, then surround the deviant function with appropriate **#defines** and **#undefs.**

Or suppose you are working with a large system of programs. You want to define a macro, but you aren't sure whether or not your definition is usurping a definition elsewhere in the system. Then simply undefine your macro at the point it is no longer needed, and the original macro, if any, will still hold for the rest of the system.

The other directives we mentioned let you set up conditional compilations. Here is an example:

```
#ifdef MAVIS

#include   "horse.h"          /* gets done if MAVIS is #defined */
#define  STABLES     5

#else

#include "cow.h"            /* gets done if MAVIS isn't #defined */
#define  STABLES   15

#endif
```

The **#ifdef** directive says that if the following identifier **(MAVIS)** has been defined by the preprocessor, then follow all the directives up to the next **#else** or **#endif,** whichever comes first. If there is an **#else,** then everything from the **#else** to the **#endif** is done if the identifier isn't defined.

The structure is much like that of the C **if-else.** The main difference is that the preprocessor doesn't recognize the **{}** method of marking a block, so it uses the **#else** (if any) and the **#endif** (which must be present) to mark blocks of directives.

These conditional structures can be nested.

The **#ifndef** and **#if** directives can be used with **#else** and **#endif** the same way. The **#ifndef** asks if the following identifier is *not* defined; it is the negative of **#ifdef.** The **#if** directive is more like the regular C **if.** It is followed by a constant expression which is considered to be true if nonzero:

```
#if SYS == "IBM"
#include "ibm.h"
#endif
```

One use for these "conditional compilation" features is to make a program more portable. By changing a few key definitions at the beginning of a file, you can have different values set up and different files included for different systems.

These brief examples illustrate C's marvelous ability for sophisticated and close control of programs.

WHAT YOU SHOULD HAVE LEARNED

How to **#define** symbolic constants: **#define FINGERS 10**
How to include other files: **#include "albanian.h"**
How to define a macro function: **#define NEG (X) (−(X))**
When to use symbolic constants: often
When to use macro functions: sometimes
The dangers of macro functions: side effects

QUESTIONS AND ANSWERS

Questions

1. Here are groups of one or more macros followed by a source code line that uses them. What code results in each case? Is it valid code?
   a.
   ```
   #define FPM  5280     /* feet per mile */
   dist = FPM * miles;
   ```
   b.
   ```
   #define FEET 4
   ```

```
#define POD FEET + FEET
plort = FEET * POD;
```

c.
```
#define SIX = 6;
nex = SIX;
```

d.
```
#define NEW(X) X + 5
y = NEW(y);
berg = NEW(berg) * lob;
est = NEW(berg) / NEW(y);
nilp = lob * NEW(-berg);
```

2. Fix the definition in 1.d. to make it more reliable.
3. Define a macro function that returns the minimum of two values.
4. Define a macro to take the place of the **whitesp(c)** function in the program to count whitespace characters.
5. Define a macro function that prints the representations and the values of two integer expressions.

ANSWERS

1. a. **dist = 5280 * miles;** Valid.
   b. **plot = 4 * 4 + 4;** This is valid, but if the user really wanted 4 * (4 + 4), she should have used **#define POD (FEET + FEET).**
   c. **#define SIX 6;** Not valid; apparently the user forgot that he was writing for the preprocessor, not in C.
   d. **y = y + 5;** Valid. **berg = berg + 5 * lob;** Valid, but probably not the desired result. **est = berg + 5 / y + 5;** Ditto. **nilp = lob *−berg + 5;** Ditto.
2. `#define NEW(X) ( (X) + 5 )`
3. `#define MIN(X,Y) ( (X) < (Y) ? (X) : (Y) )`
4. `#define WHITESP(C) ((C) == ' ' || (C) == '\n' || (C) == '\t')`
5. `#define PR2(X,Y) printf("X is %d and Y is %d.\n", X, Y)` Since X and Y are never exposed to any other operations (such a multiplication) in this macro, we don't have to cocoon everything in parentheses.

EXERCISE

1. Start developing a header file of preprocessor definitions you wish to use.

12

ARRAYS AND POINTERS

In this chapter you will find

- Arrays
    - Initialization and Storage Classes
- Pointers to Arrays
- Functions, Arrays, and Pointers
- Using Pointers To Do an Array's Work
- Pointer Operations
- Multidimensional Arrays
    - Initializing a Two-Dimensional Array
- Pointers and Multidimensional Arrays
    - Functions and Multidimensional Arrays
- What You Should Have Learned
- Questions and Answers
- Exercise

12. ARRAYS AND POINTERS

CONCEPTS

Arrays
Multidimensional arrays
Initializing arrays
Pointers and pointer operations
The array-pointer connection

OPERATORS

`&` `*` (unary)

Arrays and pointers have an intimate (but not indelicate) relationship to each other, so traditionally they are discussed together. Before we explore that relationship, however, we will review and augment our knowledge of arrays. Then we study the connection with pointers.

ARRAYS

By now you are familiar with the fact that an array is composed of a series of elements of one data type. We use declarations to tell the compiler when we want an array. The compiler needs to know the same things about an array that it needs to know about an ordinary variable (known as "scalar" variables in the trade): the type and storage class. In addition, it needs to know how many elements the array has. Arrays can have the same types and storage classes as ordinary variables, and the same default rules apply. Consider the following example of array declarations:

```
  /* some array declarations */
int temp[365];   /* external array of 365 ints  */
```

```
main()
{
   float rain[365];  /* automatic array of 365 floats */
   static char code[12]; /*static array of 12 chars */
   extern temp[];    /* external array; size given above */
```

You recall, too, that the brackets (**[ ]**) identify **temp** and the rest as arrays; and that the enclosed number indicates the number of elements in the array. We identify an individual element by using its subscript number, also called an index. The numbering starts with 0. Hence **temp[0]** is the first element of **temp** and **temp[364]** is the 365th and last element.

This is rather old hat; let's learn something new.

Initialization and Storage Classes

Often we use arrays to store data needed for a program. For instance, a 12-element array can store the number of days in each month. In cases like these, we would like to have a convenient way to initialize the array at the beginning of a program. There is a way, but only for static and external storage classes. Let's see how it is done.

We know that we can initialize scalar variables in a declaration with expressions like

```
int fix = 1;
float flax = PI*2;
```

where, we hope, **PI** was defined earlier as a macro. Can we do something similar with arrays? The answer is that old favorite, yes and no:

External and *static* arrays *can* be initialized.

Automatic and *register* arrays *cannot* be initialized.

Before trying to initialize an array, let's see what's in it if we don't put anything there.

```
 /* arraypeek */
main()
{
   int fuzzy[2];            /* automatic array */
   static int wuzzy[2];     /* static array    */

   printf("%d %d\n", fuzzy[1], wuzzy[1]);
}
```

The output is

```
525 0
```

This reflects the following rules. If you do nothing, external and static arrays are initialized to zero. Automatic and register arrays get whatever garbage happens to be left over in that part of memory.

Great! We now know how to initialize a static or external array to 0: just do nothing. But what if we want some other values, say the number of days in each month. Then we can do this:

```
 /* daysofmonth */
int days[12] = {31,28,31,30,31,30,31,31,30,31,30,31};
main()
{
  int index;
  extern int days[];  /* optional declaration */

  for ( index = 0; index < 12; index++)
     printf("Month %d has %d days.\n", index + 1,
             days[index]);
}
```

The output:

```
Month 1 has 31 days.
Month 2 has 28 days.
Month 3 has 31 days.
Month 4 has 30 days.
Month 5 has 31 days.
Month 6 has 30 days.
Month 7 has 31 days.
Month 8 has 31 days.
Month 9 has 30 days.
Month 10 has 31 days.
Month 11 has 30 days.
Month 12 has 31 days.
```

Not quite a superb program, but it's wrong only one month in every four years. By defining **days[ ]** outside the function, we made it external. We initialized it with a list enclosed in braces; commas are used to separate the members of the list.

The number of items in the list should match the size of the array. What if we count wrong? Let's try the last example again with a list that is too short (and two short, too):

```
 /* daysofmonth */
int days[12] = {31,28,31,30,31,30,31,31,30,31};
main()
{
  int index;
  extern int days[];  /* optional declaration */

  for ( index = 0; index < 12; index++)
     printf("Month %d has %d days,\n", index + 1, days[index]);
}
```

This time the output looks like this:

```
Month 1 has 31 days.
Month 2 has 28 days.
Month 3 has 31 days.
Month 4 has 30 days.
Month 5 has 31 days.
Month 6 has 30 days.
Month 7 has 31 days.
Month 8 has 31 days.
Month 9 has 30 days.
Month 10 has 31 days.
Month 11 has 0 days.
Month 12 has 0 days.
```

As you can see, the compiler had no problem. When it ran out of suggestions from the list, it initialized the rest to 0.

The compiler is not so forgiving if you have too many list members. This overgenerosity is considered an ERROR. There is no need, however, to expose yourself to the ridicule of your compiler. Instead, let the compiler match the array size to the list:

```
 /* daysofmonth */
int days[] = {31,28,31,30,31,30,31,31,30,31};
```

```
main()
{
  int index;
  extern int days[];  /* optional declaration */

  for ( index = 0; index < sizeof days/(sizeof (int)); index++)
     printf("Month %d has %d days,\n", index + 1, days[index]);
}
```

There are two main points of note in the program.

First, if you use empty brackets when initializing an array, it will count the number of items in the list and make the array that large.

Second, notice what we did in the **for** control statement. Lacking (justifiably) faith in our ability to count correctly, we let the computer give us the size of the array. The **sizeof** operator gives us the size, in bytes, of the object or type following it. (We mentioned this way back in Chapter 3.) On our system, each **int** element occupies 2 bytes, so we divide the total number of bytes by 2 to get the number of elements. But other systems may have a different size **int.** Therefore, to be general, we divide by **sizeof (int).**

Here is the result of running this program.

```
Month 1 has 31 days.
Month 2 has 28 days.
Month 3 has 31 days.
Month 4 has 30 days.
Month 5 has 31 days.
Month 6 has 30 days.
Month 7 has 31 days.
Month 8 has 31 days.
Month 9 has 30 days.
Month 10 has 31 days.
```

Oops! We just put in 10 values. But our method of letting the program find the array size kept us from trying to print past the end of the array.

There is one more short method of initializing arrays, but since it works only for character strings, we will save it for the next chapter.

Finally, we should point out that you can *assign* values to array members, regardless of storage class. For example, the following fragment assigns even numbers to an automatic array:

```
 /* array assignment */
main()
```

```
{
   int counter, evens[50];

   for ( counter = 0; counter < 50; counter++)
        evens[counter] = 2 * counter;
    . . .
}
```

POINTERS TO ARRAYS

Pointers, as you may recall from Chapter 9, give us a symbolic way of using addresses. Since the hardware instructions of computing machines use addresses heavily, pointers allow us to express ourselves in a way that is close to how the machine expresses itself. This makes programs with pointers efficient. In particular, pointers offer an efficient way to deal with arrays. Indeed, as we shall see, our array notation is simply a disguised use of pointers.

An example of this disguised use is that an array name is also a pointer to the first element of an array. That is, if **flizny[ ]** is an array, then

```
flizny == &flizny[0]
```

and both represent the memory address of that first element. (Recall that **&** is the address operator.) Both are pointer *constants,* for they remain fixed for the duration of the program. However, they can be assigned as values to a pointer *variable,* and we can change the value of a variable, as the next example shows. Note what happens to the value of a pointer when we add a number to it.

```
 /* pointer addition */
main()
{
  int dates[4], *pti, index;
  float bills[4], *ptf;

  pti = dates;   /* assign address of array to pointer */
  ptf = bills;
  for (index = 0; index < 4; index ++)
       printf("pointers + %d: %10u %10u\n",
              index, pti + index, ptf + index);
}
```

Here is the output:

```
pointers + 0:     56014     56026
pointers + 1:     56016     56030
pointers + 2:     56018     56034
pointers + 3:     56020     56038
```

The first line prints the beginning addresses of the two arrays, and the next line gives the result of adding one to the address, and so on. What?

```
56014 + 1 = 56016?
56026 + 1 = 56030?
```

Pretty dumb? Like a fox! Our system is addressed by individual bytes, but type **int** uses two bytes, and type **float** uses four bytes. What is happening here is that when you say "add one to a pointer," C adds one *storage unit.* For arrays, this means the address is increased to the address of the next *element,* not just the next byte. This is one reason we have to declare what sort of object a pointer points to; the address is not enough, for the computer needs to know how many bytes are used to store the object. (This is true even for pointers to scalar variables; otherwise the ***pt** operation to fetch the value wouldn't work.)

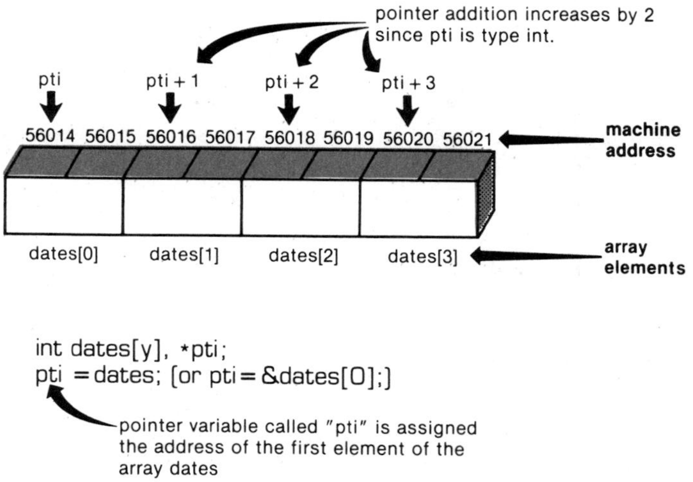

Figure 12.1
An array and pointer addition

As a result of this cleverness of C we have the following equalities:

```
dates + 2 == &dates[2]  /* same address */
*(dates + 2) == dates[2]  /* same value */
```

These relationships sum up the close connection between arrays and pointers. They mean we can use a pointer to identify an individual element of an array and to get its value. In essence, we have two different notations for the same thing. Indeed, the compiler converts the array notation to pointers, so the pointer approach is the more basic of the two.

Incidentally, don't confuse ***(dates+2)** with ***dates+2.** The value operator **(*)** binds more tightly (has higher precedence) than +, so the latter means (*dates)+2:

```
*(dates + 2)  /*  value of the 3rd element of dates */
*dates + 2  /* 2 added to the value of the 1st element */
```

The relationship between arrays and pointers means we often can use either approach when writing a program. One example is when we have a function with an array as an argument.

FUNCTIONS, ARRAYS, AND POINTERS

Arrays can appear in two places in a function. First, they can be declared in the body of the function. Second, they can be arguments of a function. Everything we have said in this chapter so far pertains to arrays of the first kind; we now need to discuss arrays as arguments.

We brought up the matter of array arguments in Chapter 10. Now that we know more about pointers, we can take a deeper look. Let's begin by looking at the skeleton of a program, paying attention to the declarations:

```
 /* array argument  */
main()
{
  int ages[50];   /* an array of 50 elements */

  convert(ages);
   . . .
```

```
}
convert(years)
int years[];      /* how big an array? */
{
   . . .
}
```

Clearly, the array **ages** has 50 elements. What about the array **years?** Surprise! There is no array **years!** The declaration

```
int years[];
```

creates not an *array,* but a *pointer.* Let's see why this is so.

This is our function call:

```
convert(ages);
```

The argument is **ages.** And the name **ages,** you may recall, is a *pointer* to the first element of the 50 element array. So the function call passes a pointer, that is, an address, to the function **convert( ).** This means that the argument of **convert( )** is a pointer, and we could have written **convert( )** this way:

```
convert(years)
int *years;
{
}
```

Indeed, these two declarations are synonymous:

```
int years[];
int *years;
```

Both declare **year** to be a pointer-to-integer. The chief difference is that the first form reminds us that **year** points to an array.

How does this relate to the **ages** array? Recall that when we use a pointer for an argument, the function affects the corresponding variable in the calling function. Thus, the operations involving **years** in **convert( )** actually affect the the array **ages** in **main( ).**

Let's see how that works. First, the function call initializes **years** to point to **ages[0].** Now suppose somewhere in **convert( )** we have the expression

years[3]. Well, as we saw in the preceding section, that's the same as saying ***(years+3).** But if **years** points to **ages[0],** then **years+3** points to **ages[3].** This makes ***(years+3)** stand for **ages[3].** Put this chain of relationships together, and we find that changing **years[3]** is the same as changing ***(years+3),** which is the same as changing **ages[3].** And this is what we claimed, that operations on **years** wind up as operations on **ages.**

In short, when you use an array name as a function argument, you pass a pointer to the function. The function then uses this pointer to effect changes on the original array in the calling program.

Let's look at an example.

USING POINTERS TO DO AN ARRAY'S WORK

Here we are going to write a function that uses arrays. Then we will rewrite it using pointers.

Consider the following simple function which finds the average (or mean) of an array of integers. The input is an array name and the number of array elements. The output is the mean, which is communicated through **return.** The calling statement could be something like

```
printf("The mean of these values is %d.\n",
mean(numbs,size));
```

```
 /* finds the mean of an array of n integers */
int mean(array,n)
int array[], n;
{
   int index;
   long sum;  /* too many ints may sum to a long int */

   if (n > 0 )
          {
          for (index = 0, sum = 0; index < n; index++)
                sum += array[index];
          return( (int) (sum/n)  ); /* return an int */
         }
   else
           {
           printf("No array.\n");
           return(0);
           }
}
```

It is simple to convert this to a program using pointers. Declare, say, **pa** as a pointer to **int.** Then replace the array element **array[index]** by the corresponding value: ***(pa+index).**

```
 /* uses pointers to find the mean of an array of n

integers */
int mean(pa,n)
int *pa, n;
{
   int index;
   long sum;  /* too many ints may sum to a long int */

   if (n > 0 )
         {
         for (index = 0, sum = 0; index < n; index++)
              sum += *(pa + index);
         return( (int) (sum/n) ); /* return an int */
        }
   else
         {
         printf("No array.\n");
         return (0);
         }
}
```

Easy, but do we have to change the function call? After all, **numbs** in **mean(numbs,size)** was an array name. No change is needed, for an array name *is* a pointer. As we discussed in the preceding section, the declarations

```
int pa[];
```

and

```
int *pa;
```

are identical in effect; both say that **pa** is a pointer. We could use the first declaration and still use ***(pa+index)** in the program.

Conceptually, how does the pointer version work? A pointer points to the first element, and the value stored there is added to **sum.** Then the next element is pointed to (one is added to the pointer), and the value stored there is added to **sum**, etc. If you think about it, this is just what the array version does, with the subscript acting as the finger that points to each element in turn.

Now that we have two ways to do things, which should we use? First, although arrays and pointers are closely related, they do have differences. Pointers are more general and far-reaching in their uses, but many users (initially, at least) find arrays more familiar and obvious. Then, too, there is no simple pointer equivalent for declaring the size of an array. The most typical situation in which you can use either is the one we have just shown: a function that operates on an array defined elsewhere. We suggest you use whichever approach you want. The main advantage of using pointers in these situations is to gain familiarity with them so that they are easier to use when you *have* to use them.

POINTER OPERATIONS

Just what can we do with pointers? C offers five basic operations we can perform on pointers, and the next program shows these possibilities. To show the results of each operation, we will print out the value of the pointer (which is the address it points to), the value stored in the pointed-to address, and the address of the pointer itself.

```
 /* pointer operations */
#define PR(X) printf("X = %u, *X =%d, &X = %u\n", X, *X, &X)
/* prints value of pointer (an address), the value stored at */
/* that address, and the address of the pointer itself. */
main()
{
   static int urn[] = {100,200,300};
  int *ptr1, *ptr2;

  ptr1 =urn;          /* assign an address to a pointer */
  ptr2 = &urn[2];     /* ditto */
  PR(ptr1);    /* see macro definition above */
  ptr1++;       /* increment a pointer */
  PR(ptr1);
  PR(ptr2);
  ++ptr2;    /* going past end of the array */
  PR(ptr2);
  printf("ptr2 - ptr1 = %u\n", ptr2 -ptr1);
}
```

Here is the output:

```
ptr1 = 18, *ptr1 =100, &ptr1 = 55990
ptr1 = 20, *ptr1 =200, &ptr1 = 55990
ptr2 = 22, *ptr2 =300, &ptr2 = 55992
ptr2 = 24, *ptr2 =29808, &ptr2 = 55992
ptr2 - ptr1 = 2
```

This example shows the five basic operations we can perform with or on pointer variables.

1. ASSIGNMENT: we can assign an address to a pointer. Typically we do this using an array name or by using the address operator **(&).** In our example, **ptr1** is assigned the address of the beginning of the array **urn;** this address happens to be memory cell number 18. (On our system, static variables are stored in low memory locations. The variable **ptr2** gets the address of the third and last element, **urn[2].**

2. VALUE-FINDING: the * operator gives us the value stored in the pointed-to location. Thus ***ptr1** initially is **100,** the value stored at location 18.

3. TAKE A POINTER ADDRESS: like all variables, pointer variables have an address and a value. The **&** operator tells us where the pointer itself is stored. In our example, **ptr1** is stored in memory location 55990. The content of that memory cell is **18,** the address of **urn.**
4. INCREMENT A POINTER: we can do this by regular addition or by using the increment operator. Incrementing a pointer makes it move to the next element of an array. Thus, **ptr1++** increases the numerical value of **ptr1** by **2** (2 bytes per **int**) and makes **ptr1** point to **urn[1].** (See the figure below.) Now **ptr1** has the value **20** (the next array address) and ***ptr1** has the value **200,** the value of **urn[1].** Note that the address of **ptr1** itself remains **55990.** After all, a variable doesn't move around just because it changes value!

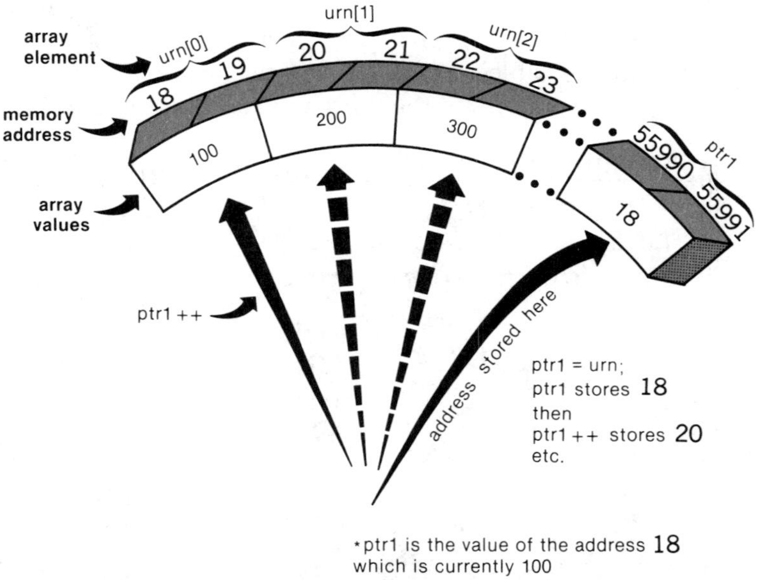

Figure 12.2
Incrementing a type int pointer

Of course you can also decrement a pointer.

There are some cautions to note. The computer does not keep track of whether or not a pointer still points to an array. The operation **++ptr2** caused **ptr2** to move up another two bytes, and now it points to whatever happened to be stored after the array.

Also, you can use the increment operator for pointer variables, but not for pointer constants, just as you can't use the increment operator on regular constants. You can use simple addition for pointer variables and constants.

VALID	INVALID
`ptr1++;`	`urn++;`
`x++;`	`3++;`
`ptr2 = ptr1 + 2;`	`ptr2 = urn++;`
`ptr2 = urn + 1;`	`x = y + 3++;`

5. DIFFERENCING: You can find the difference between two pointers. Normally you do this for two pointers to elements in the same array to find how far apart the elements were. Note that the result is in the same units as the type size.

These operations open many gateways. C programmers create arrays of pointers, pointers to functions, arrays of pointers to pointers, arrays of pointers to functions, and so on. We will stick to the basic uses we already have unveiled. The first basic use is to communicate information to and from functions. We have seen that we have to use pointers if we want a function to affect variables in the calling function. The second basic use is in functions designed to manipulate arrays.

MULTIDIMENSIONAL ARRAYS

Tempest Cloud, a weather person who takes her subject cirrusly, wants to analyze 5 years of monthly rainfall data. One of the first decisions she must make is how to represent the data. One choice is to use 60 variables, one for each data item. (We mentioned this choice once before, and it is as dumb now as it was then.) Using an array with 60 elements would be an improvement, but it would be nicer still if we could keep each year's data separate. We could use 5 arrays, each with 12 elements, but that is clumsy and could get really awkward if Tempest decides to study 50 years' rainfall instead of 5. We need something better.

A good answer is to use an array of arrays. The master array would have 5 elements, and each element would be a 12-element array. This is how it is done:

```
static float rain[5][12];
```

We can also visualize the **rain** array as a two-dimensional array consisting of 5 rows, each of 12 columns.

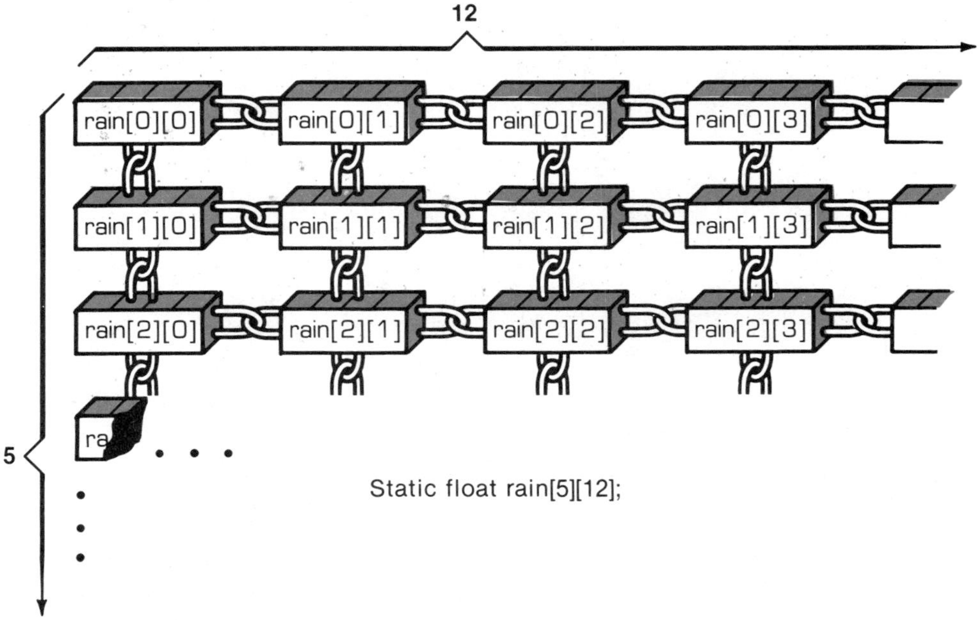

Figure 12.3
Two-dimensional array

By changing the second subscript one moves along a row, and by changing the first subscript one moves vertically along a column. For our example, the second subscript takes you through the months, and the first subscript takes you through the years.

Let's use this two-dimensional array in a weather program. Our program goal will be to find the total rainfall for each year, the average yearly rainfall, and the average rainfall for each month. To find the total rainfall for a year, we have to add all the data in a given row. To find the average rainfall for a given month, we first have to add all the data in a given column. The two-dimensional array makes it easy to visualize and execute these activities. Fig. 12.4 shows the program.

```
   /* finds yearly totals, yearly average, and monthly average */
   /* for several years of rainfall data */
  #define TWLV 12     /* number of months in a year */
  #define YRS   5     /* number of years of data    */
```

```
main()
{
 static float rain[YRS][TWLV] = {
 {10.2, 8.1, 6.8, 4.2, 2.1, 1.8, 0.2, 0.3, 1.1, 2.3, 6.1, 7.4},
 {9.2, 9.8, 4.4, 3.3, 2.2, 0.8, 0.4, 0.0, 0.6, 1.7, 4.3, 5.2},
 {6.6, 5.5, 3.8, 2.8, 1.6, 0.2, 0.0, 0.0, 0.0, 1.3, 2.6, 4.2},
 {4.3, 4.3, 4.3, 3.0, 2.0, 1.0, 0.2, 0.2, 0.4, 2.4, 3.5, 6.6},
 {8.5, 8.2, 1.2, 1.6, 2.4, 0.0, 5.2, 0.9, 0.3, 0.9, 1.4, 7.2}
                                  };
 /* initializing rainfall data for 1970 - 1974 */
 int year, month;
 float subtot, total;

 printf(" YEAR    RAINFALL  (inches)\n");
 for ( year = 0, total = 0; year < YRS; year++)
       {  /* for each year, sum rainfall for each month */
       for ( month = 0, subtot = 0; month < TWLV; month++)
             subtot += rain[year][month];
       printf("%5d %15.1f\n", 1970 + year, subtot);
       total += subtot;     /* total for all years */
       }
 printf("\nThe yearly average is %.1f inches.\n\n", total/YRS);
 printf("MONTHLY AVERAGES:\n\n");
 printf("Jan  Feb  Mar  Apr  May  Jun  Jul  Aug  Sep  Oct ");
 printf(" Nov  Dec\n");

 for ( month = 0; month < TWLV; month++ )
       {    /* for each month, sum rainfall over years */
       for ( year = 0, subtot =0; year < YRS; year++)
              subtot += rain[year][month];
       printf("%4.1f ", subtot/YRS);
       }
 printf("\n");
}
```

Figure 12.4
Weather program.

```
YEAR      RAINFALL (inches)
1970            50.6
1971            41.9
```

```
1972            28.6
1973            32.2
1974            37.8

The yearly average is 38.2 inches.

MONTHLY AVERAGES:

Jan  Feb  Mar  Apr  May  Jun  Jul  Aug  Sep  Oct  Nov  Dec
7.8  7.2  4.1  3.0  2.1  0.8  1.2  0.3  0.5  1.7  3.6  6.1
```

The main points to notice in this program are the initialization and the computation scheme. The initialization is the more involved of the two, so we will look at the computation first.

To find the total for a given year, we kept **year** constant and let **month** go over its full range. This is the inner **for** loop of the first part of the program. Then we repeated the process for the next value of **year.** This is the outer loop of the first part of the program. A nested loop structure like this is natural for handling a two-dimensional array. One loop handles one subscript, and the other loop handles the second subscript.

The second part of the program has the same structure, but now we change **year** with the inner loop and **month** with the outer. Remember, each time the outer loop cycles once, the inner loop cycles its full allotment. Thus this arrangement cycles through all the years before changing months, and this gives us a five-year total for the first month, then a five-year total for the second month, and so on.

Initializing a Two-Dimensional Array

For the initialization we included five embraced sets of numbers all enclosed by one more set of braces. The data in the first interior set of braces are assigned to the first row of the array, the data in the second interior set go to the second row, and so on. The rules we discussed about mismatches between data and array sizes apply to each row. That is, if the first set of braces encloses ten numbers, only the first ten elements of the first row are affected. The last two elements in that row would get the standard default initialization to zero. If there are too many numbers, that is an error; they do not get shoved into the next row.

We could have left out the interior braces and just retained the two outermost braces. As long as we have the right number of entries, the effect is the same. If we are short of entries, however, the array gets filled sequentially without regard to row until the data runs out. Then the remaining elements are initialized to 0. See Fig. 12.5.

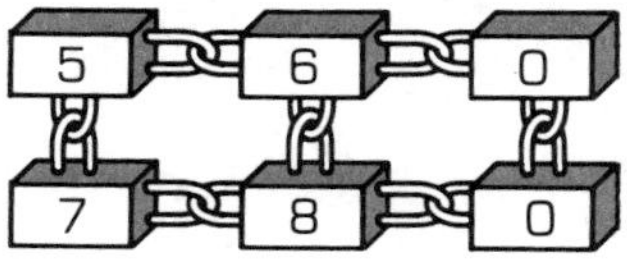


```
Static int sq[2][3] = {
                        {5,6},
                        {7,8},
                      };
```

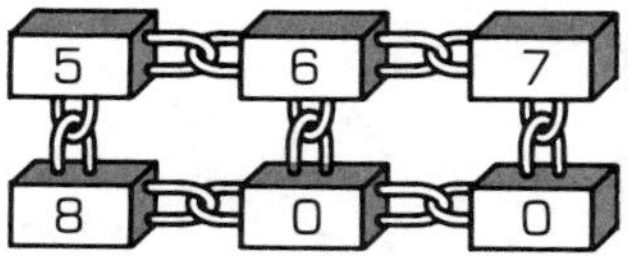


```
Static int sq[2][3] = {5,6,7,8};
```

Figure 12.5
Two methods of initializing an array

Everything we have said about two-dimensional arrays can be generalized to three-dimensional arrays and further. We declare a three-dimensional array this way:

```
int solido[10][20][30];
```

You can visualize this as ten two-dimensional arrays (each 20 × 30) stacked atop each other. Or you can think of it as an array of arrays of arrays. That is, it is a ten-element array, each element of which is an array. Each of these arrays has twenty elements, each of which is a thirty-element array. The advantage of this second point of view is that it is more easily extended to arrays of more dimensions, unless you happen to be able to visualize four-dimensional objects! We'll stick to two dimensions.

POINTERS AND MULTIDIMENSIONAL ARRAYS

How do pointers relate to multidimensional arrays? We'll look at some examples now to find the answer.

Suppose we have the declarations

```
int zippo[4][2];      /* 4 row,2 column array of int */
int *pri;             /*  pointer to int  */
```

```
Then where does
```

```
pri = zippo;
```

point? It points to the first column, first row:

```
zippo == &zippo[0][0]
```

Where does **pri + 1** point? To **zippo[0][1],** which is row 1, column2? Or to **zippo[1][0],** which is row 2, column1? To continue, we need to know how two-dimensional arrays are stored. They are stored like a one-dimensional array, the elements occupying a series of consecutive memory locations. The order is determined by letting the rightmost index vary first. That is, the internal order is

```
zippo[0][0] zippo[0][1] zippo[1][0] zippo[1][1] zippo[2][0]
 . . .
```

First the first row is stored; it is followed by the second row, then the third row, and so on. Thus, for our example

```
pri == &zippo[0][0]       /* row 1, column 1 */
pri + 1 == &zippo[0][1]   /* row 1, column 2 */
pri + 2 == &zippo[1][0]   /* row 2, column 1 */
pri + 3 == &zippo[1][1]   /* row 2, column 2 */
```

Got it? Okay, what does **pri + 5** point to? Right, to

```
zippo[2][1].
```

We have described a two-dimensional array as an array of arrays. If **zippo** is the name of our two-dimensional array, then what are the names of the 4 rows, each of which is an array of two elements? The name of the first row is **zippo[0]** and the name of the fourth row is **zippo[3];** you can fill in the other names. But the name of an array is also a pointer to that array, meaning it points to the first element of that array. This means

```
zippo[0] == &zippo[0][0]
zippo[1] == &zippo[1][0]
zippo[2] == &zippo[2][0]
zippo[3] == &zippo[3][0]
```

This feature is more than a novelty. It lets you use a function designed for a one-dimensional array on a two-dimensional array! Here's proof (although we hope you would trust us by now), using our mean program with a two-dimensional array:

```
 /* one-dimensional function, two-dimensional array */
main()
{
  static int junk[3][4] = {
                            { 2,4,6,8},
                            {100, 200, 300, 400},
                            { 10, 40, 60, 90}
                           };
  int row;

  for (row = 0; row < 3; row ++)
      printf("The mean of row %d is %d.\n",
               row, mean( junk[row],4 ) );
  /* junk[row] is a 1-dimensional array with 4 elements */
}
/*  finds mean of 1-dimensional array */
int mean(array,n)
int array[], n;
{
   int index;
   long sum;

   if (n > 0 )
        {
        for (index = 0, sum = 0; index < n; index++)
             sum += (long) array[index];
        return( (int) (sum/n) );
      }
```

```
        else
            {
            printf("No array.\n");
            return (0);
            }
}
```

The output:

```
The mean of row 0 is 5.
The mean of row 1 is 250.
The mean of row 2 is 50.
```

Functions and Multidimensional Arrays

Suppose you want a function to handle a two-dimensional array as a whole rather than piecemeal. How do you set up the function definitions and declarations? Let's get a little more specific and say we want a function that handles **junk[][]** of our last example. Let's say **main( )** looks like this:

```
 /* main junk */
main()
{
  static int junk[3][4] = {
                            { 2,4,5,8},
                            {100, 200, 300, 400},
                            { 10, 40, 60, 90}
                           };
  stuff(junk);
}
```

The function **stuff( )** takes **junk,** a pointer to the whole array, as an argument. Without worrying about what **stuff( )** does, how do we set up the function heading?

```
stuff(junk)
int junk[];
```

or

```
stuff(junk)
int junk[][];
```

No and no. The first will work after a fashion, but it will treat **junk** as a one-dimensional array of twelve elements. Information about the breakdown into rows will be lost.

The second attempt fails because although it says **junk** is two-dimensional, it doesn't tell how to break it down. Is it six rows and two columns? Two rows and six columns? Or what? The compiler needs more information.

This does it:

```
stuff(junk)
int junk[][4];
```

This informs the compiler that it should break up the array into rows of four columns.

Arrays of character strings are a special case, for the null character in each string tells the computer where the string ends. This permits declarations like

```
char *list[];
```

Character strings offer some of the most frequent uses of arrays and pointers, and we turn to this subject next chapter.

WHAT YOU SHOULD HAVE LEARNED

How to declare a one-dimensional array: **long id_no[200];**
How to declare a two-dimensional array: **short chess[8][8];**
Which arrays can be initialized: external and static
How to initialize an array: **static int hats[3] = {10,20,15};**
Another way to initialize: **static int caps[] = {3,56,2};**
How to get the address of a variable: use the **&** operator
How to get the value a pointer points to: use the * operator
The significance of an array name: **hats == &hats[0]**
Array-pointer correspondences: if **ptr = hats;** then **ptr + 2 == & hats[2]** and ***(ptr + 2) == hats[2]**

The five operations you can apply to pointer variables: see text
The pointer approach for functions operating on arrays

QUESTIONS AND ANSWERS

Questions

1. What printout will this program produce?

```
#define PC(X,Y) printf("%c %c\n", X, Y)
char ref[] = { 'D', 'O', 'L', 'T'};
main()
{
  char *ptr;
  int index;

  for( index = 0, ptr = ref; index < 4; index++, ptr++)
     PC(ref[index], *ptr);
}
```

2. In Question 1, why was **ref** declared before **main( )**?
3. What is the value of ***ptr** and of ***(ptr +2)** in each case?
   a. `int *ptr;`
      `static int boop[4] = {12,21,121, 212};`
      `ptr = boop;`
   b. `float *ptr;`
      `static float awk[2][2] = { {1.0, 2.0}, {3.0, 4.0} };`
      `ptr = awk[0];`
   c. `int *ptr;`
      `static int jirb[4] = { 10023, 7};`
      `ptr = jirb;`
   d. `int *ptr;`
      `static int torf[2][2] = { 12, 14, 16};`
      `ptr = torf[0];`
   e. `int *ptr;`
      `static int fort[2][2] = { {12}, {14,16} };`
      `ptr = fort[0];`
4. Suppose we have the declaration **static int grid[30][100];**.
   a. Express the address of **grid[22][56]** one way.
   b. Express the address of **grid[22][0]** two ways.
   c. Express the address of **grid[0][0]** three ways.

Answers

1.

```
D  D
0  0
L  L
T  T
```

2. That makes **ref** *storage class* **extern** by default, and that storage class of array can be initialized.
3. a. 12 and 121 b. 1.0 and 3.0 c. 10023 and 0 (automatic initialization to 0) d. 12 and 16 e. 12 and 14 (just the 12 goes in the first row because of the braces)
4. **a. &grid[22][56]**
   b. &grid[22][0] and **grid[22]**
   c. &grid[0][0] and **grid[0]** and **grid**

EXERCISE

1. Modify our rain program so that it does the calculations using pointers instead of subscripts. (You still have to declare and initialize the array.)

13

CHARACTER STRINGS AND STRING FUNCTIONS

In this chapter you will find

13 CHARACTER STRINGS AND STRING FUNCTIONS

CONCEPTS

Character strings
Initializing character strings
String I/O
Using string functions
Command line arguments

Character strings form one of the most useful and important data types in C. Although we have been using character strings all along, we still have much to learn about them. Of course, we already know the most basic fact: a character string is a **char** array terminated with a null character (**'\0'**). In this chapter we will learn more about the nature of strings, how to declare and initialize strings, how to get them into and out of programs, and how to manipulate strings.

Fig. 13.1 presents a busy program which illustrates several ways to set up strings, to read them in, and to print them out. We use two new functions: **gets( ),** which fetches a string, and **puts( ),** which prints out a string. (You probably notice a family resemblance to **getchar( )** and **putchar( ).)** The rest should look fairly familiar.

```
 /* stringing the user along */
#include <stdio.h>
#define MSG "You must have many talents. Tell me some."
   /* a symbolic string constant */
#define NULL 0
#define LIM  5
#define LINLEN 81  /* maximum string length + 1 */
char m1[] = "Just limit yourself to one line's worth.";
     /* initializing an external character array */
```

```
char *m2 = "If you can't think of anything, fake it.";
     /* initializing an external character pointer */
main()
{
  char name[LINLEN];
  static char talents[LINLEN];
  int i;
  int count = 0;
  char *m3 = "\nEnough about me -- what's your  name?";
        /* initializing a pointer */
  static char *mytal[LIM] = {  "Adding numbers swiftly",
          "Multiplying accurately", "Stashing data",
          "Following instructions to the letter",
          "Understanding the C language"};
        /* initializing an array of strings */

  printf("Hi! I'm Clyde the Computer. I have many talents.\n");
  printf("Let me tell you some of them.\n");
  puts("What were they? Ah, yes, here's a partial list.");
  for ( i = 0; i < LIM; i++)
       puts( mytal[i] );  /* print list of computer talents */
  puts(m3);
  gets(name);
  printf("Well, %s, %s\n", name, MSG);
  printf("%s\n%s\n", m1, m2);
  gets(talents);
  puts("Let's see if I've got that list:");
  puts(talents);
  printf("Thanks for the information, %s.\n", name);
}
```

Figure 13.1
Program using strings.

To help you see what this program does, here is a sample run.

```
Hi! I'm Clyde the Computer. I have many talents.
Let me tell you some of them.
What were they? Ah, yes, here's a partial list.
Adding numbers swiftly
Multiplying accurately
```

```
Stashing data
Following instructions to the letter
Understanding the C language

Enough about me -- what's your name?
Nigel Barntwit
Well, Nigel Barntwit, You must have many talents. Tell me some.
Just limit yourself to one line's worth.
If you can't think of anything, fake it.
Fencing, yodeling, malingering, cheese tasting, and sighing.
Let's see if I've got that list:
Fencing, yodeling, malingering, cheese tasting, and sighing.
Thanks for the information, Nigel Barntwit.
```

Let's sift through the program. However, rather than go through it line by line, we will take a more organized approach. First, we will look at ways of defining a string within a program. Then we will look at what is involved in reading a string into a program. Finally, we will study ways to output a string.

DEFINING STRINGS WITHIN A PROGRAM

You probably noticed when you read our program that there are many ways to define a string. We are going to look at the principal ways now: using string constants, using **char** arrays, using **char** pointers, and using arrays of character strings. A program should make sure there is a place to store a string, and we will take up that topic, too.

Character String Constants

Whenever the compiler encounters something enclosed in double quotes, it recognizes it as a string constant. The enclosed characters, plus a terminating **'\0'** character, are stored in adjacent memory locations. The computer counts out the number of characters so it knows how much memory will be needed. Our program uses several such character string constants, most often as arguments for the **printf( )** and **puts( )** functions. Note, too, that we can **#define** character string constants.

If you want to have a double quotation mark *in* a string, precede it with the backslash:

```
printf("\"Run, Spot, run!\" said Dick.\n");
```

This produces the output:

```
"Run, Spot, run!" said Dick.
```

Character string constants are placed in storage class **static.** The entire phrase in quotes acts as a pointer to where the string is stored. This is analogous to the name of an array serving as a pointer to the array's location. If this is true, what kind of output should this line produce?

```
  /* strings as pointers */
main()
{
printf(" %s, %u, %c\n", "We", "love", *"figs");
}
```

Well, the **%s** format prints the string, so that should produce a **We.** The **%u** format produces an unsigned integer. If the phrase **"love"** is a pointer, then this should produce the value of **"love"** pointer, which is the address of the first character in the string. Finally, ***"figs"** should produce the value of the address pointed to, which should be the first character of the string "figs". Does this really happen? Well, we got this output:

```
We, 34, f
```

Voila! Now let's turn to strings stored in **char** arrays.

Character String Arrays and Initialization

When we define a character string array, we must let the compiler know how much space is needed. One way to do this is to initialize the array with a string constant. Since **auto** arrays cannot be initialized, we need to use **static** or **extern** arrays for this purpose. For example,

```
char m1[] = "Just limit yourself to one line's worth.";
```

initialized the external (by default) array **m1** to the indicated string. This form of initialization is short for the standard array initialization form

```
char m1[] = { 'J', 'u', 's', 't', ' ', 'l', 'i', 'm', 'i',
't', ' ', 'y', 'o', 'u', 'r', 's', 'e', 'l',
'f', ' ', 't', 'o', ' ', 'o', 'n', 'e', ' ',
'l', 'i', 'n', 'e', '\'', 's', ' ', 'w', 'o', 'r',
't', 'h', '.', '\0'
};
```

(Note the closing null character. Without it, we have a character array, but not a string.) For either form (and we do recommend the first), the compiler counts up the characters and sizes the array accordingly.

Just as for other arrays, the array name **m1** is a pointer to the first element of the array:

```
m1 == &m1[0] , *m1 == 'J', and *(m1+1) == m1[1] == 'u'
```

Indeed, we can use pointer notation to set up a string. For example, we used

```
char *m3 = "\nEnough about me - what's your name?";
```

This is very nearly the same as saying

```
static char m3[] = "Enough about me - what's your name?"
```

Both declarations amount to saying that **m3** is a pointer to the string "What's you name?". In both cases the string itself determines the amount of storage set aside for the string. But the forms are not identical.

Array vs. Pointer

What is the difference, then, between these two forms?

The array form causes an array of 38 elements (one for each character plus one for the terminating **'\0'**) to be created in static storage. Each element is initialized to the corresponding character. Hereafter, the compiler will recognize the name **m3** as a synomym for the address of the first array element, **&m3[0]**. One important point here is that **m3** is a pointer *constant*. You can't change **m3**, because that would mean changing the location (address) where the array is stored. You can use operations like **m3+1** to identify the next element in an array, but **++m3** is not allowed. The increment operator only can be used with the names of variables, not with constants.

The pointer form also causes 38 elements in static storage to be set aside for the string. In addition, it sets aside one more storage location for the pointer *variable* **m3.** This variable initially points to the beginning of the string, but the value can be changed. Thus we can use the increment operator; **++m3** would point to the second character (**E**). Note that we did not have to declare ***m3** as static. That is because we are not initializing an array of 38 elements, we are initializing a single pointer variable. There are no storage class restrictions for initializing ordinary, nonarray variables.

Are these differences important? Often they are not, but it depends on what you try to do. See the box for some examples. Meanwhile, we return to the problem of creating storage space for strings.

ARRAY AND POINTER: DIFFERENCES

In the text we discuss the differences between using declarations of these two forms:

```
static char heart[] = "I love Tillie!";
char *head = "I love Millie!";
```

The chief difference is that the pointer **heart** is a constant, while the pointer **head** is a variable. Let's see what practical difference this makes.

First, both can use pointer addition.

```
for (i = 0; i < 6; i++)
    putchar( *(heart + i) );
putchar('\n');
for (i = 0; i < 6; i++)
    putchar( *(head + i) );
putchar('\n');
```

produces the output

```
I love
I love
```

Only the pointer version can use the increment operator:

```
while ( *(head) != '\0' ) /* stop at end of string */
    putchar( *(head++); /* print character, advance pointer */
```

produces

```
I love Millie!
```

Suppose we want **head** to agree with **heart.** We can say

```
head = heart;  /* head now points to the array heart */
```

but we cannot say

```
heart = head;   /* illegal construction */
```

The situation is analogous to **x = 3;** vs. **3 = x;**. The left side of the assignment statement must be a variable name. Incidentally, **head = heart;** does not make the **Millie** string vanish; it just changes the address stored by **head.**

There is a way to alter the **heart** message, and that is to go into the array itself:

```
heart[7] = 'M';
```

or

```
*(heart + 7) = 'M';
```

The *elements* of an array are variables; just the *name* isn't.

Specifying Storage Explicitly

Another way to set up storage is to be explicit. In the external declaration, we could have said

```
char m1[44] = "Just limit yourself to one line's worth.";
```

instead of

```
char m1[] = "Just limit yourself to one line's worth.";
```

Just be sure that the number of elements is at least one more (that null character again) than the length of the string. As in other static or external arrays, any unused elements automatically are initialized to 0 (which in **char** form is the null character, not the zero digit character).

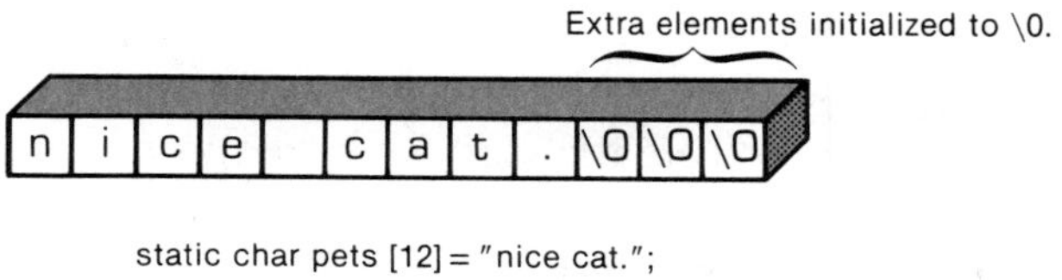

Figure 13.2
Initializing an array

Note that in our program, we had to assign a size for the array **name:**

```
char name[81];
```

Since **name** is to be read in when the program runs, the compiler has no way of knowing in advance how much space to set aside unless we tell it. There is no string constant present whose characters the compiler can count. So we took a gamble that 80 characters will be enough to hold the user's name.

Arrays of Character Strings

Often it is convenient to have an array of character strings. Then you can use a subscript to access several different strings. We used this example;

```
static char *mytal[LIM] = {  "Adding numbers swiftly",
       "Multiplying accurately", "Stashing data",
       "Following instructions to the letter",
       "Understanding the C language"};
```

Let's study this declaration. Recalling that **LIM** is **5,** we can say that **mytal** is an array of five pointers to character strings. Each character string, of course, is an array of characters, so we have five pointers to arrays. The first pointer is **mytal[0]** and it points to the first string. The second pointer is **mytal[1]** and it points to the second string. In particular, each pointer points to the first character in each string:

```
*mytal[0] == 'A', *mytal[1] == 'M', mytal[2] == 'S'
```

and so on.

The initialization follows the rules for arrays. The braced portion is equivalent to

```
{{ . . . }, { . . . }, . . . ,{ . . . } };
```

where the dots indicate the stuff we were too lazy to type in. The main point we wish to make is that the first set of double quotes corresponds to a brace-pair and thus is used to initialize the first character string pointer. The next set of double quotes initializes the second pointer, and so on. A comma separates neighboring sets.

Again, we could have been explicit about the size of the character strings by using a declaration like

```
static char mytal[LIM][LINLIM];
```

One difference is that this second choice sets up a "rectangular" array with all the rows the same length. The

```
static char *mytal[LIM];
```

choice, however, sets up a "ragged" array, with each row's length determined by the string it was initialized to. The ragged array doesn't waste any storage space.

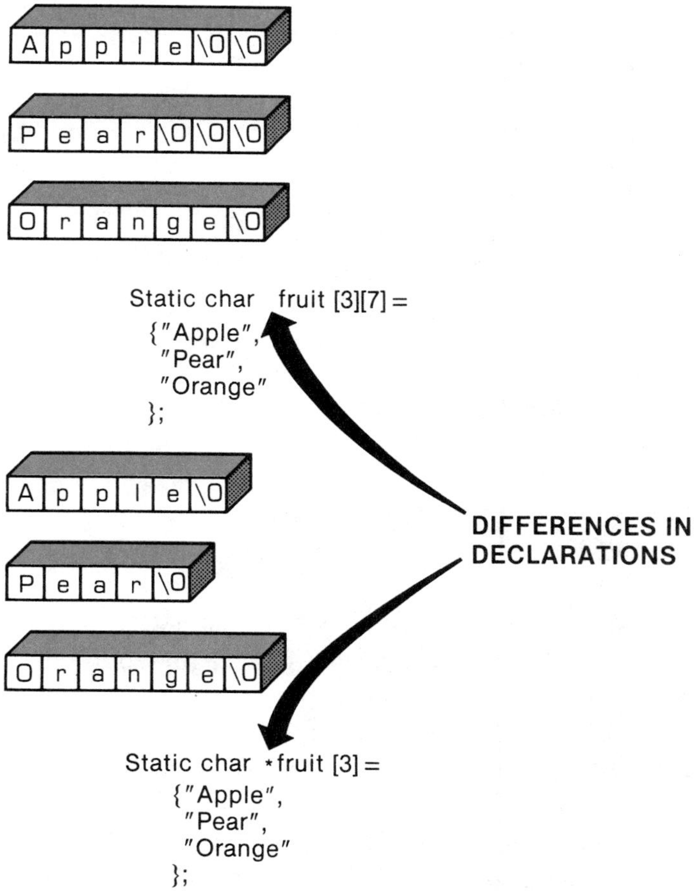

Figure 13.3
Rectangular vs. ragged array

Pointers and Strings

Perhaps you noticed an occasional reference to pointers in our discussion of strings. Most C operations for strings actually work with pointers. For example, consider the following useless, yet instructive, program.

```
 /* pointers and strings */
#define PX(X) printf("X = %s; value = %u; &X = %u\n", X, X, &X)
main()
{
  static char *mesg = "Don't be a fool!";
  static char *copy;

  copy = mesg;
  printf("%s\n", copy);
  PX(mesg);
  PX(copy);
}
```

Looking at this program, you might think it makes a copy of the string "Don't be a fool!", and your first glance at the output might seem to confirm this guess:

```
Don't be a fool!
mesg = Don't be a fool!; value = 14; &mesg = 32
copy = Dont' be a fool!; value = 14; &copy = 34
```

But study the **PX( )** output. First, **X,** which successively is **mesg** and **copy,** is printed as a string (%s). No surprises here; all the strings are "Don't be a fool!".

Next . . . well, let's come back to that later.

The third item on each line is **&X,** the address of **X.** The two pointers **mesg** and **copy** are stored in locations 32 and 34, respectively.

Now about the second item, the one we called **value.** It is **X** itself. The value of the pointer is the address it contains. We see that **mesg** points to location 14, and so does **copy.**

The meaning of this is that the string itself was never copied. All that **copy = mesg;** does is produce a second pointer pointing to the very same string.

Why all this pussy-footing around? Why not just copy the whole string?

Well, which is more efficient, copying one address or copying, say, 50 separate elements? Often, the address is all that is needed to get the job done.

Now that we have discussed defining strings within a program, let's turn to strings that are read in.

STRING INPUT

Inputting a string has two steps: setting aside space to store the string and using an input function to fetch the string.

Creating Space

The first order of business is setting up a place to put the string once it gets read. As we mentioned earlier, this means allotting sufficient storage to hold whatever strings we expect to read. Don't expect the computer to count the string length as it is read and then allot space for it. It won't (unless you write a program to do so). If you try something like this:

```
static char *name;

 scanf("%s", name);
```

it probably will get by the compiler. But when the name is read in, it will be written over data or code in your program. Most programmers regard this as highly humorous, but only in other people's programs.

The simplest thing to do is to include an explicit array size in the declaration:

```
char name[81];
```

Another possibility is to use the C library functions that allot memory, and we'll touch on that in Chapter 15.

In our program, we used an **auto** array for **name.** We could do that since we didn't have to initialize the array.

Once you have set aside space for the string, you can read the string in. As we have mentioned, input routines are not part of the definition of C. However, most systems have on tap the two library functions **scanf( )** and **gets( )**, and both can read in strings. The commonest method is to use **gets( ),** and we will discuss it first.

The *gets( )* Function

The *gets( )* (for **get** string) function is very handy for interactive programs. It gets a string from your system standard input device, which we assume is a keyboard. Since a string has no predetermined length, **gets( )** needs a way to know when to stop. Its method is to read characters until it reaches a newline (**'\n'**) character, which you generate by hitting the [enter] key. It takes all the characters before (but not including) the newline, tacks on a null character (**'\0'**), and gives the string to the calling program. Here is a simple means of using it:

```
  /* getname1 */
main()
{
  char name[81];  /* allot space */

  printf("Hi, what's your name?\n";
  gets(name);    /* place input in string "name" */
  printf("Nice name, %s.\n", name);
}
```

This will accept any name (including spaces) up to 80 characters long. (Remember to save one space for **'\0'**.)

Note that we want **gets( )** to affect something **(name)** in the calling program. This means we should use a pointer as an argument; and, of course, the name of an array *is* a pointer.

The **gets( )** function is more sophisticated than this last example suggests. Look at this:

```
 /* getname2 */
main()
{
  char name[80];
  char *ptr, *gets();

  printf("Hi, what's your name?\n");
  ptr = gets(name);
  printf("%s? Ah! %s!\n", name, ptr);
}
```

Here is a sample interchange:

```
Hi, what's your name?
Tony de Tuna
Tony de Tuna? Ah! Tony de Tuna!
```

Gets( ) gets you the input 2 ways!

1. It uses the pointer method to feed the string to **name.**
2. It uses the **return** keyword to return the string to **ptr.** Notice that **ptr** is a pointer to **char.** This means that **gets( )** must return a value that is a pointer to **char.** And up in the declaration section you can see that we so declared **gets( ).**

The declaration form

```
char *gets( );
```

says that **gets( )** is a function (hence the parentheses) of type "pointer-to-**char**" (hence the * and **char**). We got away without this declaration in **getname1** because we never tried to use the returned value of **gets( ).**

Incidentally, you can also declare something to be a pointer to a function. That would look like this:

```
char (*foop)( );
```

and **foop** would be a pointer to a function whose type is **char.** We'll talk a bit more about such fancy declarations in Chapter 14.

The structure for the **gets( )** function would look something like this:

```
char *gets(s)
char *s;
{
  char *p;
   . . .
  return(p);
}
```

The actual structure is slightly more complicated, for **gets( )** has two possible returns. If everything goes well, then it returns the read-in string, as we have said. If something goes wrong or if **gets( )** encounters an EOF character, it returns a NULL, or zero, address. Thus **gets( )** incorporates a bit of error checking.

This makes it convenient to use constructions like this:

```
while ( gets(name) != NULL)
```

where NULL is defined in **stdio.h** as **0.** The pointer aspect assigns a value to **name.** The **return** aspect assigns a value to **gets(name)** as a whole and allows us to check for EOF. This two-pronged approach is more compact than that allowed by **getchar( ),** which just has a **return** but no argument.

```
while ( (ch = getchar()) != EOF)
```

The *scanf( )* Function

We've used **scanf( )** with the **%s** format before to read in a string. The chief difference between **scanf( )** and **gets( )** lies in how they decide they have reached the end of the string; **scanf( )** is more a get word than a get string function. The **gets( )** function, we've seen, takes in all the characters up until the first newline. The **scanf( )** function has two choices. For either choice, the string starts at the first non-whitespace character encountered. If you use the **%s** format, the string runs up to (but not including) the next whitespace character (blank, tab, or newline). If you specify a field width, as in **%10s,** then **scanf( )** collects up to 10 characters or to the first whitespace character, whichever comes first.

The **scanf( )** function returns an integer value that equals the number of items read in, if successful, or an EOF character, if that's what it encounters.

```
 /* scanf() and counts */
main()
{
  static char name1[40], name2[11];
  int count;

  printf("Please enter 2 names.\n");
  count = scanf("%s %10s",name1, name2);
  printf("I read in the %d names %s and %s.\n",
           count, name1, name2);
}
```

Here are two runs:

```
Please enter 2 names.
   Jessica         Jukes
I read in the 2 names Jessica and Jukes.
```

```
Please enter 2 names.
  Liza Applebottham
I read in the 2 names Liza and Applebottham.
```

In the second example, only the first 10 characters of **Applebottham** were read, for we used a **%10s** format.

If you are obtaining only text from the keyboard, you are best off using **gets( ).** It is easier to use and is a faster, more compact function. The main use for **scanf( )** would be for inputting a mixture of data types in some standard form. For example, if each input line contains the name of a tool, the number in stock, and the cost of the item, you might use **scanf( ).** Or you might throw together a function of your own that did some entry error checking.

Now let's discuss the output process for strings.

STRING OUTPUT

Again, we must rely upon library functions, which may vary slightly from system to system. The two workhorses for string output are **puts( )** and **printf( ).**

The *puts( )* Function

This is a very easy function to use; just give it an argument that is a pointer to a string. This next example illustrates some of the many ways to do this.

```
 /* puts with ease */
#include <stdio.h>
#define DEF "I am a #defined string."
main()
{
  static char str1[] = "An array was initialized to me.";
  static char *str2 = "A pointer was initialized to me.";

  puts("I'm an argument to puts().");
  puts(DEF);
  puts(str1);
  puts(str2);
  puts(&str1[4]);
  puts(str2+4);
}
```

The output:

```
I'm an argument to puts().
I am a #defined string.
An array was initialized to me.
A pointer was initialized to me.
rray was initialized to me.
inter was initialized to me.
```

This example reminds us that phrases in quotes and the names of character array strings are pointers. Note, too, the final two examples. The pointer **&str1[4]** points to the fifth element of the array **str1.** That element contains the character **'r'**, and that is what **puts( )** uses for its starting point. Similarly, **str2+4** points to the memory cell containing the **'i'** of "pointer," and the printing starts there.

How does **puts( )** know when to stop? It stops when it encounters the null character, so there had better be one. Don't try this!

```
 /* no! */
main()
{
  static char dont[] = {'H', 'I', '!', '!' };

  puts(dont);   /* dont not a string */
}
```

Because **dont** lacks a closing null character it is not a string. Because it lacks the null character, **puts( )** won't know where to stop. It will just keep going on into the memory cells following **dont** until it finds a null somewhere. If you're lucky it might be the very next cell, but luck may fail you.

Notice that each string outputted by **puts( )** goes on a newline. When **puts( )** finally finds the closing null character, it replaces it with a newline character and then sends the string on.

The *printf( )* Function

We discussed **printf( )** pretty thoroughly elsewhere. Like **puts( ),** it takes a pointer to a string as an argument. The **printf( )** function is slightly less convenient to use than **puts( ),** but it is more versatile.

One difference is that **printf( )** does not put each string on a new line automatically. You have to indicate where you want new lines. Thus

```
printf("%s\n", string);
```

has the same effect as

```
puts(string);
```

As you can see, the first form takes more typing. It also takes longer for the computer to execute. On the other hand, **printf( )** makes it simple to combine strings for one line of printing. For example,

```
printf("Well, %s, %s\n", name, MSG);
```

combines "Well," with the user's name and symbolic character string, all on one line.

THE DO-IT-YOURSELF OPTION

You aren't limited to these library options for input and output. If you don't have them or don't like them, you can prepare your own versions, building upon **getchar( )** and **putchar( )**.

Suppose you lack a **puts( )**. Here is one way to make one:

```
 /* put1 -- prints a string */
put1(string)
char *string;
{
  while(*string != '\0')
    putchar(*string++);
  putchar('\n');
}
```

The **char** pointer **string** initially points to the first element of the called argument. After the contents of that element are printed, the pointer increments and points to the next element. This goes on until the pointer points to an element containing the null character. Then a newline is tagged on at the end.

Suppose you have a **puts( )**, but you want a function that also tells you how many characters were printed. It's easy to add that feature:

```
 /* put2 -- prints a string and counts characters */
put2(string)
char *string;
{
  int count = 0;
  while(*string != '\0')
    {
    putchar(*string++);
    count++;
    }
  putchar('\n');
  return(count);
}
```

The call

```
put2("pizza");
```

prints the string **pizza,** while the call

```
num = put2("pizza");
```

would also deliver a character count to **num,** in this case, the value **5.** Here is a slightly more elaborate version that shows nested functions:

```
 /* nested functions */
#include <stdio.h>
main()
{
  put1("If I'd as much money as I could spend,");
  printf("I count %d characters.\n",
       put2("I never would cry old chairs to mend.") );
}
```

(We **#include**d stdio.h because on our system **putchar( )** is defined there, and our new functions use **putchar( )**.)

Hmm, we are using **printf( )** to print the value of **put2( ),** but in the act of finding **put2( )'s** value, the computer first must run it, causing the string to be printed. Here's the output:

```
If I'd as much money as I could spend,
I never would cry old chairs to mend.
I count 37 characters.
```

You should be able to build a working version of **gets( )** by now; it would be similar to, but much simpler than, our **getint( )** function of Chapter 10.

STRING FUNCTIONS

Most C libraries supply string-handling functions. We'll look at the four most useful and common ones: **strlen( ), strcat( ), strcmp( ),** and **strcpy( ).**

Already we have used **strlen( ),** which finds the length of a string. We use it in this next example, a function that shortens lengthy strings.

The *strlen( )* Function

```
 /* procrustean function */
fit(string,size)
char *string;
int size;
{
    if ( strlen(string) > size)
        *(string +size) = '\0';
}
```

Try it in this test program:

```
 /* test */
main()
{
  static char mesg[] = "Hold on to your hats, hackers.";

  puts(mesg);
  fit(mesg,10);
  puts(mesg);
}
```

The output is this:

```
Hold on to your hats, hackers.
Hold on to
```

Our function placed a '\0' character in the eleventh element of the array, replacing a blank. The rest of the array is still there, but **puts( )** stops at the first null character and ignores the rest of the array.

The *strcat( )* Function

Here's what **strcat( ) can do:**

```
 /* join two strings */
#include <stdio.h>
main()
{
   static char flower[80];
   static char addon[] = "s smell like old shoes.";

   puts("What is your favorite flower?");
   gets(flower);
   strcat(flower, addon);
   puts(flower);
   puts(addon);
}
```

The output:

```
What is your favorite flower?
Rose
Roses smell like old shoes.
s smell like old shoes.
```

As you can see, **strcat( )** (for *str*ing con*cat*enation) takes two strings for arguments. A copy of the second string is tacked on to the end of the first, and this combined version becomes the new first string. The second string is not altered.

Caution! This function does not check to see if the second string will fit in the first array. If you fail to allot enough space for the first array, you will run into problems. Of course, you can use **strlen( )** to look before you leap.

```
 /* join two strings, check size first */
#include <stdio.h>
#define SIZE 80
main()
```

```
{
   static char flower[SIZE];
   static char addon[] = "s smell like old shoes.";

   puts("What is your favorite flower?");
   gets(flower);
   if ( (strlen(addon) + strlen(flower) + 1 ) < SIZE )
       strcat(flower, addon);
   puts(flower);
}
```

We add **1** to the combined lengths to allow space for the null character.

The *strcmp( )* Function

Suppose you wish to compare someone's response to a stored string:

```
 /* will this work? */
#include <stdio.h>
#define ANSWER "Grant"
main()
{
  char try[40];

  puts("Who is buried in Grant's tomb?");
  gets(try);
  while ( try != ANSWER)
      {
      puts("No, that's wrong. Try again.");
      gets(try);
      }
  puts("That's right!");
}
```

As nice as this may look, it will not work correctly. **Try** and **ANSWER** really are pointers, so what the comparison **try != ANSWER** really asks is not if two strings are the same, but if the two addresses pointed to by **try** and **ANSWER** are the same. Since **ANSWER** and **try** are stored in different locations, the two pointers are never the same, and the user is forever told that she is wrong. Such programs tend to discourage people.

What we need is a function that compares string contents, not string addresses. We could devise one, but the job has been done for us with **strcmp( )** (for *str*ing *comp*arison).

We now fix up our program:

```
 /* this will work */
#include <stdio.h>
#define ANSWER "Grant"
main()
{
  char try[40];

  puts("Who is buried in Grant's tomb?");
  gets(try);
  while ( strcmp(try,ANSWER) != 0 )
      {
      puts("No, that's wrong. Try again.");
      gets(try);
      }
  puts("That's right!");
}
```

Since nonzero values are interpreted as "true" anyway, we can abbreviate the **while** statement to **while (strcmp(try,ANSWER))**

From this example you may deduce that **strcmp( )** takes two string pointers as arguments and returns a value of **0** if the two strings are the same. Good for you for so deducing.

One of the nice points is that **strcmp( )** compares strings, not arrays. Thus, although the array **try** occupies 40 memory cells and **"Grant"** only 6 (one for the null character, don't forget), the comparison looks only at the part of **try** up to its first null-character. Thus **strcomp( )** can be used to compare strings stored in arrays of different sizes.

But what if the user answers **"GRANT"** or **"grant"** or **"Ulysses S. Grant"?** Well, that user is told he is wrong. To make a friendly program, you have to anticipate other possible correct answers. There are some tricks. You could **#define** the answer as **"GRANT"** and write a function that converts all input to upper case only. That eliminates the problem of capitalization, but you still have the other forms to worry you.

By the way, what value does **strcmp( )** return if the strings are not the same? Here is a sample:

```
 /* strcmp returns */
#include <a:stdio.h>
main()
```

```
{
   printf("%d\n", strcmp("A", "A") );
   printf("%d\n", strcmp("A", "B") );
   printf("%d\n", strcmp("B", "A") );
   printf("%d\n", strcmp("C", "A") );
   printf("%d\n", strcmp("apples", "apple") );
}
```

The output:

```
0
-1
1
2
115
```

As promised, comparing **"A"** to itself returns a **0.** Comparing **"A"** to **"B"** gives a **−1,** and reversing the comparison give a **1.** This suggests that **strcmp( )** returns a negative number if the first string precedes the second alphabetically and returns a positive number if the order is the other way. Moreover, comparing **"C"** to **"A"** gives a **2** instead of a **1.** The pattern becomes clearer: the function returns the difference in ASCII code between the two characters. More generally, **strcmp( )** moves along until it finds the first pair of disagreeing characters; it then returns the ASCII difference. For instance, in the very last example, **"apples"** and **"apple"** agree until the final **'s'** of the first string. This matches up with the 6th character in **"apple",** which is the null character, ASCII 0. The value returned is

```
's' - '\0' = 115 - 0 = 115,
```

where 115 is ASCII code for **'s'.**

Usually you don't care about the exact value returned. Typically, you just want to know if it is zero or nonzero; i.e., whether there is a match or not. Or you may be trying to sort the strings alphabetically, in which case you want to know if the comparison is positive, negative, or zero.

We can use this function for checking to see if a program should stop reading input:

```
   /* beginning of some program */
#include <stdio.h>
```

```
#define SIZE 81
#define LIM 100
#define STOP ""   /* a null string */
main()
{
  static char  input[LIM][SIZE];
  int ct = 0;

  while ( gets(input[ct]) != NULL && strcmp(input[ct],STOP)
            != 0 && ct++ < LIM)
  . . .
}
```

This program quits reading input when encountering an EOF character (**gets( )** returns **NULL** in that case), or when you hit the [enter] key at the beginning of a line (you feed in an empty string) or when you reach the limit **LIM.** Entering the empty line gives the user an easy way to terminate the entry phase.

Let's move on to the final string function we will discuss.

The *strcpy( )* Function

We've said that if **pts1** and **pts2** are both pointers to strings, then the expression

```
pts2 = pts1;
```

copies only the address of a string, not the string itself. Suppose, though, you do want to copy a string. Then you can use the **strcpy( )** function. It works like this:

```
 /* strcpy() demo */
#include <stdio.h>
#define WORDS  "Please reconsider your last entry."
main()
{
   static char *orig = WORDS;
   static char copy[40];

   puts(orig);
   puts(copy);
   strcpy(copy, orig);
   puts(orig);
   puts(copy);
}
```

Here is the output:

```
Please reconsider your last entry.

Please reconsider your last entry.
Please reconsider your last entry.
```

You can see that the string pointed to by the second argument **(orig)** is copied into the array pointed to by the first argument **(copy).** You can remember the order of the arguments by noting that it is the same as the order in an assignment statement: the string getting a value is on the left. (The blank line resulted from the first printing of **copy** and reflects the fact that **static** arrays are initialized to zeros, which are null characters in the **char** mode.)

It is your responsibility to ensure that the destination array has enough room for the incoming string. That is why we used the declaration

```
static char copy[40];
```

and not

```
static char *copy;    /* allots no space for string */
```

In short, **strcpy( )** takes two string pointers as arguments. The second pointer, which points to the original string, can be a declared pointer, an array name, or a string constant. But the first pointer, which points to the copy, should point to an array or portion of an array, of sufficient size to hold the string.

Now that we have outlined some string functions, let's look at a full program that handles strings.

A STRING EXAMPLE: SORTING STRINGS

Let's take on the practical problem of sorting strings alphabetically. This task can show up in preparing name lists, in making up an index, and in many other situations. One of the main tools in such a program is **strcmp( ),** since it can be used to determine the order of two strings. Our general plan will be to read in an array of strings, sort them, and spit them out. A little while ago we presented a scheme for reading in strings, and we

```
 /* reads in strings and sorts them */
#include <stdio.h>
#define SIZE 81        /* size limit for string length with \0 */
#define LIM 20         /* maximum number of lines to be read */
#define HALT ""     /* null string to stop input           */
main()
{
  static char input[LIM][SIZE];  /* array to store input */
  char *ptstr[LIM];  /* array of pointer variables */
  int ct = 0;    /* input count */
  int k;         /* output count */

  printf("Input up to %d lines, and I will sort them.\n",LIM);
  printf("To stop, hit the [enter] key at a line's start.\n");
  while( (gets(input[ct]) != NULL) && strcmp(input[ct],HALT)
             != 0 && ct++ < LIM)
         ptstr[ct-1]  = input[ct-1];  /*point to unsorted
input*/
  stsrt(ptstr, ct);      /* string sorter */
  puts("\nHere's the sorted list:\n");
  for ( k = 0; k < ct; k++)
       puts(ptstr[k]);    /* sorted pointers */
}
/* string-pointer-sorting function */
stsrt(strings, num)
char *strings[];
int num;
{
   char *temp;
   int top, seek;

   for ( top = 0; top < num-1; top++)
        for( seek = top + 1; seek < num; seek++)
             if ( strcmp(strings[top],strings[seek]) > 0)
                  {
                   temp = strings[top];
                   strings[top] = strings[seek];
                   strings[seek] = temp;
                   }
}
```

Figure 13.4
Program to read and sort strings.

will start the program that way. Printing the strings out is no problem, and we can use the same sorting algorithm we used earlier for numbers. We will do one slightly tricky thing; see if you can spot it.

We fed it an obscure nursery rhyme to test it.

```
Input up to 20 lines, and I will sort them.
To stop, hit the [enter] key at a line's start.
O that I was where I would be,
Then would I be where I am not;
But where I am I must be,
And where I would be I can not.
```

Here's the sorted list:

```
And where I would be I can not.
But where I am I must be,
O that I was where I would be,
Then would I be where I am not;
```

Hmm, the nursery rhyme doesn't seem to suffer much from being alphabetized.

The tricky part is that instead of rearranging the strings themselves, we just rearranged *pointers* to the strings. Let us explain. Originally, **ptrst[0]** points to **input[0],** and so on. Each **input[]** is an array of 81 elements, and each **ptrst[]** is a single variable. The sorting procedure rearranges **ptrst,** leaving **input** untouched. If, for example, **input[1]** comes before **input[0]** alphabetically, the program switches **ptrst**'s, causing **ptrst[0]** to point at **input[1]** and **ptrst[1]** to point to **input[0].** This is much easier than using, say, **strcpy( )** to interchange the contents of the two **input** strings. See the figure for another view of this process.

Finally, let's try to fill an old emptiness in our lives, namely, the void between **main( )**'s parentheses.

COMMAND-LINE ARGUMENTS

Atten-shun! The command line is the line you type to run your program. At ease! This won't be hard. Suppose we have a program in a file named **fuss.** Then the command line would look like this:

```
% fuss
```

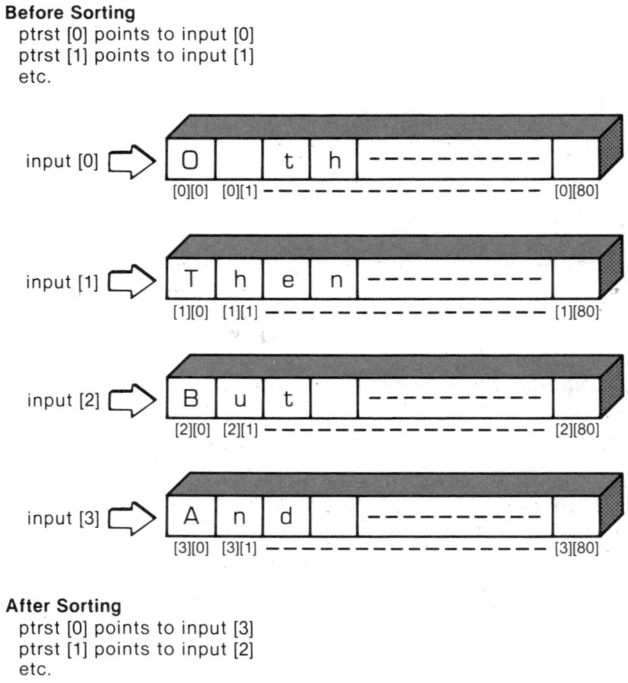

Figure 13.5
Sorting string pointers

or perhaps

```
A>fuss
```

using two common system prompts.

Command line arguments are additional items on the same line:

```
% fuss -r Ginger
```

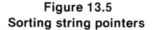

One neat thing about a C program is that it can read in these items for its own use. The mechanism is to use arguments for **main( ).** Here is a typical example:

```
 /* main() with arguments */
main(argc,argv)
int argc;
char *argv[];
```

```
{
   int count;

   for( count = 1; count < argc; count++)
      printf("%s ", argv[count]);
   printf("\n");
}
```

Put this program in an executable file called **echo,** and this is what happens:

```
A>echo I could use a little help.
  I could use a little help.
```

You probably see why it is called **echo,** but you may still be wondering how it works. Perhaps this explanation will help (we hope so).

C compilers provide for **main( )** having two arguments. The first argument represents the number of strings following the command word. By tradition (but not necessity) this **int** argument is called **argc** for *arg*ument *c*ount. The system uses spaces to tell when one string ends and the next begins. Thus our **echo** example has six strings and our **fuss** example had two. The second argument is an array of string pointers. Each string on the command line is assigned to its own pointer. By convention, this array of pointers is called **argv,** for *ar*gument *v*alues. When possible (some operating systems don't allow this), **argv[0]** is assigned the name of the program itself. Then **argv[1]** is assigned the first following string, etc. For our example, we have

```
argv[0] points to echo    (for most systems)
argv[1] points to I
argv[2] points to could
argv[6] points to help.
```

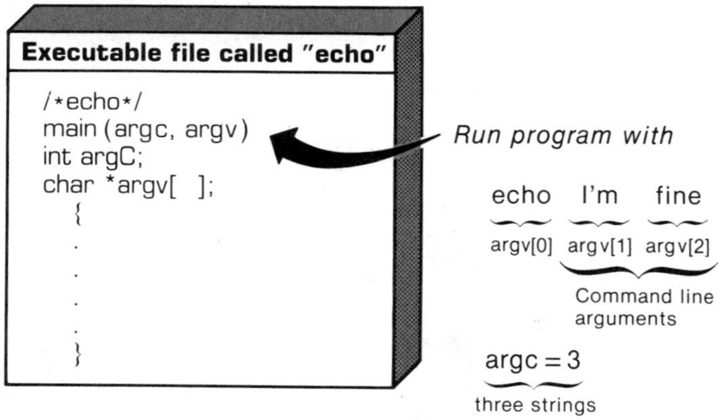

Figure 13.6
Command-line arguments.

Once you have these identifications, the rest of the program should be easy to follow.

Many programmers use a different declaration for **argv:**

```
main(argc, argv)
int argc;
char **argv;
```

The declaration for **argv** really is equivalent to **char *argv[ ];.** You would read it as saying that **argv** is a pointer to a pointer to **char.** Our example comes down to the same thing. We had an array with seven elements. The name of the array is a pointer to the first element. Thus **argv** points to

argv[0], and **argv[0]** is a pointer to **char.** Hence, even with the original definition, **argv** is a pointer to a pointer to **char.** You can use either form, but we feel the first is clearer in meaning.

One very common use for command line arguments is to indicate options for a program. For example, you might use the combination **−r** to tell a sorting program to work in reverse order. Traditionally, options are indicated using a hyphen and a letter, as in **−r.** These "flags" mean nothing to C; you have to include your own programming to recognize them.

Here is a very modest example showing how a program can check for a flag and make use of it.

```
 /* a modest beginning */
#define YES 1
#define NO 0
main(argc, argv)
int argc;
char *argv[];
{
   float array[100];
   int n;
   int flag = NO;

   if ( argv[1][0] == '-' && argv[1][1] == 'r' )
       flag = YES;
   . . .

   if flag == NO
      sort1(array,n);
   else
      sort2(array,n);
 . . .
}
```

This program checks the first string after the command file name to see if it begins with a hyphen. Then it checks to see if the next character is the code character **r.** If so it sets a flag to cause a different sorting routine to be used. It ignores strings after the first. (We said it was modest.)

If you have used the UNIX system, you probably have noticed the variety of command line options and arguments that the UNIX commands offer. These are examples of C command line arguments, for most of UNIX is written in C.

Command line arguments also can be file names, and you can use them instead of redirection to tell a program what files to work upon. We'll show you how to do that in Chapter 15.

WHAT YOU SHOULD HAVE LEARNED

How to declare a character string: **static char fun[ ]**, et al
How to initialize a character string: **static char *po = "0!"**
How to use **gets( )** and **puts( )**
How to use **strlen( ), strcmp( ), strcpy( ),** and **strcat( )**
How to use command-line arguments
How **char *bliss** and **char bliss[ ]** are similar and different
How to create a string constant: "by using quotes"

QUESTIONS AND ANSWERS

Questions

1. What's wrong with this attempted declaration of a character string?

```
main()
{
   char   name[] = {'F', 'e', 's', 's' };
```

2. What will this program print?

```
#include <stdio.h>
main()
{
   static char note[] = "See you at the snack bar.";
   char *ptr;

   ptr = note;
   puts(ptr);
   puts(++ptr);
   note[7] = '\0';
   puts(note);
   puts(++ptr);
}
```

3. What will this program print?

```
main()
{
    static char food[] = "Yummy";
    char *ptr;

    ptr = food + strlen(food);
    while ( --ptr >= food)
         puts(ptr);
}
```

4. What will the following program print?

```
main()
{
static char goldwyn[30] = "art of it all ";
static char samuel[40] = "I read p";
char  *quote = "the way through.";

strcat(goldwyn, quote);
strcat( samuel, goldwyn);
puts(samuel);
}
```

5. Design a function that takes a string pointer as argument and returns a pointer to the first blank in the string on or after the pointed-to position. Have it return a NULL pointer if it finds no blanks.

Answers

1. Storage class should be **extern** or **static**; initialization should include a '\0'.
2. See you at the snack bar.
   ee you at the snack bar.
   See you
   e you
3. y
   my
   mmy
   ummy
   Yummy
4. I read part of it all the way through.

5.
```
char *strblk(string)
char *string;
{
 while ( *string != ' ' && *string != '\0' )
     string++;    /* stops at first blank or null */
 if ( *string == '\0')
  return(NULL); /* NULL = 0 */
 else
  return(string);
}
```

EXERCISES

1. Design a function that fetches the next n characters from input, including blanks, tabs, and newlines.
2. Modify the last function so that it stops after n characters or after the first blank, tab, or newline, whichever comes first. (And don't just use **scanf( )**.)
3. Design a function that fetches the next word from input; define a word as a sequence of characters with no blanks, tabs, or newlines in it.
4. Design a function that searches the specified string for the first occurrence of a specified character. Have the function return a pointer to the character if successful, and a **NULL** if the character is not found in the string.

14

STRUCTURES AND OTHER DATA DELIGHTS

In this chapter you will find

14. STRUCTURES AND OTHER DATA DELIGHTS

CONCEPTS

Data structures
Structure templates, tags, and variables
Accessing parts of a structure
Structure pointers
Structure arrays
Functions and structures
Unions
Creating new types

KEYWORDS

struct, union, typedef

OPERATORS

->

Often the success of a program depends on finding a good way to represent the data the program must work with. C is fortunate in this respect (and not by accident), for it has a very powerful means to represent complex data. This data form, called a "structure," is not only flexible enough in its basic form to represent a diversity of data, but it also allows the user to invent new forms. If you are familiar with the "records" of Pascal, you should be comfortable with structures. Let's study a concrete example to see why a structure might be needed and how to create and use one.

EXAMPLE PROBLEM: CREATING AN INVENTORY OF BOOKS

Gwen Glenn wishes to print out an inventory of her books. There is a variety of information she would like for each book: its title, its author, its publisher, its copyright date, the number of pages, the number of copies, and the dollar value. Now some of these items, such as the titles, can be stored in an array of strings. Other items require an array of **int** or an array of **float.** With seven different arrays, keeping track of everything can get hectic, especially if Gwen wishes to have several complete lists—one sorted by title, one sorted by author, one sorted by value, and so on. A much better solution would to be use one array, where each member contained all the information about one book.

But what data form can contain strings and numbers both and somehow keep the information separate? The answer, of course, must be the subject of this chapter, the structure. To see how a structure is set up and how it works, we'll start with a limited example. To simplify the problem, we will impose two restrictions: first, we'll include only title, author, and value; second, we'll limit the inventory to one book. If you have more books than that, don't worry; we'll show you how to extend the program.

Look at the program and its output first, then we will cover the main points.

```
 /* one-book inventory */
#include <stdio.h>
#define MAXTIT  41      /* maximum length of title + 1 */
#define MAXAUT  31      /* maximum length of author's name + 1  */
struct book {   /* our first structure template: tag is book */
     char title[MAXTIT];      /* string array for title */
     char author[MAXAUT];     /* string array for author */
     float value;              /* variable to store value of book */
};                   /* end of structure template */
main()
{
     struct book libry;    /* declare variable of book-type */

     printf("Please enter the book title.\n");
     gets(libry.title);      /* access to the title portion */
     printf("Now enter the author.\n");
     gets(libry.author);
     printf("Now enter the value.\n");
```

```
    scanf("%f", &libry.value );
    printf("%s by %s: $%.2f\n",libry.title,
          libry.author, libry.value );
    printf("%s: \"%s\" \($%.2f\)\n", libry.author,
          libry.title, libry.value );
}
```

Here is a sample run:

```
Please enter the book title.
Urban Swine Raising
Now enter the author.
Godfrey Porcelot
Now enter the value.
27.50
Urban Swine Raising by Godfrey Porcelot: $27.50
Godfrey Porcelot: "Urban Swine Raising" ($27.50)
```

The structure we created has three parts: one to store the title, one to store the author, and one to store the value. The three main points we will study are

1. how to set up a format or "template" for a structure,
2. how to declare a variable to fit that template, and
3. how to gain access to the individual components of a structure variable.

SETTING UP THE STRUCTURE TEMPLATE

The structure template is the master plan which describes how a structure is put together. Our template looked like this:

```
struct book {
    char title[MAXTIT];
    char author[MAXAUT];
    float value;
    };
```

This template describes a structure made up of two character arrays and one **float** variable. Let's look at the details.

First comes the keyword **struct;** this identifies what comes next as a structure. Next comes an optional "tag," the word **book.** The tag **book** is a shorthand label we can use later to refer to this structure. Thus later on, we have the declaration

```
structure book libry;
```

which declares **libry** to be a structure of the **book** type.

Next we find the list of structure "members" enclosed in a pair of braces. Each member is described by its own declaration. For instance, the **title** portion is a **char** array with **MAXTIT** elements. The members can be any of the data types we have mentioned. That includes other structures!

Finally, we have a semicolon to close off the definition of the template.

You can place this template outside any function (externally), as we have done, or inside a function definition. If defined inside a function, then the template can be used only inside that function. If external, then the template is available to all the functions following the definition in your program. For example, in a second function, you could define

```
struct book dickens;
```

and that function would have a variable **dickens** that followed the form of our template.

We said that the tag name is optional, but one must be used when you set up structures as we did, with the template defined one place, and the actual variables defined elsewhere. We will come back to this point soon, as we look at the business of defining structure variables.

DEFINING A STRUCTURE VARIABLE

The word "structure" is used in two senses. One is the sense "structure template," which is what we just discussed. The template is a plan with no substance; it tells the compiler how to do something, but it doesn't take the next step of actually making the computer do it. The next step is to create a "structure variable"; this is the second sense of the word.

The line in our program that causes a structure variable to be created is

```
struct book libry;
```

Upon receiving this instruction, the computer creates the variable **libry.** Following the plan laid down by **book,** it allots space for a **char** array of **MAXTIT** elements, for a **char** array of **MAXAUT** elements, and for a **float** variable. This storage is lumped together under the single name **libry.** (In the next section we tell how to unlump it as needed.)

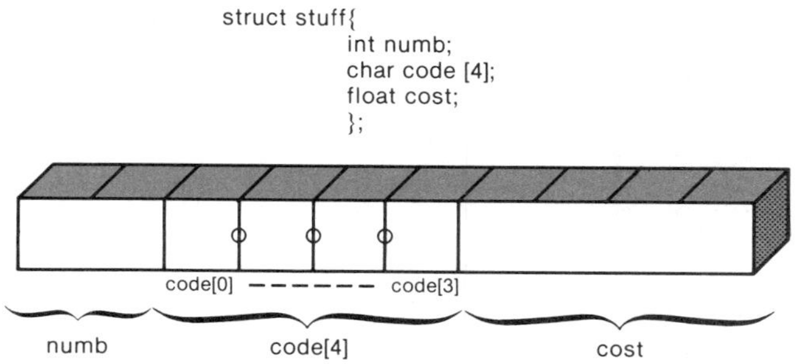

Figure 14.1
Memory allocation for a structure

In this declaration, **struct book** plays the same role that **int** or **float** does in a declaration. For example, we could declare two variables of the **struct book** type or even a pointer to that kind of structure:

```
struct book doyle, panshin, *ptbook;
```

The structure variables **doyle** and **panshin** would each have **title, author,** and **value** parts. The pointer **ptbook** could point to **doyle, panshin,** or any other **book** structure.

As far as the computer is concerned,

```
struct book libry;
```

is short for

```
struct book {
   char title[MAXTIT];
   char author[MAXAUT];
   float value;
} libry;    /* tack on variable name to template */
```

In other words, the process of defining a structure template and the process of defining a structure variable can be combined into one step.

Combining the template and the variable definitions is the one circumstance in which a tag need not be used:

```
struct  {          /* no tag */
    char title[MAXTIT];
    char author[MAXAUT];
    float value;
}  libry;
```

The tag form is much handier if you use a structure template more than once.

There is one aspect of defining a structure variable that did not come up in our example—initialization. We'll take a quick look at that now.

Initializing a Structure

We've seen how to initialize variables and arrays:

```
int count = 0;
static int fibo[] = {0,1,1,2,3,5,8};
```

Can a structure variable be initialized, too? Yes, providing the structure variable is external or static. The point to keep in mind here is that whether or not a structure variable is external depends on where the *variable* is defined, not on where the *template* is defined. In our example, the template **book** is external, but the variable **libry** is not, for it is defined inside the function and is, by default, placed in the automatic storage class. Suppose, though, we had made this declaration:

```
static struct book libry;
```

Then the storage class is static, and we could initialize the structure this way:

```
static struct book libry = {
            "The Pirate and the Damsel",
            "Renee Vivotte",
            1.95
           };
```

To make the assocations more obvious, we gave each member its own line of initialization, but all the compiler needs are commas to separate one member's initialization from the next.

Okay, let's continue with our elucidation of structure properties.

GAINING ACCESS TO STRUCTURE MEMBERS

A structure is sort of a superarray in which one element can be **char,** the next element **float,** and the next an **int** array. We can get at the individual elements of an array by using a subscript. How do we get at individual members of a structure? We use a "**.**", the structure member operator. For example, **libry.value** is the **value** portion of **libry.** You can use **libry.value** exactly as you would use any other **float** variable. Similarly, you can use **libry.title** exactly as you would use a **char** array. Thus we could use expressions like

```
gets(libry.title);
```

and

```
scanf("%f", &libry.value);
```

In essence, **.title, .author,** and **.value** play the role of subscripts for a **book** structure.

If you had a second structure variable of the same type, you would use the same system:

```
struct book spiro, gerald;

gets(spiro.title);
gets(gerald.title);
```

The **.title** refers to the first member of **book** structure.

Notice how in our initial program we printed out the contents of the structure **libry** in two different formats; this illustrates the freedom we have in using the members of a structure.

That takes care of the basics. Now we should expand our horizons and look at several ramifications of structures, including arrays of structures, structures of structures, pointers to structures, and functions and structures.

ARRAYS OF STRUCTURES

Let's fix up our book program to handle the needs of those with two or three (or perhaps even more!) books. Clearly each book can be described by one structure variable of the **book** type. To describe two books, we need to

```
 /* multiple book inventory */
#include <stdio.h>
#define MAXTIT   40
#define MAXAUT   40
#define MAXBKS   100  /* maximum number of books */
#define STOP ""      /* null string, ends input */
struct book {         /* set up book template */
    char title[MAXTIT];
    char author[MAXAUT];
    float value;
    };
main()
{
struct book  libry[MAXBKS];  /* an array of book structures */
int count = 0;
int index;

printf("Please enter the book title.\n");
printf("Hit [enter] at the start of a line to stop.\n");
while ( strcmp(gets(libry[count].title),STOP) != 0 &&
          count < MAXBKS )
    {
    printf("Now enter the author.\n");
    gets(libry[count].author);
    printf("Now enter the value.\n");
    scanf("%f", &libry[count++].value );
    while ( getchar() != '\n'); /*clear input line */
    if ( counts < MAXBKS )
          printf("Enter the next title.\n");
    }
printf("Here is the list of your books:\n");
for( index = 0; index < count; index++)
   printf("%s by %s: $%.2f\n",libry[index].title,
          libry[index].author, libry[index].value );
}
```

Figure 14.2
Multiple book inventory program.

use two such variables, and so on. To handle several books, we need an array of such structures, and that is what we have created in the next program, shown in Fig. 14.2).

Here is a sample program run:

```
Please enter the book title.
Hit [enter] at the start of a line to stop.
My Life as a Budgie
Now enter the author.
Mack Zackles
Now enter the value.
12.95
Enter the next title.
     . . . more entries . . .
Here is the list of your books:
My Life as a Budgie by Mack Zackles: $12.95
Thought and Unthought by Kindra Schlagmeyer: $33.50
The Anatomy of an Ant by Salome Deschamps: $9.99
Power Tiddlywinks by Jack Deltoids: $13.25
Unix Primer Plus by Waite, Martin, & Prata: $19.95
Coping with Coping by Dr. Rubin Thonkwacker: $0.00
Delicate Frivolity by Neda McFey: $29.99
Fate Wore a Bikini by Mickey Splats: $8.95
A History of Buvania by Prince Nikoli Buvan: $50.00
Mastering Your Digital Watch by Miklos Mysz: $13.95
```

The two main points to note about an array of structures are how to declare them and how to get access to individual members. After explaining that, we will come back to point out a couple aspects of the program.

Declaring an Array of Structures

The process of declaring a structure array is perfectly analogous to declaring any other kind of array:

```
struct book libry[MAXBKS];
```

This declares **libry** to be an array with **MAXBKS** element. Each element of the array is a structure of **book** type. Thus **libry[0]** is a **book** structure, **libry[1]** is a second **book** structure, and so on. Fig. 14.3 may help you visualize this. The name **libry** itself is not a structure name; it is the name of the array holding the structures.

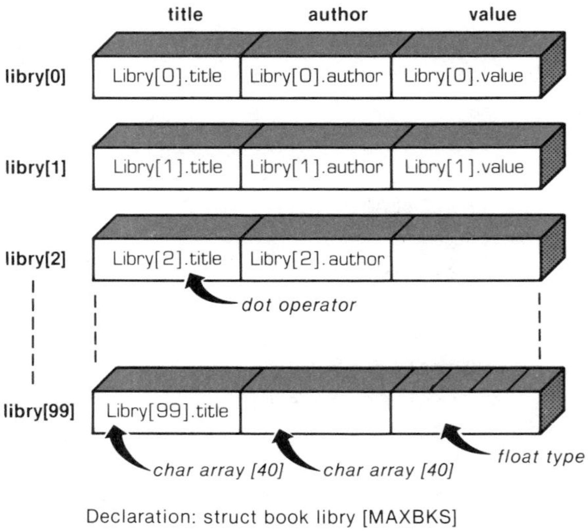

Figure 14.3
An array of structures

Identifying Members of a Structure Array

We identify members of an array of structures by applying the same rule we use for individual structures: follow the structure name with the member operator and the member name:

`libry[0].value` is the value associated with the first `array element`

`libry[4].title` is the title associated with the fifth `array element`

Note that the array subscript is attached to **libry** and not to the end of the name:

```
libry.value[2]     /* WRONG */
libry[2].value     /* RIGHT */
```

The reason we use **libry[2].value** is that **libry[2]** *is* the structure variable name, just as **libry[1]** is another structure variable name and earlier **doyle** was a structure variable name.

By the way, what do you suppose

```
libry[2].title[4]
```

would be? It would be the fifth element in the title (that's the **title[4]** part) of the book described by the third structure (that's the **libry[2]** part). In our example, this would be the character **A.** This points out that subscripts found to the right of the "." operator apply to individual members, while subscripts to the left of the operator apply to arrays of structures.

Let's finish up with the program now.

Program Details

The main change from our first program is that we put in a loop to read in successive books. We begin the loop with this **while** condition:

```
while ( strcmp(gets(libry[count].title),STOP) != 0 &&
        count < MAXBKS )
```

The expression **gets(libry[count].title)** reads an input string for the title of a book. The **strcmp( )** function compares this string to **STOP,** which is just " ", the empty string. If the user hits [enter] at the beginning of a line, the empty string is transmitted, and the loop ends. We also have a check to keep the number of books read in under the size limit of the array.

Then there is the strange line

```
while ( getchar() != '\n'); /*clear input line */
```

This is included to handle a peculiarity of **scanf( ).** The **scanf( )** function ignore spaces and newlines. When you respond to the request for the book's value, you type something like

```
12.50[enter]
```

This transmits the sequence of characters

```
12.50\n
```

The **scanf( )** function collects the **1,** the **2,** the ., and **5,** and the **0,** but it leaves the **\n** sitting there, awaiting whatever read statement comes next. If our strange line is missing, the next read statement is **gets(libry[count].title)** in the loop control statement. So it would read the leftover newline character as its *first* character, and the program would think we had sent a stop signal. So we put in our strange line. If you study it, you will see it eats up characters until it finds and gets the newline. It doesn't do anything with the character except remove it from the input queue. This gives **gets( )** a fresh start.

Now let's get back to exploring structures.

NESTED STRUCTURES

Sometimes it is convenient for one structure to contain, or "nest," another. For example, Shalala Pirosky is building up a structure containing information about her friends. One member of the structure, naturally enough, is the friend's name. The name, however, can be represented by a structure itself, with separate entries for first and last name. Fig. 14-4 is a condensed example of Shalala's work.

```
  /* example of a nested structure */
#define LEN 20
#define M1 "    Thank you for the wonderful evening, "
#define M2 "You certainly prove that a "
#define M3 "is a special kind of guy. We must get together"
#define M4 "over a delicious "
#define M5 " and have a few laughs."
struct names {              /* first structure template */
             char first[LEN];
             char last[LEN];
   };
struct guy {                /* second template */
            struct names handle;     /* nested structure */
            char favfood[LEN];
            char job[LEN];
            float income;
   };
main()
{
  static struct guy fellow = {        /* initialized a variable */
```

```
            { "Franco", "Wathall" },
            "eggplant",
            "doormat customizer",
            15435.00
        };

    printf("Dear %s, \n\n", fellow.handle.first);
    printf("%s%s.\n", M1, fellow.handle.first);
    printf("%s%s\n", M2, fellow.job);
    printf("%s\n", M3);
    printf("%s%s%s\n\n", M4, fellow.favfood, M5);
    printf("%40s%s\n", " ", "See you soon,");
    printf("%40s%s\n", " ", "Shalala");
}
```

Figure 14.4
Nested structure program

Here is the output:

```
Dear Franco,

     Thank you for the wonderful evening, Franco.
You certainly prove that a doormat customizer
is a special kind of guy. We must get together
over a delicious eggplant and have a few laughs.

                                        See you soon,
                                        Shalala
```

The first point to note is how the nested structure is set up in the template. It simply is declared, just as an **int** variable would:

```
    struct names handle;
```

This says that **handle** is a variable of the **struct names** type. Of course, the file should also include the template for the **names** structure.

The second point to note is how we gain access to a member of a nested structure. We just use the "." operator twice:

```
fellow.handle.first == "Franco"
```

We interpret the construction this way, going from left to right:

```
(fellow.handle).first
```

That is, first find **fellow,** then find the **handle** member of **fellow,** then find the **first** member of that.

For our next act, we will look at pointers.

POINTERS TO STRUCTURES

Pointer lovers will be glad to know you can have pointers to structures. This is good for at least three reasons. First, just as pointers to arrays are easier to manipulate (in a sorting problem, say) than the arrays themselves, so are pointers to structures easier to manipulate than structures themselves. Second, a structure can't be passed as an argument to a function, but a pointer to a structure can be. Third, many wondrous data representations are structures containing pointers to other structures.

The next short example (Fig. 14.5) shows how to define a pointer to a structure and how to use it to get to the members of a structure.

```
 /* pointer to a structure */
#define LEN 20
struct names {
             char first[LEN];
             char last[LEN];
    };
struct guy {
             struct names handle;
             char favfood[LEN];
             char job[LEN];
             float income;
    };
main()
{
  static struct guy fellow[2] = {
         {    { "Franco", "Wathall"  },
                 "eggplant",
                 "doormat customizer",
                 15435.00
         },
```

```
            {    { "Rodney" , "Swillbelly" },
                   "salmon mousse",
                   "interior decorator",
                   35000.00
            }
        };
    struct guy *him;  /* HERE IT IS -- a pointer to a structure */

    printf("address #1: %u #2: %u\n", &fellow[0], &fellow[1] );
    him = &fellow[0];  /* tell the pointer where to point */
    printf("pointer #1: %u #2: %u\n", him, him + 1);
    printf("him->income is $%.2f: (*him).income is $%.2f\n",
           him->income, (*him).income);
    him++;    /* point to the next structure */
    printf("him->favfood is %s:  him->names.last is %s\n",
           him->favfood,     him->handle.last);
}
```

Figure 14.5
Program with pointer to a structure

The output, please:

```
address #1: 12  #2: 96
pointer #1: 12  #2: 96
him->income is $15435.00: (*him).income is $15435.00
him->favfood is salmon mousse:  him->names.last is Swillbelly
```

Let's look first at how we created a pointer to a **guy** structure. Then we'll study how to specify individual structure members by using the pointer.

Declaring and Initializing a Structure Pointer

Declaration is as easy as can be:

```
struct guy *him;
```

First is the keyword **struct,** then the template tag **guy,** then an * followed by the pointer name. The syntax is the same as for the other pointer declarations we have seen.

The pointer **him** now can be made to point to any structures of the **guy** type. We initialize **him** by making it point to **fellow[0];** note that we use the address operator:

```
him = &fellow[0];
```

The first two output lines show the success of this assignment. Comparing the two lines, we see that **him** points to **fellow[0]** and **him + 1** points to **fellow[1].** Note that adding **1** to **him** adds 84 to the address. This is because each **guy** structure occupies 84 bytes of memory: first name is 20, last name is 20, favfood is 20, job is 20, and income is 4, the size of **float** on our system.

Member Access by Pointer

We have **him** pointing to the *structure* **fellow[0].** How can we use **him** to get a value of a *member* of **fellow[0]?** The third output line shows two methods.

The first method, and the most common, uses a new operator, ->. This operator is formed by typing a hyphen (-) followed by the "greater than" symbol (>). The example helps make the meaning clear:

```
him->income    is fellow[0].income if him = &fellow[0]
```

In other words, a structure pointer followed by the -> operator works the same as a structure name followed by the "." operator. (We can't properly say **him.income** because **him** is not a structure name.)

It is important to note that **him** is a *pointer* but **him->income** is a *member* of the pointed-to structure. Thus, in this case, **him->income** is a **float** variable.

The second method for specifying the value of a structure member follows from this sequence: If **him == &fellow[0],** then ***him == fellow[0].** This is because **&** and * are reciprocal operators. Hence

```
fellow[0].income == (*him).income
```

by substitution. The parentheses are required because the "." operator has higher precedence than *.

In summary, if **him** is a pointer to the structure **fellow[0],** then the following are all equivalent:

```
fellow[0].income == (*him).income == him->income
```

Now let's see how to handle the interaction between structures and functions.

SUMMARY: STRUCTURE AND UNION OPERATORS

I. The Membership Operator:

This operator is used with a structure or union name to specify a member of that structure or union. If **name** is the name of a structure and **member** is a member specified by the structure template, then

```
name.member
```

identifies that member of the structure. The membership operator can also be used in the same fashion with unions.

Example:

```
struct {
        int code;
        float cost;
        }   item;

item.code = 1265;
```

This assigns a value to the **code** member of the structure **item.**

II. The Indirect Membership Operator: − >

This operator is used with a pointer to a structure or union to identify a member of that structure or union. Suppose **ptrstr** is a pointer to a structure and that **member** is a member specified by the structure template. Then

```
ptrstr->member
```

identifies that member of the pointed-to structure. The indirect membership operator can be used in the same fashion with unions.

Example:

```
struct {
       int code;
       float cost;
       } item, *ptrst;
```

```
ptrst = &item;
ptrst->code = 3451;
```

This assigns a value to the **code** member of **item.** The following three expressions are equivalent:

```
ptrst->code    item.code       (*ptrst).code
```

TELLING FUNCTIONS ABOUT STRUCTURES

Recall that function arguments pass *values* to the function. Each value is a number, perhaps **int,** perhaps **float,** perhaps ASCII code, or perhaps an address. A structure is a bit more complicated than a single value, so it is not surprising that a structure itself cannot be used as an argument for a function. (This limitation is being removed in some newer implementations.) There are, however, ways to get information about a structure into a function. We'll look at three methods (actually, two with variations) here.

Using Structure Members

As long as a structure member is variable with a single value (i.e., an **int** or one of its relatives, a **char,** a **float,** a **double,** or a pointer), it can be passed as a function argument. The primitive financial analysis program of Fig. 14.6, which adds the client's bank account to his savings and loan account, illustrates this point. Note, incidentally, that we combined the template definition, the variable declaration, and the initialization into one statement.

```
 /* passing structure members as function arguments */
struct funds  {
               char *bank;
               float bankfund;
               char *save;
               float savefund;
            }     stan    =   {
                              "Garlic-Melon Bank",
                               1023.43,
                              "Snoopy's Savings and Loan",
                               4239.87
                              };
```

```
main()
{
  float total, sum();
  extern struct funds stan;  /* optional declaration */

  printf("Stan has a total of $%.2f.\n",
           sum(stan.bankfund, stan.savefund)  );
}
  /* adds two float numbers */
float sum(x,y)
float x, y;
{
  return(x + y);
}
```

Figure 14.6
Program passing structure members as function arguments

The result of running this program is

```
Stan has a total of $5263.30.
```

Ah, it works. Notice that the function **sum( )** doesn't know or care whether the actual arguments are members of a structure or not; it just requires that they be type **float.**

Of course if you want a program to affect the value of a member in the calling program, you can transmit the address of the member:

```
modify(&stan.bankfund);
```

would be a function that altered Stan's bank account.

The next approach to telling a function about a structure involves letting the summing function know that it is dealing with a structure.

Using the Structure Address

We will solve the same problem as before, but this time we will use the address of the structure as an argument. This is fine, for an address is just a single number. Since the function will have to work with the **funds** structure, it, too, will have to make use of the **funds** template. See Fig. 14.7 for the program.

```
 /* passing a structure address to a function */
struct funds  {
                char *bank;
                float bankfund;
                char *save;
                float savefund;
            }       stan     =  {
                               "Garlic-Melon Bank",
                                 1023.43,
                               "Snoopy's Savings and Loan",
                                 4239.87
                               };

main()
{
  float total, sum();

  printf("Stan has a total of $%.2f.\n", sum( &stan)  );
}
float sum(money)
struct funds *money;
```

```
{
  return( money->bankfund + money->savefund );
}
```

Figure 14.7
Program using address of structure as a function

This, too, produces the output

```
Stan has a total of $5263.30.
```

The **sum( )** function has a pointer **(money)** to a **fund** structure. Passing the address **&stan** to the function causes the pointer **money** to point to the structure **stan.** We then use the **->** operator to gain the values of **stan.bankfund** and of **stan.savefund.**

This function also has access to the institution names, although it doesn't use it.

Note that we must use the **&** operator to get the structure address. Unlike the array name, the structure name alone is not a synonym for its address.

Our next method applies to an array of structures and is a variation of this method.

Using an Array

Suppose we have an array of structures. The name of an array *is* a synonym for its address, so it can be passed to a function. Again, the function will need access to the structure template. To show how this works (Fig. 14. 8), we expand our program to two people, so that we have an array of two **funds** structures.

```
 /* passing an array of structures to a function */
struct funds  {
                char *bank;
                float bankfund;
                char *save;
                float savefund;
             }    jones[2] =  {
                                {
                                "Garlic-Melon Bank",
                                1023.43,
```

```
                                        "Snoopy's Savings and Loan",
                                        4239.87
                                        },
                                        {
                                        "Honest Jack's Bank",
                                        976.57,
                                        "First Draft Savings",
                                        1760.13
                                        }
                                      };
main()
{
  float total, sum();

  printf("The Joneses have a total of $%.2f.\n",
           sum( jones ) );
}
float sum(money)
struct funds *money;
{
   float total;
   int i;

   for( i = 0, total = 0; i < 2; i++, money++)
      total += money->bankfund + money->savefund;
   return(total);
}
```

Figure 14.8
Program passing an array of structures to a function

The output:

```
The Joneses have a total of $8000.00.
```

(What an even sum! One would almost think the figures were invented.)

The array name **jones** is a pointer to the array. In particular, it points to the first element of the array, which is the structure **jones[0].** Thus, initially the pointer **money** is given by

```
money = &jones[0];
```

Then using the -> operator lets us add the two funds for the first Jones. This is really very much like the last example. Next, the **for** loop increments the pointer **money** by 1. Now it points to the next structure, **jones[1],** and the rest of the funds can be added on to **total.**

These are the two main points:

1. We can use the array name to pass a pointer to the first structure in the array to a function.

2. We then can use pointer arithmetic to move the pointer to successive structures in the array. Note that the function call

```
sum(&jones[0])
```

would have the same effect as using the array name, since both refer to the same address. Using the array name is just an indirect way of passing the structure address.

STRUCTURES: WHAT NEXT?

We won't take the explanation of structures any further, but we would like to mention one of the more important uses of structures: creating new data forms. Computer users have developed data forms much more efficient for certain problems than the arrays and simple structures we have presented. These forms have names such as queues, binary trees, heaps, hash tables, and graphs. Many such forms are built from "linked" structures. Typically, each structure will contain one or two items of data plus one or two pointers to other structures of the same type. The pointers serve to link one structure to another and to furnish a path to let you search through the overall structure. For example, Fig. 14.9 shows a binary tree structure, with each individual structure (or "node") connected to two below it.

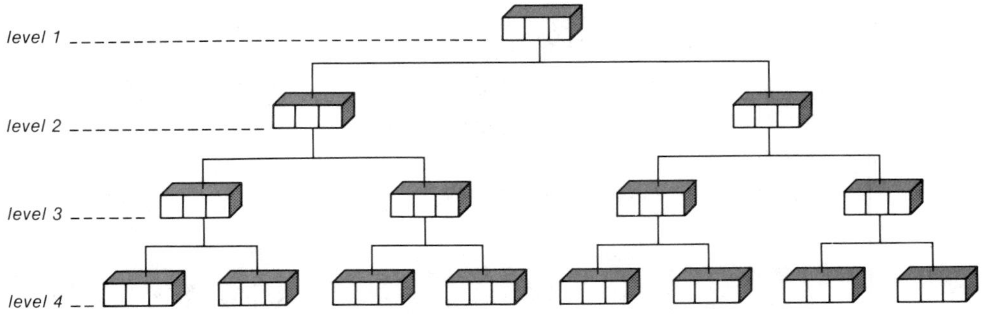

Figure 14.9
A binary tree structure.

Is such a branchy thing more efficient than an array? Well, consider the case of a tree with 10 levels of nodes. If you work it out, you find there are 1023 nodes in which you could store, say, 1023 words. If the words are arranged according to some sensible plan, you can start at the top level and find any word in at most 9 moves as your search moves down one level to the next. If you had the words in an array, you might have to search all 1023 elements before finding the word.

If you are interested in more advanced data structures, consult a book on computing science. With the C structure feature, you will be able to reproduce the forms you read about.

That's our final word on structures. Next, we will take a quick look at two other C features for dealing with data: the union and **typedef**.

UNIONS—A QUICK LOOK

A union is a device that lets one store different data types in the same memory space. A typical use would be creating a table to hold a mixture of types in some order which is neither regular nor known in advance. The union allows you to create an array of equal-sized units, each of which can hold a variety of data types.

Unions are set up in much the same way as structures. There is a union template, and a union variable. They can be defined in one step or, by using a union tag, in two. Here is an example of a template with a tag:

```
union  holdem {
                int digit;
```

```
        double bigfl;
        char  letter;
      };
```

Here is an example of defining union variables of the **holdem** type:

```
union holdem fit;  /* union variable of holdem type */
union holdem save[10];  /* array of 10 union variables */
union holdem *pu;  /* pointer to a variable of holdem type */
```

The first declaration creates a single variable **fit.** The compiler allots enough space so that it can hold the largest of the described possibilities. In this case, the biggest possibility listed is **double,** which requires 64 bits, or 8 bytes, on our system. The array **save** would have 10 elements, each 8 bytes big.

Here is how a union is used:

```
fit.digit = 23;  /* 23 is stored in fit; 2 bytes used */
fit.double = 2.0; /* 23 cleared, 2.0 stored; 8 bytes used */
fit.letter = 'h'; /* 2.0 cleared, h stored; 1 byte used */
```

You use the membership operator to show which data type is being used. Only one value is stored at a time; you can't store a **char** and an **int** at the same time, even though there is space enough to do so.

It is your responsibility to keep track of the data type currently being stored in a union; the next sequence shows what not to do:

```
fit.letter = 'A';
 flnum = 3.02*fit.double;    /* ERROR ERROR ERROR */
```

This is wrong because a **char** type is stored, but the next line assumes the content of **fit** is a **double** type.

You can use the −> operator with unions in the same fashion you did with structures:

```
pu = &fit;
 x = pu->digit;  /* same as x = fit.digit  */
```

Now let's look at another advanced data feature.

typedef—A QUICK LOOK

The **typedef** feature lets you create your own name for a type. It is a lot like **#define** in that respect, but with three differences:

1. Unlike **#define, typedef** is limited to giving symbolic names to data types only.
2. The **typedef** function is performed by the compiler, not the preprocessor.
3. Within its limits, **typedef** is more flexible than **#define.**

Let's see how it works. Suppose you want to use the term **real** for **float** numbers. Then you define **real** as if it were a **float** variable and precede the definition by the keyword **typedef:**

```
typedef float real;
```

From then on, you can use **real** to define variables:

```
real x, y[25], *pr;
```

The scope of this definition depends on the location of the **typedef** statement. If the definition is inside a function, the scope is local, confined to that function. If the definition is outside a function, then the scope is global.

Often, upper-case letters are used for these definitions to remind the user that the type name is really a symbolic abbreviation:

```
typedef float REAL;
```

The last example could have been accomplished with a **#define.** Here is one that couldn't:

```
typedef char *STRING;
```

Without the keyword **typedef,** this would identify **STRING** itself as a pointer to **char.** With the keyword, it makes **STRING** an *identifier* for pointers to **char.** Thus

```
STRING name, sign;
```

means

```
char *name, *sign;
```

We can use **typedef** with structures, too. Here is an example:

```
typedef struct COMPLEX {
                        float real;
                        float imag;
                        };
```

We then can use type **COMPLEX** to represent complex numbers.

One reason to use **typedef** is to create convenient, recognizable names for types that turn up often. For instance, many users prefer to use **STRING** or its equivalent as we did above.

Secondly, **typdef** names often are used for complicated types. For example, the declaration

```
typedef char *FRPTC () [5];
```

makes **FRPTC** announce a type that is a function that returns a pointer to a five-element array of **char.** (See our box on fancy declarations.)

A third reason for using **typedef** is to make programs more portable. Suppose, for instance, that your program needs to use 16-bit numbers. On some systems, that would be type **short;** on others it might be type **int.** If you just used **short** or **int** in your declarations, you would have to alter all the declarations when you moved from one system to the other. Instead, do this. In an **#include** file have this definition:

```
typedef short TWOBYTE;
```

Use **TWOBYTE** in your programming for those **short** variables that must be 16 bits. Then when you move the program to where type **int** is needed instead, just change the single definition in your **#include** file:

```
typedef int TWOBYTE;
```

This is an example of what makes C such a portable language.

When using **typedef,** bear in mind that it does not create new types, it just creates convenient labels.

FANCY DECLARATIONS

C allows you to create elaborate data forms. We are sticking to simpler forms, but we feel it is our duty to point out the potentialities. When we make a declaration, the name (or "identifier") we use can be modified by tacking on a modifier:

Modifier	Significance
`*`	indicates a pointer
`()`	indicates a function
`[]`	indicates an array

C lets us use more than one modifier at a time, and that lets us create a variety of types:

```
int board[8][8];  /* an array of arrays of int */
int **ptr;  /* a pointer to a pointer to int */
int *risks[10];  /* a 10-element array of pointers to int */
int (*wisks)[10]; /* a pointer to a 10-element array of int */
int *oof[3][4]; /* a 3-element array of pointers to a
                   4-element array of int */
int (*uuf)[3][4]; /* a pointer to a 3 × 4 array of int */
```

The trick to unravelling these declarations is figuring out in which order to apply the modifiers. Three rules will get you through.

1. The closer a modifier is to the identifier, the higher its priority.
2. The **[ ]** and **( )** modifiers have higher priority than *****.
3. Parentheses used to group parts of the expression have the highest priority of all.

Let's apply these rules to

```
int *oof[3][4];
```

The * and the **[3]** are both adjacent to **oof** and have higher priority than **[4]** (rule 1). The **[3]** has higher priority than the * (rule 2). Hence **oof** is a three-element array (first modifier) of pointers (second modifier) to a four-element array (third modifier) of **int** (declared type).

In

```
int (*uuf)[3][4];
```

the parentheses cause the * modifier to have first priority, making **uuf** a pointer as indicated in the description above.

These rules also yield the following types:

```
char  *fump();      /* function returning pointer to char */
char  (* frump ) (); /* pointer to a function that returns
                        type char */
char  *flump () [3]; /* function returning pointer to
a 3-element array of char  */
char *flimp[3] ();  /* a 3-element array of pointers to
a function that returns type char */
```

When you bring structures into the picture, the possibilities for declarations truely grow baroque. And the applications—well, we'll leave that for nonprimers.

With structures, unions, and **typedef,** C gives you the tools for efficient and portable data handling.

WHAT YOU SHOULD HAVE LEARNED

What a structure template is and how to define one
What a structure tag is and how to use one
How to define a structure variable: **struct car honda;**
How to access a member of a structure: **honda.mpg**
How to access a pointer to a structure: **struct car *ptcar;**
How to access a member using a pointer: **ptcar−>mpg**
How to feed a member to a function: **eval(honda.mpg)**
How to make a structure known to a function: **rate(&honda)**
How to make a nested structure
How to access a nested member: **honda.civic.cost**
How to make and use arrays of structures: **struct car gm[5];**
How to set up a union: like a structure
How to use **typedef: typedef struct car CRATE;**

QUESTIONS AND ANSWERS

Questions

1. What's wrong with this template?

```
structure {
       char itible;
       int  num[20];
       char *togs
       }
```

2. Here is a portion of a program; what will it print?

```
struct house {
                  float sqft;
                  int rooms;
                  int stories;
                  char *address;
                  };
main()
{
  static struct house fruzt = { 1560.0, 6, 1, "22 Spiffo Road" };
  struct house *sign;

  sign = &fruzt;
  printf("%d %d\n", fruzt.rooms, sign->stories);
  printf("%s \n", fruzt.address);
  printf("%c %c\n", sign->address[3], fruzt.address[4])/;
}
```

3. Devise a structure template that will hold the name of a month, a three-letter abbreviation for the month, the number of days in the month, and the month number.
4. Define an array of twelve structures of the sort in question 3 and initialize it for a nonleap year.
5. Write a function that given the month number, returns the total days in the year up through that month. Assume the structure template and array of questions 3 and 4 are declared externally.
6. Given the following **typedef**, declare a 10-element array of the indicated structure. Then, using individual member assignment, let the 3rd element describe a Remarkatar lens of focal length 500 mm and aperture f/2.0.

```
typedef struct {                /* lens descriptor */
                  float foclen;  /* focal length,mm*/
                  float fstop;   /* aperture      */
                  char *brand;   /* brand name     */
                } LENS;
```

Answers

1. The key word is **struct,** not **structure.** The template requires either a tag before the opening brace or a variable name after the closing brace. Also there should be a semicolon after ***togs** and at the end of the template.
2.
```
6 1
22 Spiffo Road
S p
```

The member *fruzt.address* is a character string, and **fruzt.address[4]** is the fifth element of that array.

3.
```
struct month {
                  char name[10];    /* or char *name;    */
                  char abbrev[4]; /* or char *abbrev; */
                  int days;
                  int monumb;
                  };
```
4.
```
struct month months[12] = {
                            { "January", "Jan", 31, 1},
                            { "February", "Feb", 28, 2},
                                    and so on
                            { "December", "Dec", 31, 12}
                          };
```
5.
```
days(month)
int month;
{
   int index, total;

   if ( month < 1 || month > 12 )
      return(-1);  /*  error signal */
   else
      for ( index = 0, total = 0; index < month; index ++)
            total += months[index].days;
       return( total);
}
```

Note that **index** is one less than month number, since arrays start with subscript 0; hence we use **index < month** instead of **index <= month.**

6. `LENS tubby[10];`

```
tubby[2].foclen = 500.0;
tubby[2].fstop = 2.0;
tubby[2].brand = "Remarkatar";
```

EXERCISES

1. Redo question 5, but have the argument be the spelled-out name of the month instead of the month number. (Don't forget about **strcmp( )**.)
2. Write a program that asks the user to input the day, month, and year. The month can be a month number, a month name, or a month abbreviation. The program then returns the total number of days in the year up through the given day.
3. Revise our book-listing program so that it prints out the book descriptions alphabetized by title and so that it prints out the total value of the books.

15

THE C LIBRARY AND FILE INPUT/OUTPUT

In this chapter you will find

15. THE C LIBRARY AND FILE INPUT/OUTPUT

CONCEPTS

The C library
Files in C
File-handling functions
Character-checking macros
Memory allotment functions

Whenever we have used functions such as **printf( ), getchar( ),** and **strlen( ),** we have used the C library. The C library contains dozens of functions and macros for you to draw upon. Libraries vary from system to system, but there is a core of functions (called the standard library) that most share. We will examine fifteen of the most common of these functions in this chapter, concentrating on input/output functions and on using files.

First, however, let's talk about how to use the library.

GAINING ACCESS TO THE C LIBRARY

How you get access to the C library depends on your system, so you will have to check yourself to see how our more general statements apply. First, there are often several different places to find library functions. For example, **getchar( )** is usually defined as a macro in the file **stdio.h,** while **strlen( )** is usually kept in a library file. Second, different systems have different ways to reach these functions. Here are three of the possibilities.

Automatic Access

On many of the larger UNIX systems, you just compile the program and the more common library functions are made available automatically.

File Inclusion

If a function is defined as a macro, then you can **#include** the file containing the definition. Often, similar functions will be collected together in an appropriately titled header file. For example, many systems have a **ctype.h** file containing several macros that determine the nature of a character: upper-case, digit, etc.

Library Inclusion

At some stage in compiling or loading a program, you may have to specify a library option. On our system, for example, there is a file **lc.lib** containing compiled versions of the library functions, and we tell the IBM PC linker to use this library. Even a system that checks its standard library automatically may have other libraries of less-frequently used functions, and these libraries will have to be requested explicitly by using a compile-time option.

Clearly, we can't go through all the specifics for all systems, but these three examples should help show you what to look for.

Now let's look at some functions.

LIBRARY FUNCTIONS WE HAVE USED

We're just going to list them briefly to give you the thrill of recollection. First, there were the I/O functions:

```
getchar()          /* fetch a character      */
putchar()          /* print a character      */
gets()             /* fetch a line           */
puts()             /* print a line           */
scanf()            /* fetch formatted input  */
printf()           /* print formatted output */
```

Then there were the string-handling functions:

```
strlen()          /* find the length of a string */
strcmp()          /* compare two strings         */
strcpy()          /* copy a string               */
strcat()          /* combine two strings         */
```

To this list we will add functions to open and close files, functions to communicate with files, functions to test and convert characters, functions to convert strings, an exit function, and functions to allocate memory.

Let's turn first to the problem of communication between a file and a program.

COMMUNICATING WITH FILES

Often we need a program to get information from a file or to place results in a file. One method of having a program communicate with files is to use the redirection operators < and >. This method is simple, but it is limited. For instance, suppose you wish to write an interactive program that asks you for book titles (sound familiar?) and you want to save the complete listing in a file. If you use redirection, as in

```
books > bklist
```

your interactive prompts also are redirected to **bklist.** Not only does this put unwanted stuff into **bklist,** it prevents the user from seeing the questions she is supposed to answer.

Fortunately, C offers more powerful methods of communicating with files. One approach is to use the **fopen( )** function, which opens a file, then use special I/O functions to read from or write to that file, and then use the **fclose( )** function to close up the file. Before investigating these functions, however, we should look very briefly into the nature of a file.

WHAT IS A FILE?

To us, a file is a section of storage, usually on disk, with a name. We think, for instance, of **stdio.h** as the name of a file containing some useful information. To the operating system, a file is a bit more complicated, but that's the system's problem, not ours. However, we should know what a file is to a C program. For those file functions we will discuss, C represents the file with a structure. Indeed, the file **stdio.h** contains a definition of a file structure. Here is a typical example taken from the IBM version of Lattice C:

```
struct _iobuf
```

```
{
char *_ptr;          /* current buffer pointer */
int _cnt;            /* current byte count */
char *_base;         /* base address of I/O buffer */
char _flag;          /* control flags */
char _file;          /* file number */
};

#define FILE struct _iobuf      /* shorthand */
```

Again, we are not going to worry about the details of this definition. The main points are that a file is represented by a structure and that the shorthand name for the file template is **FILE.** (Many systems use **typedef** to set up the same correspondence.) Thus a program that deals with files will use the **FILE** structure type to do so.

With that in mind, we can better understand file operations.

A SIMPLE FILE-READING PROGRAM: *fopen( ), fclose( ), getc( ),* AND *putc( )*

To show the rudiments of using files, we have concocted a very limited program that reads the contents of a file called **test** and prints them on the screen. You will find our explanation just after the program.

```
 /* tells us what is in the file "test"   */
#include <stdio.h>
main()
{
    FILE *in;   /* declare a pointer to a file */
    int ch;

    if ( (in = fopen("test", "r")) != NULL)
 /* open test for reading, checking to see if it exists */
 /* the FILE pointer in now points to test */
        {
        while ( (ch = getc(in)) != EOF) /* get char from in */
                putc(ch,stdout); /* send to standard output */
         fclose(in);  /* close the file */
         }
     else
         printf("I couldn't open the file \"test\".\n");
}
```

The three main points to explain are the workings of **fopen( ),** the workings of **fclose( ),** and the use of the file I/O functions. We take them in turn.

Opening a File: *fopen( )*

Three basic parameters govern **fopen( ).** The first is the name of the file to be opened. This string is **fopen( )**'s first argument; in our case it was "test".

The second parameter (and the second argument of **fopen( )**) describes the use to be made of the file. There are three basic uses:

```
"r"  :  the file is to be read
"w"  :  the file is to be written
"a"  :  the file is to be appended to
```

Some systems offer additional possibilities, but we will stick to these. Note that these use codes are strings, not character constants; hence the enclosing double quotes. The "r" choice opens an existing file. The other two choices will open an existing file, and if there is no such file, they will create one. CAUTION: If you do use "w" for an existing file, the old version is erased so that your program starts with a clean slate.

The third parameter is a pointer to the file; this value is returned by the function:

```
FILE *in;

in = fopen("test", "r");
```

Now **in** is a pointer to the file "test." (More precisely, **in** points to a structure describing the file and the I/O buffers to be used with it. Henceforth, the program refers to the file by the pointer **in** and not by its name **test.**

If you are sharp-witted right now, you might ask this question: "If **fopen( )** returns a **'FILE'** pointer for an argument, why didn't we have to declare **fopen( )** as a **'FILE'** pointer function?" Good question. The answer is that the declaration was made for us in **stdio.h,** which contains the line

```
FILE *fopen();
```

There is one more important fact about **fopen( )** that we used. If

fopen( ) is unable to open the requested file, it returns a value of 'NULL' (defined as 0 in **stdio.h**). Why could it not open a file? You might ask to read a file that doesn't exist. That is why we have the line

```
if ( (in = fopen("test", "r")) != NULL)
```

Or the disk might be full, or the name might be illegal, or some other reason might prevent the opening of the file. So check for trouble—a little error trapping can go a long way.

Closing the file is simpler.

Closing a File: *fclose( )*

Our example shows how to close a file:

```
fclose(in);
```

Just use the **fclose( )** function. Note that the argument is **in,** a pointer to the file, not **test,** the file name.

For a program less casual than this one, we would check to see if the file was closed successfully. The function **fclose( )** returns a value of **0** if successful, and **−1** if not.

Buffered Text Files

The **fopen( )** and **fclose( )** functions work with "buffered" text files. By buffered, we mean that input and output is stored in a temporary memory area called a buffer. When the buffer gets filled, the contents are passed on in a block, and the buffering process starts over. One of the main tasks of **fclose( )** is to "flush" out any partially filled buffers when the file is closed.

A text file is one in which information is stored as characters using ASCII (or similar) code. This is opposed to a binary file such as would be used to store machine language code.

The I/O functions we are about to describe also are designed to work with text files only.

File I/O: *getc( )* and *putc( )*

The two functions **getc( )** and **putc( )** work very much like **getchar( )** and **putchar( ).** The difference is that you must tell the newcomers which file to use. Thus our old buddy

```
ch = getchar();
```

means get a character from the standard input, but

```
ch = getc(in);
```

means get a character from the file pointed to by **in.**
Similarly,

```
putc(ch, out);
```

means put the character **ch** into the file pointed to by the **FILE** pointer **out.** In **putc( )**'s argument list, the character comes first, then the file pointer.

In our example, we used

```
putc(ch,stdout);
```

where **stdout** is a pointer to the standard output. Thus, this statement is equivalent to

```
putchar(ch);
```

Indeed, **putchar(ch)** is **#defined** as **putc(ch,stdout)** in **stdio.h.** That redoubtable file also **#defines stdout** and **stdin** as pointers to the standard output and the standard input of the system.

Does this seem simple enough? Good, let's add a couple of useful wrinkles.

A SIMPLE FILE-CONDENSING PROGRAM

In our example, the name of the file to be opened was built into the program. We don't have to work under that restriction. By using command line arguments, we can tell our program the name of the file we want read. Our next example (Fig. 15.1) does that. It then condenses the contents by the brutal expedient of retaining only every third character. Finally, it places the condensed version in a new file whose name consists of the old name with **.red** (for reduced) appended. The first and last features (command line argument and file name appending) are quite useful generally. The condensing feature is of more limited appeal, but it can have its uses, as you will see.

```
 /* reduce your files by 2/3rds !   */
#include <stdio.h>
main(argc,argv)
int argc;
char *argv[];
{
   FILE  *in, *out;      /* declare two FILE pointers */
   int ch;
   static char name[20];   /* storage for output file name */
   int count = 0;

   if ( argc < 2)       /* check if there is an input file */
      printf("Sorry, I need a file name for an argument.\n");
  else
      {
      if ( (in = fopen(argv[1], "r")) != NULL)
           {
           strcpy(name,argv[1]); /* copy file name into array */
           strcat(name,".red"); /* append .red to name */
           out = fopen(name, "w"); /* open file for writing */
           while ( (ch = getc(in)) != EOF)
                   if ( count++ % 3 == 0 )
                      putc(ch, out); /*print every 3rd char */
          fclose(in);
          fclose(out);
          }
      else
           printf("I couldn't open the file \"%s\". \n",
argv[1]);
      }
}
```

Figure 15.1
File reduction program.

We placed the program in a file called **reduce.** We applied this program to a file called **eddy,** which contained a single line:

```
So even Eddy came oven ready.
```

The command was

```
reduce eddy
```

and the output was a file called **eddy.red,** which contained

```
Send money
```

What luck! Our randomly selected file produced an intelligible reduction.

Here are some program notes.

Recall that **argc** is the number of arguments, including the name of the program file. Recall that, operating system permitting, **argv[0]** represents the program name, **reduce** in our case. Then recall that **argv[1]** represents the first argument, **eddy** in our case. Since **argv[1]** is itself a pointer to a string, it should not be placed in double quotes in the function call.

We use **argc** to see if there is an argument. Any surplus arguments are ignored. By putting another loop in the program, you could have the program use the further file name arguments and cycle through each of several files in turn.

To construct the new name for the output file, we used **strcpy( )** to copy the name **eddy** into the array **name.** Then we used the **strcat( )** function to combine that name with **.red.**

This program involves having two files open simultaneously, so we declared two **'FILE'** pointers. Note that each file is opened and closed independently of the other. There are limits to how many files you can have open at one time. The limit depends on the system but often is in the range of 10 to 20. You can use the same pointer for different files providing the files are not open at the same time.

We are not limited to using just **getc( )** and **putc( )** for file I/O. Next we look at some other possibilities.

FILE I/O: *fprintf( ), fscanf( ), fgets( ),* AND *fputs( )*

The I/O functions we used in the preceding chapters all have file I/O analogues. The main distinction is that you need to use a **FILE** pointer to tell the new functions which file to work with. Like **getc( )** and **putc( ),** these functions are used after **fopen( )** opens a file and before **fclose( )** closes it.

The *fprintf( )* and *fscanf( )* Functions

These two file I/O functions work just like **printf( )** and **scanf( ),** except that they require an additional argument to point to the proper file. This argument is the first in the argument list. Here is an example to illustrate the form.

```
 /* form for using fprintf() and fscanf()  */
#include <stdio.h>
main()
{
    FILE *fi;
    int age;

    fi = fopen("sam", "r");      /* read mode */
    fscanf( fi, "%d", &age  );     /* fi points to sam */
    fclose(fi);
    fi = fopen("data", "a");      /* append mode */
    fprintf(  fi, "sam is %d.\n", age);    /* fi points to data */
    fclose(fi);
}
```

Note that we could use **fi** for two different files since we closed the first before opening the second.

Unlike **putc( ),** these two functions take the **FILE** pointer as the first argument. The other two take it as the last argument.

The *fgets( )* Function

This function takes three arguments to **gets( )**'s one. Here is a sample use:

```
 /* read a file a line at a time */
#include <stdio.h>
#define MAXLIN 80
main()
{
    FILE *f1;
    char *string[MAXLIN]

    f1 = fopen("story", "r");
    while ( fgets( string, MAXLIN, f1) != NULL)
         puts(string);
}
```

The first of **fgets( )**'s three arguments is a pointer to the destination for the line that is read. Here we are placing the input into the **char** array **string.**

The second argument places a limit on the length of the string being read. The function stops after reading a newline character or **MAXLIN** – 1 characters, whichever comes first. In either case, the null character (**'\0'**) is tacked on at the very end.

The third argument is, of course, a pointer to the file being read.

One difference between **gets( )** and **fgets( )** is that **gets( )** replaces the newline character with **'\0'**, while **fgets( )** keeps the newline character.

Like **gets( ), fgets( )** returns the value **NULL** when it encounters the EOF character. This lets you check, as we have done, if you have reached the end of a file.

The *fputs( )* Function

This function is quite similar to **puts( ).** The statement

```
fputs("You did something right.", fileptr);
```

transmits the string "You did something right." to the file pointed to by the **FILE** pointer **fileptr.** Naturally, the file ought to have been opened by **fopen( )** first. The most general form is

```
status = fputs(string pointer, file pointer);
```

where **status** is an integer that is set to EOF if **fputs( )** encounters an **EOF** or an error.

Like **puts( ),** this function does not copy the closing '\0' of a string into the destination final. Unlike **puts( ), fputs( )** does not add a newline character to its output.

The six I/O functions we have just discussed should give you tools aplenty for reading and writing text files. There is one more tool you may find useful, and we discuss it next.

RANDOM ACCESS: *fseek( )*

The **fseek( )** function lets you treat a file like an array and move directly to any particular byte in a file opened by **fopen( ).** Here is a straightforward example to show you how it works. Borrowing from our earlier examples, it uses a command line argument to obtain the name of the file it will affect. Note that **fseek( )** has three arguments and returns an **int** value.

```
/* using fseek() to print the contents of a file   */
#include <stdio.h>
main(number, names)  /* you don't have to use argc and argv */
int number;
char *names[];
{
   FILE *fp;
   long offset = 0L; /* note that this is a long type */

    if ( number < 2)
         puts("I need a file name for an argument.");
    else
         {
         if ( (fp = fopen(names[1], "r")) == 0 )
              printf("I can't open %s.\n", names[1]);
         else
              {
               while ( fseek(fp,offset++,0) == 0 )
                     putchar(getc(fp));
                fclose(fp);
                }
             }
}
```

The first argument of the three arguments of **fseek( )** is a **FILE** pointer to the file being searched through. The file should have been opened using **fopen( ).**

The second argument is called the "offset" (which is why we chose that name for the variable). This argument tells us how far to move from the starting point (see below); it must be a **long** value. It can be positive (move forward) or negative (move backward).

The third argument is the mode, and it identifies the starting point:

MODE	MEASURE OFFSET FROM
0	beginning of file
1	current position
2	end of file

The value returned by **fseek( )** is **0** if everything is okay, and **−1** if there is an error, such as attempting to move past the bounds of the file.

Now we can explain our little loop:

```
while ( fseek(fp,offset++,0) == 0  )
      putchar(getc(fp));
```

Since **offset** is initialized to **0,** the first time through the loop we have the expression

```
fseek(fp,0L,0)
```

which means go to the file pointed to by **fp** and find the byte that is 0 bytes from the beginning. That is, go to the first byte. Then **putchar( )** prints the contents of that byte. Next time through the loop, **offset** has been incremented to **1L,** so the next byte gets printed. Essentially, the variable **offset** is acting like a subscript for the file elements. The process continues until **offset** tries to take **fseek( )** past the end of the file. Then **fseek( )** returns a value of **−1** and the loop halts.

This last example is purely instructional. We didn't need **fseek( )** because **getc( )** steps through the file byte by byte anyway; **fseek( )** told **getc( )** to look where it was already about to look.

Here is an example (Fig. 15.2) that accomplishes something a bit more unusual. (We thank William Shakespeare for suggesting this example in *Twelfth Night*.)

```
   /* alternating forward and backward printing */
#include <stdio.h>
main(number, names)  /* you don't have to use argc and argv */
int number;
char *names[];
{
   FILE *fp;
   long offset = 0L;

   if ( number < 2)
        puts("I need a file name for an argument.");
   else
        {
        if ( (fp = fopen(names[1], "r")) == 0 )
            printf("I can't open %s.\n", names[1]);
        else
            {
            while ( fseek(fp,offset++,0) == 0 )
                   {
                   putchar(getc(fp));
                   if ( fseek(fp,-(offset + 3), 2) == 0 )
                        putchar(getc(fp));
                   }
            fclose(fp);
            }
        }
}
```

Figure 15.2
Program alternating forward and backward printing

Applying this program to a file containing the name "Malvolio" produces this pleasing result:

```
MoaillvoovlliaoM
```

Our program prints the first character of the file, then the last character, then the second, then the next to last, and so on. We merely added these lines to the last program:

```
if ( fseek(fp,-(offset + 3), 2) == 0 )
                  putchar(getc(fp));
```

The **2** mode means we will count positions from the end of the file. The negative sign means that we will count backwards. The **+3** is there so that we start with the last regular character of the file and skip some newlines and **EOF**s at the very end of the file. (The exact value of this adjustment depends on the system. Our files happen to end with 2 newlines followed by 2 **EOF**s, so we just backed up past them.)

So this part of the program alternates printing backwards with the part that prints forwards. We should mention that some systems may not support the **2** mode for **fseek( ).**

Well, that's enough about files for awhile. Let's close the subject and move on to another section of the C library.

TESTING AND CONVERTING CHARACTERS

The header file **ctype.h** defines several macro functions that test characters to see what class they belong to. The function **isalpha(c),** for example, returns a nonzero value (true) if **c** is an alphabetic character, and zero (false) if the character isn't alphabetic. Thus

`isalpha('S') != 0,` but `isalpha ('#') == 0`

Here is a list of the functions most commonly found in this file. In each case the function returns a nonzero value if **c** belongs to the tested class, and zero if it does not.

function	**tests if c is**
`isalpha(c)`	alphabetic
`isdigit(c)`	a digit
`islower(c)`	lower case
`isspace(c)`	whitespace (blank, tab, or newline)
`isupper(c)`	upper case

Your system may have additional functions such as

function	**tests if c is**
`isalnum(c)`	alphanumeric (alphabetic or digit)
`isascii(c)`	ASCII (0–127)
`iscntrl(c)`	a control character
`ispunct(c)`	a punctuation mark

Two more functions make conversions:

`toupper(c)`	converts c to upper case
`tolower(c)`	converts c to lower case

On some systems the conversion is attempted only if the character is of the opposite case to begin with. It is safer, however, to check the case first.

Here (Fig. 15-3) is a program that uses some of these functions to convert a file to all upper case or all lower case, as you request. To provide a little variety, we use an interactive approach instead of command line arguments to feed information to the program.

```
 /* case conversion */
#include <stdio.h>
#include <ctype.h> /* include file of macros */
#define UPPER 1
#define LOWER 0
main()
{
   int crit;   /* to be set to UPPER or LOWER  */
   char file1[14], file2[14]; /* input and output file names */

   crit = choose();  /* choose upper or lower case */
   getfiles(file1,file2); /* get file names */
   conv(file1,file2, crit);  /* do the conversion */
}
choose()
{
   int ch;
   printf("The program converts a file to all upper case or \n");
   printf("all lower case. Enter a U if you want upper case \n");
   printf("or enter an L if you want lower case.\n");
   while ( (ch = getchar()) != 'U' && ch != 'u' && ch != 'L' &&
            ch != 'l' )
        printf("Please enter a U or an L.\n");
   while (getchar() != '\n')
        ; /* clear lastB */
   if ( ch == 'U' || ch == 'u')
      {
      printf("Okay, upper case it is.\n");
      return(UPPER):
      }
   else
      {
      printf("Okay, lower case it is.\n");
```

```
        return(LOWER);
        }
}
getfiles(name1,name2)
char *name1, *name2;
{
   printf(" What file do you wish to convert?\n");
   gets(name1);
   printf("That was \"%s\".\n", name1);
   printf("What name do you desire for the converted file?\n");
   while ( strcmp(gets(name2), name1) == NULL)
        printf("Choose a different name.\n");
   printf("Your output file is \"%s\".\n", name2);
}
conv(name1, name2, crit)
char *name1, *name2;
int crit;
{
    int ch;
    FILE *f1, *f2;

    if ( (f1 = fopen(name1, "r") ) == NULL)
         printf("Sorry, I can't open %s.  Bye.\n", name1);
   else
         {
         puts("Here we go!");
         f2 = fopen(name2, "w");
         while ( (ch = getc(f1)) != EOF)
              {
              if (crit == UPPER)
                  ch = islower(ch) ? toupper(ch) : ch;
               else
                  ch = isupper(ch) ? tolower(ch) : ch;
               putc(ch,f2);
               }
         fclose(f2);
         fclose(f1);
         puts("Done!");
         }
}
```

Figure 15.3
Case conversion program.

We broke the program into three parts: getting the user's decision on case, getting names for the input and output files, and doing the conversion. To keep in practice, we developed a separate function for each part.

The **choose( )** function is pretty straightforward, except perhaps for the loop

```
while( getchar() != '\n')
     ;
```

This loop is included to solve a problem we faced in Chapter 14. When the user responds to the case question with, say, the letter **U,** she hits the **U** key, then the [enter] key, which transmits a '**\n**'. The initial **getchar( )** function picks up the **U** but leaves the '\n' sitting there for the next input reader. The **gets( )** function coming up in **getfiles( )** would interpret that as an empty line, so we used the little **while** loop to get rid of the newline. Actually, a simple **getchar( );** would do if the user followed the **U** immediately with [enter]; but our version also allows for the possibility that she hits the space bar a few times before hitting [enter].

The **getfiles( )** function should have no surprises for you. Note that we have prevented the user from using the same name for the output file as for the input file. The standard version of **fopen( )** does not allow you to read and write the same file during the same opening.

The **conv( )** function is a copy function with case conversion added. The value of **crit** is used to determine which conversion to make. The work is done by simple conditional statements such as

```
ch = islower(ch) ? toupper(ch) : ch;
```

This tests if **ch** is lower case. If it is, it is converted to upper case. If it isn't, it is left as is.

The macros of **ctype.h** provide convenient, useful tools for your programming. Now let's turn to some conversion functions of a more ambitious nature.

STRING CONVERSIONS: *atoi( ), atof( )*

Using **scanf( )** to read in numeric values is not the safest course to take, for **scanf( )** is easily misled by user errors in keying in numbers. Many programmers prefer to read in even numerical data as strings and convert the string to the appropriate numerical value. Here the two functions **atoi( )** and **atof( )** are useful. The first converts a string to an integer, and the second converts a string to a floating-point number. Here (Fig. 15-4) is a sample usage:

```
  /* include atoi()   */
#include <stdio.h>
#define issign(c)      ( ((c) == '-' || (c) == '+') ? (1) : (0) )
#define SIZE 10
#define YES 1
#define NO 0
main()
{
    char ch;
    static char number[SIZE];
    int value;
    int digit = YES;
    int count = 0;

    puts("Enter an integer, please.");
    gets(number);
    if ( number[SIZE -1] != '\0' )
        {
         puts("Too many digits; you wiped me out.");
         exit(1);
         }
    while ( (ch =number[count]) != '\0' && digit == YES)
        if( !issign(ch) && !isdigit(ch) && !isspace(ch) )
           digit = NO;
    if ( digit == YES)
        {
         value = atoi(number);
         printf("The number was %d.\n", value );
         }
    else
       printf("That doesn't look like an integer to me.");
}
```

Figure 15.4
Program using *atoi( )*.

We've put in some error checking. First we check to see if the input string was too long for the destination array. Because the array **number** is static **char,** it is initialized to nulls. If the last array member isn't a null, something is wrong, and the program bails out. Here we have used the library function **exit( ),** which gets you out of the program. We'll say more about this function shortly.

Then we check to see if the string contains nothing but spaces, digits, and algebraic signs. This rejects strings such as "three" or "1.2E2". It passes mishmash like "3− 4+2", but **atoi( )** will do further screening. Recall that **!** is a negation operator, so **!isdigit(c)** means "c is not a digit."

The line

```
value = atoi(number);
```

shows how **atoi( )** is used. Its argument is a pointer to a string; in this case we used the array name **number.** It returns an **int** value for the string. Thus "**1234**", which is a string of four characters, is translated to **1234,** a single **int** value.

The **atoi( )** function ignores leading blanks, processes a leading algebraic sign, if any, and processes digits up to the first nondigit. Thus our example of " 3−4+2" would be converted to the value **3.** See the Questions at the end of the chapter for a possible implementation.

The **atof( )** function performs a similar function for floating-point numbers. It returns type **double,** so it should be declared double in a program that uses it.

Simple versions of **atof( )** will handle numbers of the form **10.2, 46,** and **−124.26.** Higher-powered versions will also convert exponential notation, that is, numbers like **1.25E−13.**

Your system also may have functions that work in the opposite direction. An **itoa( )** function would convert an integer to a string, and an **ftoa( )** function would convert a floating-point number to a string.

GETTING OUT: *exit( )*

The **exit( )** function gives you a convenient way to leave a program. Often it is used to stop a program when an error shows up. If **exit( )** is evoked from a function called by the main program, the whole program stops, not just the function. In the **atoi( )** example above, using **exit( )** let us avoid setting up an extra **else** statement to detour around the rest of the program.

One nice service **exit( )** performs is that it closes any files that had been opened by **fopen( ).** This makes your exit much tidier.

The argument of **exit( )** is an error code number. On some systems this can be passed to another program when the original is exited. Convention is that **0** indicates a normal termination, while other values indicate a problem.

Before we forget, there is one other matter we wish to discuss.

MEMORY ALLOCATION: *malloc( )* AND *calloc( )*

Your program has to set aside enough memory to store the data it uses. Some of this "memory allocation" is done automatically. For example, we can declare

```
char place[] = "Pork Liver Creek";
```

and enough memory to store that string is set aside.

Or we can be more explicit and ask for a certain amount of memory:

```
int plates[100];
```

This declaration sets aside 100 memory locations, each fit to store an **int** value.

C goes beyond this. It lets you allot more memory as the program runs. Suppose, for example, you are writing an interactive program and you don't know in advance how much input will be coming in. You can set aside what you think is a reasonable amount of memory, and then request more if you need it. Here (Fig. 15.5) is an example that uses the **malloc( )** function to do just that. Also, notice how this program uses pointers.

```
 /* add on more memory as needed */
#include <stdio.h>
#define STOP ""          /* signal for ending input    */
#define BLOCK 100        /* bytes of memory            */
#define LIM 40           /* input line length limit    */
#define MAX 50           /* max number of input lines  */
#define DRAMA 20000      /* dramatic time delay        */
main()
```

```
{
    char store[BLOCK];  /* original block of storage   */
    char symph[LIM];    /* input receptor              */
    char *end;          /* pointer to end of storage   */
    char *starts[MAX];  /* pointers to string starts   */
    int index = 0;      /* number of input lines       */
    int count;          /* counter                     */
    char *malloc();     /* memory allocator            */

    starts[0] = store;
    end = starts[0] + BLOCK -1;
    puts("Name some symphony orchestras.");
    puts("Enter them one at a time; hit [enter] at the start of");
    puts("a line to end your list. Okay, I'm ready.");
    while( strcmp(fgets(symph,LIM,stdin),STOP) != 0
          && index < MAX)
          {
          if  ( strlen(symph) > end - starts[index] )
              { /*  action if not enough memory to store input */
              puts("Wait a sec, I got to find some more memory.");
              starts[index] = malloc(BLOCK);
              end = starts[index] + BLOCK -1;
              for( count = 0; count < DRAMA; count++);
              puts("Found some!");
              }
           strcpy(starts[index],symph);
           starts[index + 1] = starts[index] + strlen(symph) + 1;
     if ( ++index < MAX)
      printf("That's %d.  Continue, if you like.\n", index);
   }
    puts("Okay, here's what I got:");
    for( count = 0; count < index; count++)
        puts( starts[count] );
}
```

Figure 15.5
Program to add on more memory as needed

Here is a sample run so you can see the output:

```
Name some symphony orchestras.
Enter them one at a time; hit [enter] at the start of
```

```
a line to end your list. Okay, I'm ready.
San Francisco Symphony
That's 1. Continue, if you like.
Chicago Symphony
That's 2. Continue, if you like.
Berlin Philharmonic
That's 3. Continue, if you like.
The Concertgebouw
That's 4. Continue, if you like.
London Symphony
That's 5. Continue, if you like.
Vienna Philharmonic
Wait a sec, I got to find some more memory.
Found some!
That's 6. Continue, if you like.
Pittsburgh Symphony
That's 7. Continue, if you like.

Okay, here's what I got:
San Francisco Symphony
Chicago Symphony
Berlin Philharmonic
The Concertgebouw
London Symphony
Vienna Philharmonic
Pittsburgh Symphony
```

First, let's see what **malloc( )** does. It takes an unsigned integer argument that represents the number of bytes of memory requested. Thus **malloc(BLOCK)** ask for 100 bytes of memory. The function returns a **char** pointer to the beginning of the new memory block. We used the declaration

```
char *malloc();
```

to alert the compiler that **malloc( )** returns a **char** pointer. We then assigned the value of this pointer to **starts[index]** with the statement

```
starts[index] = malloc(BLOCK);
```

Okay, now let's look at the program plan. Our plan is to store the input strings all in a row in the big array **store.** We will set **starts[0]** to point at the beginning of the first string, **starts[1]** to point at the beginning of the second string, and so on. As an intermediary step, the program reads a string into the array **symph.** We used **fgets( )** instead of **gets( )** so that we could limit the input string to fit **symph.**

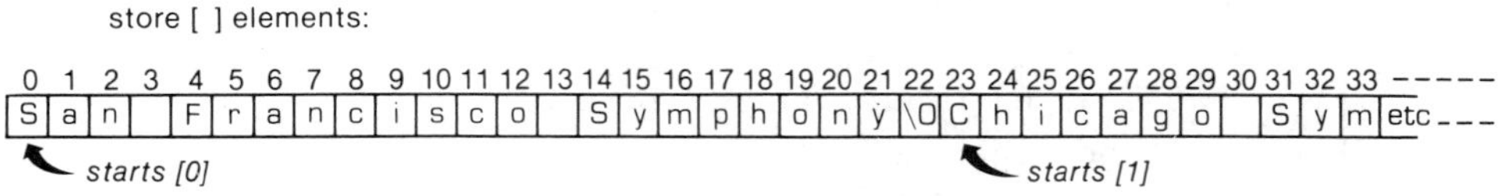

Figure 15.6
Consecutive symphs stored in store.

Before **symph** is copied into **store,** we check to see if there is enough room left. The pointer **end** points to the end of storage, and the current value of **starts[index]** points to the beginning of the unused storage. Thus we can compare the difference between these two pointers with the length of **symph** to see if enough space is left.

If there is not enough room, then we call upon **malloc( )** to prepare more storage. We set **starts[index]** to point to the beginning of the new storage block, and we reset **end** to point to the end of the new block. Note that we don't have a name for the new storage. It is not, for instance, an extension of **store.** The only identification we have are the pointers pointing to the new storage area.

As the program runs its course, each new string is pointed to by a member of the **starts** array of pointers. Some strings are in **store,** some in one or more new storage areas. But as long as we have the pointers, we can get to the strings, as the printout part of this program shows.

So that is how **malloc( )** is used. But suppose you want **int** memory, not **char.** You still can use **malloc( ).** Here is the procedure:

```
char *malloc();     /* still declare as char pointer   */
int *newmem;

newmem = (int *) malloc(100);  /* use cast operator   */
```

Again 100 bytes are set aside. The cast operator converts the returned value from a **char** pointer to an **int** pointer. If, as on our system, **int** takes two bytes of memory, then this means **newmem + 1** will increment the pointer by two bytes, just right to move it to the next integer. It also means that the 100 bytes can be used to store 50 integers.

Another option for memory allotment is to use **calloc( ).** A typical use would look like this:

```
char *calloc();
 long *newmem;

 newmem = (long *) calloc( 100, sizeof (long)  );
```

Like **malloc( ), calloc( )** returns a pointer to **char.** You must use the cast operator if you want to store a different type. This new function has two arguments, both of which should be unsigned integers. The first argument is the number of memory cells desired. The second argument is the size of each cell in bytes. In our case, **long** uses four bytes, so this instruction would set up 100 four-byte units, using 400 bytes in all for storage.

By using **sizeof (long)** instead of **4,** we made this coding more portable. It will work on systems where **long** is some size other than four.

The **calloc( )** function throws in one more feature; it sets all the contents of the block to zero.

Your C library probably offers several other memory-management functions, and you may wish to check on them.

OTHER LIBRARY FUNCTIONS

Most libraries will have several more functions in the areas we have covered. Besides functions that allocate memory, there are functions to free up memory when you are done with it. There may be other string functions, perhaps functions that search a string for a particular character or combination of characters.

Other file functions include **open( ), close( ), create( ), lseek( ), read( ),** and **write( ).** These accomplish much the same tasks as the functions we discussed, but at a more basic level. Indeed, functions like **fopen( )** typically are written using these more basic functions. They are a little more awkward to use, but they can deal with binary files as well as text files.

Your system may have a math library. Typically, such a library will contain a square root function, a power function, an exponential function, various trig functions, and a random number function.

You will have to take the time to explore what your system has to offer. If it doesn't have what you want, make your own functions. That's part of C. If you think you can do a better job on, say, an input function, do it!

And as you refine and polish your programming technique, you will go from C to shining C.

CLOSING WORDS

We've come a long way since the beginning of this primer. By now, you have encountered most of the main features of the C language. (Our main omissions—bit operations and UNIX 7 extensions—are covered briefly in Appendix F). You've seen and used C's wealth of operators, its enormous variety of basic and derived data types, its intelligent control structures, and its powerful pointer system. We hope we've helped prepare you to use C for your own purposes. So start programming, and good luck!

WHAT YOU SHOULD HAVE LEARNED

What a C library is and how to use it
How to open and close text files: **fopen( )** and **fclose( )**
What a **FILE** type is
How to read from and write to files: **getc( ), putc( ), fgets( ), fputs( ), fscanf( ), fprintf( )**
How to check character classes: **isdigit( ), isalpha( ),** et al
How to convert strings to numbers: **atoi( ), atof( )**
How to make a quick exit: **exit( )**
How to allot memory: **malloc( ), calloc( )**

QUESTIONS AND ANSWERS

Questions

1. What's wrong with this program?

```
main()
{
   int *fp;
   int k;
```

```
    fp = fopen("jello");
    for (k = 0; k < 30; k++)
        fputs(fp, "Nanette eats jello.");
    fclose("jello");
}
```

2. What would the following program do?

```
#include <stdio.h>
#include <ctype.h>
main(argc,argv)
int argc;
char *argv[];
{
int ch;
FILE *fp;

if ( (fp = fopen(argv[1], "r")) == NULL)
     exit(1);
while ( (ch= getc(fp)) != EOF )
    if( isdigit(ch) )
         putchar(ch);
    fclose (fp);
}
```

3. Is there anything wrong with expressions such as **isalpha(c[i]),** where **c** is a **char** array? What about **isalpha (c[i++])** ?
4. Use the character classification functions to prepare an implementation of **atoi( ).**
5. How could you allot space to hold an array of structures?

Answers

1. It should #**include <stdio.h>** for its file definitions. It should declare **fp** a file pointer: **FILE *fp;** The function **fopen( )** requires a mode: **fopen("jello", "w"),** or perhaps the **"a"** mode. The order of the arguments to **fputs( )** should be reversed. The **fclose( )** function requires a file pointer, not a file name: **fclose(fp);**
2. It will open the file given as a command line argument and print out all the digits in the file. It should check (but doesn't) to see if there is a command line argument.
3. The first expression is okay, since **c[i]** has a **char** value. The second expression won't choke the computer, but it may yield puzzling results. The reason is that **isalpha( )** is a macro that most likely has its argument appearing twice in the defining expression (checking for lower-case membership, then checking for upper-case membership), and this will produce two increments in **i.** It is best to avoid using the increment operator in the argument of a macro function call.

4.
```
#include <stdio.h>
#include <cytpe.h>
#define issign(c)    ( ((c) == '-' || (c) == '+') ? (1) : (0) )
atoi(s)
char *s;
{
  int i = 0;
  int n, sign;

  while ( isspace( s[i] ) )
      i++;    /* skip whitespace */
  sign = 1;
 if ( issign(s[i]) ) /* handle optional sign */
      sign = ( s[i++]=='+') ? 1 : -1;
 for (n = 0; isdigit( s[i] ); i++)
     n = 10*n + s[i] - '0';
 return( sign * n);
}
```

5. Suppose **wine** is the tag for a structure. These statements, properly placed in a program, will do the job.

```
struct wine *ptrwine;
char *calloc();

ptrwine = (struct wine *) calloc( 100, sizeof (struct wine) );
```

EXERCISES

1. Write a file copy program that uses the original file name and the copy file name as command-line arguments.
2. Write a program that will take all files given by a series of command-line arguments and print them one after the other on the screen. Use **argc** to set up a loop.
3. Modify our book inventory program of Chapter 14 so that the information you enter is appended to a file called **mybooks.**
4. Use **gets( )** and **atoi( )** to construct the equivalent of our **getint( )** function of Chapter 10.
5. Rewrite our word count program of Chapter 7 using **ctype.h** macros and using a command line argument for the file to be processed.

APPENDIX A ADDITIONAL READING

If you wish to learn more about C and programming, you will find the following references useful.

THE C LANGUAGE

Kernighan, Brian W. and Dennis M. Ritchie, *The C Programming Language.* Prentice-Hall, 1978.

This is the first and most authoritative book on C. (Note that the creator of C, Dennis Ritchie, is one of the authors.) It is practically the official definition of C and includes many interesting examples. It does, however, assume the reader is familiar with systems programming.

Feuer, Alan R., *The C Puzzle Book.* Prentice-Hall, 1982.

This book contains a large number of programs whose output you are supposed to predict. This gives you good opportunity to test and expand your understanding of C. The book includes answers and explanations.

Ritchie, D. M., S. C. Johnson, M. E. Lesk, and B. W. Kernighan, "The C Programming Language," *The Bell System Technical Journal,* Vol 57, No. 6, July-August 1978.

This article discusses the history of C and provides an overview of its design features.

***BYTE,* Vol 8, No. 8, August 1983.**

This issue of *BYTE* magazine is devoted to C. It includes articles discussing the history, philosophy, and uses of C. Twenty C compilers for microprocessors are tested and evaluated. Also included is an extensive, up-to-date bibliography of books and articles on C. Each bibliographic entry includes a short summary of the book or article.

PROGRAMMING

Kernighan, Brian W. and P. J. Plauger, *The Elements of Programming Style (Second Edition).* McGraw-Hill, 1978.

This slim classic uses examples drawn from other texts to illustrate the dos and don'ts of clear, effective programming.

Kernighan, Brian W. and P. J. Plauger, *Software Tools.* Addison-Wesley, 1976.

This book develops several useful programs and systems of programs, while emphasizing good program design. It comes in a RATFOR (rationalized FORTRAN) and in a Pascal version. Since RATFOR represents an attempt to make FORTRAN work like C, the first version is the choice of C users.

THE UNIX OPERATING SYSTEM

Waite, Mitchell, Don Martin, and Stephen Prata, *UNIX Primer Plus.* **Howard W. Sams and Company, Inc., 1983.**

This book provides an easy-to-read introduction to the UNIX operating system, including several powerful Berkeley enhancements.

APPENDIX B KEYWORDS IN C

The keywords of a language are the words used to express the actions of that language. The keywords of C are reserved; that is, you can't use them for other purposes, such as for the name of a variable.

PROGRAM FLOW KEYWORDS

Loops

```
for while do
```

Decision and Choice

```
if else switch case default
```

Jumps

```
break continue goto
```

Data Types

```
char int short long unsigned float
double struct union typedef
```

Storage Classes

```
auto extern register static
```

Miscellaneous

```
return sizeof
```

Not Yet Implemented

```
entry
```

Available on Some Systems Only

```
asm endasm fortran enum
```

APPENDIX C C OPERATORS

C is rich in operators. Here we present a table of operators, indicating the priority ranking of each and how each operator is grouped. Next, we will summarize the operators except for the bit-wise operators, which are discussed in Appendix F.

<table>
<tr><th>OPERATORS (from high to low priority)</th><th>GROUPING</th></tr>
<tr><td>()   {}   ->   .</td><td>L-R</td></tr>
<tr><td>!   ~   ++   --   - (type)   *   &   sizeof (all unary)</td><td>R-L</td></tr>
<tr><td>*   /   %</td><td>L-R</td></tr>
<tr><td>+   -</td><td>L-R</td></tr>
<tr><td><<   >></td><td>L-R</td></tr>
<tr><td><   <=   >   >=</td><td>L-R</td></tr>
<tr><td>==   !=</td><td>L-R</td></tr>
<tr><td>&</td><td>L-R</td></tr>
<tr><td>^</td><td>L-R</td></tr>
<tr><td>|</td><td>L-R</td></tr>
<tr><td>&&</td><td>L-R</td></tr>
<tr><td>||</td><td>L-R</td></tr>
<tr><td>?:</td><td>L-R</td></tr>
<tr><td>=   +=   -=   *=   /=   %=</td><td>R-L</td></tr>
<tr><td>,</td><td>L-R</td></tr>
</table>

Here is what these operators do.

I. Arithmetic Operators

- `+` Adds value at its right to the value at its left
- `-` Subtracts value at its right from the value at its left
- `-` As a unary operator, changes the sign of the value to its right
- `*` Multiplies value at its right by the value at its left
- `/` Divides value at its left by the value at its right. Answer is truncated if both operands are integers
- `%` Yields the remainder when the value at its left is divided by the value to its right (integers only)

++ Adds 1 to the value of the variable to its left (prefix mode) or of the variable to its right (postfix mode)

−− Like ++, but subtracts 1

II. Assignment Operators

= Assigns value at its right to the variable at its left

Each of the following operators updates the variable at its left by the value at its right, using the indicated operation. We use r-h for right-hand, l-h for left-hand.

+= adds the r-h quantity to the l-h variable

−= subtracts the r-h quantity from the l-h variable

*= multiplies the l-h variable by the r-h quantity

/= divides the l-h variable by the r-h quantity

%= gives the remainder from dividing the l-h variable by the r-h quantity.

Example:

`rabbits *= 1.6;` is the same as `rabbits = rabbits * 1.6;`

III. Relational Operators

Each of these operators compares the value at its left to the value at its right. The relational expression formed from an operator and its two operands has the value 1 if the expression is true and the value 0 if the expression is false.

< less than

<= less than or equal to

== equal to

>= greater than or equal to

> greater than

!= unequal to

IV. Logical Operators

Logical operators normally take relational expressions as operands. The **!** operator takes one operand, and it is to the right. The rest take two: one to the left, one to the right.

&& Logical AND: the combined expression is true if both operands are true, and it is false otherwise.

|| Logical OR: the combined expression is true if one or both operands are true, and it is false otherwise.

! Logical NOT: the expression is true if the operand is false, and vice versa.

VI. Pointer-Related Operators

& The address operator: when followed by a variable name, gives the address of that variable: **&nurse** is the address of the variable **nurse**

* The indirection operator: when followed by a pointer, gives the value stored at the pointed-to address:

```
 nurse = 22;
ptr = &nurse;  /* pointer to nurse */
val = *ptr;
```

The net affect is to assign the value 22 to **val.**

VI. Structure and Union Operators

The membership operator (the period) is used with a structure or union name to specify a member of that structure or union. If **name** is the name of a structure and **member** is a member specified by the structure template, then

```
name.member
```

identifies that member of the structure. The membership operator can also be used in the same fashion with unions.

Example:

```
  struct {
        int code;
        float cost;
        } item;

item.code = 1265;
```

This assigns a value to the **code** member of the structure **item.**

-> The indirect membership operator is used with a pointer to a structure or union to identify a member of that structure or union. Suppose **ptrstr** is a pointer to a structure and that **member** is a member specified by the structure template. Then

```
ptrstr->member
```

identifies that member of the pointed-to structure. The indirect membership operator can be used in the same fashion with unions.

Example:

```
struct {
       int code;
       float cost;
       } item, *ptrst;

ptrst = &item;
ptrst->code = 3451;
```

This assigns a value to the **code** member of **item.** The following three expressions are equivalent:

```
ptrst->code     item.code     (*ptrst).code
```

VIII. Miscellaneous Operators

`sizeof` Yields the size, in bytes, of the operand to its right. The operand can be a type-specifier in parentheses, as in **sizeof (float),** or it can be the name of a particular variable or array, etc., as in **sizeof foo.**

`(type)` Cast operator: converts following value to the type specified by the enclosed keyword(s). For example, **(float) 9** converts the integer 9 to the floating-point number 9.0.

The comma operator, like others, links two expressions into one and guarantees that the leftmost expression is evaluated first. A typical use is to include more information in a **for** loop control expression:

```
for ( step = 2, fargo = 0; fargo < 1000; step *= 2)
   fargo += step;
```

`?:` The conditional operator takes three operands, each of which is an expression. They are arranged this way:

expression1 ? *expression2* : *expression3*

The value of the whole expression equals the value of *expression2* if *expression1* is true, and equals the value of *expression3* otherwise. Examples:

`( 5 > 3 ) ? 1 : 2` has the value 1

`( 3 > 5 ) ? 1 : 2` has the value 2

`( a > b ) ? a : b` has the value of the larger of **a** or **b**

APPENDIX D DATA TYPES AND STORAGE CLASSES

THE BASIC DATA TYPES

Keywords: The basic data types are set up using the following 7 keywords: **int, long, short, unsigned, char, float, double.**

Signed Integers: These can have positive or negative values.

int : the basic integer type for a given system

long or **long int :** can hold an integer at least as large as the largest **int** and possibly larger **short** or **short int :** the largest **short** integer is no larger than the largest **int** and may be smaller.

Typically, **long** will be bigger than **short,** and **int** will be the same as one of the two. For example, IBM PC Lattice C has 16-bit **short** and **int,** and 32-bit **long.** It all depends on the system.

Unsigned Integers: These have zero or positive values only. This extends the range of the largest possible positive number. Use the keyword **unsigned** before the desired type:
unsigned int, unsigned long, unsigned short.
A lone **unsigned** is the same as **unsigned int.**

Characters: There are typographic symbols such as A, &, and +. Typically just one byte of memory is used.

char : the keyword for this type

Floating Point: These can have positive or negative values.

float: the basic floating-point size for the system

double or **long float :** a (possibly) larger unit for holding floating-point numbers. It may allow more significant figures and perhaps larger exponents.

HOW TO DECLARE A SIMPLE VARIABLE

1. Choose the type you need.
2. Choose a name for the variable.
3. Use this format for a declaration statement:
   type-specifier variable-name;

The *type-specifier* is formed from one or more of the type keywords. Here are some examples:

```
int erest;
unsigned short cash;
```

4. You may declare more than one variable of the same type by separating the variable names by commas:

```
char ch, init, ans;
```

5. You can initialize a variable in a declaration statement:

```
float mass = 6.0E24;
```

STORAGE CLASSES

I. Keywords: auto, external, static, register

II. General Comments

The storage class of a variable determines its scope and how long the variable persists. Storage class is determined by where the variable is defined and by the associated keyword. Variables defined outside a function are external and have global scope. Variables declared inside a function are automatic and local unless one of the other keywords is used. External variables defined above a function are known to it even if not declared internally.

III. Properties

STORAGE CLASS	KEYWORD	DURATION	SCOPE
automatic	`auto`	temporary	local
register	`register`	temporary	local
static	`static`	persistent	local
....			
external	`extern`	persistent	global (all files)
external static	`static`	persistent	global (one file)

Those above the dotted line are declared inside a function.
Those below the line are defined outside a function.

APPENDIX E PROGRAM FLOW CONTROL

C has several control structures for guiding the flow of a program. Here we summarize the looping statements (**while, for** and **do while**), the branching statements (**if, if else,** and **switch**), and the jump statements (**goto, break,** and **continue**).

THE *while* STATEMENT

Keyword: while

General Comments:

The **while** statement creates a loop that repeats until the test *expression* becomes false, or zero. The **while** statement is an *entry-condition* loop; the decision to go through one more pass of the loop is made *before* the loop is traversed. Thus it is possible that the loop is never traversed. The *statement* part of the form can be a simple statement or a compound statement.

Form:

```
while ( expression )
        statement
```

The *statement* portion is repeated until the *expression* becomes false or zero.

Examples:

```
while ( n++ < 100 )
      printf(" %d %d\n", n, 2*n+1 );

while ( fargo < 1000 )
      {
      fargo = fargo + step;
      step = 2 * step;
      }
```

THE *for* STATEMENT

Keyword: for

General Comments:

The **for** statement uses three control expressions, separated by semicolons, to control a looping process. The *initialize* expression is executed once, before any of the loop statements are executed. If the *test* expression is true (or nonzero), the loop is cycled through once. Then the *update* expression is evaluated, and it is time to check the *test* expression again. The **for** statement is an *entry-condition* loop; the decision to go through one more pass of the loop is made *before* the loop is traversed. Thus it is possible that the loop is never traversed. The *statement* part of the form can be a simple statement or a compound statement.

Form:

```
for ( initialize ; test ; update )
        statement;
```

The loop is repeated until *test* becomes false or zero.

Example:

```
for ( n = 0; n < 10 ; n++ )
      printf(" %d %d\n", n, 2*n+1 );
```

THE *do while* STATEMENT

Keywords: do, while

General Comments:

The **do while** statement creates a loop that repeats until the test *expres-*

sion becomes false, or zero. The **do while** statement is an *exit-condition* loop; the decision to go through one more pass of the loop is made *after* the loop is traversed. Thus the loop must be executed at least once. The *statement* part of the form can be a simple statement or a compound statement.

Form:

```
do
     statement
     while ( expression );
```

The *statement* portion is repeated until the *expression* becomes false or zero.

Example:

```
do
      scanf("%d", &number)
         while( number != 20 );
```

USING *if* STATEMENTS FOR MAKING CHOICES

Keywords: if, else

General Comments:

In each of the following forms, the *statement* can be either a simple statement or a compound statement. A "true" expression, more generally, means one with a nonzero value.

Form 1:

```
if ( expression )
       statement
```

The *statement* is executed if the *expression* is true.

Form 2:

```
if ( expression )
     statement1
else
     statement2
```

If the *expression* is true, *statement1* is executed. Otherwise *statement2* is executed.

Form 3:

```
if ( expression1 )
     statement1
else if ( expression2 )
   statement2
else
    statement3
```

If *expression1* is true, then *statement1* is executed. If *expression1* is false but *expression2* is true, *statement2* is executed. Otherwise, if both expressions are false, *statement3* is executed.

Example

```
if (legs == 4)
    printf("It might be a horse.\n");
 else if (legs > 4)
    printf("It is not a horse.\n");
 else      /* done if legs < 4 */
     {
     legs++;
     printf("Now it has one more leg.\n")
     }
```

MULTIPLE CHOICE WITH *switch*

Keyword: switch

General Comments:

Program control jumps to the statement bearing the value of *expression* as a label. Program flow then proceeds through the remaining statements unless redirected again. Both *expression* and labels must have integer values (type **char** is included), and the labels must be constants or expressions formed solely from constants. If no label matches the expression value, control goes to the statement labeled **default,** if present. Otherwise control passes to the next statement following the **switch** statement.

Form:

```
switch ( expression )
    {
     case label1 : statement1
     case label2 : statement2
     default     : statement3
     }
```

There can be more than two labeled statements, and the **default** case is optional.

Example:

```
switch ( letter )
    {
    case 'a'   :
    case 'e'   :   printf("%d is a vowel\n", letter);
    case 'c'   :
    case 'n'   :   printf("%d is in \"cane\"\n", letter);
    default    :   printf("Have a nice day.\n");
    }
```

If **letter** has the value **'a'** or **'e'**, all three messages are printed: **'c'** and **'n'** cause the last two to be printed. Other values print just the last message.

PROGRAM JUMPS

Keywords: break, continue, goto

General Comments:

These three instructions cause program flow to jump from one location of a program to another location.

break

The **break** command can be used with any of the three loop forms and with the **switch** statement. It causes program control to skip over the rest of the loop or **switch** containing it and to resume with the next command following the loop or **switch.**

Example:

```
switch (number )
    {
    case   4:    printf("Good choice!\n");
                 break;
    case   5:    printf("That's a fair choice.\n");
                 break;
    default:    printf("That's a poor choice.\n");
```

continue

The **continue** command can be used with any of the three loop forms but not with a **switch.** It causes program control to skip the remaining statements in a loop. For a **while** or **for** loop, the next loop cycle is started. For a **do while** loop, the exit condition is tested and then, if necessary, the next loop cycle is started.

Example:

```
while ( (ch = getchar()) != EOF)
      {
      if ( ch == ' ' )
            continue;
      putchar(ch);
      chcount++;
      }
```

This fragment echoes and counts nonspace characters.

goto

A **goto** statement causes program control to jump to a statement bearing the indicated label. A colon is used to separate a labeled statement from its label. Label names follow the rules for variable name. The labeled statement can come either before or after the **goto.**

Form:

```
goto label;
     . . .
label : statement
```

Example:

```
top : ch = getchar();
        . . .
if ( ch != 'y' )
        goto top;
```

APPENDIX F BIT FIDDLING: OPERATORS AND FIELDS

Some programs need (or, at least, benefit from) an ability to manipulate individual bits in a byte or word. For example, often I/O devices have their options set by a byte in which each bit acts as an on-off flag. C has two facilities to help you manipulate bits. The first is a set of 6 "bitwise" operators that act on bits. The second is the **field** data form, which gives you access to bits within an **int.** We will outline these C features here.

OPERATORS

C offers bitwise logical operators and shift operators. In the following, we will write out values in binary notation so you can see the mechanics. In an actual program, you would use integer variables or constants written in the usual forms. For instance, instead of **(00011001)**, you would use **25** or **031** or **0x19.** For our examples, we will use 8-bit numbers, with the bits numbered 7 to 0, left to right.

Bitwise Logical Operators

These four operators work on integer-class data, including **char.** They are termed "bitwise" because they operate on each bit independently of the bit to the left or right.

~: One's complement, or bitwise negation

This unary operator changes each 1 to a 0 and each 0 to a 1. Thus

```
~(10011010) == (01100101)
```

&: Bitwise AND

This binary operator makes a bit-by-bit comparison between two operands. For each bit position, the resulting bit is 1 only if both corresponding bits in the operands are 1. (In terms of true-false, the result is true only if each of the two bit operands is true.) Thus

```
(10010011) & (00111101) == (00010001)
```

since only bits 4 and 0 are 1 in both operands.

|: Bitwise OR

This binary operator makes a bit-by-bit comparison between two operands. For each bit position, the resulting bit is 1 if either of the corresponding bits in the operands are 1. (In terms of true-false, the result is true if one or the other bit operands is true or if both are true.) Thus

```
(10010011) | (00111101) == (101111111)
```

since all bit positions but bit 6 have the value 1 in one or the other operands.

^: Bitwise EXCLUSIVE OR

This binary operator makes a bit-by-bit comparison between two operands. For each bit position, the resulting bit is 1 if one or the other (but not both) of the corresponding bits in the operands are 1. (In terms of true-false, the result is true if one or the other bit operands —and not both—is true.) Thus

```
(10010011) ^ (00111101) == (10101110)
```

Note that since bit position 0 has the value 1 in both operands, that the resulting 0 bit has value 0.

Usage

These operators often are used to set certain bits while leaving others unchanged. For example, suppose we **#define MASK** to be **2,** i.e., binary 00000010, with only bit number 1 being nonzero. Then the statement

```
flags = flags & MASK;
```

would cause all the bits of flags (except bit 1) to be set to 0, since any bit combined with 0 via the **&** operator yields 0. Bit number 1 will be left unchanged. (If the bit is 1, then **1 & 1** is 1, and if the bit is 0, then **0 & 1** is 0.)

Similarly, the statement

```
flags = flags | MASK;
```

will set bit number 1 to 1 and leave all the other bits unchanged. This follows because any bit combined with 0 via the | operator is itself, and any bit combined with 1 via the | operator is 1.

Bitwise Shift Operators

These operators shift bits to the left or right. Again, we will write binary numbers explicitly to show the mechanics.

<< : Left Shift

This operator shifts the bits of the left operand to the left by the number of places given by the right operand. The vacated positions are filled with 0s and bits moved past the end of the left operand are lost. Thus

```
(10001010) << 2 == (00101000)
```

where each bit is moved two places to the left.

>> : Right Shift

This operator shifts the bits of the left operand to the right by the number of places given by the right operand. Bits moved past the right end of the left operand are lost. For **unsigned** types the places vacated at the left end are replaced by 0s. For signed types, the result is machine dependent. The vacated places may be filled with 0s, or they may be filled with copies of the sign (leftmost) bit. For an unsigned value, we have

```
(10001010) >> 2 == (00100010)
```

where each bit is moved two places to the right.

Usage

These operators provide swift, efficient multiplication and division by powers of 2:

`number << n` multiplies **number** by 2 to the **n**th power
`number >> n` divides **number** by 2 to the **n**th power if number is not negative

This is analogous to the decimal system procedure of shifting the decimal point to multiply or divide by 10.

FIELDS

The second method of manipulating bits is to use a field. A field is just a set of neighboring bits within an **int** or **unsigned int.** A field is set up via a structure definition, which labels each field and determines its width. The following definition sets up four 1-bit fields:

```
struct   {
              unsigned autfd   : 1;
              unsigned bldfc   : 1;
              unsigned undln   : 1;
              unsigned itals   : 1;
              } prnt;
```

The variable **prnt** now contains 4 1-bit fields. The usual structure membership operator can be used to assign values to individual fields:

```
prnt.itals = 0;
prnt.undln = 1;
```

Because each field is just 1 bit, 1 and 0 are the only values we can use for assignment.

The variable **prnt** is stored in an **int**-sized memory cell, but only 4 bits are used in this example.

Fields aren't limited to 1-bit sizes. We can do this:

```
struct {
             unsigned code1 : 2;
             unsigned code2 : 2;
             unsigned code3 : 8;
             } prcode;
```

This creates 2 2-bit fields and 1 8-bit field. We can make assignments such as

```
prcode.code1 = 0;
```

```
prcode.code2 = 3;
prcode.code3 = 102;
```

Just make sure that the value doesn't exceed the capacity of the field.

What if the total number of bits you declare exceeds the size of an **int?** Then the next **int** storage location is used. A single field is not allowed to overlap the boundary between two **ints;** the compiler automatically shifts an overlapping field definition so that the field is aligned with the **int** boundary. If this occurs, it leaves an unnamed hole in the first **int.**

You can "pad" a field structure with unnamed holes by using unnamed field widths. Using an unnamed field width of 0 forces the next field to align with the next integer:

```
struct {
            field1 : 1;
                   : 2;
            field2 : 1;
                   : 0;
            field3 : 1;
            } stuff;
```

Here, there is a 2-bit gap between **stuff.field1** and **stuff.field2;** and **stuff.field3** is stored in the next **int.**

One important machine dependency is the order in which fields are placed into an **int.** On some machines the order is left to right, and on others it is right to left.

APPENDIX G BINARY NUMBERS AND OTHERS

BINARY NUMBERS

The way we usually write numbers is based on the number 10. Perhaps you were once told that a number like 3652 has a 3 in the thousand's place, a 6 in the hundred's place, a 5 in the ten's place and a 2 in the one's place. This means we can think of 3652 as being

$$3 \times 1000 + 6 \times 100 + 5 \times 10 + 2 \times 1.$$

But 1000 is 10 cubed, 100 is 10 squared, 10 is 10 to the first power, and, by convention, 1 is 10 (or any positive number) to the zero power. So we also can write 3652 as

$$3 \times 10^3 + 6 \times 10^2 + 5 \times 10^1 + 2 \times 10^0.$$

Because our system of writing numbers is based on powers of ten, we say that 3652 is written in *base 10.*

Presumably, we developed this system because we have 10 fingers. A computer bit, in a sense, only has 2 fingers, for it can be set only to 0 or 1, off or on. This makes a *base 2* system natural for a computer. How does it work? It uses powers of 2 instead of powers of ten. For instance, a binary number such as 1101 would mean

$$1 \times 2^3 + 1 \times 2^2 + 0 \times 2^1 + 1 \times 2^0.$$

In decimal numbers this becomes

$$1 \times 8 + 1 \times 4 + 0 \times 2 + 1 \times 1 = 13.$$

The base 2 (or "binary") system lets one express any number (if you have enough bits) as a combination of 1s and 0s. This is very pleasing to a computer, especially since that is its only option. Let's see how this works for a 1-byte integer.

A byte contains 8 bits. We can think of these 8 bits as being numbered from 7 to 0, left to right. This "bit number" corresponds to an exponent of 2. Imagine the byte as looking like this:

bit number	7	6	5	4	3	2	1	0
value	128	64	32	16	8	4	2	1

Here 128 is 2 to the 7th power, and so on. The largest number this byte can hold is one with all bits set to 1: 11111111. The value of this binary number is

$$128 + 64 + 32 + 16 + 8 + 4 + 2 + 1 = 255.$$

The smallest binary number would be 00000000, or a simple 0. A byte can store numbers from 0 to 255 for a total of 256 possible values.

Binary Floating Point

Floating-point numbers are stored in two parts: a binary fraction and a binary exponent. Let's see how this is done.

Binary Fractions

The ordinary fraction .324 represents

$$3/10 + 2/100 + 4/1000$$

with the denominators representing increasing powers of ten. In a binary fraction, we use powers of two for denominators. Thus the binary fraction .101 represents

$$1/2 + 0/4 + 1/8$$

which in decimal notation is

$$.50 + .00 + .125$$

or .625.

Many fractions, such as 1/3, cannot be represented exactly in decimal notation. Similarly, many fractions cannot be represented exactly in binary notation. Indeed, the only fractions that can be represented exactly are combinations of multiples of powers of 1/2. Thus 3/4 and 7/8 can be represented exactly as binary fractions, but 1/3 and 2/5 cannot be.

Floating-point Representation

To represent a floating-point number in a computer, a certain number (system-dependent) of bits are set aside to hold a binary fraction. Additional bits hold an exponent. In general terms, the actual value of the number consists of the binary fraction times two to the indicated exponent. Thus multiplying a floating-point number by, say, 4, increases the exponent by 2 and leaves the binary fraction unchanged. Multiplying by a number that is not a power of 2 will change the binary fraction and, if necessary, the exponent.

OTHER BASES

Computer workers often use number systems based on 8 and on 16. Since 8 and 16 are powers of 2, these systems are more closely related to a computer's binary system than is the decimal system.

Octal

"Octal" refers to a base 8 system. In this system, the different places in a number represent powers of 8. We use the digits 0 to 7. For example, the octal number 451 (written 0451 in C) represents

$$4 \times 8^2 + 5 \times 8^1 + 1 \times 8^0 = 297 \text{ (base 10)}.$$

Hexadecimal

"Hexadecimal" (or "hex") refers to a base 16 system. Here we use powers of 16 and the digits 0 to 15. But since we don't have single digits to represent the values 10 to 15, we use the letters A to F for that purpose. For instance, the hex number A3F (written 0xA3F in C) represents

$$10 \times 16^2 + 3 \times 16^1 + 15 \times 16^0 = 2623 \text{ (base 10)}.$$

APPENDIX H IBM PC MUSIC

The IBM PC's speaker can be controlled by using the PC's I/O ports. In Chapter 6 we discussed how to use port 97 to sound the IBM PC's beeper. We used the special-purpose **inp( )** and **outp( )** I/O functions supplied with some IBM PC C compilers. Most compilers for the IBM PC also allow you to use the assembly language equivalents. We've seen how to use a time delay loop to control the duration of the sound, and in this appendix we will extend our approach to allow us to select the frequency, too. We will design a function **tone( )** whose arguments represent the frequency and duration. Then we will present a sample program using **tone( )** to turn part of the IBM PC keyboard into a simple musical keyboard.

THE *tone( )* FUNCTION

Here is the heading for our function:

```
tone(freq,time)
int freq, time;
```

The variable **freq** represents the pitch of the tone in Hz. (Hz is the abbreviation for Hertz, or what once was called cycles per second). The variable **time** represents the duration of the tone in tenths of a second; a value of 10 for **time** thus implies a duration of 10 tenths, or 1 second. Now we have to develop ways of getting this information to the sound-producing apparatus. First, let's look at duration.

Tone Duration

We can control the duration the same as we did in Chapter 6. The speaker is controlled, recall, by a device called the 8255 Programmable Parallel Interface Controller. Special I/O channels called ports connect this and other controllers to the brains of the outfit, the 8088 microprocessor. We use port 97 to turn the speaker on, use a loop to mark time, and then use port 97 to turn the speaker back off. Here's a code fragment that will do the job:

```
#define TIMESCALE 1270  /* number of counts in 0.1 second */
#define BEEPPORT 97      /* port controls speaker   */
#define ON 79            /* signal to turn speaker on */
```

```
count = TIMESCALE * time; /* convert time to timer units */
port = inp(BEEPPORT); /* save port setting */
outp(BEEPPORT,ON);    /* turn speaker on   */
for (i=0; i < count; i++)
;                         /* mark time */
outp(BEEPPORT,port);  /* turn speaker off, restore setting */
```

Here the value of **count** determines how long the speaker remains on. The **TIMESCALE** factor converts tenths of a second to an equivalent number of counts. Of course, we have to set the desired pitch before sounding the speaker, so let's have a look at that next.

Tone Frequency

The frequency of the tone can be set using another device, one known as the 8253 Programmable Interval Timer. This controller, among its other duties, determines how many pulses per second are sent to the speaker. The 8253 generates a base frequency of 1,190,000 Hz, which is far beyond the range of human hearing. But we can send the 8253 a number to divide into this base rate. For example, if we send a divisor of 5000, we get a pulse rate of

$$1{,}190{,}000/5000 = 238 \text{ Hz},$$

which is a little below middle C (the note, not a lower-class version of the language). On the other hand, if we know what frequency **freq** we want, we can calculate the divisor we need by saying

```
divisor = 1,190,000 / freq;
```

Our function will do this, so all we need to know now is how to feed the value of **divisor** to the 8253. This requires using two more ports.

The first step is to put the 8253 timer in the correct operating mode for receiving the divisor. This is done by sending the value 182 (0xB6 in hex) out port 67. Once this is done we can use port 66 to send the divisor.

Sending the divisor presents a slight problem. The divisor itself is a 16-bit number, but it must be sent in two parts. First we send the low order byte, or final 8 bits of the number. Then we send the high order byte, or initial 8 bits of the number. In the following program we call these two parts **lobyt** and **hibyt,** and we calculate their values from **divisor:**

```
lobyt = divisor % 256;
hibyt = divisor / 256;
```

Alternatively, we could use the bitwise operators:

```
lobyt = divisor & 255;
 hibyt = divisor >> 8;
```

The first statement of each pair converts the first 8 bits to 0s, leaving the last 8 bits as a 1-byte number. Check the workings of the modulus operator and of the bitwise **AND** operator to see how that works. The second statement of each pair takes the original value of **divisor** and shifts the bits 8 places to the right (which is equivalent to dividing by 2^8, or 256). The 8 leftmost bits are set to 0, leaving an 8-bit number consisting of the original leftmost 8 bits.

Here now is the complete function:

```
/* tone(freq,time) -- makes tone of given frequency,length */

#define TIMERMODE 182     /* code to put timer in right mode */
#define FREQSCALE 1190000L /* basic time frequency in Hz */
#define TIMESCALE 1230L    /* number of counts in 0.1 second */
#define T_MODEPORT 67     /* port controls timer mode */
#define FREQPORT 66       /* port controls tone frequency */
#define BEEPPORT 97       /* port controls speaker */
#define ON 79             /* signal to turn speaker on */

tone(freq,time)
int freq,time;
{
   int hibyt, lobyt, port;
   long i, count, divisor;

   divisor = FREQSCALE/freq; /* scale frequency to timer units */
   lobyt = divisor % 256;      /* break integer into */
   hibyt = divisor / 256;      /* into two bytes     */
   count = TIMESCALE * time;   /* convert time to timer units */
   outp(T_MODEPORT,TIMERMODE);   /* prepare timer for input */
   outp(FREQPORT,lobyt);  /* set low byte of timer register */
   outp(FREQPORT,hibyt);  /* set high byte of timer register */
   port = inp(BEEPPORT);  /* save port setting */
   outp(BEEPPORT,ON);     /* turn speaker on    */
   for (i=0; i < count; i++)
   ;                          /* mark time */
   outp(BEEPPORT,port);   /* turn speaker off, restore setting */
}
```

We **#define TIMESCALE** as a **long** integer so that the calculation of **TIMESCALE * time** will be done in **long** instead of **int.** Otherwise the result, if greater than 32767, will get truncated before it is placed in **count.**

USING THE tone( ) FUNCTION

Our **tone( )** function pretty much duplicates the action of the IBM PC's BASIC **SOUND** statement. Here we use it to create a rather limited (8 note, one octave) keyboard, using 8 keys in the A row to sound notes. Here's the program—some explanation follows.

```
 /* simple musical keyboard   */

#include <conio.h>  /* use unbuffered I/O */
#include <ctype.h>
#define C 262       /* define frequencies */
#define D 294
#define E 330
#define F 349
#define G 392
#define A 440
#define B 494
#define C2 524

main()
{
   int key, freq, tempo, time;

   puts("Please enter the basic tempo: 10 = 1 second.");
   scanf("%d", &tempo);
   printf("%d\n\r", tempo);   /* echo input */
   puts("Thank you. Use the key row a-k to play notes. The
\n\r");
   puts("shift key doubles the duration. A ! halts the show.");

   while ( (key = getchar()) != '!')
        {
        time = isupper(key)? 2 * tempo : tempo;
        key = tolower(key);
        switch (key)
```

```
            {
             case 'a' : tone( C, time);
                        break;
             case 's' : tone( D, time);
                        break;
             case 'd' : tone( E, time);
                        break;
             case 'f' : tone( F, time);
                        break;
             case 'g' : tone( G, time);
                        break;
             case 'h' : tone( A, time);
                        break;
             case 'j' : tone( B, time);
                        break;
             case 'k' : tone( C2, time);
                        break;
             default  : break;
             }
      }
puts("Bye bye!\n\r");
}
```

The main feature of the design is a **switch** statement that assigns different pitches to the 8 keys A–K. In addition, the program doubles the note duration if you use upper case. This duration **(time)** is set before the **switch,** then upper case is converted to lower case to reduce the number of labels we need.

The second main feature is that we used the **conio.h** header file. This file contains **#define's** that replace the usual I/O functions (such as **getchar())** with "console I/O" versions that are unbuffered. As a result, when you hit, say, the [a]-key, the note plays immediately, and you don't have to hit [enter]. Incidentally, these functions do not echo what you type, nor do they automatically start a newline. Thus we put in a **printf( )** statement to echo the **tempo** input, and we used **\n** and **\r** to move the cursor to a new line and to return it to the left of the screen. If you want the keys you hit to be echoed to the screen, insert

```
putchar(key);
```

into the program.

Although the input is not buffered, the keyboard has its own buffer. This allows you to type ahead if you like. The notes themselves will play at their own steady pace.

And here is the opening to "Joy to the World":

```
kjhGfdsA
```

We leave it to you to finish the melody.

APPENDIX I C AUGMENTATIONS

Version 7 of UNIX provides two important extensions to C. The first is that you can use a structure itself (and not just the address or a structure member) as a function argument. The second allows you to use a new data form called the "enumerated data type." We will look at these extensions now.

STRUCTURES AS FUNCTION ARGUMENTS

In unextended C we can pass the *address* of the structure to a function. For example, if **montana** is a structure variable of structure type **player,** we can have a function call like this:

```
stats(&montana);
```

The **stats( )** function would have a header like this:

```
stats(name)
struct player *name;
```

After the function call, **name** will point to the structure **montana,** and the function will use **montana** in its manipulations.

In extended C we can use the structure name itself as an argument, and this causes a *copy* of the original structure to be created in the called function. For example, a call could look like this:

```
stats(montana);
```

Now the **stats( )** function would have a header like this:

```
stats(name)
struct player name;
```

This time, after the function call, a new structure variable of type **player** is created. The new variable is called **name,** and each member of **name** has the same value as the corresponding member of the **montana** structure.

This extension allows a function to have its own private copy of a structure just as it normally has its own private copy of regular variables. The advantage, too, is the same: structures don't inexplicably alter because of some unforeseen side effect of a function.

One point of caution: Some compilers accept calls of the form

```
stats(montana);
```

but actually interpret the call as

```
stats(&montana);
```

In this case, the address is passed, and the function operates on the original structure variable, not the copy.

ENUMERATED TYPES

The **enum** keyword allows you to create a new type and specify the values it can have. Here is an example:

```
enum spectrum {red, orange, yellow, green, blue, violet};
enum spectrum color;
```

The first statement announces a new type: **spectrum.** It also lists the possible values a **spectrum**-type variable can have: **red, orange,** etc. These are **spectrum** constants, just as **4** is an **int** constant and **'g'** is a **char** constant.

The second statement declares **color** to be a variable of type **spectrum.** We can assign any of the **spectrum** constants to **color;** for example,

```
color = green;
```

At first glance, **enum** types may appear similar to Pascal's user-defined ordinal types. There are, indeed, similarities, but there also are important differences, so if you know Pascal, don't jump to conclusions.

Let's look at the nature of these new constants and at the operations we can perform with **enum** types.

enum Constants

How does the computer store something like **red?** It may look something like a string, but there are no double quotes. In fact, **red** and other **enum** constants are stored as integers. For example, try this:

```
printf("red = %d, orange = %d\n", red, orange);
```

and, with the definitions above, you will get this output:

```
red = 0, orange = 1
```

In essence, **red** and its sisters act as synonyms for the integers 0 to 5. The effect is similar to using

```
#define red 0
```

except the correspondence set up by the **enum** statement is more restrictive. For example, if **index** is an **int** variable, both of the following are illegal:

```
index = blue;     /* type clash */
color = 3;         /* type clash */
```

We'll look at further restrictions using **enum** constants and variables later. First, let's take a closer look at the values of **enum** constants.

Default Values

Our example illustrated the default values assigned to constants. The constants appearing in an **enum** declaration are assigned the integers 0, 1, 2, etc., in the order they appear. Thus the declaration

```
enum kids { nippy, slats, skip, nana, liz };
```

results in **nana** having the value **3.**

Assigned Values

You can choose the values you want the constants to have, as long as the choice is an integer-type (including **char**). Just include the desired values in the declaration.

```
enum levels { low = 100, medium = 500, high = 2000};
```

If you assign a value to one constant but not to the following ones, they will be assigned sequential values picking up after the explicitly assigned value. For example,

```
enum feline { cat = 20, tiger, lion, puma };
```

results in **tiger** having the value **21, lion** the value **22,** and **puma** the value 23.

Operations

Now let's look at some of the things you can and cannot do with **enum** types.

You can assign an **enum** constant to an **enum** variable of the same type:

```
enum feline pet;
pet = tiger;
```

You cannot use the other assignment operators:

```
pet += cat;  /* illegal  */
```

You can compare for equality or inequality:

```
if ( pet == cat)
               . . .
if ( color != violet)
               . . .
```

You cannot use the other relational operators:

```
if ( color > yellow )   /* illegal */
               . . .
```

You can use arithmetic operators on **enum** *constants:*

```
color = red + blue;
pet = puma * lion;
```

Whether or not such expressions have any meaning is another matter.

You cannot use arithmetic operators on **enum** *variables:*

```
color = color + green;    /* illegal  */
```

You cannot use the increment and decrement operators:

```
color++;   /* illegal  */
```

You cannot use an **enum** constant for an array subscript:

```
marbles[red] = 23;  /* illegal  */
```

Usage

The main reason for using **enum** types is to increase the readability of programs. If you are dealing with some sort of color code, using **red** and **blue** is much more obvious than using **0** and **4.** Note that **enum** types normally are for internal use, not for I/O. For example, if you want to input a value for the **spectrum**-type variable **color,** you would have to read in, say, the integer **1** and not the word **orange.** (Of course, you could design an input function that accepted the *string* "**orange**" and then converted it to the integer **orange.**)

APPENDIX J ASCII TABLE

Numerical Conversion

DECIMAL-HEXADECIMAL-OCTAL-BINARY-ASCII NUMERICAL CONVERSIONS

DEX X_{10}	HEX X_{16}	OCT X_8	Binary X_2	ASCII	Key
0	00	00	000 0000	NUL	CTRL/1
1	01	01	000 0001	SOH	CTRL/A
2	02	02	000 0010	STX	CTRL/B
3	03	03	000 0011	ETX	CTRL/C
4	04	04	000 0100	EOT	CTRL/D
5	05	05	000 0101	ENQ	CTRL/E
6	06	06	000 0110	ACK	CTRL/F
7	07	07	000 0111	BEL	CTRL/G
8	08	10	000 1000	BS	CTRL/H, BACKSPACE
9	09	11	000 1001	HT	CTRL/I, TAB
10	0A	12	000 1010	LF	CTRL/J, LINE FEED
11	0B	13	000 1011	VT	CTRL/K
12	0C	14	000 1100	FF	CTRL/L
13	0D	15	000 1101	CR	CTRL/M, RETURN
14	0E	16	000 1110	SO	CTRL/N
15	0F	17	000 1111	SI	CTRL/O
16	10	20	001 0000	DLE	CTRL/P
17	11	21	001 0001	DC1	CTRL/Q
18	12	22	001 0010	DC2	CTRL/R
19	13	23	001 0011	DC3	CTRL/S
20	14	24	001 0100	DC4	CTRL/T
21	15	25	001 0101	NAK	CTRL/U
22	16	26	001 0110	SYN	CTRL/V
23	17	27	001 0111	ETB	CTRL/W
24	18	30	001 1000	CAN	CTRL/X
25	19	31	001 1001	EM	CTRL/Y
26	1A	32	001 1010	SUB	CTRL/Z

27	1B	33	001 1011	ESC	ESC, ESCAPE
28	1C	34	001 1100	FS	CTRL<
29	1D	35	001 1101	GS	CTRL/
30	1E	36	001 1110	RS	CTRL/=
31	1F	37	001 1111	US	CTRL/-
32	20	40	010 0000	SP	SPACEBAR
33	21	41	010 0001	!	!
34	22	42	010 0010	’’	’’
35	23	43	010 0011	#	#
36	24	44	010 0100	$	$
37	25	45	010 0101	½	½
38	26	46	010 0110	&	&
39	27	47	010 0111	‘	‘
40	28	50	010 1000	(	(
41	29	51	010 1001	)	)
42	2A	52	010 1010	*	*
43	2B	53	010 1011	+	+
44	2C	54	010 1100	,	,
45	2D	55	010 1101	-	-
46	2E	56	010 1110	.	.
47	2F	57	010 1111	/	/
48	30	60	011 0000	0	0
49	31	61	011 0001	1	1
50	32	62	011 0010	2	2
51	33	63	011 0011	3	3
52	34	64	011 0100	4	4
53	35	65	011 0101	5	5
54	36	66	011 0110	6	6
55	37	67	011 0111	7	7
56	38	70	011 1000	8	8
57	39	71	011 1001	9	9
58	3A	72	011 1010	:	:
59	3B	73	011 1011	;	;
60	3C	74	011 1100	<	<
61	3D	75	011 1101	=	=
62	3E	76	011 1110	>	>
63	3F	77	011 1111	?	?
64	40	100	100 0000	@	@
65	41	101	100 0001	A	A
66	42	102	100 0010	B	B
67	43	103	100 0011	C	C
68	44	104	100 0100	D	D
69	45	105	100 0101	E	E

70	46	106	100 0110	F	F
71	47	107	100 0111	G	G
72	48	110	100 1000	H	H
73	49	111	100 1001	I	I
74	4A	112	100 1010	J	J
75	4B	113	100 1011	K	K
76	4C	114	100 1100	L	L
77	4D	115	100 1101	M	M
78	4E	116	100 1110	N	N
79	4F	117	100 1111	O	O
80	50	120	101 0000	P	P
81	51	121	101 0001	Q	Q
82	52	122	101 0010	R	R
83	53	123	101 0011	S	S
84	53	124	101 0100	T	T
85	55	125	101 0101	U	U
86	56	126	101 0110	V	V
87	57	127	101 0111	W	W
88	58	130	101 1000	X	X
89	59	131	101 1001	Y	Y
90	5A	132	101 1010	Z	Z
91	5B	133	101 1011	[	[
92	5C	134	101 1100	\	\
93	5D	135	101 1101	]	]
94	5E	136	101 1110	^	^
95	5F	137	101 1111	—	—
96	60	140	110 0000	`	`
97	61	141	110 0001	a	a
98	62	142	110 0010	b	b
99	63	143	110 0011	c	c
100	64	144	110 0100	d	d
101	65	145	110 0101	e	e
102	66	146	110 0110	f	f
103	67	147	110 0111	g	g
104	68	150	110 1000	h	h
105	69	151	110 1001	i	i
106	6A	152	110 1010	j	j
107	6B	153	110 1011	k	k
108	6C	154	110 1100	l	l
109	6D	155	110 1101	m	m
110	6E	156	110 1110	n	n
111	6F	157	110 1111	o	o
112	70	160	111 0000	p	p

113	71	161	111 0001	q	q
114	72	162	111 0010	r	r
115	73	163	111 0011	s	s
116	74	164	111 0100	t	t
117	75	165	111 0101	u	u
118	76	166	111 0110	v	v
119	77	167	111 0111	w	w
120	78	170	111 1000	x	x
121	79	171	111 1001	y	y
122	7A	172	111 1010	z	z
123	7B	173	111 1011	R	R
124	7C	174	111 1100	¦	¦
125	7D	175	111 1101	T	T
126	7E	176	111 1110	~	~
127	7F	177	111 1111	DEL	DEL,RUBOUT

Index

P

R

In this card we emphasize simple, typical examples rather than overly abstract generalizations. Thus some of the rarer or more complex possibilities are omitted.

TYPICAL PROGRAM FORMS

A simple program consists of one function (**main( )**). The statements of the function are enclosed between opening and closing braces:

```
main()  /* function name includes parentheses */
{   /* opening brace */
   int n;   /* declaration statement */

   for ( n = 1; n < 12; n++)
       printf("%d %d\n", n, 2*n + 1);
}     /* closing brace */
```

Programs may include preprocessor directives and more than one function. Function definitions follow one another. Do not embed one function definition within another function definition. Execution starts at the beginning of **main( )** regardless of the order of the functions.

```
#define LIMIT 12    / *preprocessor directive */
main()
{
   int n;

   for ( n = 1; n < LIMIT, n++)
       printf("%d %d\n", n, oddn(n) );
       /* invoking the oddn(n) function */
}  /* end of main() */

oddn(k)     /* function with argument */
int k;      /* declare argument */
{   /* begin function definition */
      int j;  /* declare variables */

       j = 2 * k + 1;
       return( j );
}      /* end of oddn() */
```

Functions with arguments have the arguments declared before the body of the function, as marked by the opening brace, begins. See above.

STATEMENTS

Simple statements consist of an instruction followed by a semicolon:

```
float x;        /* declaration statement */
x = 3.2857;      /* assignment statement */
putchar('A');      /* function statement */
```

Structured statements typically consist of a keyword (**if, while,** etc.) followed by a condition within parentheses followed by a statement. (See **FLOW CONTROL.**)

```
if ( idnumber == 12321 )
    salary = salary + bonus;
```

A compound statement consists of one or more statements enclosed in braces. It counts as one statement and is used in structured statements to allow more than one action be included in the statement:

```
if ( idnumber == 10007 )
      {
      salary = salary + bonus;
      status = status + 1;
      }
```

FUNDAMENTAL TYPES

Variables come in two basic varieties: integer and floating point. Not all compilers recognize all the variations below.

Integer types:

```
char
 short
 int
 long
 insigned, unsigned int
 unsigned short
 unsigned long
```

Floating-point types

```
float
double, long float
```

STORAGE CLASSES

Variables have one of the following storage classes:

```
auto
 register
 external
 static
 external static
```

auto and **register** variables are created each time the function containing them is evoked, and they vanish each time the function finishes. The others last for the duration of the whole program.

DECLARING VARIABLES

A variable can be single-valued (a scalar variable) or contain several values (an array). A variable has a *type* (**int, char,** etc.) and a *storage class* (**auto, static,** etc.). See above. A declaration statement declares these attributes. (By default, a variable is storage class **auto** if declared inside a function and **extern** if declared outside a function.) A general form for declaring a scalar variable is

storage-class   type-specifier   variable-name;

An array is indicated by following the variable name with brackets containing the number of elements.

Variables in a function normally are declared after the opening brace:

```
main()
{
```

Making Computers Simple

The Waite Group

Mitchell Waite
Stephen Prata
Donald Martin

C
Primer Plus

Reference Card

Owned or Sponsored by:

Howard W. Sams & Co.
4300 W. 62nd Street
Indianapolis, IN 46268

```
int n;  /* auto by default */
static float val;
char name[40];  /* array of 40 char values */
```

Scalar variables can be initialized in the declaration:

```
int n = 2;  /* n declared and set to 2 */
```

Arrays can be initialized if they are of storage class **extern** or **static.** If the array size is omitted, the size is determined by counting the number of elements in the initialization:

```
static int codes[4] = {2, 3, 7, 8};
static int ids[] = {11,13,15}; /* ids
has 3 elements */
```

A **char** array can be initialized as a string:

```
static char name[] = "Donald Druck";
```

Use the indirection operator ('*') to declare pointers:

```
int *pn; /* pn is a pointer to an integer */
```

STRUCTURES

A structure is a data object capable of holding more than one type of value. A structure *template* establishes the type of data the structure can hold. The structure definition is enclosed in braces. A structure *tag* gives a short-hand name for the form. A structure *variable* is one whose type is given by a structure template. The template must include a tag or a variable name or both.

No tag: Here we declare a variable **fish** to be a structure of the indicated form. No tag is used, and the variable name follows the structure definition:

```
struct  {
        float length;
        float weight;
        char name[40];
        }  fish;   /* fish is a structure
variable */
```

Tag: Alternatively, use a tag name before the opening brace, then use the tag name later in declaring the variable:

```
struct critter {    /* critter is the tag name */
                float length;
                float weight;
                char name[40];
                };
struct critter fish, seal; /* declaring two
structures */
struct critter birds[5]; /* an array of 5
structures */
```

All the structures here are of the **critter** form.

FLOW CONTROL

Loops:

while loop:

```
while (condition)
       statement
```

Example:

```
while ( i++ < 20 )
       q = 2 * q;
```

for *loop:*

```
for (initialize ; test ; update )
     statement
```

Example:

```
for ( n = 0; n < 10; n++ )
       printf("%d %d\n", n, 2*n-1);
```

do while *loop:*

```
do
   statement
      while ( condition );
```

Example:

```
do
        printf("Hello, Molly\n");
               while ( i++ < 10 );
```

Branching

if forms:

```
I.  if ( expression )
    statement

II. if ( expression )
    statement
    else
    statement

III. if ( expression )
    statement
    else if ( expression )
    statement
    else
    statement
```

Example:

```
if (amt > 400)
        rate = .0056;
else
        rate = .0062;
```

switch:

```
switch ( expression )
     {
     case label1 : statement1
  case label2 : statement2
   . . .
   default : statement
   }
```

Example:

```
switch ( letter )
      {
       case 'a'  :  act++;
                    break;
       case 'b'  :  bct++;
                    break;
       case 'c'  :  cct++;
                    break;
       default   :  restct++;
       }
```

Jumps

I. **break** is used inside a loop or **switch.** It causes program control to skip the rest of the loop and to resume with the next command following the loop or **switch.**

II. **continue** is used inside a loop. It causes program control to skip the rest of the loop and to initiate the next cycle of the loop.

III. **goto** causes program control to jump to a statement bearing the indicated label. A statement label is followed by a colon.

```
top : ch = getchar();  /* top is a label */
      . . .
if ( ch != 'y' )
      goto top;
```

OPERATOR PRIORITIES

<table>
<tr><th>OPERATORS (from high to low priority)</th></tr>
<tr><td>() { } -> .</td></tr>
<tr><td>! ~ ++ -- - (type) * & sizeof (all unary)</td></tr>
<tr><td>* / %</td></tr>
<tr><td>+ -</td></tr>
<tr><td><< >> (bit shifts)</td></tr>
<tr><td>< <= > >=</td></tr>
<tr><td>== !=</td></tr>
<tr><td>& (bitwise and)</td></tr>
<tr><td>^ (bitwise not)</td></tr>
<tr><td>d | (bitwise or)</td></tr>
<tr><td>&&</td></tr>
<tr><td>||</td></tr>
<tr><td>?:</td></tr>
<tr><td>= += -= *= /* %=</td></tr>
<tr><td>,</td></tr>
</table>

FORMATS FOR printf( )

`printf` *(controlstring, expression1, expression2, . . .*);

The *controlstring* (in double quotes) consists of characters to be printed literally and of conversion specifications, which begin with a %. There should be one conversion specification for each expression value to be printed. The value of each expression is printed in the location indicated by the conversion specification.

The basic conversion specifications:

%d —print an integer
%u—print an unsigned integer
%f—print a floating-point number
%e—print floating-point in exponential form
%g—chooses **%e** or **%f** depending on number size
%c—print a character
%s—print a string
%o—print unsigned octal integer
%x—print unsigned hexadecimal integer

Modifiers may be placed after the % to indicate field width, precision, justification, and if an **int** is long:

%10d—print an integer in a field 10 spaces wide
%5.2f—print 2 decimal places; field width = 5
%-6d—print an integer left-justified
%1d—print a **long** integer

Example:

```
printf("%s's score is %d out of 90.\n", name,
score);
```

could produce

Jim Dandy's score is 43 out of 90.

FORMATS FOR scanf( )

The **scanf( )** function works much like **printf( ).** Here are the main differences.

1. The arguments following the control string must be addresses. They can use the address operator, as in **&n,** or they can be array names, which are pointers to the first array element.
2. There is no **%g** option.
3. Both **%e** and **%f** work the same, accepting either format.
4. A **%h** conversion specification exists for reading **short** integers.

Example:

```
int n;
char title[20];
scanf(''%d %s'', &n, title);
```